Antonin Maurel, Patrick Costelloe

**The Christian Instructed in the Nature and Use of Indulgences**

Antonin Maurel, Patrick Costelloe

**The Christian Instructed in the Nature and Use of Indulgences**

ISBN/EAN: 9783337022679

Printed in Europe, USA, Canada, Australia, Japan

Cover: Foto ©Lupo / pixelio.de

More available books at **www.hansebooks.com**

# THE CHRISTIAN
## INSTRUCTED IN THE NATURE AND USE OF
# INDULGENCES

### BY THE
## REV. A. MAUREL, S.J.

"*Dei amorem et cœlum quœrentibus, Indulgentiœ sunt ingens thesaurus, et gemmœ pretiosœ.*"

"To those who seek God's love and the glory of Heaven, Indulgences are a rich treasure, and may be compared to so many precious gems."

St. Ignatius of Loyola—(*Letter to a Friend*).

### An Approved Translation of the Fourteenth French Edition

### BY THE
## REV. PATRICK COSTELLOE

Revised and Enlarged according to the latest *decisions* of the S. Cong. R.

**FOURTH EDITION.**

COLL. CHRISTI REGIS
BIB. MAJ.
TORONTO

DUBLIN
M. H. GILL AND SON
50 UPPER SACKVILLE STREET
1885

JESUITS
Upper Canada Province

**Nihil Obstat:**
>P. J. TYNAN, S.T.D.
>>Censor Theol. Deput.

**Imprimatur:**
>GULIELMUS J. CANON. WALSH,
>>Vic. Cap. Dublinensis.

*Dublini,
Die 29 mens. Junii 1885.*

[*The right of reproduction is reserved.*]

# PREFACE TO THE SECOND ENGLISH EDITION.

In publishing this New Edition, it becomes my painful duty I regret, to notice the death of the dear lamented author, the Very Rev. Father Maurel. He died on the 26th of December 1874, after a short illness. Let us hope that his soul is now in the enjoyment of the beatific vision, free of suffering, by those Indulgences whose doctrine and use he so extensively and effectually propagated, and to which, no doubt, he was careful to have recourse. *Requiescat in pace.*

The numerous and valuable Approbations of the Cardinal, Archbishops, and Bishops of Ireland, prefixed to the present Edition, render prefatory remarks on my part superfluous, for they speak eloquently of the superior excellence of the Original and of the fidelity of the Translation, and, moreover show the high value that should be set upon Indulgences by the Faithful. I am deeply grateful to their lordships for the unreservedly kind manner in which they received and approved the English version, especially to my own beloved Bishop, whom I have the honour to venerate as a Superior, love as a father, and esteem as a dear, sincere friend.

Some of the good, zealous Priests of the Irish Church, mindful of the teaching of St. Alphonsus Liguori—viz., to become saints, persons need only gain as many Indulgences as possible—have happily employed the Work as an instrument or auxiliary to advance the sanctification of the souls committed to their pastoral charge. In more instances than one they have issued orders for as many as one hundred copies, to circulate them amongst their respective Flocks, and thus stimulate the Faithful to have recourse to the precious Treasury of the Church, "replete with the gold of the merits of our Divine Redeemer, of his Blessed Mother, and of the Saints."*

* Maurel, p. 19, First Edition.

*Ballinasloe, Ash-Wednesday,*
   *February 14th, 1877.*

---

N.B.—The latest concessions and modifications as regards certain points in Indulgences have been inserted in the fourth edition of this work, with the added merit of having been revised by the learned and distinguished President of Maynooth College, the Very Rev. Dr. Walsh.

*June, 1883.*

# APPROBATIONS.

Enniscorthy, Sept. 22nd, 1876.

Rev. dear Sir,—Please accept my best thanks for your English version of Father Maurel's invaluable treatise on Indulgences, with which, in its original language and earlier Editions, I have long been familiar.

You have done a good service to religion in translating it, and I earnestly hope it will have a circulation commensurate with its great utility.—I remain, your faithful servant,

✠ Michael Warren.

The Rev. P. Costello, C.C.

Diocese of Cloyne,
Queenstown, Oct. 17th, 1876.

My dear Father Costello,—Permit me to congratulate you on the valuable service you have rendered to religion in this country by your excellent Translation of Father Maurel's standard Work on Indulgences. It supplies a Manual much needed by those of the faithful who wish to secure for themselves a participation in those abundant treasures of expiation and atonement, which the Church has so mercifully placed at their disposal, by the numerous Indulgences she has annexed to the prayers and practices of Christian piety which she recommends.

I am glad to learn that your Book has already secured for itself that best appreciation of its merits—a demand for a Second Edition—which I hope is but a forerunner of a circulation as wide and as extended as its usefulness and the conscientious care bestowed on it deserve.—I am, my dear Father Costello, yours very sincerely,

✠ JOHN MACCARTHY.

The Rev. P. Costello, C.C., Ballinasloe.

---

Kilkenny, **April 8th, 1876.**

REV. AND DEAR SIR,—On my return from Rome I found your little volume awaiting me. It will be a valuable addition to our Ecclesiastical libraries, and will do much good.—Believe me to remain, your faithful servant,

✠ PATRICK F. MORAN, Bishop of Ossory.

Rev. P. Costello, C.C., Ballinasloe.

---

Killaloe, May 1st, 1876.

DEAR FATHER COSTELLO,—Father Maurel, writing on the intended Translation of his Work on Indulgences, expressed a hope that our Clergy would be grateful for your services. That hope, I think, is fully gratified, for they have ready at hand, in one small volume, a mass of information only to be gleaned with trouble from a variety of sources.

Your accurate and conscientious rendering from French into English bids me give expression to the wish that it will come to as many editions as the original.—I am, dear Father Costello, your very faithful servant,

✠ JAMES RYAN

I shall not fail to recommend to the Priests of Ross this invaluable manual on Indulgences.—I remain, Rev. dear sir, your faithful servant,

✠ M. O'Hea.

The Rev. P. Costello, C.C., Ballinasloe.

---

Galway, Dec. 15th, 1875.

My dear Father Costello,—On my return here this evening, after a day's absence, I found your letter and book before me. I am much obliged to you for so nice a gift. I have not had time to read it; but from looking over it here and there, I am much pleased with it. It is very creditable to you to have devoted your spare hours to labours so useful and edifying.—Very faithfully yours,

✠ John MacEvilly.

Rev. P. Costello.

---

Sligo, April 29th, 1876.

Rev. and dear Sir,—I am in receipt of the copy of Father Maurel's treatise on Indulgences, with which you have kindly favoured me. I am happy to express my approval of this valuable Work, and of your accurate translation of it; and I beg to recommend it to the Clergy and laity of this diocese of Elphin.—I remain, Rev. and dear sir, your faithful servant,

✠ S. Gillooly.

Rev. P. Costello, Ballinasloe.

---

Violet Hill,
Newry, Jan. 9th, 1876.

Rev. dear Sir,—You have performed a very meritorious work of charity in rendering Father Maurel's excellent treatise available to English-speaking Catholics. It will inspire the faithful with fresh ardour to gain for themselves the invaluable treasures which the Church offers with such generous liberality, and to aid in shortening, or, at least, mitigating the fearful sufferings of the poor souls in Purgatory.—Trusting that your Work will have an extensive circulation, I am, Rev. dear sir, yours truly in Christ,

✠ JOHN P. LEAHY.

Rev. Patrick Costello.

---

The Palace,
Killarney, Jan. 22nd, 1876.

DEAR REV. SIR,—The Abbe Maurel's treatise on Indulgences translated by you is a very useful book. The teaching of the Church is made intelligible to the laity, and the conditions required for gaining Indulgences are laid down clearly and accurately.

The copious collection of the Second Part will lead devout souls to the practice of *approved* devotions.

I have not seen the Original Work, but I can say that the style of your translation is excellent.—I am, yours faithfully in Christ,

✠ DAVID MORIARTY.

Rev. Patrick Costello, C.C., Ballinasloe.

---

The Palace,
Thurles, May 2nd, 1876.

REV. AND DEAR SIR,—I am deeply indebted to you for the copy of your Work on Indulgences, which you were kind enough to send me. It cannot but be useful. Even the best instructed of our people will find in it much that is new, and many explanations that were greatly needed.

The Catholic doctrine on Indulgences, so wickedly impugned in our times by the enemies of the Christian

Church, and occasionally misapprehended by certain of the faithful, is clearly, and, I might say, authoritatively set forth in this little volume; and the many religious confraternities that are now, thank God, so flourishing amongst us, can learn from it at a glance what are the precise privileges which they enjoy, and under what conditions these privileges may be availed of.

I bespeak for your book a large circulation, and earnestly recommend the perusal of it to both Priests and people. I remain, Rev. and dear sir,

✠ T. W. CROKE, Archbishop of Cashel.

Rev. P. Costello, Ballinasloe.

---

St. Jar'ath's,
Tuam, Sept. 19th, 1876.

REV. DEAR SIR,—For Father Maurel's valuable book on Indulgences, which you have so creditably translated for the benefit of English readers, I beg to convey my most grateful acknowledgments. To bring this pious work within the reach of the simple faithful, as you have done, entitles you to the gratitude of the many readers who will not fail to derive much profit from its perusal.

Along with my best thanks, I beg you to accept the expression of my regret for the tardiness of the acknowledgment.—Your faithful and obliged servant,

✠ JOHN MACHALE, Archbishop of Tuam.

Rev. Patrick Costello, C.C.

---

Dublin, Jan. 8th, 1876.

REV. AND DEAR SIR,—I feel much obliged to you for your kindness in sending me a copy of your translation of Father Maurel's Work on Indulgences. As your translation has merited the approval of such high Ecclesiastical and theological authorities, I am sure it must do a great deal of good, and I hope it will be widely circulated. I am happy to recommend its use to the Clergy and laity of this diocese, being persuaded that the perusal of so valuable a Work will throw light upon the nature and advantages of Indulgences, and induce many of the faithful to perform the works of piety or charity which are required of those who wish to participate in the treasures placed under the control of the Church by her Divine Founder, Jesus Christ.

Congratulating you on the good work which you have performed, I wish you every happiness and blessing, and remain, your faithful servant,

✠ PAUL CARDINAL CULLEN.

The Rev. P. Costello, C.C., Ballinasloe.

NIL OBSTAT.

> EDMUNDUS O'REILLY, S.J.,
> Censor Theol. Deputatus.

---

*Loughrea, Oct. 30, 1875.*

MY DEAR FATHER COSTELLO,

    In according the requisite "approval" of the publication of your translation of the "Christian Instructed in the Nature and Use of Indulgences," I take the opportunity of expressing my deep appreciation of the religious zeal with which, in the midst of your Missionary duties, you have made time to give the English-reading public the advantage of being enabled to profit by the perusal of this valuable treatise.

    The rapidity with which so many editions of the original work of the learned Jesuit have been exhausted is satisfactory evidence of the esteem in which it is held by discerning readers. The fruits to be derived from the use of Indulgences, so abundantly placed by the Church at the disposal of the faithful, are, by too many, not sufficiently estimated. When too late, thousands will have to deplore the fatuity with which they neglected to avail themselves during life of this means of expiation. I earnestly recommend the book to all the faithful of this Diocese.

    Faithfully yours in Christ,

    ✠ PATRICK DUGGAN,
        Bishop of Clonfert.

Rev. Patrick Costello.

Lyon—Terrasse De Fourviere, 8.
8 Oct. 1871.

Monsieur L'Abbé.

Très-volontiers, je consens à ce que vous traduisiez en Anglais mon livre intitulé : *Le Chrétien éclairé sur la nature et l'usage des Indulgences*. C'est la *quatorzième édition* qu'il faut traduire, elle est plus complète, et le *Supplément*, que j'avais ajouté à la 12e, et 13e éditions, a été fondu dans le corps de l'ouvrage, de sorte qu'il n'y a qu'une table plus détaillée. Si vous n'avez pas cette 14e edition, veuillez la demander. . . . . . Quand vous aurez traduit ce ivre, vous pourrez, si vos occupations vous le permettent, traduire mon ouvrage qui a pour titre : "Guide pratique de Liturgie Romaine," et puis, mon "Catéchisme raisonné sur l'Eglise et le Souverain Pontife, corrigé d'après les définitions du Concile du Vatican." Le clergé Irlandais sera, je l'espère, content du service que vous lui rendrez.

Je vous remercie d'avance, Monsieur L'Abbé, et, me recommandant à vos prières, je suis avec respect votre très-humble et dévoué serviteur,

A. Maurel, S.J.

# TRANSLATOR'S PREFACE.

The idea of reproducing this valuable treatise on Indulgences was first suggested to me by some of the much esteemed and beloved Superiors of Maynooth, who labour so unceasingly to promote the welfare of the universal Church, particularly of that portion of it in which they are specially interested, the Church of Ireland. Printed above is the reply of the pious author to my application for permission to undertake the task. In preparing it for press, I had been greatly assisted by a very worthy Priest, the Rev. Father Sebastian, then Prior of the Carmelite Convent, Loughrea; and the learned Jesuit, the Very Rev. Father O'Reilly, has done me the honor of revising the proof-sheets and of correcting several "slips" and errors in the translation. His signature and my Bishop's seal are a guarantee, that the public may at least safely read the Original in the novel version or garb under which it is now presented to them.

No addition or alteration of any kind has been made in the text, but I have varied, in a slight degree, the arrangement of a few sentences and paragraphs, and, with the kind permission of the late F. Ambrose St. John of the Oratory, Birmingham (Translator of the "Raccolta"), have adopted his approved translation of some of the Indulgenced prayers.* Hence the Original Work remains totally integral and unaltered.

I have deemed it expedient to advance these statements for two reasons:—First, because the Church is very strict and emphatic in Her injunctions, to have translations of prayers of and books on Indulgences *faithful versions* of the Original;† and, secondly, because the present treatise is of such great value and importance. In my opinion, "*The Christian Instructed in the Nature and Use of Indulgences*," is at once the most methodical, the most full and accurate work yet pub-

---

\* A Decree of the Sacred Congregation, dated July 11, 1856, has declared that " the collection of pious prayers, &c.," then in the Rev. F. Maurel's book, *was genuine*, and that the version of the prayers he had extracted from the thirteenth Roman edition of the Raccolta and embodied in his own book, *was faithful*. See also Decree of Dec. 18, 1857 (Decreta Authentica, p. 272, n. 1570).

† Indulgentiarum Libri omnes, Diaria, Summaria, Libelli, Folia, &c. in quibus earum concessiones continentur, non edantur absque licentia Soc. Congregationis Indulgentiarum (Decreta de libris prohibitis § III, n. 12). Read p. 87, n. 4, of the present work.

lished in an abridged form on the subject of Indulgences. To estimate its worth we have only to read in its introductory pages the Approbations sanctioning its authority and recommending its use, and to bear in mind that, since its first appearance a few years ago, it has passed through as many as sixteen or seventeen editions,* "and is in the hands of ecclesiastics and lay people everywhere."†

It expounds the Doctrine of Indulgences in a concise and comprehensive style, yet with unusual clearness and precision. It contains no unnecessary repetitions that might weary, no digressions that might burden, no redundancy and ambiguity of language or expression that might tend to confuse and embarrass the reader. Nothing is to be found there but what is solidly practical, truthful, and simple, and adapted to the capacities of all. "My desire has been," says the learned author, "to render myself useful to the people;" and this desire he seems to have attained in a pre-eminent degree.

It differs, in many respects, from other works of the same kind. Some authors treat merely of the *nature* or doctrinal portion of Indulgences, without caring to exhaust the subject; others merely of the *use* or practical portion of them, and this on a limited scale, with the omission of several charming devotions of great utility and esteem to Christians; while others again combine both the doctrinal and practical portions, but in a manner unsuited to ordinary readers. We know that much of what concerns Indulgences is contained in Rescripts emanating from, and positive decisions issued by the Sacred Congregations, under the direction of the Holy See, and these authors may have written at a time when the subject had not been so fully discussed and developed as at present; thus they might have securely advanced opinions then that are now exploded and obsolete—they might have introduced into their works a considerable amount of irrelevant matter, or clothed their ideas in obscure phraseology, or stated things inaccurately.

Let us take e. g. the prayer called the "Angelus." Most of the treatises that I have seen, lay down that, to gain the 100 days' Indulgence attached to its recitation, it should be said "morning, noon, *and* evening," whereas our author properly

* I hold in my hand just now a copy of the sixteenth edition.
† See Preface to the present edition.

states that it suffices to say it "morning, noon, *or* evening."\*
In like manner a certain treatise, justly, perhaps, styled "a standard work on Indulgences" about the year 1850,† mentions, that, to acquire the Indulgences of the Via Crucis or Way of the Cross, it is necessary "to meditate on *each* mystery of the Passion," while going through the Stations; but Father Maurel, p. 145, *note*, proves conclusively from the words of the Sacred Congregation, from the prevailing impression in Rome, and from reason, that it is enough *to meditate on the Passion in general.* St. Alphonsus Liguori, that great Doctor of the Church, states, also, relying on the authority of Ferraris. I presume, in his excellent little book on the Commandments (p. 230, n. 68, of the edition in my hands), that "he who hears Mass gains an Indulgence of 3800 years." Now it is almost an undoubted fact that no Pope ever granted a partial Indulgence of so great a number of years as this,‡ and that, in general, there is no Indulgence at all, as such, obtained by hearing Mass.§ And so in numerous instances to be met with in Indulgence-books generally.

But the present publication appears to obviate these various inconveniences. Every assertion put forward in it seems based upon solid reasoning and authority; every sentence is plain and intelligible; and every word has its peculiar force and meaning. It would be difficult perhaps to find, on the same subject, a work so exhaustive and so satisfactory in almost every detail. Truly its title, "*The Christian instructed in the Nature and Use of Indulgences,*" is peculiarly expressive and appropriate.

The treatise, as may be perceived, is divided into three parts: the first, or dogmatic portion, extends over nine chapters, which treat of the *nature* of Indulgences, with a short notice of Indulgences that are false or apocryphal; in the second or practical portion, is embodied almost everything appertaining to the *use* of Indulgences; it details, for instance, the Indulgenced prayers, the Beads, Scapulars, Confraternities, &c., and other devotions of various kinds in common

---

\* Having referred to the *Decreta Authentica*, p. 20, n. 62, I find the words of the Decree (Dec. 5, 1727) are '*mane, meridie, aut vespere.*'
† See "*Bouvier on Indulgences,*" edited by Canon Oakely. *Preface.*
‡ Read the end of p. 52, present treatise.
§ Refer to p. 139, No. 56, "The Christian Instructed," &c.

use among the Faithful; and, in the third or formulary division, is given a large number l of Formulas for blessing Rosaries, Scapulars, &c., and enroling in different Sodalities, which renders the work immensely valuable to Priests as well as lay people.

Some persons may charge me with exaggeration in these remarks on its merit or excellence. But if they take the trouble of comparing it with other books on Indulgences, I am sure they will fully endorse everything said in its favour. To me it appears the most complete work of the sort in the English language. It is, in truth, just what we wanted—a work setting forth in a judicious, clear, accurate manner the true nature and use of Indulgences. And I have no doubt but that, through the Divine economy, it will become, in the hands of many Catholics, a happy medium or occasion of procuring numberless graces for themselves, and of rescuing thousands of souls from the excruciating tortures of the fire of Purgatory.

Ah! did we but consider that the ways of God are widely different from the ways of men—that His judgments are strict and terrible beyond description—that His infinite sanctity requires unblemished stainless purity, and His infinite justice an adequate expiatory punishment for every offence— did we but bear in mind that "*nothing defiled shall enter in,*" and that, as gold is refined in a furnace here on earth, so souls stained with the dross and filth of sin, in the other life, must be purged in a raging fire, until the last farthing shall have been paid to the Sovereign Master—did we but realize to ourselves that perhaps one hour's suffering in that fire would be incomparably greater than a thirty years'-long suffering in the fire of this world, and that, as is evident from the Revelations to some of the Saints, the souls of many renowned for virtue and sanctity—souls of great perfection— may be, and doubtless oftentimes are, deprived for a notable time of the Beatific Vision, on account of trivial faults far less heinous and numerous than several of our own faults— we should have a much deeper appreciation of Indulgences, we should be anxious to read and hear more about them, in the hope of being enabled to acquire more for ourselves and apply more to the helpless souls of Purgatory.

*Ballinasloe, Feast of All Souls,* 187

## APPROBATIONES

Opusculi duodecies edendi R. P. Antonini Maurel e Societate Jesu, emissæ a duobus infrascriptis S. Congregationis Indulgentiarum Consultoribus.

## APPROBATIONS

Of the twelfth edition of the work compiled by the Rev. F. Antonine Maurel, of the Society of Jesus, given by the two undersigned Consultors of the S. Congregation of Indulgences.

---

### APPROBATIO PRIMA.

EMINENTISSIME PRINCEPS—

Quum duodecimam editionem revisam, emendatam, et Supplemento auctam operis: "*Le Chretien eclaire sur la nature et l'usuage des Indulgences,*" a R. P. Antonino Maurel Soc. Jesu conscriptam, majori qua potui attentione ac diligentia perlegerim, nedum aliquid in ea censura dignum inveni, quin potius ad augendam fidelium erga sacras Indulgentias fidem, pietatemque in eorum cordibus fovendam quam maxime idoneam omnino existimo. Proindeque nihil obstare puto, ut iterum typis imprimi et vulgari possit.

Hanc vero sententiam meam, ea qua par est humilitate subjicio sapientissimo Eminentiæ Vestræ judicio, cui sacram purpuram obsequentissimo animo deosculor.

E Conventu S. Bartholomæi in Insula, 5 Martii, 1864. F. Antonius Maria Testa Ordinis Minor. observ. S. Congregationis Consultor.

### FIRST APPROBATION.

MOST ILLUSTRIOUS PRINCE*—

Having as carefully and diligently as possible read the twelfth edition —revised, corrected, and enlarged, with a supplement—of the work entitled "The Christian Instructed in the Nature and Use of Indulgences," written by F. Antonine Maurel of the Society of Jesus, not only have I not found anything censurable in it but on the contrary, am fully convinced that it is highly calculated to augment the faith of the people in the matter of holy Indulgences, and to nourish the spirit of piety in their hearts. Wherefore I think there is nothing to prevent its being newly printed and published.

However, I hereby dutifully submit this my opinion to your Eminence's most prudent judgment, at the same time, in a spirit of most profound submission, respectfully kissing your sacred purple.

Convent of St. Bartholomew in *Insula*, March 5, 1864. F. Anthony Mary Testa, *of the Order of Friar Minor Observant, and Consultor of the S. Congregation.*

---

* His Eminence Cardinal Panebianco, Prefect of the S. Congregation of Indulgences and Holy Relics. Having been called to other duties, he was succeeded in that dignity by His Eminence Cardinal A. Bizzari.

## APPROBATIO ALTERA.

**Eminentissime Princeps—**

Ex mandato Eminentiæ Tuæ Reverendissimæ, maturo examine perpendi duodecimam editionem revisam et emendatam operis, cui titulus: "*Le Chretien eclaire sur la nature et l'usuage des Indulgences*," quod opus conscripsit R. P. Antonius Maurel, Societatis Jesu: unaque simul perlegi Supplementum ejusdem editionis quod auctor præstantissimus composuit, et typis mandare nunc valde cupit. Testor me nihil invenisse censura dignum, ac omnia esse conformia concessionibus ac decretis Romanorum Pontificum, et sacrarum Congregatiorum præsertim Congregationis SS. Indulgentiis et Reliquiis præpositæ. Insupe en inservire ad confirmandos fideles in fide erga sacras Indulgentias, eosque non parum fovere ad bona opera peregenda, ut sacras Indulgentias a Matre Ecclesia tam benigniter ac copiose concessas consequi valeant. Quapropter putarem ut tam jam editum opus quam supplementum novum in lucem edi posse.

Hoc tamen meum judicium humiliter submitto sapientiæ Eminentiæ Tuæ, cui sacram purpuram reverenter ac in obsequentissimi animi mei testimonium deoscular.

Ex Conventu S. Mariæ supra Minervam Romæ, die 15 Martii, 1864.

Fr. Hyeron.-Pius Saccheri, Sacræ Theologiæ Magister in Ordine Prædicat, et S. Congregationis Consultor.

## SECOND APPROBATION.

**Most Eminent Prince—**

In obedience to the mandate of your Eminence, I have minutely examined the twelfth edition—revised, and corrected—of the work styled, "The Christian Instructed in the Nature and Use of Indulgences," compiled by the Rev F. Antonine Maurel, S. J.; I have also attentively read the supplement, which the Illustrious author has annexed thereto, and which he now anxiously desires to publish. I hereby certify, that I have discovered therein nothing deserving of censure, and that everything it contains is in strict conformity with the grants and decrees of the Roman Pontiffs and Sacred Congregations, particularly the Congregation presiding over Indulgences and Sacred Relics. Furthermore, it is my belief, that the work will tend very much to strengthen the faith reposed by the people in Indulgences, and stimulate them to perform good works in order to avail themselves of these favours, so copiously and graciously dispensed by our Holy Mother the Church. Wherefore, in my opinion both the work itself, which has been already published, and the supplement attached, may be issued forthwith to the public.

Nevertheless, this decision I humbly submit to the wisdom of your Eminence, whose sacred purple I reverently kiss, in testimony of my most devoted attachment.

Convent of St. Mary *Supra Minervam* at Rome, March 5, 1864.

Fra Jerome-Pius Saccheri, *Master of Sacred Theology in the Order of Preachers, and Consultor of the S. Congregation.*

## DECRETUM.

Cum opusculum gallico idiomate conscriptum, auctore R. P. Antonino Maurel, e Societate Jesu, et jam undecies editum, cui titulus: "*Le Chretien eclaire sur la nature et l'usuage des Indulgences*," a supraenunciatis duobus sacrae Congregationis Indulgentiarum Consultoribus revisum ac cum authenticis decretis compertum sit convenire, quoad Indulgentias, permittitur ut typis edatur.

Datum Romae, ex secretaria ejusdem sacrae Indulgentiarum Congregationis, die 17 Martii, 1864.

*Locus Sigilli.*

Ant.-Maria Card. Panebianco, Praef.
▲ Archipr. Prinzivalli, Substitutus.

## DECREE.

Whereas, the little French treatise entitled, "*The Christian Instructed in the Nature and Use of Indulgences*," written by the Rev. F. Antonino Maurel of the Society of Jesus—the eleventh edition of which is already before the public—has been examined by the two above mentioned Consultors of the Sacred Congregation of Indulgences, and found to agree with authentic decrees, as regards the Indulgences, we hereby grant permission to have it newly published.

Given at Rome, from the Secretary's office of the said Holy Congregation of Indulgences, this 17th day of March, 1864.

*Place of Seal.*

Anthony-Mary Card. Panebianco, *Prefect.*
Aloysius Prinzivalli, Archipresbyter, Substitute.

## OTHER APPROBATIONS.

Lewis James Maurice De Bonald, Archbishop of Lyons and Vienne, Primate of Gaul, &c.

The treatise styled "The Christian Instructed in the Nature and Use of Indulgences," composed by R. F. Maurel, S.J., has been repeatedly approved by the Sacred Congregation of Indulgences. We have in like manner not unfrequently recommended it to the public. Wherefore, on that account, as also because of the ends proposed in the Preface of this new edition, we now unhesitatingly authorise its publication, thus once more recommending it to all the faithful.

✠ L. J. M. Card. De Bonald, Archbishop of Lyons.

*Lyons, Jan.* 17, 1869.

---

Cum librum cui titulus est: "*Le Chretien eclaire,*" &c, a P. A. Maurel nostræ Societatis Sacerdote compositum, aliqui ejusdem Societatis Theologi quibus id commissum fuit recognoverint et in lucem edi posse probaverint; facultatem concedimus, ut typis mandetur, si ita iis, ad quos pertinet, videbitur.

Hæc nostra approbatio spectat ad præsentem præfati libri editionem.

In quorum fidem has litteras manu nostra subscriptas et sigillo Societatis nostræ munitas dedimus.

Romæ, die 19 Martii, 1864.

*Locus Sigilli.*

Petrus Beckx, *Præp. Gen. S.J.*

Whereas certain Theologians of our Society, who were commissioned for that purpose, have declared, after a careful perusal of the book called, "The Christian Instructed in the Nature and Use of Indulgences," that it may be safely placed in the hands of the public, we accordingly permit it to be printed, provided it seems well to those whose province it is to authorise its publication.

This approval has reference to the present edition of the work.

In testimony whereof is given this letter from under our hands and stamped with the Seal of our Society.

Rome, March 19, 1864.

*Place of Seal.*

Peter Beckx, *General of the Jesuits.*

To the Very Reverend Father Beckx, General
of the Society of Jesus.

My Very Reverend Father,

You have vouchsafed to approve and bless this little work; I could not aspire to a sweeter recompense, since a Father's blessing is always a pledge of happiness.

In the rules which St. Ignatius has framed for us, to the end that we might always cherish the same sentiments as the true Church, he recommends us particularly to extol Indulgences—*laudare . . . Indulgentias*—which he regarded as an immense treasure, and precious pearls. This spirit of our holy Founder has ever been that of all the Generals, as also of all the Theologians, Preachers, and Missionaries of our Order; for they have not alone commended Indulgences, but even earnestly solicited them from the Apostolic See, and unceasingly defended them against the attacks of innovators.

The same spirit has animated you, my Very Rev Father, who, by your encouragement, your writings and example, unremittingly labour to strengthen more and more the sacred bonds that inviolably unite all your children to the doctrines of the Church of Rome and its chief Pastor.

May this little work correspond to the wishes of your heart, by even slightly contributing to the maintenance and spread of that holy spirit of faith, love and devotion! And may Almighty God long preserve to us a Father whom His goodness has bestowed upon us, and of whom I shall ever remain a most respectful, obedient, humble child!

A. MAUREL, S.J.

*The Roman College, July* 16, 1856.

# PREFACE.

ALL editions of "*The Christian instructed in the Nature and Use of Indulgences,*" from the second to the thirteenth inclusively, have the same Preface. But seeing that the work has met with a most benevolent reception, and is in the hands of ecclesiastics and lay people everywhere, I deem it useless to repeat that Preface, at least integrally, in the edition now presented to the public. I may, however, mention a few facts which prove conclusively, that the work has been compiled with great care and attention, and that the faithful are warranted in giving it such a favourable reception.

As is stated in the former introduction, I wrote the first edition at Rome, where, as regards the dogmatic and general principles, I had been aided by the lights of distinguished Theologians, but, in the special practical points, by the learning and long experience of Monsignor Aloysius Prinzivalli, Delegate of the Sacred Congregation of Indulgences and Holy Relics, whose death is so deeply lamented in the Eternal City. For my own part, I shall ever cherish a fresh remembrance of his goodness, his virtues, and the valuable services which he kindly rendered to me. It was he that published the thirteenth edition of the "*Raccolta, or Collection of Prayers and Pious Works to which Indulgences have been annexed by the Sovereign Pontiffs.*" The compiler was the venerable and virtuous Canon D. Telesphorus Galli, Consultor of the Sacred Congregation of Indulgences, who, during his whole life, had a most tender devotion to the Souls in Purgatory, to whom he dedicated his precious little work.

The first edition of it issued from the press of M. Perego Salvioni, at Rome, in the year 1807. Towards the end of 1855, was printed the thirteenth edition, for which, as well as for the preceding, we are indebted to the exertions of Mgr.

Prinzivalli. Having been most carefully corrected, it was enlarged with some new general grants of Indulgences, accorded by his Holiness Pius IX., who never leaves undone anything that may tend to promote the glory of God and the interests of souls. The Sacred Congregation has not only recognised this thirteenth edition as authentic, but also specially approved of it, as being most useful to the living and the dead. *Prædictum opus omnibus Christi fidelibus vivis ac defunctis maxime perutile fore probavit, et ut authenticum recognovit.*\* Moreover the Sacred Congregation desires that, to remove any doubts which may hereafter arise in the editions or translations of the work, as regards the Indulgences contained therein, recourse be unhesitatingly had to the grants given down in the edition of 1855. Accordingly, wherever there is mention of the "Raccolta" in the course of the present treatise, the reference is invariably to the thirteenth edition.†

To M. Prinzivalli are we likewise indebted for the magnificent work entitled: *Decreta authentica sacræ Congregationis Indulgentiis sacrisque Reliquiis præpositæ, ab anno 1668 ad annum 1861.*‡ This voluminous collection, compiled with rare discrimination, cost the venerable author an amount of trouble, labour, and sacrifice, which his intimate friends alone can appreciate. It is needless to remark, that I have frequently drawn from that pure genuine source.

The first edition of "*The Christian Instructed,*" &c., had the approbation of his Eminence Card. Asquini, Prefect of the Sacred Congregation of Indulgences. In fact, this was the chief title on which it had been recommended to the favourable reception of its readers. One of the first of these was the Rev. F. Ravignan, of so illustrious and pious a memory. Soon after its publication he wrote to me in these terms. "I. have read the entire of your little volume; you have really

---

\* Decree of the Sacred Congregation of Indulgences, Dec. 15, 1854.
† *Roma Typografia Perego alvioni, piazza di S. Ignazio*, n. 153.—1855.

The "Raccolta" has been translated into French by the Abbe Louis Pallard, Doctor of Theology, and in both one and the other law. The translation was approved by a Decree of the Sacred Congregation of Indulgences, dated March 28, 1856. It may be had at the establishment of the Widow Poussielgue-Rusand in Paris.

‡ *Romæ, ex officina societatis Hurelianæ, anno* 1862.

done a great service to souls; I sincerely wish to have it circulated and well known amongst the people at large." But as the first was imperfect and incomplete, I again went to Rome to make other researches, as well in the dogmatic, as in the practical part of Indulgences. The result was, that the second edition, compiled as the former in the Roman College, had been considerably enlarged, and in many points corrected. The visit also served to solve many of the other difficulties that had been proposed to me both verbally and in writing.

Thus were issued in rapid succession, several editions of " *The Christian Instructed*," &c. It has been even translated into several languages. The twelfth edition—revised, corrected, and enlarged, with a supplement of fifty pages—appeared in 1864. It had been newly examined and approved at Rome. Shortly after, a new Roman Ritual was published at the Propaganda, with an appendix approved by the Sacred Congregation of Rites. Accordingly, I availed myself of it to modify the third part, or the *Formulary*, of the thirteenth edition, which I enriched with several forms of blessings.

After these different successive improvements, one would imagine that the work was both large and accurate enough for the use of the Clergy and simple faithful. So too thought Canon Philip Cossa, who, on account of his acquirements and learning, was chosen to succeed Mgr. Prinzivalli, as Substitute of the Sacred Congregation of Indulgences.* Nevertheless, according to the earnest wishes of many worthy ecclesiastics, I have determined to present to the public this Fourteenth Edition, in which the supplement is embodied in the original part of the volume, so that there no longer exists the inconvenience of having two Indexes to it. Furthermore, having on another occasion visited Rome, for the purpose of composing my Catechism on the Church and Sovereign Pontiff,† I there received some fresh positive decisions on certain points which had been groundlessly disputed.

---

* The Holy City then mourned the loss of that virtuous and learned Priest. He died on the 7th of Nov., 1868, deeply regretted through the entire world.

† *L'Eglise et le Souverain Pontife, Catéchisme raisonné* by **Rev.** Antonine Maurel of the Society of Jesus, one vol., 12mo. Lyons, M Pelegaud, 1868.

I was also favoured with some new decrees and Indulgences. Hence, at least as far as I can believe, my readers are more than ever justified in placing unbounded confidence in this treatise on Indulgences. For since the additions and slight alterations introduced into this edition are most authentic, they in no way affect the various approbations given of it by the Roman Authorities.*

I have also taken the liberty of saying, that the venerable and holy Pontiff Pius IX. has not disdained to bless it, thereby assuring it a success, which I have ambitioned for no other object than the well-being of the faithful on earth, and of the poor souls in Purgatory.

Finally, since Providence has once more situated me near the Church of our Lady of Fourviere—a place abounding with all the riches of Heaven—I again put this entire work, in a special manner, under the patronage of the glorious Queen, who, I am inclined to believe, first inspired me with the thought of it, on that dear holy eminence.

*Fourviere, Dec.* 8, 1868.

---

* I may observe that I there made use of a little book called:— "*Nuove Indulgenze concesse del Sommo Pontefice Pio IX. dopo la publicazione della decimaterza edizione Romana dell' anno 1855, fin oal mese di maggio del 1865.* This is the Appendix to the "Raccolta:" it was approved on the 12th of May, 1865.

# THE CHRISTIAN,

## INSTRUCTED IN THE NATURE AND USE

# OF INDULGENCES.

---

### PART I.

DOGMATIC AND GENERAL PRINCIPLES.

---

#### I.

##### DEFINITION OF AN INDULGENCE.

The word *Indulgence* is derived from the Latin verb *Indulgere*, to which sacred as well as profane authors have attached various significations, all having substantially the same meaning. *Indulgere* generally signifies to treat with kindness, condescension, and gentleness, to pardon.* Thus a king who liberates a rebellious subject; a creditor who remits part of a debt to his debtor; a shepherd who, after having found a lost

---

\* In Sacred Scripture and other writings, particularly in Ecclesiastical authors, *Indulgence* commonly signifies remission, ease, or condescension, so to speak.—(*Bellarmine de Indulg.* lib. I. cap. 1.)

sheep, instead of striking it with his crook, takes it on his shoulders and carries it to the fold; all exercise acts of indulgence.

In a theological sense the word *Indulgence* expresses at once an act of clemency and mercy, a remission, a condonation, a pardon granted by the Church. To express what is meant by an Indulgence, the early Councils and Fathers frequently used the words "peace" (ειρηνη), "remission," "donation, or condonation," which fact induced the Fathers of the Council of Trent to annex the epithet *insigne* to the word Indulgence. *Insigne hoc Indulgentiarum nomen* (Sess. xxv. Decree on Indulg.).

Our present aim is to explain what that pardon means; to point out the precise nature of that condonation, that act of clemency and goodness. It will be easy to understand it, if we set before our eyes certain principles which are defined truths or dogmas of faith in the Catholic Church.

*First Truth.*—In sin, whether mortal or venial, we distinguish two things—the *guilt* and *punishment*. The *guilt* or offence is the injury done to God by sin; the penalty or *punishment* is the chastisement which the Almighty has a right to inflict on the sinner, even in the event of the sin being pardoned. When the sin is mortal the offence is grievous; it breaks the bonds that unite us to our Creator, thereby depriving us of the favour of sanctifying grace, which constitutes the life and beauty of our souls. The penalty incurred in this case is an everlasting punishment to be undergone in hell, without any alleviation or hope of pardon: "In hell there is no redemption" (Office of the Dead). But if the sin be only venial, it neither destroys the friendship of God nor merits eternal torments. "Although," says the Council of Trent, "during this mortal life holy and just men sometimes fall into venial faults, they do not on *that account* cease to be just" (Sess. vi. chap. 11).*

Sacramental absolution, worthily received, reconciles us with God, and consequently remits the guilt or offence of sin, as also the eternal punishment. The same wonderful effects result to the repentant sinner, from an act of perfect contrition or of perfect charity, which, implicitly at least, includes a *desire* of the Sacrament (Council of Trent, Sess. xiv. chap. 4). Thanks for ever to our loving Saviour, who, in His infinite mercy, has had regard to the dust of which we are formed! At the same time, we should bear in mind that we are still bound to confess the very sins thus remitted by an act of perfect contrition.

The remission of the guilt or offence of venial sin is, of course, obtained in like manner by means of the Priest's absolution. But it may be also procured by an act of contrition, or by various other practices of piety and charity, as the devout hearing of Mass, the pious recital of the Lord's Prayer, &c., because such acts procure for us an amount of love or repentance sufficient to remit these lesser faults.†

---

\* Both here and elsewhere the translator has adopted, for the most part, Waterworth's version of the "Canons and Decrees of the Council of Trent."

† Venial sins by which we are not excluded from the grace of God .... although they be rightly and profitably declared in confession, as the custom of pious persons demonstrates, may yet be omitted without guilt, and expiated by many other remedies (C. Trent, Sess. xiv. chap. 5).

In the Catholic Church there are certain ceremonies or sacred rites called *Sacramentalia*—Sacramentals. She has instituted them in order to dignify and render more solemn the administration of the Sacraments,

*Second Truth.*—Through the aid of Divine grace, the sinner, in receiving absolution, or eliciting an act of the love of God, may have for his sins a sorrow so intense, or a degree of charity so perfect, that the Almighty will grant him an entire and absolute remission of all the punishment due to his sins, as in the case of baptism and martyrdom.* But ordinarily speaking, the sinner's justification and the total remission of all the punishment exacted by Divine justice, do not take place at one and the same time. True, indeed, God in restoring the sinner to His friendship, abandons the right He has to condemn him to eternal torments. But, nevertheless, He does not omit to subject him to some temporal chas-

---

the oblation of the Holy Sacrifice, and the rites of Benedictions. They serve to inspire respect and devotion during Divine Service; they help to instruct the ignorant by reminding them of the sublime mysteries of our Redemption: they also increase faith and nourish piety. *Careant proinde*, says Voit (Tholog. mor. de Sacram. n. 114). *Ministri ecclesiæ, ne neglectim ac contemptim Ritus et Ceremonias peragendo, piam Matrem suo fine defraudent. Fideles æquè ac infideles scandalizent, et sancta fidei mysteria ludibrio exponant.*

In a more extended sense the term *Sacramentalia* is applied to other sacred rites besides those of the Sacraments. For example, to the sprinkling of holy water, the eating of blessed bread, or the pious use of any other object that has been blessed; the Confiteor or General Confession recited publicly; the various benedictions of water, wine, vestments, &c.

The effects attributed to these "Sacramentals" are to obtain for us:—1, special graces; 2, contrition, and consequently pardon of venial faults; 3, a remission of part of the temporal punishment due to sin; 4, estrangement from the devil, and preservation against his wiles or artifices; health, and other temporal advantages. But these results are obtained only by *way of suffrage*, or in virtue of the prayers used by the Church in performing these sacred rites; for those prayers, being most salutary in themselves, have great influence at the seat of Divine Mercy. Hence, the Sacramentalia do not confer grace after the manner of the Sacraments, i. e. *ex opere operato*, as the schoolmen say. Moreover, their effect entirely depends on their nature, and on the end the Church had in view in instituting them.

* God sometimes moves the heart of the sinner with such compunction that he is at once completely restored to justification, not alone as regards the remission of guilt, but also as to the removal of all relics of sin. (St. Thomas, 3rd part, Quæst. 86, Art 5.)

tisement; thus, adds Bourdalone, showing forth His wisdom at the same time that He exercises His mercy. "O Lord," exclaims St. Augustine, "Thou dost not leave unpunished the sins of even those to whom Thou grantest pardon: *Impunita peccata etiam eorum quibus ignoscis non reliquisti*" (Comment on Ps. 50, n. 11). Several examples taken from the sacred volumes clearly demonstrate the same truth. It is also expressly laid down by the Council of Trent.*

*Third Truth.*—The temporal punishment due to sin must be undergone either in this life by means of works of satisfaction or in the next by the pains of Purgatory. This is formally expressed by the same holy teacher (Sess. vi. canon 30).† And in the eighth chapter of the fourteenth Session, after having stated that in pardoning sin God does not always thereby remit the entire punishment, it gives the following convincing reason:—"And truly the nature of Divine justice seems to demand, that they who through ignorance sinned before Baptism, be received by God into grace in one manner, and in another, those who, after having been freed from the servitude of sin and of the devil, and having received the gift of the Holy Ghost, have not feared knowingly to 'violate the temple of God' and to 'grieve the

* "The Holy Synod declares that it is wholly false and alien to the word of God, that the guilt is never forgiven by the Lord without the whole punishment being therewith pardoned. For clear and illustrious examples are found in the *Sacred Writings*, whereby, besides by Divine tradition, this error is refuted in the clearest manner possible." (Sess. xiv. chap. 8.)—See likewise Canons 12 and 15 of same Session.

† "If any one saith that, after the grace of justification has been received, to every penitent sinner the guilt is remitted, and the debt of eternal punishment is blotted out in such a wise, that there remains not any debt of temporal punishment to be discharged either in this world or in the next in Purgatory, before the entrance to the kingdom of Heaven can be opened (to him); let him be anathema."

Holy Spirit.' And it becomes the Divine clemency, that sins be not so remitted to us without any satisfaction, as that having taken occasion thence, thinking sins lighter, we, injurious as it were, and contumelious to the Holy Spirit, should fall into more grievous sins, treasuring up to ourselves wrath against the day of wrath."

According to the same infallible guide, the satisfactory good works by which we may in this life discharge the debt of punishment due to our sins, are:—1, the penances voluntarily undertaken by ourselves; 2, those imposed by our confessors in the Sacred Tribunal; 3, calamities, maladies, and whatever other scourges it may please Providence to send upon us, provided we endure them with patience and resignation. For by these painful exercises we can make satisfaction to God the Father through Jesus Christ—*apud Deum Patrem per Jesum Christum satisfacere valeamus* (Sess. xiv. chap. 9)—and in Jesus Christ *in whom we live, in whom we merit, in whom we satisfy, bringing forth fruits worthy of penance* (ibid. cap. 8). By the latter words the Holy Council would have us understand that, in order to have our works satisfactory, we should be in a state of grace while performing them, for it is by charity we are enabled to live the life of our Divine Redeemer. For if we be not in the state of grace, our satisfaction will not avail in the least before the Most High; because, says the Angelic Doctor, in that case God would not accept it (Suppl. 3, part Q. xiv. art. 2). Let us, therefore, be careful to have our souls constantly united to Him by charity that we may be able to redeem some of the punishment which may, perhaps, be hereafter very rigorous, and of long duration.*

Having these principles before our minds, we can easily arrive at a correct notion of Indulgences. Suppose, then, the case of one who has had the misfortune of offending God. If the sin be mortal, the injury done to the Divine Majesty is grievous; consequently, this person has both lost sanctifying grace, and merited eternal chastisements. But should it be merely venial, the friendship of God is not lost, so that in this case he incurs only a temporal penalty. In the former supposition, the Sacrament of Penance, or an act of perfect contrition reconciles the sinner with his Creator, and obtains for him pardon as to the eternal punishment. But since a temporal penalty is ordinarily substituted for this eternal chastisement, the offender, though reconciled to God, must pay that fine either in this life by means of works of penance, or hereafter by the pains of Purgatory.

---

* Nevertheless, although works performed by a person in the state of mortal sin are not accepted by God, either as rendering satisfaction to Him or meriting eternal life, we must not imagine that they are, therefore, altogether useless. On the contrary, they are most useful, and even necessary, in order to draw down upon us the favour of Divine mercy, to soothe or disarm His anger, and thereby to procure the grace of conversion.

In Suppl. 3, part Q. xv. Art 3, St. Thomas classifies under three heads the good works by which we may satisfy God for our sins; these are, prayer, fasting, and alms-deeds. Under the first may be comprised meditation, retreats, spiritual reading, visits to the Blessed Sacrament, Mass, &c.; under the second, all mortifications of the body and of the spirit; and under the third may be reckoned not alone all corporal works of mercy, such as to feed the hungry, to harbour the harbourless, to visit the sick and those who are in prison, to clothe the naked, to give drink to the thirsty, to dress the sores of the wounded, and to bury the dead; but also all spiritual works of mercy, as to instruct the ignorant, to admonish or correct sinners, to comfort the afflicted, to give counsel to those in need of it, to protect those wrongfully persecuted, to bear patiently the faults of others, to forgive injuries, and pray for our enemies (See Duclot's "Explanation of the Christian Doctrine." clxxv. Discourse)

Blessed be God! by an inestimable benefit, whose worth and greatness are beyond expression, or, as Bourdalone says, *by a favour calculated to call forth all the envy of demons against man*, the Almighty graciously remits that debt by means of Indulgences. In fact, Indulgences are nothing else than this remission. At the very moment the sinner separates himself from God by sin, God may abandon and deliver him up to the rigour of His inexorable justice But far from doing this, He says to him: "Do penance, and you will thereby avert the arrows of my vengeance." Not only that, but since the reconciliation of the soul to God by penance entails a length of painful sufferings which the transgressor must undergo in order to make satisfaction, Our Divine Lord, on that account, vouchsafes to give up the strict right He has to exact such a penalty. Accordingly, to supply the insufficiency of the sinner's satisfaction, to facilitate the total expiation of his sins, and thus to complete his justification, so to speak, through the hands of His Church, He holds out to him a treasure of Indulgences.\*

An Indulgence, then, is "a remission of the *temporal punishment* for which the sinner remains indebted to the Divine Justice on account of *sins already pardoned as to their guilt and eternal chastisement*." This remission is effected by means of the application of the satisfactions contained in the *Spiritual Treasure* of the Church: it takes place outside the Sacrament of Penance—*extra Sacramentum*—but always in virtue of the *Power of the Keys*, that is, through the medium of those empowered to

---

\* See Bourdalone's Sermon for the Feast of Our Lady of Angels, part iii.

unlock and dispense this Grand Treasure. Hence, an Indulgence remits neither mortal sin, nor venial sin, nor the eternal chastisement; neither does it bring about or effect justification; on the contrary, it presupposes and follows it.*

The following chapters will develop and elucidate these several propositions, so as to clearly exhibit them in their true light. We shall first glance at the foundation of Indulgences, or, in other words the source whence they derive their efficacy.

* There are certain Rescripts of Indulgences which, at one and the same time, accord a remission both of guilt and punishment—*à culpâ et a pœnâ*. But in the opinion of Benedict XIV., such Rescripts are spurious, and should be attributed rather to those Quaestors who, before the Council of Trent, went about collecting and publishing Indulgences. "Such a mode of speech," writes the learned Pontiff, "is to be ascribed to the Quaestors of by-gone days, who may be said to have been the real cause of the many calamities that befel the Church on account of Indulgences" (De Synodo Diocees. lib. xiii., chap. 18, n. 7). It is plain, then, that these Quaestors or Indulgence-preachers brought great evils on the Church. Hence they were suppressed for ever by a decree of the Council of Trent (Sess. xxi., chap. 9, de Reform).

Clement V. also (Clem. 2 De Pœnit et Remiss) declared that this form of expression—*à culpâ et pœnâ*—is altogether improper—*incongruum omnino hujusmodi dicendi formula*. No doubt the words *peccata* and *culpa* are often employed to denote the *penalty* of sin; they have this meaning in various passages of Sacred Scripture. Whence it follows that the Rescripts, in which it is stated that such or such an Indulgence remits a part or the whole of the sins, refer, not to the offence itself, but to the temporal penalty exacted as a rigorous, indispensable expiation of it.

Cardinal Bellarmine gives another explanation of the phrase *à culpâ et à pœnâ*. If, says he, the Sovereign Pontiffs sometimes make use of the formula, it is because an Indulgence is generally linked to confession, so that thus by the Sacrament of Penance a person is first cleansed from his sins—*à culpâ*, and then, by means of Indulgences, afterwards released from the punishment—*à pœnâ*.

## II.

### GROUNDS OF INDULGENCES.

The doctrine of Indulgences rests on two points of Catholic faith, as on its proper immovable basis. These are the dogmas regarding *the Communion of Saints* and the existence of a *Spiritual Treasure in the Church*, composed, as it is, of the infinitely superabundant satisfactions of Christ, to which are added the satisfactions of the Blessed Virgin and Saints. Of both we shall briefly treat in order.

1. *The Communion of Saints.*—We make a profession of it in the Symbol of the Apostles, who have coupled it with the article on the Church, as essentially belonging to it. The word *communion* or common union denotes a binding together, a society of many individuals united in one, as various members in the same body. Hence it is applied to the Society of the Faithful forming only one Church or one body, having Christ Jesus for its head, and the Holy Ghost animating and enlivening it.

In this Creed the faithful are, indeed, honoured with the title of Saints, as is frequently the case in the Epistles of the inspired Apostles. This, however, does not imply that they all actually live that life of grace which constitutes saints: unhappily they do not; but they are so styled in this sense, that at least they have been all sanctified by Baptism; again, even those members that may afterwards happen to be oppressed with the weight of sin have for their head Jesus Christ, in whom dwells the plenitude of justice and sanctity. Moreover, they belong to a Church that is One and Holy, and are by vocation pledged to lead a life of sanctity: *you are a chosen generation . . . . a holy nation* (I Peter ii. 9).

The Church may be viewed under three different aspects: those of the faithful who, having ended the term of their mortal career, now happily enjoy the beatific vision in Heaven, constitute what is called the *Church Triumphant;* those detained in Purgatory to pay any debts they may have contracted by sin, compose the *Suffering Church;* in fine, those mortals who, surrounded by trials and vicissitudes of all kinds, have still to fight against temptations, make up what is known as the *Church Militant.* Yet these three bodies, distinct at present by reason of their different positions, in reality form only one Church, one body, whose head is Jesus Christ, from whom, as also from His Holy Spirit, it receives life and animation.

But to confine ourselves to the members of the *Church Militant.* The closest relations exist amongst them; relations which neither distance of place, nor difference of language, nor diversity of manners or customs can alter, since, to use the words of St. Paul, the Scythian and barbarian, the free man and slave, are all one in Jesus Christ; *but Christ is all, and in all* (Coloss. iii. 11).

Now, the Communion of Saints is the happy result of that union, or rather of that perfect unity which the Holy Ghost forms amongst all His members; a unity which, on the eve of His death, our Divine Saviour solicited from His Father for all His own: "Father, I pray to you for them, that My disciples may be all one, as Thou, Father, in Me, and I in you, that they also may be one in us . . . . I in them and Thou in Me, that they may be made perfect in unity (St. John, xvii. 21-23)."* Hence that Godlike unity exhibited, and, as it were, reproduced in the Church wherein all tends to, or is unity, agreeably to what the Great Apostle wrote to the Ephesians: "Carefully preserve the unity of the Holy Spirit in the bond of peace. One Body, and one Spirit, one Lord, one Faith, and one Baptism" (Eph. 3-5). Behold what we find in the Catholic Church, and what is to be found in and by it alone. Next to the Divinity, says Bossuet, there is nothing so beautiful as the Church, wherein is displayed a heavenly or divine unity.†

But what most enhances the value of the Communion of Saints for us is, that, if by grace we are living members of the Church—the mystic body of Christ—we, in the first place, have thereby an imme-

---

\* Wherever, in the course of this treatise, the learned author cites any texts of S. Scripture, I have scrupulously adhered to the authorised version of the Vulgate.—*Translator.*

† *Discours sur l'unité de l'Eglise.* In the same lecture, the immortal Prelate again cries out: "O holy Church of Rome, Mistress of Churches, and Mother of all the Faithful! O Church selected by God for the union of His children in the same faith and charity! To Thy unity shall we always cling with all the earnestness of our heart. 'If I forget thee, O Church of Rome, may I forget myself; may my tongue become parched and remain immovable in my mouth, if thou be not ever foremost in my memory, if I give thee not first place in all my canticles of joy!' (Ps. 136.)"

From the fact that this perfect unity exists therein, the same author concludes that the Church is indefectible, and that the gates of hell shall never prevail against it; in other words, that division, the source of weakness and characteristic of hell, shall never destroy unity, which is the touchstone or principle of power, and a mark of the true Church. Hence we see that all sects that separate themselves from the Catholic Church or from holy unity, become, by that very fact, detached bodies, disunited amongst themselves, and destined to give way sooner or later (*Histoire des Variations*).

diate participation in all of her spiritual favours, the holy Sacrifice of the Mass, the Sacraments, Divine Offices, &c.; for all these are the property, and, as it were, the dowry of that Heavenly Spouse, from which, in virtue of that holy alliance, each one of us derives his share. Then, again, as members of the Church, we are made partakers of all the merits of the righteous; just as in the human body each member performs its proper functions for the advantage and common benefit of the entire frame. Appositely, then, does St. Paul, speaking of the unity of the Church, often adduce this comparison borrowed from the members of the human body. Witness chapter xii. ver. 5 of the Epistle to the Romans; I. to Cors., chap. xii. ver. 27; likewise chap. i. v. 22, 23 of the Ep. to the Ephesians. The Angelic Doctor also speaks of it in similar terms: "As in the natural body," says he, "the action of each member contributes to the well-being of the whole frame, so likewise in the spiritual body, that is, in the Church, for since all the Faithful constitute only one body, the property of one is communicated to another; thus writes St. Paul to the Romans : ' *We are all everyone members of one another.*' Hence one of the articles of faith bequeathed to us by the apostles is the Communion of Saints or the communion of goods in the Church" (Opusculum 7).

Such is the beauteous harmony of the body of the Church; by his prayers, by his works of penance, zeal, and charity, the true Christian assists in promoting the welfare of the whole body, and that of each of its members; in praying for himself he prays for all; he imparts strength to his weaker brethren, and shares his wealth with those who are in need, for to all these is he linked by charity or sanctifying grace.\*

Much more, as a result of this royal economy, by means of our works of expiation, that is, by troublesome or painful exercises of humiliation and penance, we can make satisfaction for one another, and thus reciprocally discharge the debt of temporal punishment we may owe to the Divine justice, so that, agreeably to the design of the apostle, the members of the Church bear one another's burdens. "Bear ye one another's burdens" (Gal. vi. 2). And has not the same inspired writer said in his Epistle to the Colossians, "I now rejoice in my sufferings, and fill up in my flesh those things that are wanting of the sufferings of Christ for His body, which is His Church" (ch. i. v. 24). That is, as explained by Saints Augustine, Gregory the Great, Anslem, and Thomas, I offer my sufferings for the members of the Church, in order that those of Christ may be of avail to them. "We are all one body," writes St. John

---

\* These inestimable advantages of the body of the Church are not communicated, at least directly or integrally, to any except living members, or those united to the Head by grace or charity. Nevertheless, since sinners (dead members) are not wholly excluded from this Fellowship of Saints, they derive great benefit from the prayers and good works of the just, inasmuch as the Almighty, out of regard for these supplications and pious exercises, grants them the grace of conversion or a return to life. Thus is a plank of safety held out by charitable souls to their brethren shipwrecked in virtue. But for those who may have suffered shipwreck as regards the faith, or in the obedience due to the pastors of the Church—I mean heretics, schismatics, apostates, excommunicated persons, &c.—they are cut off from the body of the Church, and do not share with ordinary sinners these means of conversion. They are like poor sheep that defencelessly abandon themselves to ravening wolves in pursuit of them. Yet if they choose they may at any moment come back to the true fold. The Church ardently desires their conversion, and the Good Shepherd continually opens to them the bosom of His mercy, as He does to all, even to infidels. Hence on Good Friday, the day on which our loving Redeemer shed His precious blood for the salvation of all mankind, holy Church prays even for heretics, schismatics, Jews, pagans, &c.

Chrysostom, "though some members may be more distinguished than others; hence by reason of the union which makes this body unique in itself yet common to all, we are enabled to obtain forgiveness for one another by means of prayer, alms, &c." (Homil. 41, I. to Cor.).

Moreover, it has ever been the belief of the Church that, in virtue of the Communion of Saints, the Faithful have power mutually to assist one another, in such a way that some of them can actually pay the temporal penalty incurred by others. "We cannot," says the Roman Catechism, "sufficiently extol the ineffable goodness of God, who, compassionating human weakness, has bestowed on man the privilege, that one man may satisfy for another, so that those endued with Divine grace can pay for another what is due to His Supreme Majesty."\* Hence we see, on the testimony of Tertullian, St. Cyprian, and others, that, in the days of persecution, the Pastors of the Church, at the entreaties of Confessors who were on the point of receiving the crown of martyrdom, and in consideration of their sufferings, oftentimes granted to repentant public sinners a relaxation of the severe canonical punishments to which, conformably to the laws of the Church, they had been wisely subjected; the Martyrs kindly took upon themselves to expiate the crimes of those transgressors; thus they offered their tortures in payment for the debts contracted by

---

\* *Part II. de Sacr. Pœnit*, chap. v. n. 72 : In his valuable Treatise on Indulgences, chap. 1. art. v., Father Theodore of the Holy Spirit proves very clearly the truth of this doctrine, so essentially connected with the nature of Indulgences.

N.B.—Throughout, the extracts from the Roman Catechism are given almost verbally as rendered by the learned Doctor O'Donovan.—*Translator.*

their weaker brethren, especially by apostacy. So much for the dogma relating to the Communion of Saints.

2 *The Spiritual Treasure of the Church.*—As already stated, it is composed of the superabundant satisfactions of the Man-God, together with those of the Blessed Virgin and Saints. Let us now see *how* this is so.

By sin we had contracted towards the Divine Justice a debt such as all our works of satisfaction could never fully repay. But in offering Himself to His Heavenly Father as a victim of propitiation, He atoned or satisfied for us: " He is a propitiation for our sins; and not for our sins only, but also for those of the entire world" (1 John ii. 2). It is plain that, being sanctity itself, our Divine Redeemer had nothing to atone for, as regards Himself personally; yet, it was only by a life of suffering and a most cruel death, He expiated our sins, and reconciled us with our Creator: "With His own blood," says St Paul, "hath God purchased His Church" (Acts xx. 28). Now, we know that, because of the infinite dignity of His person, one single sigh from our Blessed Saviour, a single tear, or even one drop of His blood, would have been sufficient to redeem a thousand worlds. Therefore it follows that, being of infinite value, His satisfaction was not only amply sufficient to make atonement for the sins of the whole human race, and to cancel the punishment due to them, but also superabundant, nay infinitely superabundant. "For, where sin hath abounded, grace did more abound" (Rom. v. 20).

Listen to the words of Pope Clement the Sixth: " In redeeming us on the Altar of the Cross, the

Son of God has shed, not merely one drop of His precious blood, which, nevertheless, on account of its union with the Word, would have been sufficient for the redemption of all mankind, but He has spilt it even to the last drop. Accordingly, since the grace or merit of such a sacrifice cannot remain fruitless and unprofitable, how great must be the treasure with which He has endowed His Church! This treasure He has neither laid up in a napkin, nor buried in a field, for He has committed to blessed Peter, the key-bearer of heaven, and to his successors, His Vicars here on earth, power to distribute its riches to the faithful, so as to remit, either totally or in part, the temporal punishment due to their sins."\*

I pass by the testimonies of the Fathers, though they too loudly extol the efficacy of the merits of Christ, proclaiming them to be much more than sufficient for the expiation of our sins and the punishment due to them. St. Gregory Nazianzen, for instance, calls a few drops of our Saviour's blood the reparation of the entire human race: *Guttæ sanguinis paucæ mundum universum reformantes* (*Orat. in Sanct. Pasch.*).

To this essential, real fund of the treasure confided to the Church, are added the satisfactions of the Blessed Mother of God. As regards herself, the ever pure and Immaculate Virgin had never even a shadow of an imperfection to atone for; she was more holy than the Cherubim and Seraphim. Yet her life was one of prayer, privation, and sacrifice.

---

\* Etravag. Decretal.—Constit. *Unigenitus*, tit. de pœnit et remiss, cap. ii.

O how often did the sword of sorrow pierce her soul! Now, inasmuch as Mary's virtues, good works, and heroic actions were *meritorious*, they have received their recompense, such a recompense as is proportionate to their excellence and value; but, in so far as they are *satisfactory*, they have not been at all applied; consequently, since in this respect they could not be lost or of no avail, they are annexed or joined to the merits of Christ.\*

In fine, to swell still more this mysterious Capital, the satisfactory good works furnished by the Martyrs, the Virgins, and by all the Elect, are superadded to

---

\* All the good actions of the just, as almsdeeds, fasting, &c., have a distinct twofold price or value—namely, that of *merit* and *satisfaction*. This teaching is both founded on S. Scripture and upheld by the early Fathers. St. Cyprian, for example, speaking of works of penance, positively lays down that they not only procure forgiveness for those performing them, but also a crown: Qui sic Deo satisfecerit . . . . nec jam solam Dei *veniam* merebitur, sed *coronam* (In Serm de Lapsis Extremo).

Furthermore, it is certain that a good act done by a person in a state of grace *truly merits eternal life and an increase of glory* (Trent, Sess vi. can. 26 and 32); but, undoubtedly, such an act loses none of its value or efficacy by the mere fact of the Most High accepting it in compensation for some chastisement deserved by sin Therefore the same act may be at once both *meritorious* and *satisfactory*.

Again, by praying for another, I can obtain from the Almighty such or such a particular favour for him, without, on that account, forfeiting the intrinsic merit or reward of my prayer; thus my prayer will, at one and the same time, be *meritorious* and *impetratory:* why then should it not be *meritorious* and *satisfactory*, when, in praying, I purpose to make atonement for the sins of others?

I may observe, however, that the *merit* of a good action cannot be applied to another. Because, since the act itself necessarily belongs to him who places it, he alone is worthy of the recompense due to its performance. And a person could not be deprived of his own peculiar merit, Hence the declaration of St. Paul to the Corinthians: "Each one will have his own reward" (1 Cor. iii. 8). But as to the satisfaction, i. e. the atonement, the compensation for or the payment of some debt, it evidently can be applied to another, in such a manner that it may be said this other has really satisfied. Of course, it is needless to remark that he who makes satisfaction for another cannot. by the same act, satisfy for himself.

it. Many of them, as St. Joseph, St. John Baptist, St. Aloysius Gonzaga, St. Agnes, &c., performed good works far beyond what was requisite to satisfy for their own personal faults. Is it not just, therefore, that, through the Communion of Saints, the excess of their satisfactions should revert to their brethren? Surely, the Saints in heaven, our friends and advocates, being no longer able to make satisfaction of undergo sufferings in our behalf, ardently wish that the Church should deal out to us the rich fund or sacrifices which they have left to her as an inheritance.\*

Such, then, is this admirable Treasure, replete, so to speak, with the gold of the merits of our Divine Redeemer, of His Blessed Mother, and of the Saints. We shall see, in the next chapter, that the power of dispensing it has been confided to the Chief Pastors of the Church: "For (God) hath given to us the ministry of reconciliation" (2 Cor. v. 18). Thence do they draw, without ever impoverishing it, every time they grant one or more indulgences, thus substituting for that which we ourselves should personally render to the justice of God, a ransom paid by another. Think you, therefore, that, if the Church

---

\* St. Pius V. condemned the following proposition:—"By the satisfactions of Christ alone is remitted the temporal punishment, but the sufferings of the Saints are offered to God, to the end that, having regard to them, He may apply to us the merits of Christ." Hence the merits of the Saints really form part of the TREASURE, which the Church applies to us by means of Indulgences.

"There is no need," writes Cardinal Bellarmine, "to unite the sufferings of the Saints with those of our Divine Lord, as if the latter were not sufficient in themselves; they are joined to them, however, because it is fitting that their sufferings should not be unprofitable before God, particularly since such a course, besides tending in a high degree to glorify the Redeemer, from whom these holy ones derive all their blessings, redounds very much to the honour of the Saints themselves" (De Indulg. lib. i., cap. 7).

has this power, if our adorable Saviour has left at her disposal the infinite riches of His own satisfaction, together with those of His divine mother and the elect, she would be acting wisely, directed and enlightened as she is by the Holy Ghost, in neglecting to make them available to those of her children who, not unfrequently, have enormous debts to liquidate?

I have said that the satisfactions of holy Mary and the Saints constitute a part of the Treasure of the Church. To this heretics object, by saying that we thereby diminish and obscure the value of the infinite satisfaction of Christ. But they are mistaken. On the contrary, we thus enhance their merit and excellence. For, in the words of Bossuet, the grace bestowed by God on the Saints is a result growing out of the efficacy of Our Lord's precious blood, the price and power of which are so great, that it imparts its value to the sufferings and blood of the Saints, coupled as they are with His own. In this, doubtless, partly consists the Communion of Saints, by virtue of which no member in the mystic body of Christ has any property in which all the others may not have a share Thus the Divine complacency, moved on the one hand (by the good works and supplications of the righteous), shows mercy (to sinners) on the other.\* And lower down in Art. I. of his *Instructions for a Jubilee*, he adds, that, to "gain Indulgences we ought to unite our tears, sighs, groans, mortifications, and labours, to the sufferings of all the Martyrs and Saints, especially to the Agony and Dereliction, the Passion and Death of

---

\* *Meditations pour le temps du Jubil. v. point.*

Christ, in, and by whom, all the satisfactions and good works of the just are accepted by the Father."

The Holy Council of Trent, in like manner, speaking of the fruits of Penance, and of the efficacy they derive from the *Lamb that was slain*, expresses itself thus: " All our glorying is in Christ, in whom we live, in whom we merit, in whom we satisfy, bringing forth fruits worthy of Penance, which from Him have their efficacy, by Him are offered to the Father, and through Him are accepted by the Father" (Sess. xiv. c. 8).

Lastly, it is worthy of note, that Leo X., condemned Luther's 19th Article, which denied there exists in the Church a Spiritual Treasure such as defined by us.\* In his Bull *Auctorem Fidei*, Aug. 28, 1794, Pius VI. has also condemned a similar proposition of the Synod of Pistoia as false, temerarious, and derogatory to the merits of Christ and the Saints.

### III.

#### POWER OF GRANTING INDULGENCES—EXERCISE OF THAT POWER.

THE Catholic Church has this power. It would be an error in faith to maintain the contrary. A queen in her realms, a mother in her family, enjoys the

---

\* In the article to which there is reference, Luther declared that "The Treasure of the Church, whence the Pope dispenses Indulgences, is not the merits of Christ and the Saints."

esteemed prerogative of conferring a favour. Why, then, should we deny it to the spouse of the King of Kings, the dispenser of His graces and the mother of all the faithful? Truly, it was befitting that this ministry of charity should have been confided to the Church, which is here on earth the impersonation, as it were, of the goodness, the tenderness of the compassionate Lamb; but to crown all, the Eternal Son has put no bounds to His goodness, His mercy. *I desire mercy.* He came down from heaven to seek out and save that which was lost; unmindful of the ingratitude, the injustice, and the profligacy of the prodigal son, He ran to meet him; through briars and precipices, He pursued the lost sheep, and, having found it, He again opened to it His arms and His bosom. He granted pardon to Magdelene, the Paralytic, Peter and the Penitent Thief, &c. Now, this kindness on the part of our loving Jesus to seek, welcome, and pardon sinners, has passed into the very bosom of our holy mother the Church. Moreover, to render more salutary and efficacious this tenderness of His Immaculate Spouse, our Lord has promised, that He will loose in heaven whatever she should loose on earth. "Whatsoever thou shalt loose on earth, it shall be also loosed in heaven" (Math. xvi. ver. 18). Consequently, since He has made no exception, the Church can loose or remit both sin and the punishment due to it.

Again, hear the words of our Divine Master in another place. "All power is given to me in heaven and on earth" (St. Matth. xxviii. 18). "As the Father hath sent me, I also send you" (St. John xx. 21). Decidedly, those words, while they constitute her the depositary of the very power of Christ Himself, invest the Church with the right and power to forgive sinners the punishment merited by their crimes, a prerogative which nobody could dare refuse to the adorable Son of God.

Still more, our Saviour gave to His Church, in the person of St. Peter and the Apostles, the keys of the kingdom of heaven, therefore He has also conferred on her the power of opening that blessed abode to penitent sinners, and, therefore, the power of removing every obstacle that may obstruct their entrance into it; but, undoubtedly, one of the chief obstacles is, the obligation of paying their debts, *even to the last farthing*, i. e. the obligation of redeeming the penalty of sin, before presenting themselves at the Gates of Paradise. Hence, we rightly infer, that she has received from her Divine Founder power to release souls, not alone from the guilt and eternal chastisements, but also from the temporal punishment, and, consequently, to break the spiritual bond that impedes or retards their entry into the heavenly Jerusalem.

Why, then, should we limit or restrict the faculties accorded by our Redeemer to His Church? His language is clear and precise. In no other sense have they been understood by the Church or tradition. Accordingly, we see, that, in the first ages of Christianity, the Apostles and Bishops of the Church granted real Indulgences to repentant or well-disposed sinners. But they would never have exercised this power had they not been fully convinced it came to them from our Divine Lord Himself. Thus everybody admits that St. Paul truly accorded an Indulgence to the incestuous Corinthian, when, moved by the entreaties of the Faithful, and out of regard for themselves, he remitted to that poor sinner, who had by this time become an humble penitent, the remainder of the punishment to which he had been previously subjected. Bear in mind, also, that he granted this favour in the name and in the person of Jesus Christ, or as dispenser of His holy mysteries. "What I have pardoned, if I have pardoned anything, for your sakes have I done it, in the person of Christ" (2 Cor. ii. 10). Tradition, in truth, leaves no doubt on the point.*

Thus, happily, the pious use of indulgences had been constantly growing and spreading amongst the Faithful, until the blasphemous attacks of modern heretics obliged the Church to define their divine origin, utility, and efficacy. Witness the ensuing decree of the holy Council of Trent, to which every true Catholic must adhere with a firm hearty assent: "Whereas the power of conferring Indulgences was granted by Christ to the Church, and she has, even in the most ancient times, used the said power delivered unto her by God; the Holy Synod teaches,

---

* Tertulian (libi. ad. Martyres, cap. 1). St. Cyprian (libi. iii. Epist. 15, vol. 11). id (Serm de lapsis extremo). I Concil Niceno, can. 11, vol. 12. Concil Aucyran, can. 5. Concil Laodic, can. 2, &c., &c. Notwithstanding all the documents establishing the antiquity and divine origin of Indulgences, Kemnitzius has had the audacity to assert that they had not been dispensed before the year 1200. Yet he maintains, with Catholics, that the Vaudois were the first who combated the doctrine of the Church touching Indulgences. But these sectarians commenced to spread their errors about 1170. How, then, could he make out that Indulgences originated in 1200, whereas, thirty years previously, they were an object of contempt, and open to the attacks of the sect just mentioned? (See Bellarmine, de Indulg., lib. I., cap. 3, n. s.)

The same writer dates the origin of Confession from the fourth Council of Lateran, which was held under Innocent III., 1215; whilst the more enlightened Protestants "are unable to withstand the weight of historical evidence, clearly showing that it was one of the chief points of Catholic teaching *during even the four first centuries.*" I quote the very words of Gibbon, who was himself a Protestant (see his "History of the Fall of the Roman Empire").

and enjoins, that the use of Indulgences for the Christian people, most salutary and approved by the authority of sacred Councils, is to be retained in the Church; and it condemns with an anathema those who assert that they are useless, or who deny that there is in the Church the power of granting them (Sess. xxv. chap. 21).*

Prior to his final outburst with the Church, even Luther himself said: "If anyone denies the truth of the Pope's indulgences, let him be an anathema!" Hence, then, at least, he admitted the Roman Pontiff, had *power* to confer them. Soon after, however, this apostate friar, instigated by jealousy and spite, attacked both Indulgences themselves and the right of the chief pastor to grant them. In truth, his virulent and unwarranted censure of Indulgences was the ever-deplorable cause of all the incredible excesses of blindness, effrontery, and rage, into which he afterwards irrevocably precipitated himself. O, how wholesome the admonition of St. Paul: "He that thinketh himself to stand, let him take heed lest he fall" (1 Cor. x. 12) †

---

* In the Profession of Faith enjoined by Pius IV. (Bull Injunctum Nobis, Nov. 18, 1567), it is given down in express terms: *I affirm. . . . that the power of granting Indulgences was left by Christ to His Church.*

N.B.—See "Waterworth's Canons and Decrees," p. 277—*Translator.*

† Not content with treating Indulgences as mere human inventions, Luther and his partizans, through a sheer malicious spirit of slander, moreover proclaimed them to be nothing more than a mere selfish mercenary traffic—a sacrilegious and demonical negotiation of sacred th ngs. Wherefore, it may not be out of place here, to remind our readers of the incident that gave rise to this odious, oft-repeated calumny, which, unfortunately, has not failed to make a sinister impression on a great number of badly-instructed and unwary Catholics. I leave yourselves to judge, whether it were not of a most trivial character.

Full of lofty ideas respecting the grandeur and majesty of religion, Pope Leo X. wished to complete the magnificent Basilica of St. Peter in Rome—a temple, which, by reason of its outward splendour should be, as far as possible, an image as it were of the pre-eminence

The power then of granting Indulgences belongs to the Church—I mean to its Chief Pastors—who were entrusted with the charge of governing and directing the Flock, and in whose hands were left the Keys of the Kingdom of Heaven (S. Matth. xviii. 18).

and dignity of the Church herself. To accomplish this holy design, he held out a grant of Indulgences to everybody who should freely contribute something towards the building of this splendid fabric. Moreover, his Holiness had been just then witnessing, with deep regret, the rapid progress of the Turks, who, after having destroyed the Grecian Empire, after having conquered the King of Persia and the Sultan of Egypt, threatened to direct their victorious arms against the whole of Europe, and to abolish Christianity therein. Alarmed at this, he invited all the Christian Princes to unite in a common league against Selim I., to obviate the evil results of the designed invasion. He also granted an Indulgence to all those who being unable, on account of their age, office, or peculiar circumstances, actually to engage in it, should, by their contributions, forward the success of so useful and holy an enterprise. Now, who could imagine that charitable aid, so reasonable, so legitimate, and so well-applied, became the deadly source of Lutheranism? Yet it is under this pretext alone the loud cry has been raised that the Popes sell the grace of our Redeemer, and that they make an infamous and sacrilegious traffic of Indulgences!

No doubt some shocking abuses unfortunately crept into the mode of collecting or receiving these alms. Alas! what have not the base passions of man abused at all times? But the Church never authorised these scandalous proceedings. On the contrary, long before the time of the so-called Reformers, they had been condemned by Popes Innoc. III., in the Council of Lateran, by Innoc. IV., at the Council of Lyons, and by Clem. V., at that of Vienna. Later still, as already noticed, the holy Council of Trent both strictly prohibited all extortions of this nature, and totally abolished the office of quæstor.

Before Martin Luther, the Vaudois—also called the Poor of Lyons—John Wickliffe, and the Hussites, had denied to the Pope and Bishops, the power to accord Indulgences. Wickliffe's errors were repudiated and condemned in the Council of Constance (Sess. 8 and 19).

With reason, therefore, was M. de Maistre astounded at the furious manner in which Protestants combat the doctrine of Indulgences. "Still," continues he, "there is not a single Protestant head of a family who has not accorded some Indulgences, even in his own house; not one who has not pardoned a guilty child, either through the intercession, or in virtue of the merits of another child, with whom he had reason to be well pleased. Nor is there a Protestant Sovereign who has not endorsed fifty Indulgences during his reign, by giving employment, by remitting or commuting a certain penalty, &c.; and all this in consideration of the *merits* of some parents, or sons, or brothers, ancestors, &c. The blind and rebellious may then, as much as they please, dispute the principle of Indulgences. Let them have it so. But ours is that of *Reversion*" (Soirees de Saint Petersbourg, Tom, 10 entretien 1.

These are the Bishops, the successors of the Apostles (Act. xx. 28), having at their head the Bishop of Bishops, the Roman Pontiff, the successor of St. Peter, and Christ's vicar upon earth. To them alone appertains the right to apportion the spiritual Treasure of the Church.*

The bestowal of Indulgences is an act of jurisdiction or of authority that may be exercised even by delegation. Therefore, it is not an act of sacramental administration, which would require the sacerdotal or episcopal character. This, Theologians say, arises out of the nature of the thing that is to be loosed or remitted—*Debent omnia solvi, sicut exigit eorum natura*.† Accordingly, since mortal sin is not remitted without the infusion of sanctifying grace (into the soul), it is not pardoned except through the Sacraments of Baptism or Penance, by means of which this infusion takes place. But after the sin has been forgiven the remission of the temporal penalties due thereto does not require a fresh infusion of grace; rather it presupposes that the soul is already adorned with grace. Hence the reason why this absolution or remission takes place outside the sacrament by the application of the satisfaction of Christ; in other words, by means of Indulgences. It requires, however, that the jurisdiction reside in the legitimate dispensers of the Treasure of the Church, from which it follows, said Alexander III., that only those subject to the Bishop who grants the Indulgences can gain them, because nobody can be distrained or acquitted except by his own judge:

---

* Cap. *Cum ex eo*, et cap. *Nostro*, de pœnit et remission—et cap. *Indulgentiae*, eodem in 6.
† See Bellarmine, *De Indulg.* lib. 1, cap. 3, n. 3

cum a non suo judice ligari nullus valeat vel absolvi.*

A series of results grows out of this. In the first place, a Bishop-elect, or one canonically appointed, though not consecrated, can grant Indulgences. But a Bishop *in partibus Infidelium*, a mere titular Bishop, even a coadjutor-bishop, with the right of future succession, or a dimissory bishop—one who has resigned his See—possesses not this power, because he has no subjects over whom to exercise jurisdiction.

Hence, also, since the Roman Pontiff is the only person vested with a universal jurisdiction, he alone has power to dispense Indulgences for the entire Catholic world. Furthermore, as Supreme Pastor and judge of all the Faithful, and Sovereign Administrator of the spiritual goods of the Church, he can accord all kinds of Indulgences.† Of course, a General Council, without the Pope, enjoys not this power (Suarez, Bellarmin, &c.).

Again, according to the present discipline of the Church, as regulated by the fourth General Council of Lateran, held in 1215, under Innocent III., Bishops can grant only an Indulgence of one year, on the occasion of the dedication or consecration of

---

* Et cap. iv. *Quod autem*, de pœnit et remissionib. lib, 5, Decretal.

† This entire treasure, writes St. Thomas—the doctor of doctors—composed of the merits of Christ and the saints, is confided to the administration of him who presides over the universal Church. Hence we see that our Lord committed to St. Peter the keys of the kingdom of heaven (Matth. xvi). When, therefore, the utility or requirements of the Church demand it from this infinite treasure he can, at discretion, communicate to a member linked to her by charity a portion equivalent in effect, either to a total or partial remission of the punishment merited by that member; so that, forsooth, the Passion of Christ and the Saints is thereby as effectually applied to him as if he himself had suffered as much as would suffice for the remission of his sins; just precisely as happens when one person makes satisfactions for another (Quodlib. 2, q. 8, art. 16, in corp.)

a church, and at all other times merely forty days, and this to those alone under their jurisdiction. But should an Indulgence be attached by a Bishop to a church, oratory, or crucifix, &c., that is, if it be *local*, it may be gained also by strangers or persons not belonging to the diocese, provided they visit that place or that object.* His successor, however, is not at liberty to annex forty other days' Indulgence to the same object or to the same pious exercise. For such an accumulation has been interdicted by several Popes, amongst the rest by Clement IX. (Decree of Nov. 20th, 1668).† See also Decree of Dec. 17, 1838.

Archbishops are empowered to grant the same Indulgences as Bishops, as well in their own dioceses as in those of their respective provinces, even though not in the course of their visitation.‡ But Vicars-General, Vicars Capitular Generals of Orders, Abbots, Visitors, Provincials, approved Confessors, &c., have not, by common law, power to accord any Indulgences. In truth, neither Canon Law, nor custom, nor Theologians, recognise this faculty in them. Hence it is only as delegates of the Holy See or of Bishops they enjoy it.§ It follows, too, that the participation in the merits of their order, sometimes accorded by the superiors of certain religious Institutes to some worthy benefactors, is not an Indulgence. It must be said, writes Suarez, that whatever Religious Prelates do, or can do, in

---

* Eus. Amort, Theolog. mor. tom. iii., disput viii., quæritur 88.
† Theod. A. S. Spiritu *Tract. de Indulg.* cap. iii., art 2, quæres 6.
‡ Ex cap *Nostro* de posuit et remissionib. lib. 5. Decretal.
§ Ex. cap. *Acrodentibus de excessib. Praelator.* tit. x. Amort. loco it quærtur 87. S. Thomas, S. Bonaventura, Suarez. . . . et Theologi assim.

this way, is only a bestowal of suffrages or a mere gift, not a real grant of Indulgences.*

Cardinals, besides the Indulgences which it is competent for them to grant in their dioceses or provinces, should they be Bishops or Archbishops, have power to annex a hundred days' Indulgence to the churches of which they may be titular; and this though they be not Bishops or even Priests. In like manner, the Grand Penitentiary in Rome can grant a similar Indulgence of one hundred days.

Moreover, in virtue of concessions made to them by the Holy See, Nuncios and Apostolic Legates may, in the districts under their jurisdiction, attach to any good work whatever an indulgence of 100, 200, or 300 days, &c., provided the number amounts not to as many as there are days in the year. They have also power to annex to a church or chapel an Indulgence of seven years and seven Quarantines, which may be gained by all the Faithful, who, having confessed and communicated, shall visit that sanctuary, and pray there for the intention of his Holiness (Suarez, Lacroix, &c., Ferraris).

It is a well known fact that though the use of Indulgences has always flourished in the Church, yet it was not so frequent in the first ages of the Christian era as it had been at a later period, or as it is at present. This, however, is not a matter of surprise. For when there is question of what is left to her free disposition, and is not necessary as regards salvation, before extending or contracting the circle of her gifts or graces, holy Church is always sure to make inquiries respecting the wants of her children, the

* Disp. 55, sect. 5, n. 2. For more ample details, see Theodore of the Holy Spirit (Tract. de Indulg. tom. 1, cap. iii.).

opportunities of time, circumstances, &c.; she then in her wisdom afterwards deals out to, or withdraws her favours from them. Now, in the early ages of Christianity the Faithful were animated with a more lively faith; the Precious Blood of our Saviour, with which they daily replenished themselves, enkindled in their breasts a sacred fire that rendered them capable of doing and suffering all things for the Most High. Not seeking any alleviation from or mitigation of penal rigours, they desired rather to avenge upon themselves, by undergoing the canonical punishments, all the outrage done to the Divine Majesty by their sins. Our holy Mother was well aware that then, as now, she had power to dispense favours and Indulgences; but she wished to maintain, as far as possible, the rigour of her discipline. Consequently, in those days of ardent faith and primitive fervour, Indulgences were less necessary than at a more recent date.

In the course of time, however, public penances fell into disuse, and the austerities of former ages were no longer practised, though the people had not become less culpable before the Almighty. "The Church could undoubtedly abandon sinners to all the rigour of the chastisements they deserved to have inflicted upon them, both in this life and in the next. But full of beneficence towards her children and compassionating their infirmity, she prefers to supply them with Indulgences that they may be thereby induced to make at least some efforts to become thoroughly converted to God. . . . Moreover, although in consideration of the need we have of them, she dispenses these favours with a more lavish hand now than formerly: she, nevertheless, confers them only within fixed limits on certain occasions, and for legitimate reasons."*

All obstacles being removed, it is infallibly certain that the Faithful on earth obtain the fruit of an Indulgence which the Church makes applicable to the *living*. For as regards the living who may be subject to her jurisdiction, Indulgences are real juridical absolutions—*juridicæ absolutiones*—certain relaxations or condonations resulting from the *power of the keys*, and based on the judicial power with which Christ invested His Spouse in these memorable words: "I will give to thee the keys of the kingdom of heaven, and whatsoever thou shalt loose upon earth it shall be loosed also in heaven" (Matth. xvi. 19). Besides, conformably to the Sacred Canons, a person cannot accord Indulgences to any except his own subjects, because a judge has power to condemn or acquit only those subject to his jurisdiction. Hence we find that several Popes, amongst others, Martin V. and Gregory VII., have given the title of *absolutions* to the Indulgences accorded by them. Therefore, in granting an Indulgence to any one of her children here on earth, the Church directly remits to him, *by way of absolution*, a penalty corresponding to this Indulgence.

But recollect, she advances payment at the same time that she absolves; in other words, from the inexhaustible mine or treasure composed of the satisfactions of Christ and the Saints, she takes a portion equivalent in value to the Indulgence accorded, and applies it to the repentant sinner, saying to him, at least in effect: "Behold, my child, you have been

---

* *Exposition de la Doctrine Chrétienne*, by R. Fr. Bougeaut, S. J. tom. 2.

released from a part or the entire of the punishment due to your sins; your debt has been totally or partially liquidated; Jesus Christ, the Blessed Virgin, and the Saints, have satisfied for you; be sure to testify your gratitude to them, particularly by the future amendment and innocence of your life."[*]

The reason of all this is, that the Prelates of the Church, even the Popes themselves, are not such absolute masters as to be able, at pleasure, and without any compensation, to remit or cancel the transgressions and penalties for which sinners are answerable before the Sovereign Judge. Doubtless, they are *divinely appointed judges*, who, by virtue of the *power of the keys* with which they are invested, can truly remit both sin itself and its punishment, in the name of God; but, at the same time, this must be *in a manner* that will satisfy His justice. Thus, for example, when a Priest, in the tribunal of Penance, absolves a penitent from his faults and part of the temporal penalty, he does not do so without any compensation, for, to satisfy the Divine justice, he applies to that soul the price of our Blessed Redeemer's Precious Blood. It is precisely the same in the case of Indulgences, because, through them as a means, the Chief Pastors of the Church remit the temporal penalties due to sin, by paying them, if the expression be allowable, with the satisfaction of

---

[*] In this paraphrase or admonition is contained the reason why theologians style an Indulgence at once an *absolutio* and a *solutio*—an acquittal or payment, "An Indulgence is necessarily an *absolution* which has annexed to it a payment taken from the treasure made up of the merits of Christ and the Saints" (Theodore of the Holy Spirit Suarez, Lugo, &c.).

"It must be remarked that a relaxation, i. e. a grant of Indulgences implies two things—namely, a communication of the treasure of the Church, and a certain judicial absolution (S. Bonav. in iv. sent diat. 20, p. 2, quæst. 5).

Jesus Christ and His Saints. For the inspired words of the great Apostle admit of no exception: "Without shedding of blood there is no remission" (Heb. ix. 22).*

This is also the reason why the Church, in granting Indulgences, by no means intends to dispense us from every other obligation. Surely it is not her design thereby to release us from the obligation of doing penance, of carrying our cross in the footsteps of Christ, and of uniting our satisfaction to His; in fact, she *could not* dispense us from these all-important duties. She simply comes to the assistance of well-disposed persons, in such a way that she enables them to free themselves before the justice of God, even as regards the life beyond the grave. Without this goodness on the part of our loving mother, we could never, except by works of penance, fill up the exact measure of the punishment due to our sins.

---

## IV.

#### SALUTARY EFFECTS OF THE USE OF INDULGENCES.

Doubtless, from what has been already said, we have a clear conception of the principal and direct fruit of Indulgences. Yet it may be useful to recur here to the same important matter, and to impress it vividly on our minds.

---

\* See Bellarmine (*De Indulg.* lib. i. cap. 5, n. 3.) In a subsequent chapter we shall see how the Church applies Indulgences to the Faithful departed.

Whenever we confess our sins in order to obtain absolution, the Priest imposes on us a penance, the performance of which is necessary and sufficient for the integrity of the Sacrament. But, generally, this penance is not enough to cover fully our liabilities before the just Judge. For seldom is the penance enjoined by the confessor proportioned to the penalties incurred by the sinner and exacted by the Almighty, especially since the Penitential Canons have practically ceased to be enforced in the Church. Hence the holy Council of Trent, well aware of that, so strongly admonishes Priests to enjoin salutary penances, adapted to the nature of the crimes and the strength of the penitents, yet such as the spirit of God and prudence may suggest.*

In connection with this matter, I may remark incidentally, that when a penitent complains of the penance imposed on him in the Sacred Tribunal, when he murmurs at and censures the rigour of the confessor, he evidently shows he is ignorant both as to the heinousness of sin and the weight of the obligations contracted by him in its commission. "Could penitents rightly understand how beneficial it would be to them to make satisfaction in this life for their sins, they would not content themselves with an exact performance of the light penances imposed on them by the minister of reconciliation; but would spontaneously undertake other austerities, to give stronger evidence of their sorrow for having offended

---

* These are the very words of the Council : "Therefore the Priests of the Lord ought, as far as the Spirit and prudence may suggest, to enjoin salutary and suitable satisfactions, according to the quality of the crimes, and the ability of the penitents; lest, if haply they connive at sins and deal too indulgently with penitents, by enjoining certain very light works for very grievous crimes, they be made partakers of other men's sins" (Sess. xiv. chap. 8).

God, as also of the feelings of love and gratitude with which they ought to be animated on account of His unspeakable mercy.*

Did we duly perform, here on earth, all the works of penance prescribed for us in the holy tribunal, together with even other exercises freely added by ourselves, still it would be to be feared we should have to endure very severe chastisements in the life to come. Accordingly, what has the Church done in the name and by the authority of her Divine Spouse? Full of tenderness and love, and compassionating our weakness, our good mother has enriched us with the marvellous gift of Indulgences, thereby supplying the inefficiency of our penances, which may be either too light or badly performed by us. She thus actually acquits us before the Most High, and completes our justification.† Her conduct in this respect is an exact imitation of that of God Himself in the adorable mystery of the world's redemption; for, in truth, this Divine redemption is nothing else than an immense Indulgence accorded to guilty man, in consideration of the Precious Blood shed by our Saviour for him on Calvary.

But to resume our subject: From this essential fruit, which is inherent in the nature of an Indulgence, spring others that are most valuable. It has been objected by certain heretics, and even by some Catholics, unworthy of the name, that in unlocking her Spiritual Treasures for her children, the Church merely paves the way to relaxation. They have

---

\* Abbe Duclot (*Explication de la Doctrine chretienne, Discours* 175).

† Luther affirmed that, "for persons who truly gain them, Indulgences do not avail unto the remission of the penalty due to actual sin before the Divine Justice." Leo X. has condemned this proposition (Bull, *exurge Domine*, June 11, 1520)

furthermore advanced that the bestowal of Indulgences is only a permission to sin with impunity. We answer, that this might be so, if, as our enemies blush not to affirm, Indulgences exonerated us from the obligation of doing penance and of leading Christian lives. But, should the very reverse be the case, then we are justified in inferring that these rash, fickle-minded beings blasphemously comment on what they are totally ignorant of, or, at least, what they affect to ignore. We, moreover, emphatically assert, that the conditions to be fulfilled in order to gain Indulgences would exact from most of these libertines sacrifices from which their corrupt nature would shrink with horror. In one word, this is the great secret of the calumnies with which they cloak their repugnance to everything that mortifies the flesh and brings the spirit under subjection.

Yes, happily, it is beyond doubt that Indulgences, be they what they may, are not obtained without a spirit of penance and a life of Christian virtue. As has been stated, an Indulgence remits neither sin itself nor its eternal penalty, but merely the temporal punishment not yet expiated. Now this chastisement can be remitted only to sinners already reconciled to God; because, while the sinner is at enmity with his Creator, there can be no Indulgence for him, since our Lord will never cancel the penalty of sin as long as the sin itself subsists, or as long as the stain or guilt is not blotted out.* But, pursuant to this Catholic teaching, which is expressly given down in the Apostolic Bulls, an Indulgence can be

---

* Nobody can obtain remission of the punishment, until he shall have first got forgiveness of the offence (St. Thomas, Supplement, 3 par quæst. 27, art. 1).

acquired only by a heart that is truly contrite and penitent—*vere pænitentibus et confessis, vere contritis* . . . . . by a soul in the friendship of God and adorned with His grace. How then could it do away with penance, or open a doorway to relaxation? How could that give leave to outrage the Divine Majesty with impunity, which presupposes that sin is destroyed in the soul, and which, to use the words of Bourdaloue, implies a *true conversion*, the most difficult, the most heroic, and the greatest attainment in all religion.*

This is not all. A participation in Indulgences, especially in those that are plenary, requires not alone a *sincere conversion*, or as Bossuet has it, *the perfect love of God*, but also a faithful accomplishment of certain works of piety, charity, and mortification, to which are nearly always added confession and communion. Now, I repeat, are such works as these, think you, done with a view to foster relaxation and irregularity? Far otherwise did Clement VI. reason when, in his Bull for the Jubilee of the year 1350, he said: "We grant those Indulgences *in order that the piety of the Roman people and of the faithful at large may be augmented, that their faith may light up with renewed splendour, that their hope may become stronger, their charity more ardent and enlivened.*" Hear what

---

* *Sermon pouri l'overture die Jubile*, 2. parte. The illustrious preacher clearly proves there also, "that it is rather in the principles of the Heresiarchs, and in their scandalous tenets, the palpable relaxation, and even the total abolition of penance are to be found. If we have good faith, we shall readily see, on a little reflection, that a religion which has robbed penance of all its works of humiliation, of all that is arduous and painful about it—inasmuch as it has abolished confession, suppressed the rigour of satisfaction, censured bodily mortifications, dispensed with the obligation of fasting, &c., is not the religion of Jesus Christ." "The kingdom of heaven suffereth violence, and the violent bear it away" (Matth. ix. 12).

Bellarmin also said at the beginning of the seventeenth century: "This year of Jubilee has been productive of such extraordinary works of penance, of such wonderful conversions, such excellent and numerous works of piety, that it may well be called a *holy year*, a year rich and fertile, and pleasing to the Almighty." Elsewhere he cites a pamphlet which specifies in detail the *remarkable and almost countless religious exercises* performed during the Jubilee celebrated in the Pontificate of Gregory XIII.

Nor should we omit the testimony of an illustrious English prelate, not less distinguished for his learning than for his virtues. Speaking as an eyewitness of the effects produced at Rome by the Jubilee of Leo X., he says: "I wish you had seen the Confessionals beset on all sides, and the altars thronged with the crowds that flocked to the Holy table. I wish you had been witness of the restitutions made, and of the conversion of obdurate sinners, for you would then understand why persons undertake this arduous pilgrimage, and you would see whether the nature of such an institution is an incentive to vice, and a license to commit sin.* Even infidels themselves are forced to admit openly the efficacy of Indulgences as regards both the maintenance and increase of faith and virtue. M. D'Alembert, e.g., complains of the Jubilee of 1775 *as having retarded the progress of the Revolution by twenty years.* "*Such another Jubilee,*" said Voltaire, "*would put an end to philosophy.*"

* Cardinal Wiseman, 12th Homily, tom II. In his sermon for the Feast of Our Lady of Angels, Fr. Bourdalon frequently notices the signal effects of graces, produced in souls by the holy Indulgence of the Portinuncula (3rd part). The same may be said of other plenary Indulgences.

Far, then, from being an inducement to discontinue the performance of good works and the exercise of Christian virtues, the grace of an Indulgence, on the contrary, serves to promote their practice, and, consequently, to excite the fervour, the devotion, and zeal of the people.* Daily experience proves this. For never do we do greater violence to ourselves, never are we more energetic in our struggles against the bent of our evil habits, or more guarded against relapses; in a word, never have we more fervour in forming our resolutions to begin a new life than when we prepare to gain a plenary Indulgence. Aptly, therefore, does Bossuet conclude his *meditations for a time of Jubilee* by this beautiful prayer: "O my God, an Indulgence cannot but be most salutary to me, since it is at once calculated to appease your anger and excite my love. O my Jesus! O Divine Spouse! all needy as I am I accept in a spirit of faith, humility, and compunction, the Indulgences of thy holy Church, in order to unite myself more perfectly to thee, and, if possible, to leave nothing between us both—not even the least relic either of sin or its penalty—that may separate us for one moment. O my God, my only refuge, and my support! I desire to be entirely thine. I consecrate to Thee my heart, that I may love Thee with all my strength, for Thou art my God, my most amiable Creator, who art infinitely good and perfect, to whom be honour and glory for ever and ever. Amen."

Finally, it may be well to note that in granting Indulgences the Vicars of Christ grant them only for some pious ends that tend to advance the glory

---

* See how St. Francis Xavier appreciated Indulgences. (His letters tom. ii. book 7. letter xx.)

of God and the salvation of souls. Thus, for example, they invite us to contribute towards the Propagation of the Faith in distant pagan countries—to take part in so charitable and holy a work as the baptism of children belonging to the Chinese or Indians—to procure the conversion of sinners through the intercession of the Immaculate Heart of Mary—to induce the people to enrol themselves in the Associations of the Sacred Heart, of the Blessed Sacrament, or in the confraternities of Holy Mary—to encourage devout pilgrimages—to frequent the Sacraments—to assist the poor souls in Purgatory, &c., &c.; doubtless, if by dispensing Indulgences, holy Church attains these happy results, we ought to bless our tender Mother as also the Indulgences, and to proclaim with the Fathers of the Council of Trent that their use is most salutary for the Christian people: *Christiano populo maxime salutarem.*

## V.

#### APPLICATION OF INDULGENCES TO THE SOULS IN PURGATORY.

The destiny of all men is not the same after death, for "the Son of Man will render to everyone according to his works" (St. Matth. xvi. 27). Happy are those good and faithful servants who keep themselves not only in the state of grace but also cleansed from every fault, and released from all liabilities to the Divine Justice! At the very moment of their blessed death, they enter into heaven and into the joy of their Lord. But unhappy those who depart this life, having their souls contaminated by mortal sin, at enmity with their Creator. Like the Rich Man of the Gospel, they are then instantly buried in the flames of hell.

There is, however, a third or middle class, composed of those souls that are not pure enough to enter heaven immediately—*into which nothing defiled shall enter* (Apoc. II. 27). They have, it is true, some lesser faults to atone for, some temporal punishment to endure, but yet they leave this world in a state of grace, and in the friendship of the Almighty. Accordingly, they are detained in a place of suffering called Purgatory, until, having fully satisfied the justice of God, they are admitted into the mansions of eternal bliss.

Such, briefly, are the teachings of our holy religion, as inviolable and immutable as the Being who revealed them. Now, we pray not for the Saints in Heaven, since they have no need of our prayers, nor for the Reprobate, as our prayers would be of no avail to them, for the smoke of their torments shall ascend up for ever and ever (Apoc. xiv. 11). But we pray for the souls in Purgatory.

That there is such a place, and that the souls detained there can be assisted and relieved in their sufferings by the prayers or suffrages of the Living, by their fasting, alms-deeds, and other good works, particularly by the oblation of the holy Sacrifice of the Mass, is an article of faith founded on Sacred Scripture, the tradition of the Fathers, the teaching of Councils, notably on that of the Council of Trent.*

---

* Trid. Sess. xxv. Decret. de Purgat.—Sess. vi., can. 30—Sess. xxii. can. 3—et cap. 2, where it is said: "Therefore not only for the sins

From time immemorial, writes Tertullian, to offer prayers and suffrages for the Dead has been considered a divine tradition and a repository of faith—*fides servatrix*. Even in the Old Law it was customary to pray and offer sacrifices for the Departed; in fact, the people doubted not that it was a holy, salutary thought, inspired by God: "It is therefore a holy and a wholesome thought to pray for the Dead that they may be loosed from their sins" (2 Machab. xii. 16). Hence the Church has never omitted to pray for them during the celebration of the divine Mysteries. A mere glance at her ancient liturgies will convince us of this. And the reason is, because there has been always a universal belief in the existence of Purgatory, or in some place or state where, to borrow the expression of St. Augustine, the Almighty sets things to rights. There He completes the punishment of those faults that may not have been sufficiently expiated here on earth; there he puts holy souls to their last test, inasmuch as he wipes away their least flaws and imperfections, thus enabling them to acquire, through fire, that consummate degree of purity requisite for the enjoyment of the Beatific Vision. Is not this conduct on the part of the Most High supremely just and equitable? Let us, then, console ourselves with the thought that, should we be one day of the number of those Suffering Souls, the whole Church will offer prayers for us; for this tender Mother ever solicitous for her children, never ceases to assist them, until she has safely landed them in the bosom of a blessed immortality.

punishments, satisfactions, and other necessities of the faithful who are living, but also for those who are departed in Christ, and who are not as yet fully purified, is it rightly offered, agreeably to a tradition of the Apostles" (Sacrifice of the Mass).

Notwithstanding the various strong, irrefragable proofs in favor of Purgatory, many heretics, and amongst them Protestants, have rejected it altogether. It seems they prefer to do so, rather than unite their prayers with those of the Catholic Church in behalf of their deceased relatives and friends, who may, perhaps, be greatly in want of help. Thus they forsake those poor souls at death, and think no more of them. Why? Because heresy is not a true parent; it possesses not the tenderness or love of a mother.

Moreover these Holy Souls can be aided and succoured in, as also totally released from their pains by means of Indulgences. The Church has never had a doubt on this point. Hence, for many centuries she has granted Indulgences applicable to the Faithful Departed. Is it not, then, in the words of the Doctor of Grace, an unheard-of madness to call in question what the universal Church believes and practices through the entire world?\* Copying the example of Luther, the Synod of Pistoia had the effrontery to maintain that the application of Indulgences to the departed was a mere chimera.† But Pius VI., in his Bull *Auctorem Fidei*, has censured and condemned that proposition as false, rash, offensive to pious ears, injurious to the Roman Pontiff, as well as to the general practice and feelings of the Church at large.

Again, if our prayers and good works taken separately in themselves, are beneficial to the souls in Purgatory, are we not warranted in the belief, that Indulgences, which are an application of the *satis-*

---

\* Si quid tota perorbem frequentat Ecclesia quin ita faciendum sit disputare insolentissimae insaniae est (Aug. Epist. 54, alias, 118, n. 6).

† Luther said: "For six classes of persons, Indulgences are neither necessary nor useful, viz.—the dead," &c. The proposition was condemned by Leo X., in the Bull *Exurge Domine*, already cited

*factions* of Christ, of the Blessed Virgin and Saints, will be much more profitable to them, since the Church herself makes this application? Independently of that, the power of alleviating and abridging the pains of the Souls in Purgatory, is a happy result which grows out of the doctrine of the Communion of Saints. The souls of the Faithful who die in a state of grace, says St. Augustine, are not separated from the Church; they are members of the same body, united to the Faithful on earth, by the same bond of faith and charity: Neque enim piorum animæ mortuorum separantur ab Ecclesiâ.* Hence the grounds of all our pious efforts to assist them.

The Church, however, does not apply Indulgences to the Dead by way of judgment or *absolution*, as it does in the case of the living, but by way of *suffrage*, or intercession, or succour, or offering. Being no longer under her jurisdiction, as they are not subjects of her realm, but belong only to the empire of the Eternal King, she cannot release or deliver them *directly* from their pains, but only indirectly, that is to say, in consequence of an Indulgence gained by the Living, and applied by them to the Departed, the Church takes out of her Treasure, a portion of the merits and satisfactions which may correspond to that Indulgence, and presenting it to God, supplicates Him

---

* De Civit. Dei, lib. xx. c. 9. Item ex Litteris Decret. Leonis X. ad Cardinalem Cajetanum. It may not be amiss to cite here the beautiful words of Count J. de Maistre: "What a grand spectacle, that immense city of spirits, with its three ranks ever linked to each other! The *fighting* world presents one hand to the *suffering* world, and with the other takes hold of the world *triumphant*. Thanksgiving, prayers, satisfactions, succours, inspirations, faith, hope, and love, all pass on from one to one in regular succession, closely resembling beneficent rivers. Nothing there is isolated, but the spirits, not unlike the bars of a magnetic battery, join their own powers to those of all the others (Soirees de St. Petersburgh, tom. 11, 10 entretien.)

to vouchsafe so much relief to the suffering souls. If, then, the Almighty accept the offering thus presented to Him by Holy Church, the souls in Purgatory, to whom the Indulgence shall have been applied, will receive either a total or partial remission of the temporal punishment which they would otherwise be obliged to undergo. And we have every reason to believe that He really does accept it. Is not the dogma of the Communion of Saints, a guarantee for this belief? Are not the merits of Christ, the Blessed Virgin, and the Elect, infinitely dear to the Divine Complacency? Is not the Church who offers them a most amiable Bride, the glorious, blessed, immaculate Spouse of His only Son? When she prays and offers, is it not the Holy Ghost that prays and offers in her and by her? "It is the dove that coos," adds St. Augustine, "and God always graciously hears her voice." *

Nevertheless, our Lord is not bound by any formal express promise, to accept the offered price, and hence this acceptation depends altogether on His adorable will, and perhaps, also, on the amount of care which the Dead may have taken during life to render themselves worthy of such relief. On the other hand, the person desirous to gain the Indulgence for the Holy Souls, may, through ignorance, or forgetfulness, omit one or more of the prescribed conditions, or fulfil them negligently. Therefore we

---

* In the present matter, by the *Church* I mean the Sovereign Pontiff or Chief Head, who alone has power to dispense in an absolute manner the treasure composed of the merits of our Lord and the Saints. Bishops, or any other prelates inferior to the Roman Pontiff, cannot accord Indulgences applicable to the faithful departed. As already noticed, they can grant them only for the living to those under their jurisdiction, and in a measure determined by the Apostolic See ("Bellarmin de Indulg." lib. 1, cap. 14, n. 8.—"Ex Navarro de Jubil." notab. 22, n. 4).

have no absolute certainty that an Indulgence applied by us to such or such a soul in Purgatory has had its full effect.* The same applies to *privileged altars*, of which hereafter. Accordingly, it cannot be positively asserted, that the plenary Indulgence annexed to them in behalf of the Dead, infallibly leads to heaven the soul to whom it may have been applied by a Priest. Yet for reasons before assigned, we should entertain strong hopes that such is the case.

In like manner, we should not imagine that, because of the infinite merit of the Sacrifice of the Cross, which is identically the same as that of the altar, wherein Christ is the High Priest and Victim, it is always enough to have merely one Mass said for the repose of a certain soul in Purgatory. For though the value of the Sacrifice of Calvary is infinite, the application made of it by means of the Holy Sacrifice of the Mass is not so: rather it is His will to proportion, so to speak, this application or efficacy of the adorable Sacrifice to the fervour and piety of our dispositions. This is the opinion of St. Thomas.† Hence it is most useful to have Mass frequently celebrated for the Departed, and also, if the Rescripts of the Holy See permit, to apply to them the greatest possible number of both partial and plenary Indul-

* Several distinguished Theologians are of a different opinion They maintain that the effect in their regard is infallibly certain, even *ex justitia et condigno*, as scholastics have it. Bellarmin styles this opinion *admodum piam*, a very pious one, but the other adopted by me in the present article, *valde rationabilem*—a well grounded opinion. In truth, it enables us to meet any difficulty that may present itself in the former view.

† Although, by reason of its infinitude, this oblation would be sufficient to cover all liabilities, yet, to those for whom, or even to those by whom it is offered, it is applied only in proportion to the measure of their devotion, and not so as to redeem the whole penalty (St. Thomas, 3 pars, quærst. 79, art. 5).

gences. Should it happen that the souls for whom we pray are in the company of the Blessed, then, through the goodness of God, the fruit of these Masses and Indulgences will be available for other souls.

Let us, then, be assured, that, far from being prejudicial to ourselves, our charity towards the Departed, will, on the contrary, be most advantageous to us, because merit is proportioned to the ratio of charity. But, decidedly, there is more charity in sacrificing a person's own interest to relieve his suffering brethren, than in reserving it to himself. "There is very little virtue in giving what is superfluous to the poor," remarks a judicious author, "but a great deal in bestowing on them part of what is necessary for oneself." We should likewise reckon on the special protection of the Righteous, whose pains we may have assuaged, and whose deliverance we may have accelerated. Having once entered into glory, they will become our most faithful intercessors before the Eternal Father. We perhaps know them not, but they know us well, and will never forget us. Neither will they be alone in discharging this their debt of gratitude. Our blessed Lord Himself, whose interests and glory were immensely promoted and advanced by our devotion towards those Holy Souls, will assist them in repaying the kind services we may have rendered them.*

---

* See n. 83, part 2nd, "An Heroic Act of Charity," to which is annexed an immense number of Indulgences for the holy souls. In his admirable work, entitled "All for Jesus," the Rev. F. F. W. Faber, of the Oratory of St. Philip Neri, beautifully developes the six advantages arising from the application of Indulgences to the souls in Purgatory (chap. ii. s. 4). Read these pages, and you will be greatly stimulated to be generous to these Daughters of God, these Spouses of the Holy Ghost, who continually wail afar off from the Paradise above, a prey to torments such as the Martyrs never endured. Perhaps, too, these poor souls whom, according to the laws of His Justice, our Saviour is obliged to afflict and punish, are our own parents or friends! Blessed for ever be the Most

## VI.

**VARIOUS KINDS OF INDULGENCES—IMPORTANT OBSERVATIONS REGARDING THEM.**

THERE are two sorts of Indulgences, namely, those that are *plenary* or general, and those that are *partial* or limited. In according one or other of these, the Church, in her wisdom, exercises the power she has received from our Divine Redeemer Himself. Call to mind the well-known words of St. Thomas, which are cited in a note, page 28, Pope Clement VI., after having defined the Treasure confided to St. Peter and his successors, to be distributed to the Faithful, adds, "in such a way, that at one time they might grant a total, at another a partial remission of the temporal chastisement due to sin, as well in a general as in a special manner, just as they may see it conducive to the glory of God" (Extravag. *Unigenitus* de Pœnit et Remission).

A plenary Indulgence is so called because it remits the whole of the temporal punishment due to sins already forgiven. Accordingly, a person who may have been fortunate enough to gain such an Indulgence, and receive its full application, would be like a newly baptised adult—free from sin and its penalty; so that if he were to die in this happy state,

---

High for having empowered us to intercede for them, to petition for and procure their release! Let us then avail ourselves of this prerogative, by oftentimes helping them with our prayers, offering for them our Indulgences and the *satisfaction* of our good works, without fearing that we shall lose any of the fruit as regards ourselves. Nothing is ever lost that is done for God and for the souls whom He loves with a most sincere and tender love!

he would mount up directly to heaven, without passing through the fire of Purgatory.

Amongst the plenary Indulgences, the principal and most solemn is that of a Jubilee.* I say the

---

* This word is derived from the Hebrew *Jobel*. According to the Rabbins, it signifies a *Ram's horn*; because, to announce the year of Jubilee, the priests in the Old Law made use of a trumpet shaped in the form of a ram's horn. But other Hebrew scholars derive it from the Hebrew verb *Hobil*, to restore, recall—from the fact, that on such occasions everything used to be restored to its former owner (See Calmet's "Dictionary of the Bible").

Cardinal Bellarmin traces its etymology from the Hebrew *Jabal*, to produce or bring forth, whence the substantive *Jabul*, which designates every species of fruits. In this view a Jubilee would mean a productive, useful, fruitful year, in which the people, without labouring, lived on the produce of the preceding years; then, too, all lands and houses hitherto alienated, were restored *gratis* to their original proprietors; slaves, in like manner, without molestation, recovered their liberty (De Indulg. lib. 1, cap. 1, n. 3).

At present, the more common and probable derivation given of it, is from the word *Jobel*, which taken separately by itself, does not signify as the Rabbins maintain, a *ram's horn*, but rather *joy jubilation—a joyous acclamation*. To convey their meaning, it should be joined to the word *queren* (horn), expressed, or at least understood. It is nearly certain the Latins have taken the word *jubila, orm*, from the Hebrew Jobel. As a matter of fact, the jubilee year was to the Jews a time of joy, of grace and general pardon. We see its origin and institution in ch. xxv. of Leviticus. From that of the Jewish law is borrowed the word used to denote the Christian jubilee, which is likewise an occasion of spiritual joy, grace, and forgiveness.

The *ordinary* Jubilee is that which is published at Rome every twenty-five years, commencing from the Pontificate of Sixtus IV. It continues for the space of a year in the Holy City, during which the people visit and venerate the tombs of the Apostles; by a special Bull it is then extended to all the Catholic universe. The first of these Jubilees dates from 1475. Boniface VIII. ordained that the ordinary Jubilee should take place every succeeding hundredth year, down from the famous one of the year 1300. But by a Bull, dated Jan. 8, 1343, Clement VI. reduced this period, and decided that it should be henceforward celebrated every fiftieth year. Hence it was observed at Rome in 1350, being then much more numerously attended than in 1300. Urban VI. abridged this term still more, purposing that in memory of the thirty-three years our Saviour lived on earth, the interval should be thirty-three years. At last Paul II. and Sixtus IV. arranged that the celebration of the Jubilee should occur every twenty-fifth year. This rule has been observed ever since by all succeeding Popes.

An *extraordinary* Jubilee is one that is accorded for some particular occasion, as the crowning of a new Pope, an urgent want on the part of the Church or State, the averting of some public calamity, &c. Since his glorious elevation to the throne, his present Holiness Pius IX. has granted several Jubilees of this kind.

*principal and most solemn*, not indeed as regards the essence of the Indulgence or the entire remission of the penalty, for this is common to all plenary Indulgences, but on account of certain circumstances peculiar to a Jubilee. Thus, for example, a Jubilee generally extends to the faithful at large, and may be obtained indiscriminately in all Churches; it is also accompanied with more imposing ceremonies; it is published, celebrated, and brought to a close, with a display of pomp better calculated to inspire devotion; while it lasts, the whole Church is in prayer and penance, and everywhere is preached the inspired Word, calling on the people to raise their suppliant hands to the most High, to propitiate Him by their humiliations and fasts. Furthermore, a Jubilee brings also in its train special privileges, as the power conferred on ordinary confessors to absolve from all reserved cases and censures, that of commuting simple vows, and so on, agreeably to the clauses contained in the Bull.

At the time of a Jubilee, the Constitutions of the Sovereign Pontiffs and the Bishops' Pastorals determine the works to be performed in order to participate in its signal favours. Those prescribed for the ordinary Jubilee are: 1, the procession by which the Jubilee is opened; 2, Confession; 3, Communion; 4, the Stations or a visitation of certain fixed Churches, in which prayers are to be said for the intention of his Holiness. Fasting and alms-deeds are works peculiar to an extraordinary Jubilee. The chief thing on such occasions is to attend to the conditions laid down in the Pontifical Bulls and Bishops' Pastorals, and to adhere strictly to them.

A *partial* Indulgence is one that remits only a

portion of the penalty due to sin. We oftentimes hear of an Indulgence, for instance, of forty or a hundred days, seven weeks, a year, &c. But in thus granting an Indulgence of a certain defined number of days, weeks, or years, the Holy See does not thereby intend a corresponding abridgment of the pains of Purgatory. Such phraseology has reference merely to the penance enjoined by the ancient rules or canons of the Church. All are agreed in this. Wherefore an Indulgence of a hundred days or a year, for example, is the remission of as much temporal punishment as would have been formerly atoned for, before God, by a canonical penance of a hundred days or a year.\* Hence it would be useless to try to ascertain the amount of purgatorial sufferings, redeemed or remitted by such a penance. God alone knows this, and we accordingly ought to leave it to His infinite mercy. All that may be in general said on the matter, is, as has been just stated, that an Indulgence which remits a penance of so many days or years in this life, remits in the other a penalty corresponding to this penance. But the real specific value of this penalty, in relation to the life to come, is wholly unknown to us.

The longest partial Indulgences ordinarily granted by the Vicars of Christ are of seven, ten, fifteen, or twenty years, rarely more. Rightly, then, do the most learned authors concur with Benedict XIV., in regarding as false or suspicious Indulgences of 1,000, and, *a fortiori* those of 10,000, or 100,000

---

\* To Indulgences of years in length, the Holy Father often adds an equal number of *Quarantines*. The Quarantines have reference to the Lenten fast. Accordingly, an Indulgence of seven years and as many Quarantines, e. g. means the remission of a temporal penalty corresponding to seven years of canonical penances, joined to the special austerities of seven Lents.

years, such as are mentioned in certain pamphlets or loose papers that are hawked about and sold to simple, credulous people, not unfrequently, also, to the great disedification of many, and the detriment of true devotion.*

Thus it becomes necessary to cite here different Indulgences which are false, null, and in many instances condemned by positive Decrees of the Sacred Congregations of the Holy Office and Indulgences. Notwithstanding the various proclamations against them, they are still, even at the present day, printed and spread amongst the Faithful, with no other result than to render piety a matter of superstition, to bring religion into ridicule, as also to expose it to the attacks of heretics and the ungodly. From this it appears that Pastors cannot be too diligent in their efforts to abolish and prevent the use of apocryphal Indulgences. Hence the Sovereign Pontiffs themselves have most frequently exercised their zeal in this important matter. In the notes prefixed to the second part of this treatise, I have cited a Decree of Bened. XIV. on the publication of Indulgences, which has been renewed and confirmed by his Holiness Pius IX. The following Indulgences are both false and prohibited.

Those attached to rosaries, crowns, crosses, images, and grains, blessed before the Decree of Clement VIII. (19th Jan. 1597), *De forma Indulgentiarum*—those annexed to the Cross of St. Thuribius, by Urban VIII.

---

* See Benedict XIV. De Synod Diocesaná, lib. xiii., c. 18, n. 8. According to several able Theologians quoted by him, these Indulgences of 1,000, 10,000 years, &c., are pure fictions of Quæstors. . . . . mere forged and counterfeit grants, which should by no means be attributed to the Apostolic See. In truth a Decree of Sept. 18, 1669, has already declared partial Indulgences of 1,000 years apocryphal.

—the Indulgences *of the crosses of Carraca, which originated in Spain, granted by Pius V., &c.* Also those said to have been granted by Pope Eugene III., at the request of St. Bernard, for the recitation of three Paters and Aves in honour of the wound in our Redeemer's shoulder—the 1,000 years' Indulgences accorded to persons carrying the measure of the wound in His side—those ascribed to the measure of His stature, &c.—the Indulgence of six Paters, Aves, and Glorias, to be said kneeling before the Blessed Sacrament, as a reparation, conceded by Leo X., Innoc. XI., Innoc. XII., &c. The Indulgences granted by John XXII. to those who kiss the measure of our Blessed Lady's foot—those annexed to the recital of the Angelic Salutation at the sound of the clock, and to the image of the Conception of Immaculate Mary painted within a circle and having the moon under her feet—Indulgences ascribed to grains, crosses, or chaplets of Louisa of the Ascension, a Spanish Poor-Clare—those said to have been annexed, at the instance of the grand duke of Tuscany, to the chaplets of our Lord's Passion—the Indulgences of the prayer reputed to have been found in His Sepulchre, pursuant to the revelations of SS. Bridget, Machtilda, and Elizabeth—as also of other *prayers at the Holy Sepulchre of Jesus, in honour of God and for the salvation of my soul*—those contained in a little work entitled: "Directorium Spirituale" (Spiritual Directory); the Indulgences reported to have been held out to all, who, during Lent, shall visit Franciscan Churches; in like manner, to persons wearing the cord of St. Francis, &c. (see Decree of S. Congreg. of Indulgences, March 7, 1678, *Decreta Authentica*, n. xvii.). I shall hereafter mention the genuine Indulgences attached to the Archconfraternity of the Cord of St. Francis.

These Indulgences are likewise false which release two, three, or five souls from Purgatory, particularly if they purpose to do so every day, week, year, &c.—those too accorded by Clem. VIII. to all wearing the livery of the holy *winding sheet*—those attached to five prayers revealed by our Saviour to St. Bridget, Queen of Sweden; nothing is more absurd or opposed to the principles of our holy Faith than the promises made to whomsoever should recite these prayers for the space of a year—Indulgences which preserve from thunder—those promised to all who give a certain sum of gold, &c.*

Furthermore, by a declaration of 23rd Feb., 1856, the S. Congregation of Indulgences established, and afterwards notified to the Bishops, the falsity of an Indulgence of 1080 days, inscribed on a medal representing the Blessed Virgin holding on her knees the dead body of her Divine Son taken down from the cross. The inscription on the other side lays down that, to gain the Indulgence, it is necessary to recite a Pater and Ave in presence of the image. We should, then, endeavour to prevent the sale of this medal which is to be found in all places, under every variety of shape and size. It has been copied in engravings.

Amongst apocryphal Indulgences should, in like manner, be ranked: 1, those attributed to the Litanies

---

* In March, 1567, Pius V. revoked all Indulgences which Religious quæsters pretended to distribute. The Council of Trent (Sess. xxi. cap. 9) had already decided that Indulgences were to be everywhere given *gratis*. Hence the "*gratis ubique*," affixed to all grants of Indulgences sent from Rome. At the same time, as the authorities there have to incur considerable expenses, such as the cost of postage, agents, commissioners, &c., persons asking for any graces of this sort must necessarily help to defray them.

of Our Lady of Pity, said to have been composed by Pius VII. during his captivity, who annexed to their recital a plenary Indulgence available on all Fridays. They were printed and circulated in Naples, and elsewhere, even as late as 1821. Having been asked whether he was the real author, Pius VII. replied: " I have not dreamt either of composing or applying Indulgences to them." Accordingly he had a letter sent to the Archbishop of that city, that he might prohibit such litanies in his diocese (Secretary of the S. Congregation of Indulg.); 2, those of a little chaplet called " the Crown of Mary's Virtues," said to have been authorized by Alexander VII. and Leo X. The former was said to have attached 10,000 days' Indulgence to each Ave Maria, and the latter 10,000 years', together with 1,000 years to all the faithful who carry about them this Crown ; 3, an Indulgence of 200 days for every *letter*, granted by his Holiness Pius VII., to the recital of a prayer to the Holy Virgin : in French, Que ta pureté soit bénie, &c. (may thy purity be blessed, &c.); 4, we should also esteem as counterfeit favours supposed to have been affixed to copies of a letter which the same Holy Mother is said to have addressed to the inhabitants of Messina, the original of which is kept in that town.

In France and other places, has been circulated a certain sort of crucifix, accompanied with a scrap of paper, on which are inscribed these words : " By a special faculty obtained June 1, 1804, from our Holy Father Pope Pius VII. confirmed by a Rescript dated Nov. 6, 1805, and renewed again by his Holiness Pius IX., Nov. 15, 1852, the following Indulgences are annexed to this crucifix: 1, A plenary Indulgence at the moment of death to everybody who shall kiss it or have it on his bed. 2, 100 days' Indulgence to all who recite three Paters, Aves, and Glorias, before the crucifix, for the intention of his Holiness, and this as often as they shall recite them. 3, One hundred days' Indulgence for any person who shall kiss it, invoking, at least in heart, the aid of God, and this whenever it shall have been kissed. 4, A plenary Indulgence twice a month, at the choice of each one, by going to holy Communion. 5, An Indulgence of seven years and seven quarantines for everybody who, after a sermon, shall receive the blessing given by the same crucifix. 6, Those Indulgences are annexed directly to the crucifix, and not to the cross, so that they are not lost, though the Christ be affixed to another cross. 7, The proprietor of the crucifix enjoys these Indulgences during his life. 8, The crucifix retains the Indulgences in favour of every person to whom the proprietor may deem it proper to bequeath, bestow, or sell it. In fine, the proprietor, but not those to whom it may have been sold, can, in case of lawful hindrance, gain the Indulgences of the Stations, by saying seven Paters and Aves; also the Indulgences of the Viæ Crucis, by saying fourteen."

The S. Congregation assembled on the 31st of March, 1856, declared all these Indulgences apocryphal: *Non esse attendendas utpote apocryphas;* and on the 14th of April, same year, his Holiness Pius IX. gave this decree his entire approbation: *Ormnino approbavit.** But to return to our subject

* There are many other spurious Indulgences which, though regarded as true, are not really so. Several of them will be found in the second part of this work.

" We should keep the people on their guard against the fraudulency

A person may gain several partial or plenary Indulgences on the same day. Yet, should he have gained one plenary Indulgence in its full extent (which will be known to the Almighty alone), he cannot gain another for himself on the same day, unless he may have committed fresh sins and obtained forgiveness of them as to the guilt, because, without this, the second plenary Indulgence would not have its effect. Consequently, after having tried to gain a plenary Indulgence for himself, if it be allowable, he ought to apply all the other Indulgences that he may gain on the same day to the souls in Purgatory.

True it is that Communion is ordinarily required for a plenary Indulgence, but according to various decrees of the S. Congregation of Indulgences, one Communion may serve to gain all the plenary Indulgences occurring on the same day: for example, all those to which a person may be entitled, as a member of different Confraternities, or in virtue of his having practised various devotions during a given period, &c. In like manner, the same confession suffices (see the ensuing No). Indulgences, whether partial or plenary, may be local, personal, real, perpetual, or temporary. A few observations on each of these classes.

A *local* Indulgence is one that is attached to a certain place, for instance, to a church, an altar, a statue or image erected in a chapel, placed on a

---

of certain traders in devotional objects. Every means seems honest for the interests of that unbridled avarice, which barters things sacred and profane in the pursuit of its guilty traffic. False indulgences, false prophecies, false prayers, false miracles, all these deceitful sacrileges repudiated and condemned by the Church, form part of the criminal intrigues of avarice, to ensure success in its labours " (Lettre Circulaire of His Eminence Cardinal de Bonald, Archbishop of Lyons, addressed to the clergy of his diocese, 14th April, 1857).

pillar, &c. It may be gained by visiting the place, image, altar. &c., and fulfilling the other conditions of the *grant*. Should the place to which the Indulgence is inherent be totally, or almost totally, destroyed, the privilege ceases. It likewise ceases when, in the case of an Indulgenced church, it is converted to any profane purpose. But if the church were merely repaired, it retains the Indulgence, even though it were entirely renewed by successive repairs. A church that may have once belonged to some Religious Order, but subsequently becomes the parochial church or chapel of a secular community, no longer enjoys the privileges it had before its destination was altered (Decree of 10th Feb. 1819).*

A *personal* Indulgence is that accorded to one or more individuals, but not to the entire body of the Faithful. Such are those granted to Religious of different Orders, to members of Confraternities of the Blessed Virgin. &c. The person possessed of this favour carries it with him, thus to speak, so that he can avail himself of it wherever in the world he may chance to be, provided the requisite conditions be complied with.

An Indulgence is *real* when it is attached to certain portable objects of devotion, as a crucifix, chaplet, medals, statues, &c. This Indulgence is nearly always both real and personal, because, with few exceptions, it is only the owners of these objects who can gain the Indulgences annexed to them. Should

---

* However, as will be noticed in its own place, on account of the Indulgence of the Portinucula, there is an exception in favour of those churches in France which belonged to the Franciscans prior to the Revolution of '89.

the Indulgenced object be morally destroyed, or have lost its natural form, the Indulgence is no longer attached to it. Such would be the case if a cross or medal, say, were broken in two or three pieces, or if a Rosary had its parts so detached from one another that it existed only in fragments, or if the berries were wholly separated, &c.

An Indulgence is said to be *perpetual* whenever it is granted without any limitation as to the term of its duration. Hence it holds good until positively revoked, and dies not with the person who accorded it; because an Indulgence is a favour conferred by the Chief Pastors of the Church, as Lieutenants or Vicars of Jesus Christ. Then, according to Canon Law, gifts or graces do not expire at the death of the donor : decet concessum a principe beneficium esse mansurum.\* Therefore the same should be said of Indulgences, whose Rescripts end in these words. Ad beneplacitum Romani Pontificis, seu Sedis Apostolicæ (during the pleasure of the R. Pontiff or Holy See), because such a clause has reference, not to the person, but to the supreme dignity of the R. Pontiff, which never dies.†

A *temporary* Indulgence is a favour bestowed only for a definite time, as for three, five, seven years, &c. It ceases at the expiration of the period for which it was granted. We should recollect, that, conformably to a decision of the S. Congregation of Indulgences, August 3rd, 1711, the time must be computed from the date of the Rescript or Brief conceding the

---

\* De Regulis Juris in sexto. Regula xvi.
† Theodore of the Holy Spirit, cap. xiii. art. 1. Suarez de Legib. lib. 8, cap. 5, art. 1.

Indulgence, and not from the day of its publication or receipt.*

Lastly, some Indulgences are granted only for the Living, and some only for the Dead; whilst others again are granted to the Living, with power to apply them to the Dead. It appertains to the Church to determine them in this manner. In the specification of Indulgences, I shall take care always to indicate those that are applicable to the souls in Purgatory.

---

## VII.

#### DISPOSITIONS NECESSARY FOR GAINING INDULGENCES.

THEY are three in number: the intention, the state of sanctifying grace, and a faithful accomplishment of the works or conditions prescribed. Of these in order:

1st. *The intention.* In fulfilling the conditions, the person who desires to participate in an Indulgence ought to propose to himself to gain it effectively. For it is thus the conditions or works enjoined are directed to the end proposed by the Pope or Bishop in granting the Indulgence. Nevertheless, it is not necessary that the intention be *actual*, or that one should say to himself at the very moment:

---

* But in the case of a Rescript conferring the favour of a privileged altar for a fixed term, the time commences only on the day on which the Rescript shall have been presented to the Bishop. This, however, holds for distant countries alone: Tempus non a die datæ sed a die præsentationis Brevis Ordinariis, esse computandum in regionibus remotis tantum (Decree of 4th Feb., 1736, quoted by Amort, Disputat-vii. de Indulg. quærit. 78).

"I purpose to offer this prayer, to give this alms, to receive this Communion, &c., in order to share in such an Indulgence." A *virtual* intention suffices—that is, an intention which was at first *actual* on the part of the person wishing to obtain the Indulgence, and which, not having been revoked by any contrary act of the will, morally perseveres so as to really determine him to comply with the requisite conditions.

Thus St. Leonard of Port Maurice used to advise the Faithful to form each day, at morning prayer, an intention of gaining all the Indulgences annexed to the various practices of piety and good works which they might perform in the course of the day. Because this intention, if not recalled, morally or virtually perseveres during the day, and, according to the common opinion of Theologians, suffices to make us sharers in those different Indulgences. Hence it is not necessary to know positively, what precise Indulgence is attached to such or such an act of virtue, nor even to know whether there is one attached to it at all: it is enough to have the will or intention of gaining it, if it really exists, and such as it exists. Let us, then, follow the counsel of that holy Missionary, by adopting so easy a means of satisfying the justice of God in our own behalf, and of affording relief to our deceased parents or friends.

Speaking of these poor Souls, it may be desirable to remark, that we should not forget to particularize in our minds the exact individual or individuals to whom we wish to apply such Indulgences as may be available for the Departed, this determination being left by the Church to the choice of the person fulfilling the conditions For it is quite certain, that Indulgences always chiefly benefit those souls for whom a person designs to gain them. Such is the will of the Supreme Pontiffs and the belief of the Universal Church. Yet there is nothing to hinder him from directing his intention in such a way, as to offer these Indulgences to God for the relief of the most neglected souls in Purgatory, or for the Dead of such a parish, of such a community, of such a family, or even for the Departed in general. Because the Almighty, whose knowledge, wisdom, and clemency are infinite, knows full well how to select amongst the Holy Souls those that stand most in need of succour.*

2nd. *The state of grace.* " Provided," says St. Thomas, " the recipient be endowed with charity."† Elsewhere he gives the reason of this. A lifeless member, he writes, is in no way influenced by living members; but he who is in a state of grievous sin is like a lifeless member. Therefore the merits of the living members have no influence over him by way of Indulgences.‡

Again, we know that the fruit of Indulgences depends on the Superiors who dispense them. But assuredly the Chief Pastors of the Church never intended to apply, by means of Indulgences, the merits of Christ and His Saints to souls tainted with mortal sin. An Indulgence is designed to favour the friends or children of God, and not His enemies. Besides, how could the temporal penalty be remitted to him who is still a debtor for the eternal? In one word,

---

* This assertion is altogether conformable to a decision of the S. Congregation of Rites (Sept. 2, 1741); it runs thus: Hodie—All Souls' Day, 2nd of Nov.—Missa potest applicari tam in genere pro omnibus, quam in specie pro aliquo defuncto. Still, as will be seen farther on, all altars are privileged on that day.

† Supplem. Quaest. 25, art. 2. ‡ Supplem. Quaest. 27, art. 1.

so long as the sin itself subsists, the Judge remits not its penalty.

A state of grace either conserved after baptism, or recovered by penance, is therefore indispensable. Hence a single mortal sin on the soul would be an obstacle to the gaining of the smallest Indulgence. Nay more, a single venial sin, for which a person retains even a secret affection, renders him incapable of acquiring a plenary Indulgence in its entirety. For, as the stain or guilt of this fault is not yet effaced, the punishment due thereto cannot be remitted. "Such," declares Bourdaloue, "is the all-just ordinance of the Most High; He relaxes the punishment, only in the ratio and proportion in which we detest the offence itself."*

This abhorrence of sin ought to be true and sincere—*vere contritis*. Our renunciation of it and of the occasion thereof should, in like manner, be real and efficacious; a mere outward show, or a fair semblance of contrition, will not be enough. On the occasion of a Jubilee many persons are anxious to make general confessions; this is all very fine, provided the general confessions conduce to *general conversions*.

Nevertheless, should a plenary Indulgence require the fulfilment of several works of piety, as does that of a Jubilee, though it would be very profitable, and in fact one ought to strive to perform all of them in a state of grace, a person is not ordinarily bound to do so under pain of forfeiting the Indulgence. Nearly all are agreed that it suffices to have the soul free from sin at the moment in which the last of these works shall have been accomplished, for it

---

* Sermon for the Opening of a Jubilee. Part ii.

is only then the fruit of the Indulgence is applied.* Many eminent Theologians even lay down, that it is not necessary to be in a state of grace, in order to gain Indulgences for the souls in Purgatory. Because, argue they, the sin of the person placing the conditions could not impede the application of the Indulgence to those guiltless holy souls that are capable, on account of their being guiltless, of participating in the satisfactions of others.† As this opinion is only *probable*, it would be better to adopt the contrary one in practice, since it is safer.

Wherefore, previous to our trying to acquire Indulgences even for the Departed, let us purify our souls, become reconciled to God by a good confession, or, at least, excite in our hearts a sincere sorrow for our sins, and promise to have recourse, as soon as possible, to the Sacrament of Penance. Thus our charity towards our suffering brethren shall become the source of our own sanctification. Furthermore, since most plenary Indulgences require, as conditions,

---

* St. Antoninus, Suarez, Theodore of the Holy Spirit, &c., are of this opinion. Sometimes, however, the Apostolical Letters order the prescribed works to be done in a state of grace. In the Constitutions, e. g. of Clem. VII., Julius III., and other Popes, relative to Jubilees, it is expressly declared, that those desirous to gain the Indulgence must visit churches, pray, &c., *being truly penitent and having confessed*—vere pœnitentes et confessi. Hence, in all such instances, we should adhere to the regulations specified in the Bulls or Papal Indults.

† Theologia Wireeburgensis, tom. v., p. 229, Billuart, Suarez, &c. The state of grace, writes Suarez, is required merely to remove the obex or obstacle to an Indulgence, and consequently, in itself, is a disposition necessary only in him who is about to obtain the benefit of an Indulgence; now, pursuant to the present hypothesis, it is not the person fulfilling the prescribed conditions, who will reap the fruit of the Indulgence, but another for whom it is procured. Therefore it is not incongruous to suppose, that a person in mortal sin may obtain the fruit for another, and not for himself, as he himself has an impediment in the way, while the other has not; especially since this fruit is independent of the merits of the person complying with the conditions (Disp. iii. de Defunct, sect. 3).

confession and communion, it is evident, that, to gain them, one should be in a state of grace. Hearken, then, to the advice of the great Apostle of the Indies to his neophytes. "You are solicitous," says he, "for your brethren who suffer beyond the grave: you have a religious ambition to succour them; but attend to yourselves first, for God listens not to him who appears in his presence with a guilty conscience. Before attempting to release any souls from the pains of Purgatory, begin by delivering your own from the fire of Hell. For surely it is fitting, that he who would liberate the soul of another from the prison of Purgatory should previously rescue his own from Hell."*

3rd. *A faithful accomplishment of the works* enjoined by the Bulls or Briefs according the Indulgences: they should be performed really and integrally at the appointed time, as also, no doubt, with piety and in a spirit of penance; because works done without devotion, or recollection, perhaps through vanity, would badly correspond with the designs of the Chief Pastors in bestowing Indulgences. Moreover, since, in this matter, everything depends on the will of the Donor, a voluntary or involuntary omission of any of the conditions, even through ignorance or inability, would hinder the acquisition of an Indulgence. Yet, if the omission were comparatively very slight, it would not have this effect; as, for illustration, if, owing to distraction or negligence, a person omitted one or two Hail Marys in the recitation of the Rosary. Because a trifle is reckoned as nothing—*parum pro nihilo reputatur*. But the

---

* Letter of St. Francis Xavier to St. Ignatius. Goa, 21st Oct., 1542.

*trifle* should be always estimated relatively to the works or conditions enjoined.

In connection with this subject, I may mention, that a person cannot acquire an Indulgence by doing a work already obligatory, except in the case in which the Pope may have so ordained by a particular grant or Rescript. For, by one single act, a person cannot satisfy two obligations, each of which requires a separate act by itself. Again, the conditions implied for the acquisition of Indulgences, are works of supererogation; but, doubtless, those that are obligatory or indispensable are not works of this kind. Thus, e.g. neither the Lenten Fast, nor that of Quatuor-Tense or of a Vigil, would do instead of a fast prescribed for gaining an Indulgence. Nor could a Priest substitute the Office for prayers enjoined by the Holy Father.* Hence we see, that, for a participation in the Jubilee of 1825, Leo XII. ordered a special Communion, independently of that commanded by the Paschal Precept. The same regulation has been occasionally renewed ever since.

Note, however, that a decision of the S. Congregation, dated 19th March, 1841, and addressed to the Bishop of Munster, lays down that a Communion received on Easter Sunday will be sufficient, both to comply with the Paschal duty, and gain the plenary Indulgence attached to the Papal Benediction. Another decision of May 10, 1844, to a learned professor of Louvain, declares that the Easter Communion may serve to obtain any plenary Indulgence

---

* "By prayers that are obligatory, for instance, the Canonical Hours, one cannot comply with a condition requiring prayers ordered by the Supreme Pontiff for the acquisition of a Plenary Indulgence." (Decree, 29th May, 1841).

whatever, which is not conceded in the form of a Jubilee—*in forma Jubilæi*. There is also a special Indult, dating Jan. 25, 1842, directed to Mgr. Darcimoles, then Bishop of Puy, allowing persons to satisfy, by one Communion, as well the Paschal obligation, as the condition requiring them to communicate in order to partake of the Jubilee celebrated that year in the church of Our Lady of Puy. Evidently, then, above all in the field of Indulgences, we should scrupulously conform to the designs of the Holy See.

In Religious Communities, since the Rules do not generally bind under sin, the prayers and other devotional exercises prescribed by Rule, may serve to gain all the Indulgences annexed to all these pious practices. It is sufficient merely to have the intention of gaining them. Quite a similar impression prevails at Rome, in reference to the prayers and acts of virtue enjoined as penances at the Sacred Tribunal. Hence the Confessors there almost prefer to impose penances enriched with Indulgences. In fact, we are told by the learned Eusebius Amort, that, in his time, it was a common thing amongst them to give as penance the recital of certain prayers designed to serve for the obtaining of Indulgences. And this usage, he thought, was at least implicitly sanctioned by the R. Pontiffs (Theol. Mor. tom. iii., Disp. vii., q. 32).

The grants or acts of concession nearly always prescribe Confession, Communion, and Prayers for the intention of his Holiness, as essential conditions for attaining Indulgences. Hence it may not be out of place to cite here various decisions of the S. Congregation, all approved and confirmed by the Supreme Pontiffs.

*Decree of* 19*th May*, 1759. It supposes that, to obtain a plenary Indulgence, attached to a certain feast, it is necessary to go to confession on the very day of the feast. But if the Indulgence were not affixed to the feast, one should confess on the day on which he might wish to gain it; and he was obliged to do this on every occasion—*toties quoties*. So that as many Confessions were required as Communions. At the same time, it was customary then, as now, always to interpret the obligation of confessing on the day of Communion, by comprising under the word *day*, the vigil of the same day. The Decree itself allows this. It was confirmed by Clement XIII., who, at the prayer of several Bishops, Priests, and Religious Communities, &c., afterwards modified it by a perpetual Indult, dated Dec. 9, 1763.

*Indult Dec.* 9, 1763, *and Decree* 12*th March*, 1855. All persons who have the praiseworthy custom of going to confession *at least once a week*, except in a case of lawful hindrance, can gain all the plenary Indulgences occurring in the interval between one confession and another, without being obliged to confess each time an Indulgence may be available.* We except, however, the Indulgence of a Jubilee, whether ordinary or extraordinary, as also those accorded in the form of a Jubilee, for these require a fresh con-

---

* Observe the expression *once a week;* it is not said once in every eight days. Thus, agreeably to the terms of the Indult, a person may go to confession on the Monday of one week, say, and not again until Saturday of the ensuing week, which would be the thirteenth day after his last confession. Yet it would be true to say, he had confessed every week, or once a week, which is all that the Rescript requires.

In February, 1868, I again submitted this note to the S. Congregation of Indulgences. The reply was, that it gives the true sense of the clause, "Saltem semel in habdomada," and that those who interpret it otherwise, confining it solely to an interval of eight days, are quite mistaken.

fession, irrespective of any others. There is likewise an exception, of course, in the case of one who may have become guilty of some mortal sin since his last confession. Nay more, it is not a rare thing, to see, particularly in France, this privilege of weekly confession extended by the Holy See, at the request of some Bishops, to a confession made only *twice a month.*\* The Holy Father confers this favour chiefly on Bishops who have the care of large Dioceses, or who are in need of Confessors. Hence it may be well for devout souls to ascertain from the Parish Priests or Confessors, whether or not this prerogative has been vouchsafed to their respective localities. His Eminence the Cardinal Archbishop has obtained it for the Diocese of Lyons.

*Decree of June* 12, 1822: for the benefit of persons living in places where, by reason of a scarcity of Confessors—*ob inopiam Confessariorum*—it is impossible to go frequently to the Holy Tribunal. Pius VII. permits them to confess at any time within the *eight days* immediately preceding the feast endowed with a plenary Indulgence, and still, by that confession, to share in the Indulgence.† It is needless to remark, that the Decree does not contemplate

---

\* Note again the clause, "*twice a month*"—*bis in mesne*—it does not say every fifteen days.

† By *Feast*, in this Decree, is meant, not alone one that is of precept, but any feast whatever, whether of obligation or otherwise, as those of our Lord, Holy Mary, the Saints, &c. In one word, it comprises any festival whatsoever, on which a person may purpose to gain a plenary Indulgence.

With regard to the class of persons who, as the Decree supposes, cannot, on account of a dearth of confessors, go frequently to confession, it may be beneficial to know, that the words "*infra hebdomadam*" include the eight days directly preceding the feast. Such is the declaration of a Decree of December 15, 1841. But this does not in any way weaken the force of the Indult of Clem. XIII., in favour of those who confess at least once a week. Why not then leave the pious Faithful to

Indulgences conceded in forma Jubilæi, since, as stated above, they demand a separate confession.

*Decree 15th Dec.*, 1841. This confession made within the eight days before a feast, will suffice to enable persons, who, through want of Confessors, are unable to confess often, to participate in all the plenary Indulgences occurring in that limit.

*Decree of August* 20*th*, 1822, *and the same Decree of Dec.* 15, 1841. Should a person have only light faults to accuse himself of, it will not be necessary to receive absolution in order to reap the benefit of an Indulgence: simple confession suffices.

*The same Decree of June* 12, 1822. When Communion is enjoined as a condition for a plenary Indulgence inherent to a feast, the rule is to receive on the very day. This decree, however, authorizes persons to communicate on the eve or vigil of the festival. Should the Indulgence commence at First Vespers, the prescribed works may be performed any time between that hour and sunset of the Feast itself. First Vespers begin with the afternoon, i. e. at the moment in which Priests are allowed to recite them privately—extra chorum—consequently, whenever an Indulgence is available from the hour of First Vespers, one may begin to fulfil the conditions at noon. But to continue.

According to the Decree of July 3, 1754, ordinary Indulgences commence with the natural day, or at sunrise—ab ortu solis. The predominant feeling at Rome is, that, in this case, the conditions may be

---

enjoy, peaceably and without scruple, a privilege accorded to them by the Holy See?

In fine, these plenary Indulgences comprehend all local and personal Indulgences, for which confession may be required as a condition (See the Decree of December 4, 1843).

complied with at any time between midnight and midnight. As a general principle, the Indulgence always commences at First Vespers, whenever it is granted in consideration of some Saint or Mystery that is honoured on a given festival. In all other instances, it is necessary to consult the Rescript or Grant. One thing is certain, at all events, that unless the favour be expressly mentioned in the petition sent to Rome, the authorities there never concede an Indulgence beginning at First Vespers, for mere ordinary Sundays of the year. Thus, though amongst the general concessions, neither the six Sundays of St. Aloysius Gonzaga, nor the seven of St. Joseph, enjoy that prerogative.

*Decree of 10th May*, 1844. The Paschal Communion may serve to acquire a plenary Indulgence available on a day on which it is received, provided the Indulgence be not accorded in the form of a Jubilee.

*Decree of 30th Aug.* 1847. One Communion will suffice to obtain several Indulgences occurring on the same day, either for oneself or the Souls in Purgatory, even though, as commonly happens, Communion were prescribed for each of them. But, bear in mind, that it is necessary to fulfil the other enjoined works, as often as there are Indulgences to be gained; in other words, for each Indulgence we ought to repeat those conditions that may be repeated on the same day.

In general, it is not requisite to communicate in the church to which the Indulgence is annexed. It will be enough to go there and pray for the intention of his Holiness, which may be done either before or after Communion, or in the course of the day. Moreover, should the Communion be received in the Indulgenced Church, and the prayers offered then and there for the Pope's intention, it will not be necessary to go there a second time, since the condition of the prescribed visit is, by that very fact, sufficiently complied with.

Finally, I may observe, that those unable to communicate at the hour of death can still gain all the plenary Indulgences to which they might be entitled on many grounds, by simply invoking the Sacred Name of Jesus, if not by word of mouth, at least with a contrite heart. This will be seen in its own place.

*Prayers for the Intention of the Holy Father.*—There are no special ones appointed. Hence we are at liberty to say, for that end, any prayers we please. Nearly all are agreed that five Paters and Aves fully satisfy this condition. In truth Suarez, Theodore of the Holy Spirit, and other eminent writers, maintain that it may be complied with by even a much shorter prayer—*per orationem quantumvis modicam*—for, argue they, the prayer prescribed for acquiring an Indulgence is not to be estimated according to the length of time spent in reciting it, but rather by the amount of devotion and fervour with which it is recited.*

Note, likewise, when an Indult does not specify that the prayer is to be said in the Church to which

---

* "Theodore à Spiritu Sancto, tract de Indulg." cap. xi, art. 2, quærit 3. He also cites Suarez, Bonacina, Fillucius, &c. In the same article, quærit 1, he adopts the opinion of those who hold, that meditation or *mental prayer* would suit the requirements of this condition or prayer for the Pope—*oratio*. The opposite view, which we follow, is surer. It sets forth, that it is requisite to pray *vocally*, recommending us, at the same time, particularly to recite the Lord's Prayer and the Angelical Salutation, prayers that are so pleasing to our Divine Saviour and His Blessed Mother, as also so salutary in themselves.

a certain Indulgence is attached, it may be recited anywhere, provided, however, a visit to some church or public oratory, *together with prayers for the intention of His Holiness*, be not enjoined.

Should a person purpose to partake of several plenary Indulgences on the same day, it will be necessary for him to pray for the ends intended by the Church, as often as there are Indulgences to be gained, available, of course, on the condition of a prayer for Her pious designs. The ends or intentions of the Supreme Pontiffs in these prayers so generally exacted as conditions, are, the exaltation of holy Church, the propagation of the Faith, the extirpation of heresy and schism, peace and concord amongst Christian princes, including the other wants of the Faithful. But it is not necessary to have all these ends definitely before our minds in order to gain an Indulgence. It will be sufficient to pray with and for the intention of the Supreme Head of the Church.

Observe, however, that one may recite the prayers required for obtaining an Indulgence, either separately by himself or alternately with others. In fact, since it is sanctioned by our holy Mother, there is nothing more laudable than this method of alternate recitation, so often employed in the saying of the Rosary, Litanies, Angelus, &c. See the words of the "Raccolta," pursuant to a Decree of the Sacred Congregation, dated February 29, 1820. It is noticeable, too, that, conformably to a recent declaration of the same S. Cong. of Indulgences, August 11, 1862, unless the contrary be expressly stated in the grant, Indulgenced prayers need not be said *kneeling*. The decision was approved by His Holiness on the 18th of September in the same year.

*Decree in Favour of Deaf Mutes*—Having been issued by the S. Congregation of Indulences, February 16, 1852, it was confirmed by Pius IX. on 15th March ensuing. It ordains : 1. That whenever a visit to a church is prescribed, deaf and dumb people need only make the visit, taking care there to raise up their hearts and souls to the Almighty; 2. Should public prayers be commanded, it will then be enough for them to pray in heart and spirit, provided they are present in body with the rest of the faithful; 3. If the prayers are to be said privately, their confessors have power to substitute for them some other external works of piety.

*The Visit to a Church or Public Oratory*—Treating of this visit, so often put forth as one of the conditions for acquiring Indulgences, I should cite a Decree of the S. Congregation, framed in August 22, 1842. It decides that those chapels attached to Monasteries, Seminaries, &c., to which the Faithful have not free and public access, are not to be regarded as public Oratories.* Nevertheless, as the Supreme Pontiffs do not like to deprive those living in communities of the Indulgences conceded to the people at large, the authorities at Rome readily allow such persons, who are not at liberty to visit a parochial church or public Oratory, to comply with this condition by simply visiting their own chapel. Consequently, chapels

---

* The following is the Decree of the S. Congregation : it is entitled "*In Virdunensi.*" The question proposed runs thus : "In granting Indulgences, the Holy See often enjoins a devout visit to a parochial church, or public Oratory; it is asked, then, whether, in order to the fulfilment of this condition, those Oratories canonically erected in Monasteries, Seminaries, or in other religious houses, may be esteemed public, even though the Faithful have not public access to them ?

After mature deliberation, and having taken the votes of the consultors, the Sacred Congregation replied to said doubt *in the negativ.* (Decree of 22nd August, 1842).

belonging to Religious Convents, Hospitals, Prisons, Boarding-schools, &c., may be considered public Oratories, as regards the individuals residing in these places, since they are not free to go beyond their boundaries. By a similar privilege, members of all Confraternities, who cannot visit a church or sanctuary of their respective Associations to participate in certain Indulgences, may satisfy this condition by visiting either the parish church or that of their convent. In a case of infirmity, it will suffice to perform, instead of the visit, some good work marked out by one's confessor.

It may be asked, whether the visit ought to be formally *repeated*, as often as there are Indulgences to be gained on the same day? Theologians are divided on the point. Hitherto I myself have followed the opinion of those on the negative side, because it seemed to have been generally enough adopted at Rome, and safe in practice. But this is no longer the case, since, by a Decree of the S. Congregation, February 29, 1864, it was decided, that, for each visit prescribed, it is necessary actually to leave the church and re-enter it, with the intent of reiterating the visit and the prayers for the Pope's intention.

Before dismissing this subject, I may be permitted to make one other remark. In many countries it is no uncommon practice for Pastors of souls not to bring the Blessed Eucharist to persons habitually disabled or labouring under any chronic infirmity, except on the principal Festivals of the year. Thu' it would be impossible for invalids to partake of an immense number of Indulgences available on the condition of communicating and of visiting a church or public Oratory. To obviate this inconvenience, our Holy Father Pius IX., at the request of certain worthy, zealous ecclesiastics, deigned to furnish them with an easy means of obtaining all such favours. At present, therefore, it is quite enough for them to comply with the other conditions, and faithfully discharge some pious works enjoined by their confessors, as a substitution for Communion and the visitation of a church. (It is scarcely necessary to say, of course, that persons living in Religious Communities enjoy not this privilege, since they have an opportunity of frequently approaching the Holy Table.) (Pius IX., in audience of September 18, 1862), Prior to this Clem. XIII. had conferred a similar favour on all members—*Confratribus et consororibus*—of any confraternities or congregations canonically erected (in case these members were either in prison, or affected by some bodily ailment) (August 2, 1760).

N. B.—The question has been several times asked of the S. Congregation of Indulgences, whether or not could a person gain the Indulgence of a Jubilee as often as he may have performed the prescribed works within the term of its duration? The reply has invariably been, that it is necessary to keep to the letter of the grant—*Standum est concessioni;* should the Brief be silent on the matter, the prevailing opinion is, that, at least as regards extraordinary Jubilees, it can be gained but once. However, during the Holy Year, or on the occasion of an ordinary Jubilee, the Faithful at Rome may reap the benefit of the Indulgence as often as they repeat the thirty visits to each of the four Basilicas—those of St. Peter, St. Paul, St. Mary Major, and St. John Lateran—as also Confession and Communion (Bened. XIV.).

## VIII.

#### THE TRANSFERRING OF INDULGENCES.

Some years ago, the doubt had been more than once proposed both to the Sacred Congregations of Rites and of Indulgences, whether in the event of a feast being transferred from that on which it fell to some other day, would the Indulgences annexed to it be also transferred? They uniformly answered, that the Indulgence was not transferred with the feast, and that, in particular instances, recourse should be had to the Holy See to procure a special grant. Accordingly, up to a recent date, these decisions, given at different periods, were adhered to in practice, so that if, in certain dioceses, the Indulgence accompanied the feast, the transfer took place in virtue of a Special Indult. There never had been any general Decree issued on the subject.

Recently, however, considering the circumstances of the times, above all the various Concordates entered into between the Holy See and different nations, anxious moreover to stimulate more and more the devotion of the Faithful, his present Holiness Pius IX. settled the whole matter by the Decree *Urbis et Orbis*, dated August 9, 1852. Therein he has laid down, that all Indulgences hitherto attached to certain feasts, or which might hereafter be attached to them, as also those accorded, or to be in future accorded, to certain Churches or public Oratories for such feasts, including likewise, yet with the consent of the Ordinary, those granted for Processions,

Novenas, and Triduums, which may be held either before or after the feasts, or during the Octave, shall follow these festivals to the days to which they may have been lawfully transferred as to their exterior pomp and solemnity—*quoad solemnitatem et externam celebrationem.* Thus, in all such cases, the Indulgences cannot be gained on the proper or primarily fixed days of these feasts.\*

In France, therefore, there is no longer any difficulty respecting the feasts of the Epiphany, Corpus Christi, SS. Peter and Paul, and the Patron of a parish. Because the solemnity of these having been transferred to the ensuing Sundays, the Indulgences annexed to them are similarly transferred.

But when only the Office and Mass are postponed, without the exterior solemnity, there is no postponement of the Indulgences, and hence, in this instance, they are to be gained on the day originally assigned to the festival. "*Cum vero,*" says the Decree, "*transfertur tantum Officium cum Missa, non autem solemnitas et exterior celebratio festi, Indulgentiarum nullam fièri translationem decrevit*" (SS. Dominus Noster, Pius Papa IX.).

---

## IX.

### RECAPITULATION.

Such are the explanations of Indulgences in general

\* The Decree has reference to Indulgences dispensed to the Faithful at large, and in consideration of any given feast. For, as regards the special ones accorded to this or that Religious House, Congregation, &c., it allows them to continue attached to the day itself of the feast, which is transferred as to exterior solemnity, and permits these to accompany the feast to the day appointed for its celebration as to its outward ceremony.

which I have deemed proper to offer in the first part of this treatise. Let us read them over carefully, and we shall be thereby induced ever to appreciate more fully the immense benefit which Holy Church, the dispenser of the Divine Mysteries, the Depositary of the Keys of the Kingdom of Heaven, confers on her children, in unlocking to them the Treasury of Indulgences. For, in reality, what are Indulgences? They are the fruit of the sufferings and of the Precious Blood of our Divine Redeemer; the fruit of Mary's Dolors and Merits, joined to that of the penances and martyrdom of the Saints.

What advantage do we derive from them? They purify our Souls from the dross of sin, by paying the debts we owe to the Divine Justice; they cause us to live constantly in a state of sanctifying grace, to practise works of piety, charity, and Christian mortification; they abridge for us the excruciating pains of the other life, or even altogether preserve us from them; lastly, in them we have at our disposal a most excellent means of affording relief to the Souls of our relatives, friends, and benefactors, who might be undergoing punishment in the fire of Purgatory, and of thus hastening their entrance into the blissful region of light, rest, and peace.

Would it not then be doing an injury to the bounty of the Most High and the tenderness of His Church, would it not even be cruelty towards ourselves and those belonging to us, to neglect a gift so salubrious? O! let us call to mind all that true Christians have done in every age, in order to acquire and share in them. It is related by F. Segneri, that, in Rome, during the famous Jubilee accorded by Clem. VI., there were over 800,000 pilgrims at the Feast of Pentecost alone. The concourse there was larger still in the reign of Pope Nicholas V.* Thus, not recoiling at any sacrifice, immense crowds of fervent Christians flocked from all parts of the world to the Eternal City! O let us take care never to despise this inestimable blessing, for otherwise we should be marching into the ranks of the Innovators of the sixteenth century, whose contempt for Indulgences led them into heresy, and thereby cast them out from the haven of salvation. Nor let us either accuse the Church of being too lavish of Indulgences; but rather, let us weigh well the sublime end She has in view in dispensing them, as also the varied conditions required for their attainment. In short, let the Faithful enter into the designs of a good Mother, who is no less full of wisdom than of anxious care for their well-being; above all, let them endeavour to acquire the many Plenary Indulgences which She graciously tenders to them, and God will then be richly glorified by their prayers, their efforts, and their virtues. Amen!

Finally, to conclude this First Part, I add to the preceding reflections, those beautiful words of Perè Bourdalone, exhorting his audience to profit by the grace of a Jubilee; "Therefore, let us receive this Indulgence with respect, gratitude, and thankfulness—with all docility and submission of faith. Let us carefully treasure it up: as Christians, with respect; as sinners, with gratitude and thankfulness; with all submission of faith, as Catholics. As Christians, I repeat, let us accept it with profound reverence, for it is an application made to us of the

---

* "Il Cristiano Istruito," by Father Paul Segneri, Ragionamento, xxi.

superabundant satisfactions of Jesus Christ; it is a precious streamlet emanating from the Divine Fountains of our Saviour, which are spoken of by the Prophet, and which we shall never exhaust; it is a fresh proof of the virtue and efficacy of His Precious Blood, the least drop of which would have sufficed to redeem a thousand worlds. O! with what sentiments of veneration would I not have received the priceless drops of that adorable Blood when He shed it for me on the cross! Could I be so senseless and hard-hearted, as to neglect the means instituted by Him for applying it to me? As sinners, let us in like manner receive it with thankfulness, since it is it that crowns the mercy of God, completes our own justification, and supplies the inefficiency of our own satisfaction; in short, it is a help given to us by the Almighty for acquitting ourselves in His ineffable presence. Were an angel to announce to a damned soul that such a remission is granted to it, what would be its transports of gratitude and joy! But surely we too are sinners, and perhaps much greater sinners than many of the Reprobate whom His Majesty preserved not by His prevenient grace as much as us, for whom He waited not as He waits for us, for whom he had not the same predilection that He has for us. O! what an advantage to be able to pay so heavy a debt by so easy a means! How have we merited it? Consequently, the less we have deserved it, the more ought we to redouble our efforts to make a sincere return of gratitude and love. As Catholics, let us embrace it with all docility and submission of faith, for, as it was contempt of Indulgences that lately gave rise to schism and total separation from the Church; so should our regard for them prove our inviolable attachment to Her, and our zeal for Her unity. His daring malevolent censure of Indulgences was the chief source of all Luther's misfortunes. Let his example be our instruction; and to render it salutary, as well in this matter of Indulgences as in others, let us ever believe what She believes, practise what she practises, venerate what She renders sacred by Her authority. After all, what risk do we run by attaching ourselves to Her. But, O! what risk do we run if we swerve, even ever so little, from the docile submission which She demands of us?"*

Truly, then, may we repeat with St. Ignatius: "Indulgences are an immense treasure, precious pearls to those who seek the love and Kingdom of God."

* "Sermon for the Opening of a Jubilee." End of Part 1.

# PART II.

## SPECIAL PRACTICAL POINTS.

#### PRELIMINARY OBSERVATIONS.

**1.** It is not my design to enumerate here all the prayers and religious practices, all the works of zeal, all the pious Associations and Confraternities, to which the Roman Pontiffs have annexed Indulgences. This would be an arduous task, which, besides being beyond my power, would not attain the end I had in view when framing this Collection. For, as may be inferred from the foregoing, my desire has been, to render myself useful to the people, by enlightening them in and riveting their attention on the Indulgences affixed to those prayers, those acts of devotion, those works of charity and zeal most in use amongst them, as also to those Associations and Confraternities most commonly known and warmly patronised. This, too, is the reason why I have not given at length several prayers and pious exercises, which every good Christian knows by heart, or at least, which he may readily find by opening his Prayer Book or Manual of Devotion.

**2.** Our Holy Father Pius IX., by a Decree *Urbis et Orbis*, dated April 14, 1856, exhorts all the Bishops of the Catholic world to endeavour by every means in their power, *pro eâ quâ pollent et quâ uti debent sollicitudine*—not alone to prevent the circulation of false and apocryphal Indulgences, and forbid them to the Faithful, but also to carry out the salutary Decrees of the S. Congregation, particularly in reference to the printing and publishing of these Indulgences, above all, the Decree of January 19, 1756, which was sanctioned by Bened. XIV. on the 28th of the same month; these are its very words: "Whereas daily experience proves that a great many general grants of Indulgences are expedited without the knowledge of the S. Congregation, which has occasioned numerous doubts and abuses, it has been ordained, after mature reflection, that all those who may hereafter obtain similar concessions of Indulgences, shall be bound under pain of nullity as regards the favour received, to deposit a copy of the grant with said Congregation." Note, Indulgences accorded by *general grants* are those available to the Faithful indiscriminately.

3. Whenever persons receive from Rome any Briefs or Receipts conferring Indulgences on a certain Parish, Confraternity, &c., they ought not to publish or propose them to the people until their authenticity shall have been certified by the Bishop of the place or by his Vicars-General.\* The Council of Trent even requires that the Diocesan be assisted by two members of the Chapter.† However, unless

---

\* ecrees of July 1, 1839, and Jan. 28, 1842. They should present to him either the very grant itself, or at least a copy of it, which must be certified as conformable to the original.

† "But as to Indulgences, or other spiritual graces, of which the faithful of Christ ought not on this account to be deprived, it decrees that they are henceforth to be published to the people at the due times by the Ordinaries of the places, aided by two members of the Chapter (Sess. xxi., De Reform, cap. 9).

the Brief have an express declaration to the contrary, the validity of the Indulgence does not depend upon this attestation on the part of the Ordinary, and hence it would not be null or of *no avail*, even prior to his declaration.\*

Furthermore, should there be question of personal Indulgences or faculties, as an Indulgence for the hour of death, the power of applying the Indulgence of a privileged altar, of blessing Beads, Medals, &c., if there be no mention of it in the Brief or

---

\* The question was asked by the Archbishop of Rouen, "whether local Indulgences, that is, such as those attached, e.g. to a certain church or altar, are null and void, so that, as long as the Bishop of the place does not permit them to be published, in vain would the Faithful strive to gain them?" Having previously taken the counsel of the Consultors, the Sacred Congregation responded in the negative—*negative*—as regards the invalidity of the Indulgences; nevertheless, the publication made by the Ordinary, after he shall have proved them to be genuine, should be waited for, that the people may know whether the Indulgences are plenary or partial, and what conditions required to gain them. In truth, this is the sense of the answer given Jan. 28, 1842, addressed to the same Church, for the circle of local Indulgences, but, as will be said just now, not in respect of those that are general or personal (Aug. 31, 1844).

The same Prelate desired to ascertain "whether personal Indulgences, privileges, or faculties, that is to say, those accorded merely to some individuals, as an Indulgence conceded to a person for the moment of death, a personal Indult of a privileged altar, the faculty of blessing Beads of the Blessed Virgin and of enriching them with Indulgences, are null and void, so long as the Bishop of the diocese does not recognise them as authentic and permitted their use?" The S. Congregation replied in the negative-*negative* (Aug. 31, 1844). A similar response was given in reference to Indulgences conceded to all the Faithful of the world by the Roman Pontiffs, through the medium of Bulls or Rescripts already published, and cited by authors the most approved. They are valid, so that the people may gain them, even before they may have been promulgated by the Ordinaries of the various districts.

An Ecclesiastic of the Diocese of Valence also proposed a doubt: "whether a person who has obtained different faculties from the Apostolic See, forsooth, the faculties of a personal privileged altar, of erecting the Stations of the Cross, of blessing crucifixes and medals, ought to present said faculties to the Ordinary, even though there be no mention of it in the acts of concession?" The Sacred Congregation answered *affirmative*, in reference to the erection of the Viæ Crucis, but *negative* as to the other faculties, unless it be ruled otherwise in the grants procured (Feb. 5, 1844).

Rescript, the authentication or authorization of the Bishop are not necessary, though expediency may demand them. But, should the grant require his *visa* and his permission, the faculties become null by the mere fact of their not having been obtained. In reality, all Briefs now-a-days, empowering persons to bless said indulgence-crosses, medals, chaplets, &c., contain this very clause in express terms: *Ac de tui Ordinarri Consensu (quem nisi obtinueris, has itteras nullas volumus)*. In like manner, if, as sometimes happens, the faculties of blessing and annexing Indulgences to crosses, chaplets, medals, &c., have inserted the term *privatim*, a Priest not otherwise possessed of power, cannot bless these objects publicly, as, e. g. from a pulpit, whilst the people hold them in their hands (Decree, Jan. 7, 1843). Nay more, he could not place them on the altar, and bless and indulgence them at the conclusion of a public office or ceremony (Decree Feb. 16, 1852).

4. To gain an Indulgence attached to a certain prayer, it ought to be recited in the language in which the Indulgence had been applied to it. The reason of this is evident, from the fact that the Church has ever a special dread against anything liable to tarnish Her stainless faith; but we know it is very easy to slip error into translations, and thus seduce and lead astray incautious or ill-instructed people. The only exception is, in the case of those prayers which the Popes allow to be said in any language whatever, provided the translation be what is called a *faithful version: quocumque idiomate dummodo versio sit fidelis*.

Treating of this matter, I may remark that, in virtue of a special concession made by Pope Pius IX to Monsignor Prinzivalli in September, 1852, all the prayers given in the thirteenth Roman edition of the "Raccolta" are privileged in this way. Hence they may be recited in any language—*quocumque idiomate*—if the versions be faithful and also approved of by the S. Congregation of Indulgences: *ed approvate dalla S. Congregazione delle Indulgenze* (See Preface to the Italian edition, p. xv., on the Decree subjoined). But, observe, the words relating to the approbation contemplate merely a translation of the whole work: "Moreover," continues the Decree of Sept. 30, 1852. "His Holiness has ordered that, should this collection be translated into another tongue, the new version shall not be published without the approval of this S. Congregation." Consequently, if there be question only of one or more prayers taken from the "Raccolta," and rendered in a strange language, the Indulgences may be gained by reciting them in this language, yet after the Ordinary shall have certified that it is a *versio fidelis*—a faithful version.

5. The same may be inferred from a recent but long expected Decree, issued by the S. Congregation of Indulgences, Dec. 14, 1857, and approved by His Holiness Pius IX., Jan. 22, 1858. It is an answer to a doubt laid before the S. Congregation by the Bishop of Perigueux. The illustrious Prelate sought to ascertain the meaning of No. 12, Sect. III., of the Decrees given down after the Rules of the Index: "Let no books, diaries, summaries, pamphlets, loose-papers, &c., conveying Indulgences, be published without the leave of the S. Congregation of Indulgences." He desired to know whether the prohibition were absolute, so as to take away all

power from Bishops in the matter. The decision ordains that it is to be interpreted and executed in the following manner :—

1. If there be question of an Indulgence accorded by an Apostolic Brief or Rescript, or of a number of Indulgences extracted from a Collection already before the public with the approbation of the S. Congregation, it is competent for the Bishop to authorize the publication of such an Indulgence or Summary of Indulgences, provided it come not within the range of a given list or catalogue of Indulgences, respecting which there may be some particular prohibition.*

2. On the other hand, should the reference be to a Summary or Collection previously published, but without the approval of the S. Congregation, or to a compilation about being issued for the first time, the license of the Ordinary would not be sufficient, even though he had the very Rescripts themselves. The publication must be expressly authorized by the Sacred Congregation. *E Contra vero si sermo sit de Summario vel antea collecto, sed nunquam approbato, vel nunc primum ex diversis concessionibus colligendo, requiritur expressa Sacræ Congregationis Indulgentiarum licentia.*

In practice, then, applying these decisions to the translation of the different prayers which may be recited in any supposed language, without prejudice to the Indulgences attached to them, it is plain a Bishop or his Vicar-General may authorize the print-

---

*As a matter of fact, such a prohibition exists in regard to the translation of the *entire* Italian " Raccolta" into another language (Decree 30th Sept. 1852). The same applies to the List of Indulgences annexed by the Sovereign Pontiffs to medals, crosses, chaplets, &c.; accordingly, each new version, before being printed, ought to have received the approbation of the Holy See, or of the S. Congregation of Indulgences.

ing and publication of such versions, provided he is certain that the indulgences attached to these prayers are genuine or authentic, and also that he himself shall have recognized them as being *faithful*. Thus, recourse need not be had to the S. Congregation, except when there is question of a translation of prayers whose Indulgences are either doubtful or unapproved, or of a Summary of Indulgences, which has never been approved, or which is being now compiled for the first time from various Briefs or grants. Such was the reply vouchsafed to me by M. Prinzivalli shortly before his death.

6. Whenever the Briefs, Indults, or Summaries specify that a *plenary* Indulgence may be obtained on all the Feasts of our Lord, the reference is merely to the Festivals of Christmas Day, the Circumcision, Epiphany, Easter Sunday, the Acension and Corpus Christi. And should they connote a *partial* available on the same days, the understanding is, that those alone celebrated by the Universal Church are included. So, too, the feasts of our Blessed Lady comprise, for a *plenary* Indulgence, only the Conception, Nativity, Annunciation, Purification, and Assumption; and, as regards a *partial* one, all the feasts solemnized by the entire Church. Similarly, by an Apostle's feast, in the case of a plenary Indulgence, is meant the principal feast—*natale*—and not the secondary ones, such as the Chair of St. Peter, the Conversion of St. Paul, St. Peter in Chains, St. John before the Latin Gate, &c. (Pius IX. in an audience Sept. 18, 1862).

7. When the Holy See accords an Indulgence *for ever*, it means without any limitation as to time. Hence in such cases, it will not be necessary to have

the favour renewed after a term of twenty years, or of even a much longer period (Decree of Feb. 14, 1842).

8. At present it is not through the medium of the Sacred Congregation of Indulgences and of the Holy Relics the Pope bestows any Indulgence solicited from Rome, but rather through the Congregation of Briefs, the first mentioned one still remaining charged with the examination and solution of al the difficulties raised so frequently on this subject

9. All Decrees cited in this Second Part, whose source is not formally pointed out, are Decrees or Rescripts emanating from the S. Congregation of Indulgences. They are for the most part preceded by the names of the Supreme Pontiffs who may have authenticated and approved them.

10. The capital letter A, placed at the end of any particular Number, indicates the Indulgences applicable to the Souls in Purgatory. May this little volume contribute to succour and release from their pains a vast multitude of these Holy Souls ! We are too forgetful of our deceased friends, said St. Francis of Sales. We take delight in performing works of mercy, continued he in another place, yet never realize to ourselves that, in the relief of those poor souls, nearly all kinds of works of mercy are included ; let us then do for these predestined Souls, these Elect of

* The Sacred Congregation of Indulgences and Holy Relics, in virtue of its institution by Clement IX., by his Constitution commencing thus: "At the very beginning of our Pontificate," July 6, 1669, is invested with power to solve every doubt and difficulty that may arise regarding Indulgences or the Relics of the Saints; also, should any abuses have crept into them, to rectify and correct them ; to forbid the printing of false, apocryphal, and indiscreet Indulgences; to recognise and examine those printed, and, having referred the matter to the Roman Pontiff, to set them aside altogether by his authority" (Decree *Urbis et Orbis*, April 14, 1856).

God, what we shall desire others may one day do for ourselves. O "Blessed are the merciful, for they shall obtain mercy" (Matt. v. 7).

N.B. There is a slight difference between a Decree and a Rescript. The latter presupposes a petition or application, and is therefore given in the form of a response; it vouchsafes, modifies, or refuses the favours sought for in the supplication. While the former is an ordinance, decision, or law enacted irrespective of any previous request. But, since Decrees are not unfrequently elicited by applications made, or doubts proposed, to the Congregations at Rome, the two words are sometimes used indiscriminately. The privileges obtained through Rescripts are called Indults.

## ARTICLE I.

### Prayers.

#### 1. ANGELIC TRISAGION.

| | |
|---|---|
| Sanctus, Sanctus, Sanctus, Dominus Deus Exercituum : plena est terra gloriâ tuâ: Gloria Patri, gloria Filio, Gloria Spiritui Sancto. | Holy, Holy, Holy, Lord God of Hosts: earth is full of Thy Glory; Glory be to the Father, glory be to the Son, glory be to the Holy Ghost. |

I. An Indulgence of 100 days, *once a day*, to all those who, in order to render homage to the Adorable

Trinity, shall recite with contrite hearts the Angelic Trisagion.

II. The same Indulgence may be gained *thrice* every Sunday, as also on the Festival and each day during the Octave of the Most Holy Trinity.

III. A plenary Indulgence *once a month*, available to those who shall have said it every day of the month, provided that on some day of their own choosing, they confess, communicate, visit a church, and pray there for the intention of the Sovereign Pontiff (Clement IX., Decree of June 26, 1770). A—applicable to the Souls in Purgatory.*

---

* The "Raccolta" says: *accorded afresh for ever.* The Indulgence is then *perpetual*, as are all those mentioned in this Book. Should it happen to be otherwise in any particular instance, notice will be given to that effect.

In the course of the treatise, there will often be question of a plenary Indulgence to be gained *once a month*, by those who, *during the entire month*, may have daily recited such or such a prayer, or practised a certain pious work. But it is necessary to observe, once for all, that, before being entitled to it, one must really have said the prayer or practised the work, throughout the whole month, should he have begun the exercise on the first day of the month ; or at least during thirty consecutive days, if he commenced it on any other day of the month. Hence the mere intention of continuing the prayer or devout exercise would not suffice to obtain the Indulgence.

As regards the Confession and Communion prescribed to acquire it, generally speaking, these conditions must be fulfilled *after* the expiration of the month, on any day selected by oneself—*un giorno ad arbitrio*—says the "Raccolta" repeatedly. Such is the sentiment of the S. Congregation of Indulgences, and in fact the sense of most of the Rescripts, with the exception of a few in which it is enjoined to confess and communicate in the course of the month—*infra mensem*—*in un giorno di detto mese*—or one of the three last days of it. However, in these instances the Indulgence is not gained on the day of Communion, which is received before the end of the month, but on the last day of the month, or the last of the thirty days, that is to say, when, conformably to the designs of the Supreme Pontiffs, the prayer shall have been said or the work performed *throughout the entire month*.

To this again there is an exception in favour of the Month of May, for the plenary Indulgence can be obtained only on a day within the month, on which a person may choose to confess and communicate, so that, in this case, the Communion should be made either during the month, or at any event, on the last day of the month. Because the

## 2. THREE GLORIA PATRIS, &c.

To be said in thanksgiving to the most Holy Trinity for the special graces and privileges bestowed on Holy Mary, particularly in her glorious Assumption into Heaven.

1. An Indulgence of 300 days if they are recited morning, noon, and evening.

2. An Indulgence of 100 days for each of the three times.

3. A plenary Indulgence, *once a month*, to persons who shall have said it daily during the month, at the three aforesaid hours—Confession and Communion being supposed—(Pius VII., Rescript of the Sacred Congregation of Indulgences, July 11, 1815). A.*

Rescript of Pius VII. does not make the Indulgence depend on the practice of the devotion through every day of the month. This is so true that, at Rome, where it is usual to terminate the Month of May on the first Sunday of June, whenever it approximates to the 31st of May, they invariably petition His Holiness to empower them to partake of the Indulgence by communicating on that Sunday. Clearly, this faculty would be needless, if, to acquire the Indulgence, *every day of the month* should have been consecrated to our Blessed Lady, since pursuant to the explanation given in the first part of the note, each person would be free to receive the Communion on the first Sunday of June— *un giorno ad arbitrio*,

N.B.—This Indulgence may be likewise gained on the 1st day of June. but only on that day (Pius IX., August 8, 1869). As will be noticed further on, there is another exception respecting the Month of St. Joseph.

* The Indulgence of 30 days, which, according to many writers, may be gained by those who recite the Gloria Patri, &c., inclining the head at the same time, is not authentic. They all cite Ferraris as their authority, whilst he himself refers to John XXII., without indicating either the Bull or the Brief wherein the Indulgence may be seen. The truth is, that, as regards the question of Indulgences, Lucius Ferraris, in his "Bibliotheca Canonica," deserves not the confident reliance centred in him by several French authors, who have even recently written on the subject. Had they taken the trouble of examining his Article on Indulgences, as embodied in that work, they would be easily convinced that, in many instances, they should not rely entirely on the mere statements of the compiler Take, for illustration, a few of

## 3. THREE OFFERINGS TO THE MOST HOLY TRINITY.

*With three Paters, Aves, and Glorias, to obtain a good death.*

I. We offer to the most Holy Trinity the merits of Jesus Christ, in thanksgiving for the most Precious Blood which He shed in the garden for us; and by His merits we beseech the Divine Majesty for pardon of our sins. Pater, Ave, Gloria.

II. We offer to the Most Holy Trinity the merits of Jesus Christ, in thanksgiving for His most precious death endured on the cross for us; and by His merits we beseech the Divine Majesty for the remission of the pains due to our sins. Pater, Ave, Gloria.

III. We offer to the Most Holy Trinity the merits of Jesus Christ, in thanksgiving for His unspeakable charity, by which He descended from heaven to earth to take human flesh, and to suffer and die for us upon the cross; and by His merits we beseech the Divine Majesty to bring our souls to the glory of heaven after our death. Pater, Ave, Gloria.

the Indulgences given down by him as genuine, and you will see, at a glance, that it would be difficult to establish their authenticity:

"Persons hearing or celebrating Mass devoutly, 30,800 years' Indulgence, applicable by way of suffrage to the Souls in Purgatory." And lower down, "Joannes XXII. concessit sacerdotibus devote post Missam orationem sequentem recitantibus veniam pœnæ debitæ mille peccatis lethalibus, necnon genuflexis Indulgentiam annorum 10,000:
'Anima Christi, sanctifica me,
Corpus Christi, salva me, &c.'"
The writer does not say where this unheard-of prerogative may be found; in reality it was never bestowed.

Again: "Ex concessione Clementis VIII., consequuntur remissionem omnium commissorum, seu omissorum in Missa, necnon 2,300 annorum Indulgentiam sacerdotes omnes recitantes sequentem orationem: 'Obsecro te, Dulcissime Jesu Christe, &c.'" Where is the concession of Clem. VIII.? (See the true Indulgences accorded to this beautiful prayer by Pius IX., No. 15.)

1. An Indulgence of 100 days, *every time* a person devoutly recites these offerings.

2. A plenary Indulgence at the end of the month, to all who shall have said them daily during that time : the conditions being Confession, Communion, and prayers for the intention of His Holiness (Leo XII., Rescript from under his own hand, Oct. 21, 1823. The original is preserved in the Archives of the Fathers Observant of *Ara Cœli* at Rome). A.

### 4. TRIDUO OR NOVENA IN HONOUR OF THE MOST HOLY TRINITY.

Which may be celebrated just immediately before the Feast of the most Blessed Trinity, or at any other time of the year, either in public or private. The prayers to be said are left to one's own choice:

1. An Indulgence of seven years and seven Quarantines each day of the Triduo or Novena.

2. A plenary Indulgence at the end of it, on the condition of Confession, Communion, and visit to a Church in which a person shall pray according to the Pope's intention (Pius IX., Decree of Aug. 8, 1847; at the prayer of the Procurator-General of the Discalced Trinitarian Fathers). A.

### 5. PRAISES TO THE HOLY NAME OF GOD.

Blessed be God.
Blessed be His Holy Name.
Blessed be Jesus Christ, true God and true man.
Blessed be the Name of Jesus.
Blessed be Jesus in the most Holy Sacrament of the Altar.

Blessed be the incomparable Mother of God, the Most Holy Mary.
Blessed be her Holy and Immaculate Conception.
Blessed be the Name of Mary, Virgin and Mother.
Blessed be God in His Holy Angels and in His Saints.

For the love we owe to God, and for the honour due to His most adorable Name, let us recite these acts of praise to repair the outrages done to it by blasphemers.

1. One year's Indulgence, *each time* (Pius VII.—Rescript, dated July 23, 1801).

2. A plenary Indulgence *once a month* to all who recite them at least once a day, provided they confess, communicate, visit a Church or public Oratory and there pray for the intention of the Sovereign Pontiff (Pius IX.—Decree of Aug. 8, 1847). A.*

### 6. PRAYERS AND PETITIONS.

O Father! O Son! O Holy Ghost!
O Holy Trinity! O Jesus! O Mary!
O ye blessed angels of God, all ye Saints of Paradise, men and women, obtain for me these graces, which I ask through the Precious Blood of Jesus Christ:

1. Ever to do the holy will of God.
2. Ever to live in union with God.
3. Not to think of anything but God.
4. To love God alone.
5. To do all for God.

\* In all Churches at Rome, the Priest usually recites them aloud, alternately with the people, after Benediction, but before replacing the Blessed Sacrament in the Tabernacle. The same custom prevails at Florence.

6. To seek only the glory of God.
7. To sanctify myself solely for God.
8. To know well my own utter nothingness.
9. Ever to know more and more the will of my God.

Mary, most holy, offer to the Eternal Father the most Precious Blood of Jesus Christ for my soul, for the holy souls in purgatory, for the needs of Holy Church, for the conversion of sinners, and for all the world.

*Then say three* Gloria Patris *to the most holy Blood of Jesus Christ;  one* Hail Mary, *to the sorrows of the most holy Mary; and one* Requiem æternam, &c., *for the holy souls in purgatory.*

1. An Indulgence of 300 days, *once a day* to everybody who, with contrite heart and devotion, recites these prayers.

2. A plenary Indulgence, *once a month*, to such as shall have repeated them daily; the conditions require Confession, Communion, visit to a Church or public Oratory, and to pray there for the intention of the Holy Father. Note, that in this case the Communion should be received on some one of the last three days of the month (Leo XII., Rescript March 3, 1827). It, moreover, expresses a wish that copies of these prayers and petitions be distributed gratis. A.

### 7. ACTS OF FAITH, HOPE, AND CHARITY.

In annexing Indulgences to acts of the Theological Virtues, Benedict XIV. prescribed no particular form of words in which they should be made Hence a person may use any formula he pleases, provided it expresses the respective motives of the three virtues. The favours vouchsafed are :—

1. An Indulgence of seven years and seven Quarantines, *every time* the faithful devoutly make them in their hearts, and say them with their lips.

2. A plenary Indulgence, *once a month*, to those who shall have recited them daily, if they confess, communicate, and pray for holy Church.

3. A plenary Indulgence, at the hour of death, to all who may have frequently repeated them during life (Bened. XIV., Decree, January 28, 1756). A.

### 8. AN ACT OF CONFORMITY TO THE WILL OF GOD.

| | |
|---|---|
| Fiat, laudetur, atque in æternum superexaltetur justissima, altissima, et amabilissima voluntas Dei in omnibus. | May the most just, most high, and most amiable will of God be in all things done, praised and magnified for ever. |

1. An Indulgence of 100 days, to be gained *once a day only*.

2. A plenary Indulgence, *once a year*, to those who shall have made that act every day, provided that, on some day of their own selection, they go to Communion, and pray according to the design of the Head of the Church.

3. A plenary Indulgence, *at the hour of death*, to anybody who shall have often repeated it through life, if he accept death with resignation from the hand of God (Pius VII., Decree of May 10, 1818). A.

### 9. USE OF INDULGENCED PRAYERS
*during our daily occupations.*

We ought to accustom ourselves to practise them in such a way, that their frequent use will become quite easy to us. Every one knows that aspirations of the heart, proceeding directly from the Holy Ghost, are eminently calculated to obtain for us light, strength, and consolation. Select, then, dear reader, for that purpose, certain pious ejaculations, and thus, whilst perfecting your own sanctification, you will be enabled to relieve the suffering souls in Purgatory. With a view to this, see Nos. 1, 17, 18, 21, 22, 23, 24, 25, 27, 28, 36, 40, &c.

### 10. PRAYER IN THE FORM OF AN OFFERING.

Eternal Father, we offer Thee the Blood, Passion, and Death of Jesus Christ, the Sorrows of Most Holy Mary and St. Joseph, for the remission of our sins, the deliverance of the souls in Purgatory, the wants of our holy Mother the Church, and the conversion of sinners.

By a Rescript of April 30, 1860, His Holiness Pius IX. granted to all the Faithful, *every time* they recite this prayer with devotion, 100 days' Indulgence. They are exhorted, moreover, to repeat it sixty-three times a day, in the form of a Rosary.

### 11. PRAYER OF ST. FRANCIS XAVIER.

*For the conversion of Infidels.*

| | |
|---|---|
| Æterne rerum omnium effector Deus, memento abs te animas infidelium procreatas, easque ad imagineum et similitudinem tuam conditas. Ecce Do- | O God, who bringest all things into existence, remember that the souls of unbelievers have been called into existence by Thee, and that they have |

mine, in opprobrium tuum his ipsis infernus impletur. Memento Jesum Filium tuum pro illorum salute atrocissimam subiisse necem. Noli, quæso, Domine, ultra permittere, ut Filius tuus ab infidelibus contemnatur; sed precibus sanctorum virorum et Ecclesiæ sanctissimi Filii tui Sponsæ placatus, recordare misericordiæ tuæ, et oblitus idololatriæ et infidelitatis eorum, effice ut ipsi quoque agnoscant aliquando, quem misisti Dominum Jesum Christum, qui est salus, vita et resurrectio nostra, per quem salvati et liberati sumus: cui sit gloria per infinita sæcula sæculorum. Amen.

been made after Thy own image and likeness. Behold, O Lord, to the dishonour of Thee, with these very souls hell is filled. Remember, O God, that for their salvation Thy Son Jesus Christ underwent the most cruel death. Let it not then, I entreat Thee, O Lord, be any longer permitted by Thee that Thy Son should be despised by the unbelievers; but, appeased by the prayers of holy men and of the Church, the Spouse of Thy most holy Son, do Thou remember Thy own pity, and, forgetting their idolatry and their unbelief, bring it to pass that they too may some time acknowledge Thy Son Jesus Christ, who is our salvation, life, and resurrection through whom we are saved and set free; to whom be glory from age to age without end. Amen.

By a Rescript from his own hand, the Sovereign Pontiff, Pius IX., accorded, to every person who shall recite this prayer devoutly, an Indulgence of 300 days. The Rescript is dated 28th July, 1847, and was registered in the Segretaria of the Sacred Congregation of Indulgences, Sept. 30th, 1862.*

## 12. THE HYMN "VENI CREATOR SPIRITUS," AND THE SEQUENCE "VENI SANCTE SPIRITUS."

Veni Creator Spiritus,
Mentes tuorum visita,
Imple superna gratia,
Quæ Tu creasti pectora.

Come, O Creator Spirit blest!
And in our souls take up Thy rest;
Come with Thy grace and heavenly aid,
To fill the hearts which Thou hast made.

Qui diceris Paraclitus
Altissimi Donum Dei,
Fons vivus, Ignis, Charitas,
Et spiritalis Unctio.

Great Paraclete! to Thee we cry:
O highest gift of God most high!
O fount of life! O fire of love!
And sweet Anointing from above.

Tu septiformis munere
Digitus Paternæ dexteræ,
Tu rite promissum Patris,
Sermone ditans guttura.

Thou in Thy sevenfold gifts are known;
Thee Finger of God's hand we own;
The promise of the Father Thou!
Who dost the tongue with pow'r endow.

Accende lumen sensibus,
Infunde amorem cordibus,
Infirma nostri corporis
Virtute firmans perpeti.

Kindle our senses from above,
And make our hearts o'erflow with love;
With patience firm, and virtue high,
The weakness of our flesh supply.

---

\* His Holiness Pius IX., by a Rescript of May 9th, 1850, granted 300 days' Indulgence to all who pray for the conversion of England. And by another Rescript, Nov. 16th, 1857, he extended this favour to those who *associate* together, to pray for the conversion of all dissenting from the Catholic Church,

| | |
|---|---|
| Hostem repellas longius, | Far from us drive the foe we dread, |
| Pacemque dones protinus, | And grant us Thy true peace instead; |
| Ductore sic Te prævio | So shall we not, with Thee for guide, |
| Vitemus omne noxium. | Turn from the path of life aside. |
| | |
| Per Te sciamus da Patrem, | O, may Thy grace on us bestow, |
| Noscamus atque Filium, | The Father and the Son to know, |
| Teque utriusque Spiritum | And Thee through endless times confess'd. |
| Credamus omni tempore. | Of Both th' eternal Spirit blest. |
| | |
| Deo patri sit gloria, | All glory while the ages run |
| Et Filio, qui a mortuis | Be to the Father, and the Son, |
| Surrexit, ac Paraclito | Who rose from death; the same to Thee, |
| In sæculorum sæcula. Amen.* | O Holy Ghost, eternally. |

### THE SEQUENCE.

| | |
|---|---|
| Veni Sancte Spiritus, | Holy Spirit! Lord of light! |
| Et emitte cœlitus | From Thy clear celestial height |
| Lucis tuæ radium. | Thy pure beaming radiance give: |

---

\* Outside Paschal time, the Doxology is:—

| | |
|---|---|
| Deo Patri Sit Gloria, | Glory to God the Father be, |
| Ejusque soli Filio, | And to his sole begotten Son, |
| Cum Spiritu Paraclito, | The same O Holy Ghost to Thee, |
| Nunc et per omne seculum. | While everlasting ages run. |
| Amen. | Amen. |

By a Decree of the S. Congregation of Rites, 28th July, 1832 (Gardelini, 3, 4545 ad 4 et 5 4713 ad 11); 1, the Indulgences will not be gained, if the Hymn be recited pursuant to the ancient rhythm; 2, the variation of the Doxology, during and outside Paschal time, does not hinder them from being gained; 3, every other sort of Doxology would prevent them, even though it were sanctioned by episcopal authority (Pius IX., Decree March 12, 1855).

| | |
|---|---|
| Veni, Pater pauperum, | Come, Thou Father of the poor, |
| Veni, dator munerum, | Come, with treasures which endure! |
| Veni, lumen cordium. | Come, Thou life of all that live! |
| | |
| Consolator optime, | Thou, of all consolers best, |
| Dulcis hospes animæ, | Visiting the troubled breast, |
| Dulce refrigerium. | Dost refreshing peace bestow; |
| | |
| In labore requies, | Thou in toil art comfort sweet; |
| In æstu temperies, | Pleasant coolness in the heat; |
| In fletu solatium. | Solace in the midst of woe. |
| | |
| O lux beatissima, | Light immortal! Light Divine! |
| Reple cordis initima, | Visit Thou these hearts of Thine |
| Tuorum fidelium. | And our inmost being fill: |
| | |
| Sine tuo numine, | If Thou take Thy grace away, |
| Nihil est in homine, | Nothing pure in man will stay. |
| Nihil est innoxium. | All his good is turn'd to ill. |
| | |
| Lava quod est sordidum, | Heal our wounds—our strength renew; |
| Riga quod est aridum, | On our dryness pour Thy dew; |
| Sana quod est saucium. | Wash the stains of guilt away: |
| | |
| Flecte quod est rigidum, | Bend the stubborn heart and will |
| Fove quod est frigidum, | Melt the frozen, warm the chill; |
| Rege quod est devium. | Guide the steps that go astray. |
| | |
| Da tuis fidelibus | Thou on those who evermore |
| In te confidentibus | Thee confess and Thee adore, |
| Sacrum septenarium. | In Thy sevenfold gifts, descend: |
| | |
| Da virtutis meritum, | Give them comfort when they die: |
| Da salutis exitum, | Give them life with Thee on high; |
| Da perenne gaudium. | Give them joys which never end. |
| Amen. | |

The Indulgences accorded to the recitation of the "Veni Creator," or the "Sequence," are:

1, An Indulgence of 100 days, *each time* and for very day of the year.

2, Three hundred days' Indulgence on Whit-Sunday, and on each day within the Octave.

3, A plenary Indulgence, *once a month*, to all who shall have, one or more times, daily recited either the Hymn or Sequence, *with* the intention of praying for concord amongst Christian Princes, &c., after having approached the Sacraments. Remark that, in saying these prayers, it is necessary to have the intention of praying, at the same time, for the wants of Holy Church, but there is no need to add any other prayer for that end (Pius VI., Brief, May 25, 1796; the original is kept in the Archivium of the Congregation called *Prima Primaria* in the Roman College). A.

13. PRAYER, "EN EGO," &C., BEFORE A CRUCIFIX.

Every person who, after Confession and Communion, shall recite with at least a contrite heart, and devoutly, the following prayer, before any image whatever of Jesus crucified, can gain a *plenary Indulgence*, accorded for ever by Pius VII. (Decree of April 10, 1821). But conformably to a Decree dating 31st July, 1858, it is necessary, in order to participate in it, to add some other prayer for the Pope's intention.* A.

* The *short Meditation* on the five wounds of our Redeemer, required by some authors for acquiring this precious Indulgence, is by no means necessary. Moreover the Sovereign Pontiff has declared, that those who may not be aware of the Decree of July 31st, 1858, can still share in the Indulgence, by fulfilling the other conditions (Confession, Communion, and a recital of the "En Ego," before a Crucifix). The

En ego, O bone et dulcissime Jesu, ante conspectum tuum genibus me provolvo ac maximo animi ardore te oro atque obtestor ut meum in cor vividos fidei, spei, et charitatis sensus, atque veram peccatorum meorum pœnitentiam, eaque emendandi firmissimam voluntatem velis imprimere: dum magno animi affectu et dolore, tua quinque Vulnera mecum ipse considero, ac mente contemplor, illud præ oculis habens, quod jam in ore ponebat suo David Propheta de Te, O bone Jesu: "Foderunt manus Meas

O good and sweetest Jesus, before Thy face I humbly kneel, and with all fervour of soul I pray and beseech Thee to vouchsafe to fix deep in my heart lively sentiments of faith, hope, and charity, true contrition for my sins, and a most firm purpose of amendment; whilst I contemplate with great sorrow and love Thy five Wounds, and ponder them over in my mind, having before my eyes the words which, long ago, David the Prophet spoke in his own person concerning Thee, O good Jesus: "Foderunt manus Meas et

prayer itself "En Ego," may be said before or after Mass or Communion.

et pedes Meos; dinumeraverunt omnia ossa Mea." pedes Meos; dinumeraverunt omnia ossa Mea." "They digged My hands and My feet; they numbered all my bones" (*Ps.* xxi. 17, 18).

14. PRAYER, "EGO VOLO CELEBRARE MISSAM," &c.

Ego volo celebrare Missam, et conficere Corpus et Sanguinem Domini nostri Jesu Christi juxta ritum sanctæ Romanæ Ecclesiæ, ad laudem omnipotentis Dei, totiusque Curiæ triumphantis; ad utilitatem meam totiusque Curiæ militantis; pro omnibus qui se commendarunt orationibus meis in genere et in specie, ac pro felici statu sanctæ Romanæ Ecclesiæ. Amen.

Gaudium cum pace, emendationem vitæ, spatium veræ pœnitentiæ, gratiam et consolationem Sancti Spiritus, perseverantiam in bonis operibus tribuat nobis omnipotens et misericors Dominus. Amen.

An Indulgence of fifty *days* to all Priests, secular and regular, who, before celebrating the Holy Sacrifice of the Mass, shall say this prayer devoutly. A. *Decr. S.R.C.*, January 13, 1879.

15. PRAYER, "OBSECRO TE, DULCISSIME," &c.

Obsecro te, dulcissime Domine Jesu Christe, ut Passio tua sit mihi virtus qua muniar, protegar atque defendar: vulnera tua sint mihi cibus potusque quibus pascar, inebrier, atque delecter: aspersio sanguinis tui sit mihi ablutio omnium delictorum meorum; mors tua sit mihi refectio, exultatio, sanitas et dulcedo cordis mei. Qui vivis et regnas in sæcula sæculorum. Amen.

An Indulgence of *three years* for all Priests who, after having celebrated Mass, recite the foregoing prayer (Pius IX., Decree of 11th December, 1846). A.

Moreover, he directed that the Decree of this grant should be hung up in the Sacristies of all Churches and public Oratories, for the reason that to this prayer have been attributed some apocryphal Indulgences, which are set forth on old cards used by several of the clergy, when preparing for Mass. Read the note of No. 2.

### 16. PRAYER "ANIMA CHRISTI," &c., "SOUL OF CHRIST," &c.

Pope Pius IX., annulling all other Indulgences previously annexed or attributed to the subjoined prayer, so often employed by St. Ignatius, in his spiritual exercises, granted afresh:—

1, An Indulgence of 300 days to all the Faithful, *every time* they repeat it with contrite hearts.

2, An Indulgence of *seven years* to all Priests who shall say it after Mass, and to the laity after Holy Communion.

3, A plenary Indulgence, *once a month*, to all in the pious habit of reciting it at least once a day; it being understood that they Confess, Communicate, visit a Church or public Oratory, and pray there for the intention of the Holy Father (Decree of January 9, 1854). A.

| | |
|---|---|
| Anima Christi, Sanctifica me. | Soul of Christ, be my sanctification; |
| Corpus Christi, salva me. | Body of Christ, be my salvation; |
| Sanguis Christi, inebria me. | Blood of Christ, fill all my veins; |
| Aqua lateris Christi, lava me. | Water of Christ's side, wash out my stains, |

| | |
|---|---|
| Passio Christi, conforta me. | Passion of Christ, my comfort be; |
| O bone Jesu, exaudi me. | O good Jesus listen to me; |
| Intra tua vulnera absconde me. | In Thy wounds I fain would hide, |
| Ne permittas me separari a Te | Ne'er to be parted from Thy side; |
| Ab hoste maligno defende me. | Guard me, should the foe assail me; |
| In hora mortis meæ voca me, | Call me when my life shall fail me; |
| Et jube me venire ad Te, | Bid me come to Thee above, |
| Ut cum sanctis tuis laudem Te | With Thy saints to sing Thy love |
| In sæcula sæculorum. Amen. | World without end. Amen. A. |

### 17. EJACULATORY PRAYER, OR OFFERING OF THE PRECIOUS BLOOD OF OUR SAVIOUR JESUS CHRIST.

Eternal Father! I offer Thee the precious blood of Jesus, in satisfaction for my sins, and for the wants of Holy Church.

An Indulgence of 100 days to all the Faithful *each time* they piously repeat this ejaculation (Pius VII., Rescript, March 29, 1817; signed by his own hand). A.

### 18. EJACULATION TO THE BLESSED SACRAMENT.

Blessed and praised every moment, be the most Holy and Divine Sacrament!

To the pious recital of this ejaculation or Eucharistic tribute, are attached:

1, An Indulgence of 100 days, available *once* a day.

2, An Indulgence of 300 days every Thursday of the year, and on all days during the Octave of Corpus Christi, to persons repeating it *thrice* on said days.

3, A plenary Indulgence, *once a month*, to anybody who may have recited it daily, if he Confess, Communicate, and pray for our Mother the Church (Pius VI., Rescript, May 24, 1776).

4, In addition to that, Pius VII. (Decrees of June 30, 1818, and December 7, 1819), ever desiring to stimulate more and more the devotion of the Faithful towards the most adorable Eucharist, conceded 100 days' Indulgence to anyone, who, at the sound of a bell announcing that the Blessed Sacrament is exposed, or that Benediction is being given in some Church, shall adore our Divine Lord, with a contrite heart, and recite the aforesaid ejaculation. The same favour is held out to all who, while assisting at Mass, say this prayer at the Elevation of the Host and Chalice, meanwhile adoring our Blessed Redeemer present on the altar.

Prior to this, Gregory XIII. (Constitution, April 10, 1580), had granted:

1, *One year's Indulgence*, whenever, at the sound of a bell giving the signal for the Elevation at High Mass, whether conventual or parochial, the Faithful, wherever they chance to be, adore on their knees Jesus in the Blessed Sacrament, saying, at the same moment, some short prayer.

2, *An Indulgence of two years*, should they enter a Church for this purpose, and there, as specified, adore our loving Saviour during the Elevation. A.

### 19. THE HYMN "PANGE LINGUA," OR THE "TANTUM ERGO."

| | |
|---|---|
| Pange lingua gloriosi | Sing, my tongue, the Saviour's glory, |
| Corporis Mysterium, | Of His Flesh the mystery sing; |
| Sanguinisque pretiosi, | Of the Blood, all price exceeding, |
| Quem in mundi pretium, | Shed by our immortal King, |
| Fructus ventris generosi | Destin'd for the world's redemption, |
| Rex effudit gentium. | From a noble womb to spring. |

Nobis datus, nobis natus
  Ex intacta Virgine,
Et in mundo conversatus
  Sparso verbi semine,

Sui moras incolatus
  Miro clausit ordine.

In supremæ nocte cœnæ
  Recumbens cum fratribus,
Observata lege plene
  Cibis in legalibus,

Cibum turbæ duodenæ
  Se dat suis manibus.

Verbum caro, panem verum
  Verbo carnem efficit;
Fitque Sanguis Christi merum
  Et si sensus deficit,

Ad firmandum cor sincerum
  Sola fides sufficit.

Of a pure and spotless Virgin
  Born for us on earth below,
He, as Man with man conversing
  Stay'd, the seeds of truth to sow;
Then He clos'd in solemn order
  Wondrously His life of woe.

On the night of that Last Supper,
  Seated with His chosen band,
He the paschal victim eating,
  First fulfils the Law's command;
Then as food to all his brethren
  Gives Himself with His own hand.

Word made Flesh, the bread of nature
  By His word to Flesh he turns:
Wine into His Blood He changes—
  What though sense no change discerns?
Only be the heart in earnest
  Faith her lesson quickly learns.

(Tantum ergo Sacramentum.)

Tantum ergo Sacramentum
  Veneremur cernui:
Et antiquum documentum
  Novo cedat ritui:
Præstet fides supplementum
  Sensuum defectui.

Down in adoration falling,
  Lo! the sacred Host we hail;
Lo! o'er ancient forms departing,
  Newer rites of grace prevail;
Faith for all defects supplying,
  Where the feeble senses fail.

| | |
|---|---|
| Genitori Genitoque<br>  Laus et jubilatio, | To the everlasting Father,<br>  And the Son who reigns on high, |
| Salus, honor, virtus quoque | With the Holy Ghost proceeding |
|   Sit et benedictio,<br>Procedenti ab utroque<br>  Compar sit laudatio. Amen. | Forth from each eternally,<br>Be salvation, honour, blessing,<br>Might, and endless majesty.<br>                Amen. |
| v. Panem de cœlo præstitisti eis. | v. Thou gavest them Bread from heaven. |
| r. Omne delectamentum in se habentem. | r. And therein was sweetness of every kind. |

*Oremus.*                *Let us pray.*

Deus, qui nobis sub Sacramento mirabili, Passionis tuæ memoriam reliquisti : tribue, quæsumus, ita nos Corporis et Sanguinis tui sacra mysteria venerari, ut redemptionis tuæ fructum in nobis jugiter sentiamus. Qui vivis et regnas, &c.

O God who under this wonderful Sacrament has left unto us the memorial of Thy Passion; grant us, we beseech Thee, so to venerate the sacred mysteries of Thy Body and Thy Blood, that we may constantly experience within us the fruit of Thy redemption, Who livest and reignest, &c.

    1, Three hundred days' Indulgence, *once a day*, to all who, with contrite hearts, piously recite that entire hymn, with the Versicle, Response, and prayer of the Blessed Sacrament.

    2, An Indulgence of 100 days, if they say only the two last stanzas or the *Tantum Ergo*, &c., with the Versicle and Prayer.

    3, A plenary Indulgence, *three times a year*, namely, on Holy Thursday, Corpus Christi, or some day in its Octave, and on one other day at their own option, should they have the devout habit of repeating often, or at least ten times a month, tho whole Hymn, or the *Tantum Ergo* alone. To acquire this Indulgence, one must go to Confession and Communion, visit a Church, and pray there for the intentions of the Head of the Church (Pius VII., Decree, August, 25, 1818). A.

### 20. OFFERING TO JESUS CHRIST.

My loving Jesus, out of gratitude to Thee, and to make reparation for my unfaithfulness to grace, I (N.N.) give Thee my heart, and I consecrate myself wholly to Thee, and with Thy help I purpose never to sin again.

This offering or act of consecration should be made before an image or picture of the Sacred Heart of Jesus. The Indulgences annexed to it are:

1, An Indulgence of 100 days, *once a day*, to those who make it with contrite hearts.

2, A plenary Indulgence, *once a month*, if it be made every day during that period, on condition of Confession, Communion, and prayers for the intention of the Supreme Pontiff (Pius VII., Rescripts, June 9, 1807, and September 26, 1817). A.

### 21. PIOUS EJACULATION: *"My Jesus, Mercy."*

An Indulgence of 100 days *every time* a person repeats it. (Leo XII., by word of mouth, 1824, confirmed for ever by Pius IX., Decree, September 23, 1846). A.

St. Leonard, a celebrated Missionary of the last century, made frequent use of this short invocation; recommending it particularly to the dying, who may be unable to say long prayers.

### 22. ANOTHER INVOCATION.

Jesu, Deus meus, super omnia amo te.
Jesus, my God, I love Thee above all things.

An Indulgence of 50 days to all who recite this ejaculation, with sentiments of compunction and thanksgiving, in any language whatever. Moreover, persons charged with the care of souls or labouring for their salvation, may partake of the same Indulgence, by exhorting others to elicit it (Pius IX. Rescript, May 7, 1854).

### 23. DEVOUT ASPIRATION.

Dulcissime Jesu, ne sis mihi Judex, sed Salvator.
My sweetest Jesus, be not to me a Judge, but a Saviour.

1, Fifty days' Indulgence *every time* a person says this little prayer of St. Jerome Emiliani.

2, A plenary Indulgence to those who repeat it at least once a day for a year, to be gained *once* only, on the feast of the Saint (20th July), or on some day of the Octave, on condition that they approach the Sacraments on that day, visit a Church, and pray there for the wants of Holy Church (Pius IX., Decree, August 11, 1851, and Nov. 29, 1853). A.

### 24. THE HOLY NAMES OF JESUS AND MARY.

1, An Indulgence of 50 days *every time* two persons saluting each other should say, the one: Laudetur Jesus Christus—Praised be Jesus Christ; the other by way of answer : In Sæcula Sæculorum. Amen—For evermore. Amen—or Be it ever praised.

2, An Indulgence of 25 days *every time* any one devoutly invokes the Holy Name of Jesus or that of Mary.

3, A plenary Indulgence, *in articulo mortis*, to all who, during their lifetime, may have had the pious practice of saluting reciprocally, as above, or of invoking frequently these Holy Names, if, in that last hour, they also invoke them with at least contrite hearts, should they be unable to do so with their mouths.

Lastly, the same Indulgences are available to preachers and others who exhort the Faithful to salute one another in this manner, and to often invoke the most Sacred Names of Jesus, and Mary (Sixtus V., and afterwards Bened. XIII., Decree Jan. 12, 1728, and Clem. XIII., Sept. 5, 1759). A.

### 25. ANOTHER PIOUS SALUTATION.

An Indulgence of 50 days, *as often as* two persons salute each other, the one saying, in any language whatever : "Praised be Jesus and Mary ;" and the other replying, " Now and for ever," or in some other similar form of words (Pius IX., Rescript, September 26, 1864).

### 26. LITANY OF THE SACRED NAME OF JESUS.

It is quite certain that, with the exception of some special concessions made by the S. Congregation of Rites to the Bishops of Germany, the Litany of the Sacred Name had not been universally approved until very recently. But, on the occasion of the solemn canonization of the Japanese Martyrs, a great number of illustrious Prelates, seeing the people were accustomed to recite it in almost all the Dioceses of Christendom, solicited His Holiness for a general approbation of it. Accordingly, the august Pontiff, Pius IX., graciously consented to comply with their wishes. From the different Litanies of the Sacred Name, the Congregation of Rites selected and approved the one commonly used in France. To the recitation of this the Holy Father vouchsafed to apply 300 *days' Indulgence.*

Still the Dioceses enjoy not the privilege of reciting or of chanting the Litany in Churches, at processions, &c., only as far as the respective Bishops may have procured faculties for doing so, by application to the S. Congregation of Rites. It is *only then* the Faithful can partake of this Indulgence.

Note, also, that the Bishops can procure faculties from the Holy See, to enable their flocks to recite it in the Vernacular, without forfeiting the Indulgence. Only that then, it is said in private.\* In point of fact, His Eminence the Cardinal Archbishop of Lyons has obtained these two faculties for his own Diocese.

### 27. EJACULATION TO THE SACRED HEART OF JESUS.

Jesu mitis et humilis corde, fac cor meum sicut cor tuum.

Jesus meek and humble of heart, make my heart like to Thine.

---

\* Every one knows the Decree of the Church, prohibiting the use of all Litanies, except those that are most ancient and in common use amongst the Faithful, which are inserted in the Breviaries, Missals, Pontificals, and Rituals, excepting also the Litany of the Blessed Virgin, which is usually sung in the Holy House of Lorretto (Decrees given down at the end of the Rules of the Index, p. iv., n 3).

However this Decree was modified by Pius IX. (1861), so that any Litanies examined and approved by the Bishops of the various districts, cease to be on the *Index*. The people may then, of course, recite them privately. But to use them as the Litany of the Church, one should have the permission and approbation of the Holy See (See the *Revue des Sciences Ecclesiastiques*, Dec., 1861).

An Indulgence of 300 days for the devout recital of this prayer (Pius IX., Jan 25, 1868). A.

### 28. INVOCATION OF JESUS, MARY, AND JOSEPH.

Jesus, Mary, Joseph, I offer you my heart and my soul.
Jesus, Mary, Joseph, assist me in my last agony.
Jesus, Mary, Joseph, may I breathe forth my soul with you in peace.

1, An Indulgence of 300 days *every time* a person recites these three aspirations, with at least a contrite heart (Pius VII., Decree of April 28, 1807).

2, The same Pope likewise attached 100 days' Indulgence to the recitation of one of them. A.

### 29. THE PRAYER "SACROSANCTÆ," &c.

Leo X. accorded to all persons obliged to the Divine Office, or the Office of the Blessed Virgin, a remission of the faults committed through human frailty in reciting it, provided that, on bended knees, they devoutly say at the end of it the prayer *Sacrosanctæ*, composed by St. Bonaventure, together with the Pater and Ave. And, as this grant is more a kind of compensation for the defects incurred in the recitation of the Office than an Indulgence (*a compensation* or *a supplying*, says the "Raccolta," p. 245), it is not suspended during the holy year of the Jubilee at Rome.

Furthermore, conformably to a new decision of March 12, 1855, approved by his Holiness Pius IX., this prayer must be said *kneeling*. But, at the request of his Eminence Cardinal Asquini, Prefect of the Congregation of Indulgences, the Pope was pleased to make one exception (July 12, 1855), in favour of sick persons only who could not repeat it on their knees—*infirmitatis tantum causâ*. Hence travellers or persons on a journey are not excepted, for they can say it kneeling, at the end of the journey. The prayer is at the commencement of all Breviaries.*

### 30. PRAYER FOR CONFESSORS.

Pope Pius IX. (Decree, March 27, 1854), has granted 100 days' Indulgence, *available once a day only*, to all Priests who, prior to their sitting in the Sacred Tribunal to hear Confessions, shall devoutly recite the following prayer, with at least contrite hearts :—

Da mihi, Domine, sedium tuarum assistricem sapientiam, ut sciam judicare populum tuum in justitiâ, et pauperes tuos in judicio. Fac me itâ tractare Claves regni cœlorum, ut nulli aperiam cui claudendum sit, nulli claudam cui aperiendum sit. Sit intentio mea pura, zelus meus sincerus, charitas mea patiens, labor meus fructuosus. Sit in me lenitas non remissa, asperitas non severa, pauperem ne despiciam, diviti ne aduler. Fac me ad alliciendos peccatores suavem, ad interrogandos prudentem, ad

---

* It is sufficient to say the *Sacrosanctæ* once only, at the end of the Office, after Complin, with the intent of obtaining pardon of all the defects a person may have been guilty of in saying the entire Office. Yet it may be repeated after each Hour, e. g. after Matins and Lauds, after the Small Hours and after Complin, in which case one would thereby get forgiveness of the faults committed during the part of the Office recited. This explanation has been given by the Holy Father himself.

The usage amongst the members of the Chapters at Rome, as at St. Peter's, St. Mary's in Cosmedin, &c., is to recite it every time they leave choir.

instruendos peritum. Tribue, quæso, ad retrahendos à malo solertiam, ad confirmandos in bono sedulitatem, ad promovendos ad meliora industriam: in responsis maturitatem, in consiliis rectitudinem, in obscuris lumen, in implexis sagacitatem, in arduis victoriam, inutilibus colloquiis ne detinear, pravis ne contaminer, alios salvem, meipsum non perdam. Amen. A.

### 31. OFFICE OF THE BLESSED VIRGIN.

The Roman Office is the proper one, for, pursuant to a late decision approved by Pius IX., March 12, 1855, the Indulgences cannot be gained by reciting any other Office of the Blessed Virgin, even though it were authorized by the Diocesan.

1, An Indulgence of 100 days, every time persons bound thereto shall piously recite the Office of the Blessed Virgin on the days prescribed by the Rubrics of the Roman Breviary.

2, An Indulgence of fifty days, *each time*, to all who say it out of devotion merely (S. Pius V., Bull *Quod a Nobis*, July 9, 1568; also the Bull *Superni omnipotentis Dei*, dated April 5, 1571). A.

### 32. LITTLE OFFICE OF THE IMMACULATE CONCEPTION.

An Indulgence of 300 days each time a person recites it (Gregory XVI., orally, Dec. 5, 1837).*

---

* It may be found duly approved by the Congregation of the Holy Office, in a small work entitled: "The Immaculate Conception of the Most Blessed Virgin," by F. A. Maurel, S. J., at Madame widow Niccoll's, rue Merciere, Lyons, 2nd edition. It has subjoined a faithful translation into French

## 33. LITANY OF THE BLESSED VIRGIN.*

1, An Indulgence of 300 days *every time* it is recited.

2, A plenary Indulgence on the five Feasts of the Blessed Virgin, of obligation according to the Roman Calendar—viz., the Immaculate Conception, the Nativity, the Annunciation, the Purification, and the Assumption, to all who shall say it every day, on condition that, on these days, they approach the Sacraments, visit a public Church, and pray there for the intention of his Holiness (Pius VII., Decree of September 30, 1817). A.

Note, it is not necessary to add the prayer, "Pour forth," &c.

## 34. THE "ANGELUS DOMINI," OR THE "REGINA CŒLI," &C.

St. Bonaventure, in the General Chapter of his Order, held at Pisa, in the year 1262, directed his Religious to induce the faithful to honour the sublime Mystery of the Incarnation, by reciting three Ave Marias in the evening at the sound of the bell. The devotion was afterwards introduced into France, and approved by John XXII., in a Bull dated from Avignon, October, 13, 1318. His Holiness likewise attached to it an Indulgence of some days. Hence the origin of the "Angelus." By a Brief, *Injuncta Nobis*, September 14, 1724, Bened. XIII. enriched it with the following Indulgences:—

1, An Indulgence of 100 days, *every time* the faith-

---

* The word Litany is derived from the Greek verb λιτανευω, *supplico*, I pray. The Litany of our Blessed Lady is also styled, "The Litany of Loretto," in the Bulls of the Roman Pontiffs, Sixtus V., Clem. VIII., and Alex. VII. This title has been given to it, because, from time immemorial, it is sung with great solemnity every Saturday in the Holy Chapel of our Lady of Loretto, near Ancona.

This prayer comprises the most glorious titles, eulogies, and appellations that could possibly be applied to the Mother of God. It dates from a remote period of antiquity, has been always dearly cherished by the faithful, and specially approved by the Church.

ful say the "Angelus" on their knees, with contrite hearts, and at the sound of the bell, morning, noon, or evening, no matter whether the bell be blessed or not; and consequently 300 days' Indulgence to all who may thus recite it thrice each day, at the three hours specified.*

2, A plenary Indulgence, *once a month* to all repeating it daily as aforesaid—viz., morning, noon, or night (after sunset); the conditions being Confession, Communion, and prayers for the Church. A.

*Important Remarks*: I. Agreeably to a declaration of the Sovereign Pontiffs, Bened. XIV., Clem. XIV., and Leo XII., these Indulgences are not suspended during the Holy Year. And instead of the "Angelus," the "Regina Cœli," with its proper versicle and prayer, should be said during Paschal-tide. Yet those who know not the "Regina Cœli" by heart, may obtain the Indulgences by continuing to say the "Angelus" (Decision of Bened. XIV., April 20, 1742). The same Pope also declared, that the "Angelus" ought to be said standing, every Sunday in the year, beginning at first Vespers, or Saturday evening, each week, to Sunday evening inclusively. The "Regina Cœli" is always said standing.

II. Observe again that Religious, and others living in Community, who, when the Bell tolls the "Angelus" or "Regina Cœli," may be engaged in some exercises prescribed by their Rule, can still gain the Indulgence by saying it immediately after—*flexis genibus et devote*—(Concession of Bened. XIII., Rescript, December 5, 1727).

* Persons prevented by any reasonable obstacle from complying with the usual conditions, may gain the Indulgences without saying the "Angelus" on bended knees, or at the sound of the bell. Moreover, if one does not know by heart, or cannot read the "Angelus," he can gain the Indulgences by devoutly reciting five Hail Marys at the hours or time of the Angelus. (*Decr. S.C. Indulg.*, 3 April, 1884).—*Translator*.

III. The faithful who happen to be dwelling where there is no "Angelus"-bell rung, may acquire the benefit of these Indulgences by reciting it at the hours at which it is wont to be rung, or thereabouts, according to the diversity of season (Pius VI., Rescript of March 18, 1781).

IV. As regards the "Angelus," it is optional to add, or omit the verse, "Pray for us," &c., and the prayer "Pour forth," &c. But the versicle, "Rejoice and be glad," &c., and the prayer "O God, woe," &c., constitute an integrant part of the "Regina Cœli."

Lastly, it is enough to hear the sound of any bell ringing the "Angelus," so that a person need not wait until the bell of a certain Church or religious house be rung.

### 35. THE "SALVE REGINA," &c., AND THE "SUB TUUM," &c.

All those who, with the intent of repairing the outrages done to the Mother of God and the Saints, as also of defending and propagating the worship and veneration of their sacred images, shall recite in the morning the *Salve Regina*, &c., and in the evening *Sub tuum*, &c., may gain these Indulgences accorded by Pope Pius VI. (Decree, April 5, 1786).

1, For every day in the week, an Indulgence o 100 days.

2, An Indulgence of seven years and seven Quarantines, on each Sunday of the year.

3, A plenary Indulgence twice a month, to be gained on any two Sundays of one's own selection, by going to Confession and Communion, and praying for the Pope's intention.

4, A plenary Indulgence, on the same conditions,

on all Feasts of the Blessed Virgin, and on all Saints' day.

5, Finally, a plenary Indulgence at the hour of death, to all who may have been accustomed through life to say these prayers, if they Confess and Communicate, or are then contrite of heart at least.

Note, that, to partake of these Indulgences, one must add to the *Salve Regina* at morn, and to the *Sub tuum* at night, the following versicles:

v. Make me worthy to praise Thee, Holy Virgin.
r. Give me strength against Thine enemies.
v. Blessed be God in His Saints.
r. Amen. A.

Without these verses, the Indulgences are not attached to the *Salve Regina* or the *Sub tuum*.*

### 36. EJACULATION, "SWEET HEART OF MARY," &c

*Sweet Heart of Mary be my salvation.*

1, An Indulgence of 300 days, *as often* as a person repeats it with contrite heart and devotion.

2, A plenary Indulgence once a month, to all who say it every day during that period, provided they Confess, Communicate, visit a Church or public Oratory, and there offer prayers for the intention of the Holy Father (Pius IX., Decree, dated Sept. 30 1852). A.

### 37. PRAYER TO THE SACRED HEART OF MARY.

"Heart of Mary, Mother of God, and our Mother Heart most amiable, on which the adorable Trinity ever looks with complacency, worthy of all the veneration and tenderness of angels and of men

---

* Also an Indulgence of 100 days once a day to all who with contrite heart and devotion recite the "Magnificat" (*Decr. S. C. Indulg.*, 20 September, 1879).—*Translator.*

Heart most like the Heart of Jesus, whose most perfect image thou art; Heart full of goodness, ever compassionate towards our miseries,—vouchsafe to thaw our icy hearts, that they may be changed entirely to the likeness of the Heart of Jesus. Infuse into them the love of thy virtues, inflame them with that blessed fire with which thou dost ever burn. In thee let the Holy Church find safe shelter; protect it, and be its sweet asylum, its tower of strength, impregnable against every inroad of its enemies. Be thou the road leading to Jesus; be thou the channel whereby we receive all graces needful for our salvation. Be thou our help in need, our comfort in trouble, our strength in temptation, our refuge in persecution, our aid in all dangers; but especially in the last struggle of our life, at the moment of our death, when all hell will be unchained against us to snatch away our souls,—in that dread moment, that hour so terrible, whereon our eternity depends, ah, yes, most tender Virgin, do thou then make us feel how great is the sweetness of thy motherly Heart, and the strength of thy power with the Heart of Jesus, by opening for us a safe refuge in the very fount of mercy itself, whereby we too may one day join with thee in Paradise in praising that same Heart of Jesus for ever and for ever. Amen.

### ACTS OF PRAISE TO THE SS. HEARTS OF JESUS AND MARY.

May the Divine Heart of Jesus and the Immaculate Heart of Mary be known, praised, blessed, loved, worshipped, and glorified always and in all places! Amen.

The Indulgences dispensed by the Sovereign

Pontiff, Pius VII., to those who piously recite this prayer, with the subjoined act of praise, are:

1, An Indulgence of sixty days once a day.

2, A plenary Indulgence to all who say it every day for a year, available on each of the three Feasts of the Nativity, Assumption, and the Immaculate Heart of Mary, should they go to Confession, Communion, visit a Church, or an altar dedicated to our Lady, and pray there according to the intention of the Sovereign Pontiff.

3, A plenary Indulgence at the moment of death, to such as may have repeated it during their life (Rescript of August 18, 1807; also Feb. 1, 1816, and Sept. 26, 1817). A.

### 38. THE "STABAT MATER."

An Indulgence of 100 days, each time a person recites it with devotion, to honour the dolours of our Blessed Lady (Innoc. XII., Brief *Commissæ Nobis* September 1, 1681). A.

### 39. THE "MEMORARE," OR "REMEMBER, O MOST PIOUS VIRGIN," &c.

1, 300 days' Indulgence every time the Faithful recite that beautiful prayer, which is ascribed to St. Bernard, and which the "Raccolta" styles "most efficacious and devout."

2, A plenary Indulgence, once a month, to all accustomed to say it at least once a day. As usual, the individual may select a day on which he is to receive Communion, visit a Church or public Oratory, and there pray for the Pope's intention.

These Indulgences were at first restricted to France alone, to which they have been accorded in compliance with the demand of his Eminence Cardinal Louis J. M. de Bonald, Archbishop of Lyons, by a Rescript, dated July 25, 1846. Soon after, however, his Holiness vouchsafed to extend the favour to the entire Catholic Universe (Pius IX., Decree of Dec. 11, 1846). A.

### 40. EJACULATIONS IN HONOUR OF THE IMMACULATE CONCEPTION.

"Blessed be the Holy and Immaculate Conception of the Blessed Virgin Mary!"

*Or,*

"In thy Conception, O Virgin Mary, thou wast immaculate. Pray for us to the Eternal Father, whose only begotten Son Jesus, conceived in thy womb by the Holy Ghost, thou didst bring forth."

Recite devoutly and with a contrite heart, one or other of these ejaculatory prayers, and you shall gain, each time, an Indulgence of 100 days (Pius VI. Rescript, Nov. 21, 1793). A.

### 41. THE PRAYER, "O MY QUEEN," &C.

"O my Queen! my Mother! I give thee all myself; and to prove my devotion to thee, I consecrate to thee this day, my eyes, my ears, my mouth, my heart, and my whole self. Wherefore, O loving Mother, as I am thine, guard me, defend me, as thy own property, and thy own possession."

*Aspiration in Temptation.*

O my Queen! my Mother! remember I am thine; guard me, defend me, as thy own property, and thy own possession.

1, An Indulgence of 100 days, to be attained once a day by everybody who recites, morning and evening, with a contrite heart, one Ave Maria, with the accompanying prayer, "O My Queen," as above, to acquire a victory over temptations, especially temptations against Chastity.

2, A plenary Indulgence once a month, to all who practise the devotion during the entire month, if, on the day of Communion, they visit a Church or public Oratory, and there pray for the intention of his Holiness.

3, An Indulgence of 40 days is annexed to the short ejaculation alone, "O my Queen, my Mother," &c., as often as it may be recited at the time of temptation (Pius IX., Decree of August 5, 1851, procured by the Very Rev. Father-General of the Society of Jesus). A.

### 42. PRAYER TO THE BLESSED VIRGIN AND TO ST. ANNE.*

"Hail, full of grace, the Lord is with thee; may thy grace be with me. Blessed art thou amongst women, and blessed be holy Anne thy Mother, from whom, O Virgin Mary, thou didst come forth free from all stain of sin; of thee has been born Jesus Christ, Son of the living God. Amen."

1, By saying this prayer, with a contrite heart and devotion, a person may gain an Indulgence of 100 days, as often as it may be repeated.

---

\* This prayer had been forbidden for a time, but having been afterwards corrected, it was approved by Pius VII. It ought to be thus addressed to the Blessed Virgin, without the image or title of St. Anne above, particularly without the proclamation of 30,000 years' Indulgence, falsely attributed to Alex. VII., in 1494 ("Manuel des Devotions," &c., by Abbe de Sambucy, p. 149).

2, A plenary Indulgence on the Feast of St. Anne —July 26th—to those who may have said it at least ten times every month; the conditions being Confession, Communion, visit to a Church, and prayers for the Pope's intention (Pius VII., Rescript of Jan. 10, 1815). A.

### 43. LITTLE CHAPLET OF THE IMMACULATE CONCEPTION.

It owes its origin to a Capuchin Friar Minor of the province of Bologna. It is composed of fifteen grains or berries, which are divided into three groups; the three separate grains denote the Pater Nosters, and the other twelve, the Ave Marias. A medal of the Immaculate Conception may be attached to it. To obtain the Indulgences annexed to the Chaplet, it should have been blessed by a Priest empowered to do so. The power has been granted by Pope Pius IX. to all priests of the Capuchin Order, with the faculty enabling their Procurator-General to delegate secular or regular Priests to exercise the same privilege.

*Mode of recitation*: Make the sign of the Cross " In the name of the Father," &c.; next say, " Blessed be the Holy and Immaculate Conception of the Blessed Virgin Mary !" Then one Pater, four Aves, and one Gloria Patri, &c. And so for the other two groups, " Blessed be," &c., Pater, Ave, and Gloria. &c.

*Indulgences*: 1, An Indulgence of 300 days every time a person shall say the Chaplet, with a contrite heart.

2, A plenary Indulgence once a month to all those who may have recited it once a day during that term, the reception of the Sacraments being implied (Pius IX.—Brief, *Longe Inter*, June 22, 1855, which the Sacred Congregation of Indulgences has recognized as authentic by a Decree of Sept. 22, 1858). A.

## 44. "THE MEMORARE," OR "REMEMBER," &C., TO ST. JOSEPH.

"Remember, O most chaste Spouse of Mary, my amiable protector St. Joseph, that never hath it been heard that anyone solicited thy protection and implored thy aid who had not been consoled. With this confidence I come before thee, and fervently recommend myself to thee. Ah! despise not my prayer, adoptive father of my Redeemer, but graciously hear and grant the object of my petition. Amen."*

300 days' Indulgence, available once a day only, to all who recite this prayer with devotion. The original is in Italian, but, it may be recited in any language, provided the translation be a faithful one (Pius IX., Brief of June 26, 1863, deposited in the Segrataria of the S. Cong. of Indulgences, 8th July, same year). A.

## 45. PRAYER, "O GLORIOUS ST. JOSEPH."

"O Glorious St. Joseph, father and protector of virgins, faithful guide, to whom God intrusted Jesus, very innocence, and Mary, the most pure of Virgins; by this twofold deposit, Jesus and Mary, so dear to thee, grant, I pray and beseech thee, that I may preserve my heart free from every defilement, pure and innocent,

---

* The Author's translation of this prayer has been approved at Rome.

and that I may continually serve Jesus and Mary in perfect chastity. Amen."

An Indulgence of 100 days, to be gained once a day, by the faithful who recite it with contrite hearts and devotion, in any language whatever (Pius IX., Brief of Feb. 3, 1863).

### 46. Prayers to St. Joseph, before and after Mass, for Priests.

*Ante Missam.*

O felicem virum beatum Joseph, cui datum est Deum quem multi reges voluerunt videre, et non viderunt, audire et non audierunt, non solúm videre et audire, sed portare, deosculari, vestire et custodire.

v. Ora pro nobis, beate Joseph;
r. Ut digni efficiamur, &c.

*Oremus.*

Deus, qui dedisti nobis regale Sacerdotium, præsta, quæsumus, ut sicut beatus Joseph unigenitum Filium tuum natum ex Mariâ Virgine suis manibus reverenter tractare meruit, et portare : ita nos facias cum cordis munditiâ, et operis innocentiâ tuis sanctis Altaribus deservire, ut sacrosanctum Filii tui Corpus, et Sanguinem hodiè dignè sumamus, et in futuro sæculo præmium habere mereamur æternum. Per Christum Dominum nostrum. Amen.

*Post Missam, et per diem.*

Virginum custos et pater, sancte Joseph, cujus fideli custodiæ ipsa innocentia Christus Jesus, et

Virgo virginum Maria commissa fuit: te per hoc utrumque charissimum pignus Jesum, et Mariam obsecro et obtestor, ut me ab omni immunditiâ præservatum, mente incontaminatâ, puro corde, et casto corpore Jesu, et Mariæ semper facias castissimè famulari. Amen.

An Indulgence of one year, accorded by Pius VII. (September 23, 1802), to all Priests piously saying the prayer "Ofelicem," &c., before Mass; he granted the same Indulgence to them as often as they repeat the "Virginum custos," &c., throughout the day. Both are applicable to the souls in Purgatory.

### 47. HYMN OF ST. MICHAEL.

To increase devotion to St. Michael the Archangel, Prince of the Celestial Army, and thereby more effectually secure his powerful patronage for the troubled times in which we live, his Holiness, Pius VII., has granted to all the Faithful:

1, An Indulgence of 200 days, once a day, for the devout recital of this hymn, with its antiphon and prayer.

2, A plenary Indulgence once a month, to those who, after having said it daily during the month, approach the Sacraments, and pray for the wants of holy Church (Decree of May 6, 1817).

#### HYMN.

| | |
|---|---|
| 1. Te splendor et virtus Patris, Te vita, Jesu, cordium, | 1. O Jesus, life-spring of the soul, The Father's power, and glory bright! |
| Ab ore qui pendent tuo Laudamus inter Angelos. | Thee with the angels we extol; From Thee they draw their life and light. |

2. Tibi mille densa millium
   Ducum corona militat :
   Sed explicat victor crucem
   Michael salutis signifer.

3. Draconis hic dirum caput
   In ima pellit tartara,
   Ducemque cum rebellibus
   Cœlesti ab arce fulminat.

4. Contra ducem superbiæ
   Sequamur hunc nos Principem,
   Ut detur ex Agni throno,
   Nobis corona gloriæ

5. Patri simulque Filio,
   Tibique, sancte Spiritus,
   Sicut fuit sit jugiter,
   Sæculum per omne gloria.
              Amen.

2. Thy thousand thousand hosts are spread
   Embattled o'er the azure sky;
   But Michael bears Thy standard dread,
   And lifts the mighty cross on high.

3. He in that sign the rebel powers
   Did with their dragon prince expel;
   And hurl'd them from the heaven's high towers
   Down like a thunderbolt to hell.

4. Grant us with Michael still, O Lord,
   Against the Prince of Pride to fight;
   So may a crown be our reward,
   Before the Lamb's pure throne of light.

5. To God the Father glory be,
   And to His sole-begotten Son;
   The same, O Holy Ghost, to Thee,
   While everlasting ages run.
              Amen.

*Ant.* Princeps gloriosissime, Michael Archangele, esto memor nostri : hic et ubique semper precare pro nobis Filium Dei.

v. In conspectu Angel-

*Ant.* Most glorious Prince, Michael the Archangel, be thou mindful of us; here and in all places pray for us to the Son of God most high.

v. I will sing praises

orum psallam tibi, Deus meus.

℟. Adorabo ad templum sanctum tuum, et confitebor nomini tuo.

to Thee, my God, before the Angels.

℟. I will adore Thee in Thy hòly temple, and praise Thy Name.

*Oremus.*

Deus, qui miro ordine Angelorum ministeria, hominumque dispensas; concede propitius, ut a quibus tibi ministrantibus in cœlo semper assistitur, ab his in terra vita nostra muniatur. Per Dominum, nostrum, &c. A.

O God, who in the dispensation of Thy providence dost admirably dispose the ministry of angels and of men; mercifully grant that the Holy Angels, who ever minister before Thy Throne in heaven, may be the protectors also of our life on earth. Through Jesus Christ our Lord. A.

### 48. PRAYER TO THE ANGEL GUARDIAN

Angele Dei, qui Custos es mei, me tibi commissum pietate supernâ, illumina, custodi, rege, et guberna. Amen.

O Angel of God, who, through divine goodness and charity, hast been constituted my guardian, enlighten and protect, direct and govern me.
Amen.

Aware of the many beneficial results issuing from devotion to our good Angel, the Sovereign Pontiffs, Pius VI. and Pius VII., have enriched the foregoing prayer with Indulgences, in order to stimulate us the more efficaciously to implore his assistance frequently.

1, An Indulgence of 100 days every time it is said devoutly and with a contrite heart.

2, A plenary Indulgence to those who may have repeated it every morning and evening in the year, available on the Feast of the Holy Guardian Angels —October 2nd—if they Communicate on that day, pray for the Pope's intention, and visit some Church or public Oratory.

3, A plenary Indulgence once a month, on a day chosen by the individual, should it have been recited at least each day, and the last mentioned conditions complied with.

4, Another plenary Indulgence, *in articulo mortis*, to all accustomed to say it often during life (Pius VI., *Motu Proprio*, Brief, Oct. 2, 1795, and Brief of Sept. 20, 1796, Pius VII., Decree of May 15, 1821). A.

### 49. PRAYER TO ST. ALOYSIUS GONZAGA, WITH A PATER AND AVE.

O blessed Aloysius, adorned with angelic virtues, I thy most unworthy suppliant recommend specially to thee the chastity of my soul and body, praying thee by thy angelic purity to plead for me with Jesus Christ the Immaculate Lamb, and His most Holy Mother, Virgin of virgins, that they would vouchsafe to keep me from all grievous sin. Never suffer me to be defiled with any stain of impurity; but when thou dost see me in temptation, or in danger of falling, then remove far from my mind all bad thoughts and unclean desires, and awaken in me the memory of eternity to come, and of Jesus crucified; impress deeply in my heart a sense of the holy fear of God; and kindling in me the fire of Divine love, enable me so to follow thy footsteps here on earth, that in heaven I may be made worthy to enjoy with thee the vision of our God for ever. Amen.

### *Pater Noster and Ave Maria.*

100 days' Indulgence to everybody who recites that prayer piously and with a contrite heart, to be gained once a day (Pius VII., Decree, March 6, 1802). A.

### 50. THREE PATERS AND AVES FOR THE FAITHFUL IN THEIR AGONY.

The three *Paters* are said for the faithful in their agony, in remembrance of the Passion and Agony of our Lord Jesus, and the three Aves in memory of the bitter sorrows experienced by our Lady at the foot of the Cross, during the agony of her Divine Son. The prayers must be recited *kneeling*, unless when one may be hindered from doing so by some indisposition.

1, An Indulgence of 300 days, every time it may be recited.

2, A plenary Indulgence once a month, on a day of their own choosing, to all who say it once a day at least during that period; Confession, Communion, and prayers for the intent of his Holiness, being understood as necessary conditions (Pius VII., April 18, 1809). A.*

* See farther on—No. 62—"Devotion to the agonizing Heart of Jesu."

### 51. THE "DE PROFUNDIS," FOR THE DEAD.

An Indulgence of 100 days to all the Faithful who, at an hour of night, that is, an hour after nightfall, or after the evening "Angelus," shall piously recite the "De Profundis," on their knees, at the sound of the bell, which must be ended by these versicles and responses:

v. Eternal rest give unto them, O Lord.
r. And let perpetual light shine upon them.
v. May they rest in peace.
r. Amen.

Note, that persons who do not know the "De Profundis," may substitute for it a Pater and Ave, with the versicles and responses, "Eternal rest," &c.

2, A plenary Indulgence once a year, on a day of their own option, to those who may have been faithful to this pious exercise through the entire year, if they approach the Sacraments (Clem. XII., Brief *Cœlestes Ecclesiæ*, August 14, 1736). A.

Observe, too, that in places where the "De Profundis," also called the signal or Ave Maria for the Dead, is rung either before or after the hour after nightfall, the same Indulgences are still available, on the same conditions (Clem. XII., Declaration of Dec. 12, 1736).

They may be gained even by those living in districts where no signal for the dead is given at all, if, about the hour specified above, they say the "De Profundis," or "Pater," &c., as aforesaid (Pius VI., Rescript of March 18, 1781).

### 52. OFFICE OF THE DEAD.

1, An Indulgence of 100 days to persons, who,

*being bound thereto*, recite the Office of the Dead, on the days prescribed by the Rubrics of the Roman Breviary.

2, Fifty days' Indulgence, every time a person recites it through devotion (St. Pius V., Bull, *Quod a Nobis*, July 9, 1568, and the Bull *Superni*, of April 8, 1571). A.

### 53. PRAYER FOR PEACE.

*Ant.* Da pacem, Domine, in diebus nostris, quia non est alius qui pugnet pro nobis, nisi tu Deus Noster.

v. Fiat pax in virtute tua.

r. Et abundantia in turribus tuis.

*Ant.* Give peace, O Lord, in our days, for there is none other to fight for us, but only Thou, our God.

v. Let peace be in Thy strength, O Lord.

r. And plenty in Thy strong places.

*Oremus.*

Deus a quo sancta desideria, recta consilia, et justa sunt opera, da servis tuis illam quam, mundus dare non potest pacem; ut et corda nostra mandatis tuis dedita, et hostium sublata formidine, tempora sint tua protectione tranquilla. Per Christum Dominum Nostrum. Amen.

O God from whom all holy desires, right counsels and just works proceed, grant unto us Thy servants that peace which the world cannot give, that our hearts may be devoted to Thy Commandments, and, the fear of our enemies being removed, our times under Thy protection may be peaceable. Through Christ our Lord. Amen.

1, An Indulgence of 100 days every time this prayer may be recited.

2, A plenary Indulgence once a month, to all who recite it at least once a day, during said term, provided they approach the Sacraments, visit a Church, and pray there for the intention of the Supreme Pontiff (Pius IX., Decree of May 18, and Sept. 18, 1848). A.

## ARTICLE II.

### Devout Exercises.

#### 54. THE SIGN OF THE CROSS.

It is the emblem of a Christian, a sacred symbol with which, on the testimony of Tertullian, our ancestors in the Faith were accustomed to sign themselves at the commencement of all their actions. Together with reminding us of the great mysteries of our holy religion, when made with recollection and piety, it also draws down upon us the blessings of Heaven, and banishes the temptations of the wicked spirits. The Holy Father, well aware of that, and anxious likewise to enkindle more and more the devotion of the Faithful towards this august sign, accorded:

1, An Indulgence of fifty days, as often as, being at least truly penitent, they make the sign of the cross, pronouncing the words, "In the Name of the Father, and of the Son, and of the Holy Ghost" (Pius IX., Brief *Quum Salutiferæ*, July 28, 1863, deposited with the S. Cong. of Indulg., August 4, ensuing). A.

2, In virtue of a Brief dated April 7, 1866, a person may gain 100 days' Indulgence whenever it is accompanied with holy water.

### 55. MEDITATION OR MENTAL PRAYER.

The illustrious and devout Pontiff, Bened. XIV., in his Bull *Quemadmodum*, December 16, 1746, strongly inculcates the practice of meditation. And with good reason. For there are very few religious exercises from which the Christian derives more real solid advantages for his advancement and perseverance in virtue. "Give me," said a great saint, "a person who makes a quarter of an hour's meditation every day, and I promise him Paradise." To encourage this salutary and holy practice, Benedict granted, by the same Bull, to all the Faithful who make meditation for half-an-hour, or, at least, for a quarter of an hour each day :—

1, A plenary Indulgence once a month, available on a day on which they shall Communicate and pray for the wants of holy Church.

2, Another plenary Indulgence once a month, on the same conditions, as well to those who frequently teach others, either in public or private, the way to meditate, as to all who often get themselves instructed in it.

3, An Indulgence of seven years and seven Quarantines, every time that, being truly contrite, and having Communicated, they teach, or are present at an instruction on the manner of making meditation or mental prayer. A.

### 56. HOLY SACRIFICE OF THE MASS.

We are not aware that there has been any authentic Indulgence accorded to the faithful at large, for assisting at the most adorable Sacrifice. True indeed, in his "Bibliotheca Canonica," Ferraris distinctly mentions an Indulgence of 30,800 years, accorded to all who piously hear or celebrate Mass, and it is ascribed to several Popes who graced the throne from the reign of Innoc. IV. to that of Eugene IV. But, as has been already remarked, grants of Indulgences of many thousand years are most improbable, suspicious, and false, and have never emanated from the Holy See. Amongst the various authentic Diplomas of Indulgences conceded by the Roman Pontiffs, there has never yet been found a single example of grants of "many thousand years." On this subject it would be well to consult a little treatise composed by the virtuous and learned Cardinal Thomasius, vol. vii. of his works. See also the "Analecta Juris Pontificii," 15th number, July, 1856.

Some time after his return to Rome, Pius VII., of glorious and happy memory, having been requested to dispense some Indulgences to the Faithful who might assist at Mass, replied that the adorable Sacrifice of the Altar contains such abundant inestimable treasures of grace, as render it sufficient of itself to excite their devotion. He accordingly declined to accede to their wishes. Nevertheless, in virtue of some special title or privilege, as, for instance, if a person were a member of a Confraternity of our Lady aggregated to the "Prima Primaria," he may partake of certain partial Indulgences by hearing Mass Observe, moreover, that when the grant requires one to be present at a solemn Mass, it is enough, in order to share in the Indulgences, to assist at a Mass chanted without sacred Ministers and Incense, or even at a low Mass, on days, and in districts where Mass is not chanted at all (Pius VII., Decree, April 11, 1820).

#### 57. FREQUENT COMMUNION.

1, An Indulgence of five years to all persons who Communicate on Sundays and Festival-days, and pray for the Sovereign Pontiff, &c., on these occasions.

2, An Indulgence of ten years, each time, to those who have the pious habit of approaching the Holy Table once a month at least, as also on the Feasts of our Lord, of our Lady, of all the Apostles, and on the Nativity of St. John Baptist; and a plenary Indulgence, once a year, on the Festival of the Patron of the city, or of the country where one lives, the usual conditions being requisite (Greg. XIII., Constitution " *Ad excitandum,*" of April 10, 1580). A.

#### 58. EXAMEN OF CONSCIENCE.

There is no concession of Indulgences for this pious practice, so much recommended by the masters of the spiritual life. Hence, as will be seen in its proper place, it is only on account of some special ground, a person may participate in certain partial Indulgences by making an examen of conscience.

#### 59. ASSISTING AT A SERMON.

1, By a Decree of July 31, 1756, Bened. XIV. granted an Indulgence of seven years and seven Quarantines, every time a person assists at the explanation of the Gospel, or at the Sermon preached in each Parish on Sundays and the more solemn Festivals of the year, agreeable to the Decrees of the Holy Council of Trent (Sess. V., de Reform, cap. 2, et Sess. xxii., cap. 8).

2, A plenary Indulgence on Christmas-day, Easter Sunday, and on the Feasts of the holy Apostles, Peter and Paul, provided they receive the Sacraments on those days, and are present at the Sermon.

3, Pius VI., by a Rescript of December 12, 1784, extended the plenary Indulgence to the Feasts of the Epiphany of our Lord and Pentecost Sunday, under the same conditions. A.

N.B.—These Indulgences may be gained by Parish Priests, and by all Priests supplying their place for the explanation of the Gospel.

## ARTICLE III.

### Special Devotions.

#### 60. WAY OF THE CROSS.

According to the great Pope Bened. XIV. (Brief *Cum tanta*, August 30, 1741), the Way of the Cross, also called the *Via Crucis* or Stations, is one of the chief devotional exercises whose object is to meditate on the sufferings, Cross, and Death of our Divine Lord—exercises that are so effectual "in reclaiming sinners, in reanimating and inflaming the tepid, and in perfecting the sanctification of the just." In its literal acceptation, the Way of the Cross is the space traversed by our Saviour loaded with the weight of the Cross, from the court of Pilate, where He had been condemned, to the summit of Calvary, whereon he was crucified. After the Ascension of her Divine Son, the Blessed Virgin, either alone or accompanied by other holy women, frequently travelled along that dreary way of sorrow. Imitating her example, the Christians of Palestine at first, and, in after ages, crowds of pilgrims even from the remotest countries in the world, used to visit these sacred places which were bedewed with the Sweat and Blood of Jesus Christ. To encourage their piety, the Church also opened to them the treasure of her spiritual favours; moreover, seeing that all could not visit the Holy Land, She vouchsafed permission to erect in other places, such as Churches or Chapels, crosses and pictures, or works of art representing the awful scenes actually gone through on the true way from Calvary to Jerusalem. These representations or Stations were afterwards introduced into Europe, and propagated primarily by the blessed Alvar, of the Order of Preachers, but subsequently through the agency of the Friars Minor Observant, who, about the year 1342, were charged with the custody of the Sacred Places. Finally, in permitting their erection, aware of the excellence and efficacy of the devotion, the Roman Pontiffs deigned also to enrich it with all the Indulgences annexed to an actual visit to Palestine. Thus, pursuant to the Briefs and Constitutions of Innoc. XI., Innoc. XII., Bened. XIII, Clem. XIII., and Bened. XIV., those performing the Way of the Cross with the proper dispositions, gain also the Indulgences accorded to the faithful who might in person visit the Holy Places in Jerusalem. These Indulgences are applicable to the Souls in Purgatory.

In the next place, as may be seen in the "Bullarium Terræ Sanctæ," it is quite certain that numerous Indulgences, whether partial or plenary, were really granted to persons visiting these hallowed spots. But the Sacred Congregation of Indulgences, in its instruction on the manner of performing the *Via Crucis*, approved of by Clem. XII., April 3, 1731, and by Bened. XIV., May 10, 1742, forbids Catechists, Preachers, and others, ever to specify in detail, particularly by writing or engraving where the Stations are, the number of Indulgences attached thereto (IX. Regulation). One of the reasons of this prohibition may have been the loss of many ancient Briefs, by which the Holy See had applied several rich Indulgences to that pious practice, and which, it is said, were destroyed at Jerusalem, on the occasion of the burning of the Archives belonging to the Franciscan Friars there. The instructions, however, assign a different reason. For in the rule referred to, it is expressly stated as having been ascertained on more occasions than one, that either through malice, negligence, or excessive zeal, the truth of the Indulgences had been so altered as to render them altogether obscure and uncertain.

*Conditions requisite for gaining these Indulgences.*— They are only two in number. They are essential, yet sufficient. The first is, to go actually through the Stations, without passing over any of them— one by one—says the VII. Rule. Hence it is necessary to rise at each Station, change one's place, and go from one to the other, unless a person be prevented from doing so by reason of some infirmity, the narrowness of the place, or a crowd of people ; because, in that case, it would be enough to make some slight movement, and turn towards the following Station. By this pious exercise, the Faithful reproduce, as it were, on a small scale, the pilgrimage of the *Via Crucis* of Jerusalem. But bear in mind, that where it is impossible to pass from one Station to another, the Decrees invariably require *some motion of the body—aliquem corporis motum* (Sept. 30, 1837; Feb. 26, 1841). Nor does such a condition import any great inconvenience, for, should there happen to be a large concourse present, the men, for example, could readily go "through the Stations," without departing from the Sanctuary, or the spot where they are located, provided they always change their place, and face in the direction of each succeeding Station. Acting in this manner, if I mistake not, they would enter into the spirit of Pope Bened. XIV., who would have two sets of Stations erected in each Church, one for men and the other for females (Rule IV.) As a matter of fact, when the devotion is gone through *publicly*, to avoid all confusion, it is permitted by a recent Decree, dated July 23, 1757, to adopt the method observed by St. Leonard of Port Maurice. It states that "all the people remain in their respective places, whilst a Priest accompanied by two Clerics or Chanters goes round the different Stations, and, stopping before each of them, recites there the usual prayers, to which the Faithful answer in their turn."

The second condition is to meditate on the Passion of Christ while going through the fourteen Stations.*

---

* The "Raccolta" merely says, that, "in performing the Way of the Cross, we should meditate on the Passion of our Redeemer, according to our abilities." Mind, it does not lay down that a special meditation ought to be made on each of the fourteen Stations. It suffices to meditate on the Passion in general, for nowhere in the Constitutions of

But persons not knowing how to meditate, may content themselves with pious thoughts on some circumstances of the Passion, according to their capacities. Nevertheless, without imposing any obligation on them, they are exhorted to recite a Pater and Ave before each cross, and to elicit an act of contrition (VI. Regulation). (Decree Feb. 16, 1839.)

Confession and Communion are not required; it is enough to be in a state of grace, and to have a sincere sorrow for one's sins. Neither is it necessary to repeat at each Station the Versicle, "We adore Thee, O Christ," &c., the Pater, Ave, Gloria, the "Have Mercy," &c., "May the Souls," &c., nor to read the accompanying considerations given down in books containing these prayers. The practice of saying these prayers and reading these points for reflection is very good in itself, and most useful in enabling persons to perform the *Via Crucis* with profit. Hence the S. Congregation has admonished them not to

the Holy See is it enjoined to meditate on each individually. True, the Sacred Congregation of Indulgences, having been consulted on the matter, replied that one should meditate on the mysteries represented by the fourteen Stations (Feb. 16, 1839). But at Rome, this declaration is regarded as a counsel, and not as an essential condition for sharing in the Indulgences, especially since the same Decree, n 3, even expressly states that a short meditation on the Passion of our Lord is what is prescribed for participating in these favours. I give the very words of the Instructions: "Any short meditation on our Saviour's Passion suffices, which is the work enjoined, for obtaining the holy Indulgences" (VI. Rule).

Add to this that, in many Churches and Chapels in France, Italy, &c., the *Via Crucis* is made up of crosses alone, without pictures or engravings. Then in such places, though some of the people know how to meditate, yet they may not be able to read, or have access to books suited to this devotion. Would it not be very difficult for them to perform the *Via Crucis*, if they were obliged to call to mind each of the fourteen stages, one after the other? It is better, therefore, to adhere to the "Raccolta," 13th edition, 1855, which has been specially approved by Pius IX. See also the end of IX. Rule.

Lastly, on October 29, 1868, Canon Cossa. substitute of the Sacred Congregation of Indulgences, had me written to, to the effect that this is the true doctrine.

neglect it. But it is not indispensable (Declaration of April 3, 1731; also Decree of June 2, 1838). Not even is it obligatory to recite at the conclusion of the Way of the Cross, six Paters, Aves, and Glorias, for the Pope's intention, whether performed publicly or privately, in a Church or Chapel where it may have been canonically established (Decree, June 2, 1838).

Up to a recent date, the prevailing impression in France had been, that it was not necessȧy to go through all the Stations at once. Accordingly, in our first edition, we affirmed "That the devotior may be extended to two or more different occasions, provided it be completed on the same day." But, by a Decree, December 14, 1857, approved by his Holiness Pius IX., January 22, 1858, the S. Congregation has decided the contrary. At present, therefore, the Indulgences are not acquired unless the Visitation of the Fourteen Stations takes place at one and the same time, i. e. continuously.* However, mere slight interruptions, which do not destroy the moral unity of the prescribed meditation, would not hinder a person from obtaining the Indulgences.† Should he perform the *Via Crucis* repeatedly on the same day he can gain the Indulgences each time. The devotion, may be practised even at night (Decree, March 1, 1819).

*Useful Observations.* — 1. The Stations of the

---

* Do the Faithful gain the Indulgences of the *Via Crucis*, if they visit the Fourteen Stations on the same day, even though it be not on one occasion, but with the lapse of a greater or lesser interval between the Stations?

In a Congregation, held the 14th December, 1857, the most eminent Fathers answered, *negative;* which response was confirmed by our Holy Father Pius IX., in an audience of June 22, 1858.

† Thus, for instance, a person may interrupt the Stations, to hear Mass, receive Communion, go to Confession, &c. (Decree, Dec. 16, 1760).

Cross may be erected in all churches, public chapels, domestic oratories, &c., and even externally to churches and oratories, in cemeteries, on hills, or in private apartments. They may be likewise established in several chapels belonging to the same community, as also in the gallery, choir, infirmary, &c., provided the place be a becoming suitable one (Decree of Aug. 4, 1767). To have them erected in these various places, it is sufficient to have a special authorization from the Holy See. At Rome there are some religious houses in which there are as many as three, four, five, and even seven sets of Stations. The permission is sought from the congregation of 'Memorials.' There should be always some little distance between the Stations (Decree Aug. 28, 1752).

2. That the Indulgences be attached to the Via Crucis, it is absolutely required to have the fourteen crosses blessed, but not the pictures or engravings, because, the Indulgences being attached to the former, the latter are not essentially necessary (Decision, March, 13, 1837, and Aug. 22, 1842). Hence, conformably to a Decree of Jan. 30, 1839, the pictures or images need not be blessed—*Minime vero imagines per quas designantur Stationes.* See also the Decree of Aug. 22, 1842. But according to the mode of erection followed by the Franciscan Fathers, and approved by the S. Congregation of Rites, the pictures may be blessed, if there be any— *Si adsunt* (see the Formula).

The crosses ought to *be of wood*,\* for this condition is indispensably required by a series of Decrees (June 20, 1838; Aug. 22, 1842; June 14, 1845). Yet the wooden crosses may be gilt, or em-

---

\* And visible to those in their presence, *under pain of nullity*, (*Decr. S. C. Indulg.*, November 23, 1878).—*Translator.*

bellished with ornaments of metal. They should not have the Christ or figure. Crosses painted on the wall would not suffice. Moreover, if pictures be used, they ought to represent the fourteen scenes known to everybody, defined by the Holy See and by Tradition. The first is the Sentencing of our Redeemer to death. They are exactly the same as the Via Crucis at Jerusalem. There has been recently invented a new system of Stations, or pictures, totally at variance with the ancient ones. Consequently, they ought to be discarded (Feb. 16, 1839).

3. Hence, the blessing or Indulgences annexed to the Via Crucis are not lost by a substitution of new pictures instead of the former ones, nor even of new crosses for some that may have been broken or impaired, provided the substitution does not imply a renewal of the greater number of them, so that all the while there subsists a larger number of old than new ones (Decisions, August 22, 1842; June 14, 1845; Sept. 20, 1839).

4. Neither are they nullified by a removal of the crosses and pictures, to clean, whiten, repair, paint or ornament the walls of a given church, if they be afterwards replaced (Decisions, March 21, 1836; Aug. 2, 1842).

5. Still more, they retain the Indulgences, although, for the purpose of arranging them in symmetrical order, the relative positions of crosses and pictures may be altered after they have been set up, on the supposition that this takes place in the same church or oratory (Decrees of Aug. 22, 1842, and August 20, 1844).

6. As regards the validity of the erection, it is

not necessary that the Priest who presides at or establishes the Via Crucis, should personally set up the different Stations. He can employ another, even a laic, to do this (Decree, March 20, 1846); or he may himself locate them privately, on a different occasion, without any ceremony, as, e.g. without witnesses, &c. (Decrees of August 22, 1842, and March 20, 1846.)* It is in virtue of this concession that, when the Via Crucis is being established in the choir or enclosure of a convent, the Priest who blesses the cross, not being at liberty to enter the enclosure, intrusts the Religious with the care of setting the Stations in their respective places. Such, in truth, is the will of the S. Congregation. Here I may also remark, that a general usage, grounded on the basis of piety and congruity, would have the first station commence at the gospel side of the church. But this arrangement is not strictly required (March 13, 1837).

7. The Priest erecting the Way of the Cross must have previously procured a special faculty for that purpose, either directly from the Pope himself, or mediately through the Congregation of Briefs, or through the very Reverend Father-General of the Friars Minor Observant, or through his Bishop.† In addition to this he should obtain the consent of the Ordinary *in*

---

* The Stations may be blessed before or after they have been set in their places. (*Decr. S. C. Indulg.*, 21 June, 1879) —*Translator*.

† The Holy See ordinarily accords to Bishops the power of erecting the Via Crucis in all the churches and chapels of their respective dioceses, and of deputing their Grand Vicars Parish Priests, Missionaries, Curates, &c., to do the same.

It is noticeable also, that the faculty of establishing it in public churches extends to all oratories erected with the authority of the Diocesan, which have a public entrance leading to them (Decree of March 12, 1855). A special permission is needed for private chapels.

N.B.—The Franciscans, who are not subject to the General of the Order of Friars Minor Observant, have not the privilege of erecting the Stations of the Cross, or of blessing the crucifix used for that

*writing,* as also the consent of the Parish Priest, or Superior of the Church or house in which the Via Crucis is about being erected. This is in strict conformity with several Decrees of the S. Congregation, notably with those of Jan. 27, 1838, Sept. 25, 1841. " Impetratis ab Apostolica Sede necessariis et opportunis facultatibus, says the latter Decree, " omnia et singula quæ talem erectionem respiciunt scripto fiant, tam nempe postulatio quam erectionis ejusdem concessio, quam instrumentum (the Proces-verbal), &c. Still, looking at the decisions issued by the S. Congregation, Jan. 27, 1838, it does not appear that these different formalities are exacted under pain of *nullity.* This may be inferred from the very words which I took down at the Segretaria of the S. Congregation of Indulgences:—

*Molinen.* Vicarius Generalis Diœcesis Molinensis sequentia dubia sacræ Congregationi solvenda proposuit :

1. Detectâ nullitate alicujus erectionis stationum Viæ Crucis ob defectum executionis conditionum in Apostolico Rescripto, vel de jure præscriptarum, estne necesse hujusmodi nullitate sanatâ iterùm benedicere cruces et pictas tabellas jàm anteà benedictas?

Sacra Congregatio respondit : *Dummodò nullitas non cadat super cruces anteà benedictas, minimè necessarium est, aliâ nullitate sanatá, iterùm cruces benedicere.*

2. Petitiones pro hujusmodi erectionibus fierine debent cui de jure in scriptis sub pœnâ nullitatis concessionis, vel sufficiat quòd factæ sint oretenùs ?

Sacra Congregatio respondit : *Quamquàm in scriptis, ac de consensu Ordinarii, et loci patroni optanda sit petitio, tamen si oretenùs, sub pœnâ nullitas negativè.*

purpose, independently of a particular Indult, which they need like other Priests (Decrees of April 25, 1735, and Nov. 28, 1742). The Father General of the Observants lives at Rome, Convent of Ara Cœli, Capitol.

\*3. Si hujusmodi erectio nulla detegatur ob omissionem documenti in scriptis talis concessionis, et secutæ executionis, poteritne hujusmodi defectus in posterùm, atque etiam post longum tempus suppleri?

Sacra Congregatio respondit: *Suppleatur documenti defectui per novas literas institutionis seu confirmationis ab Ordinario conficiendas, dummodò constet aliundè de secuta executione.*

4. Estne tempus determinatum, et quale, pro confectione documenti secutæ erectionis Stationum Viæ Crucis vigore Apostolici Indulti?

Sacra Congregatio respondit: *Negativè, sed expedit ut quamprimùm conficiatur documentum juxtà apostolicam concessionem, ne dubia in posterùm oriantur.*

These responses were given by the S. Congregation on Jan. 27, 1838.

Wherefore, to avoid any doubts that may afterwards arise from negligence in the matter, the Proces-Verbal, or report of the erection, ought to be framed as soon as possible. It should mention the Apostolic Rescript, in virtue of which the erection took place, the authorization of the Bishop, the permission of the Parish Priest or Superior, and the date of these three grants. Furthermore, it ought to be signed by the Priest so delegated, and by the Parish Priest or Superior. It would be well, too, to have some witnesses. The document, or account, must then be forwarded to the Bishop to have it deposited amongst his Archives, and a copy of it, or, at least, a certificate of the erection, is to be kept in the parish Register, or in that of the

---

\* In erecting the Stations the consent of the Bishop *in writing* is required *in each* case of erection, SUB POENA NULLITATIS, and a general permission to erect the Stations in a certain number of churches or oratories, without a special mention of the place of erection, will not suffice. (*Decr. S. C. Indulg.*, 21 June, 1879. —*Translator.*

establishment where it had been effected (Decree, Sept. 25, 1841).

8. Pious works treating of the Via Crucis, give down various ceremonies to be observed in the erection, when it takes place solemnly. Although they are not essential, yet, they ought to be rigorously attended to, being highly calculated to inspire reverence and love for this holy devotion. Of its manifold advantages we need hardly speak. It was almost a continual practice of the Blessed Benedict-Joseph Labre; from it he derived fruits of eminent sanctity.* Often did St. Leonard of Port Maurice repeat, that the sole practice of the Way of the Cross was sufficient to sanctify a whole parish.

### 61. CRUCIFIX INDULGENCED FOR THE STATIONS OF THE CROSS.

Persons who are sick or infirm, says the Raccolta, prisoners, those at sea, or living in pagan countries, and, in general, all who cannot† visit the Stations erected in a church or public oratory, may gain the Indulgences by reciting fourteen Paters, Aves, and Glorias (Pius IX., Aug. 8, 1859); then five other Paters, Aves, and Glorias; and lastly, one Pater, Ave, and Gloria for the Pope's intention, mean-

* Benedict Joseph Labre, born at Amettes, in the diocese of Bologne-sur-Mer, in 1740, was remarkable, from his infancy, for piety and innocence of life. Having gone to Rome, he there lived in poverty and the exercise of every virtue, and died in the odour of sanctity, April 17, 1783. He has been beatified by Pope Pius IX.

† A moral impossibility suffices—*ob legitimum impedimentum*—say the latest Rescripts. Thus, a person on a journey, or in the country, at a considerable distance from the parish church, may be said to be constituted in a moral impossibility of visiting the Stations. So, too, as regards a Priest or Religious, who, on account of his multiplied duties, or for other grave reasons, is unable to visit a church to go through the Stations. Accordingly, all such people may perform the Stations privately, by means of the crucifix.

while, holding in their hands a brass crucifix, specially blessed for this purpose by a person duly authorized to do so.* This favour was vouchsafed by Clement XIV., Jan. 26, 1773, at the request of the Reformed Minorites of the Monastery of St. Bonaventure, at Rome, who hold the Decree in their *Archivium*.

Formerly the person possessing the crucifix Indulgenced for the Via Crucis, could *alone* gain the Indulgences. This was changed by Decree of the 19th January, 1874. (See Translator's note, page 155.) Again, conformably to repeated Decrees, the Crucifix can neither be sold, nor given away, nor lent to others with the intent of communicating to them the Indulgences. Though strictly speaking, all crucifixes, no matter how diminutive, can be blessed for this end, it would not be becoming to apply the Indulgences to very small ones, which would scarcely be visible in the hands of those using them. In fine, recollect that, pursuant to the late Decree quoted above, the twenty Paters, Aves, and Glories should be said without, at least, any notable interruption, which might break the moral connection or unity of the Prayer.†

* According to numberless recent decisions, it is allowable to bless and Indulgence devotional objects, of whatever material, provided it be not fragile or easily broken, as would be plaster-of-Paris, hollow glass, &c. Presently, then, there is nothing to prevent one from having Indulgences applied to the crucifix, sometimes substituted for the Stations of the Cross, if it chance to be made of ivory, bone, wood, and with much greater reason if of gold, silver, &c. In fact, a Decree of Sept. 16, 1859, permits it.

As to the prayers, we ought to adhere to what is stated above, viz.—fourteen Paters, Aves, and Glorias, one for each Station—five Paters, Aves, and Glories in honour of the five wounds of our Saviour—and, finally, one Pater, Ave, and Gloria according to the intention of the Head of the Church (Pius IX. Decree Aug. 8. 1859).

† Some Priests have succeeded in obtaining the faculty of applying to that crucifix the Indulgences of the Stations, available on the sole condition, that the individuals using it say in its presence some vocal

## 62. DEVOTION TO THE AGONIZING HEART OF JESUS.

This salutary devotion has for its object, 1, to honor the Sacred Heart of Jesus enduring through life, particularly during His Passion, great interior sufferings for the salvation of souls; 2, to obtain, through the merits of that protracted agony, a happy death for the thousands who die each day throughout the universe. Those who practise it, daily repeat the subjoined prayer, which has been approved and enriched with Indulgences by our Holy Father, Pius IX. It is recited for the "Agonizing of each day," that is, for persons on the brink of eternity, or who are to expire within the twenty-four hours.

### PRAYER.

O Clementissime Jesu, amator aminarum, obsecro te per agoniam Cordis tui sanctissimi et per dolores Matris tuæ Immaculatæ, lava in sanguine tuo peccatores totius mundi, nunc positos in agonia et hodie morituros. Amen.

O most merciful Jesus, lover of souls, I pray thee, by the agony of thy most Sacred Heart, and by the sorrows of thy Immaculate Mother, cleanse in thy Blood all the sinners of the world, who are now in their agony, and are to die this day. Amen.

prayers prescribed by their confessors, always, however, only in cases where it is impossible for them to visit the Stations in some church or public chapel.

But these privileges are very rare. Hence, as a rule, we ought to regard as unauthentic the Indulgences of the Via Crucis when applied to a crucifix under any conditions differing from those specified in the Decree of Clement XIV., which was modified by Pius IX. I have referred before to an example, in the article on apocryphal Indulgences; perhaps I could cite others also like it. In the matter of Indulgences, we should distrust everything that deviates from the common ordinary grants.

When a number join in making the Stations of the Cross before a crucifix indulgenced for the purpose, it is enough if any one present hold in his hands the privileged Crucifix. A distinct Crucifix for each is no longer necessary (*Decr. S. C. Indulg.*, 19 January 1874).--*Translator*.

Cor Jesu in agoniâ factum, miserere morientium.

Agonizing Heart of Jesus, have pity on the dying.

1. An Indulgence of 100 days every time it is said with a contrite heart and devotion.

2. A plenary Indulgence once a month to all who shall have repeated it thrice every day during that limit, at three distinct intervals, should they approach the Sacraments, visit a Church or public Oratory on the day of Communion, and there pray for a time according to the intentions of his Holiness (Decree, *Urbis et Orbis*, issued from Portici near Naples, February 2, 1850). A.

The devotion originated with the Rev. Father Lyonnard, of the Society of Jesus, and is widely circulated at the present day. We can easily understand how agreeable it must be to the Heart of that Eternal Son, who descended from the habitation of His Glory and came upon earth for no other object than to save mankind. Let us then propagate it everywhere. Should we, by our united fervent prayers, succeed in saving a single soul every day, O! what a rich harvest we shall have gathered at the end of a year, of ten years, &c.!\*

### 63. PRAYER OF THE QUARANT' ORE.

I speak here of the devotion of the Forty Hours, practised on the occasion of the Carnival. Its object is to repair the wanton irregularities committed more particularly during those days of relaxation, to pre-

---

\* See the little work published at Avignon by M. Seguin, entitled "Devotion to the Agonizing Heart of Jesus. Devotion to the Compassionate Heart of Mary." The latter devotion has for its aim the conversion of all the sinners of the world, especially of those giving scandal

vent persons of the world from taking part in such scandals, and to offer prayers for those who seem, at that period, to forget and almost abjure the hallowed duties of religion.

A plenary Indulgence is granted by Pope Clem. XIII. (Decree, July 23, 1765), to all who share in the devotion, on condition that they Confess, Communicate, and visit the blessed Sacrament in some Church where it may be exposed. One visit suffices during the entire term of exposition. It is exposed for three days, from six or seven o'clock in the morning to five or six in the evening, in one or each of the weeks from Septuagesima-Sunday to Ash Wednesday exclusively, or even only on the Thursday of Sexagesima, the day commonly called "Giovedi-grasso."* A.

---

\* We must not, as is done by many authors, confound this Quarant'Ore, whose end is to make reparation to our Divine Saviour for the numerous crimes perpetrated during the days of the Carnival, with that established at Rome and elsewhere, in memory, proceeds the "Raccolta," of the forty hours our Lord's Body lay in the Sepulchre. The latter commenced at Milan, in the year 1534, whence it spread to other cities of Italy, and was introduced into several churches in Rome. By his Constitution, *Graves et Diuturnæ* of Nov. 25, 1592, Clem. VIII. instituted it for ever in the Eternal City, so that, through the whole course of the year, it is kept there in certain churches successively. It begins on the first Sunday of Advent, in the chapel of the Apostolical Palace. The public calamities then afflicting the Church, caused the Pope to establish this beautiful devotion, in order that, day and night, prostrate before our Lord exposed on the Altar, the Faithful might appease his justice, and secure the effects of his mercy by prayer. These regulations were afterwards confirmed by Paul V. (Brief, *Cum felicis recordationis*, May 10, 1606), together with the Indulgences annexed thereto by Clem. VIII., viz :—

1. A plenary Indulgence to anybody who, at the time of Exposition, approaches the Sacraments, and pays a visit to some church where the Blessed Sacrament is exposed.

2. Ten years and as many Quarantines as often as the visit is made with a strong determination of confessing.

3. By a Rescript of May 12, 1817, Pius VII. has declared all the altars *privileged* during the three days of Exposition in these churches. The Masses, however, are not said in black.

In November, 1810, a pious Association of Worshippers, or adorers of

## 64. VISIT TO THE "ALTAR OF REPOSE," ON HOLY THURSDAY AND GOOD FRIDAY.

To encourage a devotion so praiseworthy in itself and so conformable to the Christian spirit, Pope Pius VII., by a Rescript, March 7, 1815, accorded:

1. A plenary Indulgence available to all who Communicate either on Holy Thursday or Easter Sunday, on the supposition that, on Holy Thursday and Good Friday, they visit our blessed Lord in the Tomb or Altar of Repose, and there pray for some moments according to the intentions of the Holy See.

2. An Indulgence of ten years and as many Quarantines each time the visit is repeated, with a firm purpose of going to Confession. A.

## 65. FEAST OF THE BLESSED SACRAMENT, OR CORPUS CHRISTI.*

1. An Indulgence of 200 days to all the Faithful who, being truly contrite and having Confessed, shall fast on the vigil of Corpus Christi, or do some other good work pointed out by the Confessor.

2. An Indulgence of 400 days to those who, contrite in heart and after Confession, shall piously assist at Mass on the day of the Feast. The same Indulgence for being present at Vespers.

3. An Indulgence of 200 days to every Priest who, after having said Mass, and to the Faithful who

---

the Blessed Sacrament, was founded at Rome, for the purpose of spending the whole night in His Divine Presence. The last-named Pope accorded various privileges and Indulgences to them (see the "Raccolta," p. 133).

\* It was instituted, with an Octave, by Pope Urban IV. (Constitution, *Transiturus*, Aug. 11, 1264).

having Communicated, shall religiously accompany the Procession of the Blessed Sacrament on that day, or any other day within the Octave, praying for the wants of Holy Church, &c.

4. An Indulgence of 200 days, to be gained on the days during the Octave, by persons assisting at Mass or Vespers.

N.B.—There is likewise an Indulgence of 200 days for those accompanying the Procession which the Confraternity of the Blessed Sacrament is in the habit of making on the third Sunday of the month and on Holy Thursday (Urban IV., Martin V., Eugene IV., Constitution, *Excellentissimum*, May 26, 1433). A.

### 66. THE HOLY HOUR.

The devotion of the "Holy Hour" is not the same as the Confraternity of the "Holy Hour."* I speak here of an hour spent in prayer or meditation, on all the Thursdays of the year, on Holy Thursday, and the Feast of Corpus Christi, in remembrance of and in thanksgiving for the institution of the Blessed Eucharist.

1. A plenary Indulgence on Holy Thursday and the Feast of Corpus Christi, if to the Holy Hour Communion be added, either on these days, or some day of the ensuing week.

2. On all other Thursdays of the year an Indul-

* That Confraternity is established in the Convent of the Visitation, at Paray-le-Monial, in the diocese of Autun. Its object is to partake in and honor during the night, from Thursday to Friday in each week, the sorrows of the Heart of Jesus in His agony in the Garden of Olives. To be a member of it, a person should have his name inscribed in the register kept for this purpose at Paray-le-Monial.

gence of 300 days (Pius VII., Rescripts of February 14, 1815, and April 6, 1816). A.

### 67. NOVENA IN HONOR OF THE SACRED HEART OF JESUS.

It was composed by Father Charles Borgo, S. J. By using that little treatise, one may acquire :

1. An Indulgence of 300 days each day of the Novena.

2. A plenary Indulgence, available on the Feast of the Sacred Heart, or some day of the Octave, under the ordinary conditions of Confession, Communion, and prayers for the intention of the Holy Father (Pius VII., Decree of the Cardinal-Pro-Vicario, March 15, 1819; and Rescript, January 13, 1818). A.

The Novena is made immediately before the Feast, but may also be made a second time at any part of the year, the same Apostolical favours being still attainable. Persons not in possession of Father Alphonso Rodriguez's work on Christian Perfection, assigned by Fr. Borgo for a spiritual lecture, are permitted by Pius VII. to use any other pious book they please.

N.B—M. Seguin, printer at Avignon, has translated, to French, and published the Novena of Fr. Borgo.

### 68. FIRST FRIDAY OF THE MONTH.

Agreeably to the design of our loving Redeemer, it is consecrated to the honour of His divine Heart. There is a plenary Indulgence for all who receive holy Communion on that day, provided they are members of the Confraternity of the Sacred Heart, of which we shall treat hereafter. A

There is a precious practice which was suggested by our Lord Himself to Blessed Margaret Mary, telling her to hope for the grace of final repentance, and that of the reception of the last Sacraments before death, in favour of those who observe it. "It consists in nine Communions received for that end, and to honour the Sacred Heart of Jesus on the first Friday of each of nine consecutive months" ("Life of the Venerable Mother Margaret Mary," by Mgr. J. J. Languet, Bishop of Soissons, liv. vii.).

### 69. MONTH OF MARY.

The devotion of the Month of Mary consists in making the whole of May—the most charming month of the year—a continuous feast of thirty-one days in honour of the Queen of Heaven. It is productive of numerous graces and benedictions. The chief elements of the devotion are, the rich decorations of the sanctuaries, altars, and images of our Blessed Lady; the brilliant lights, which increase day after day, from the commencement to the solemn close of the month; the pious canticles harmonized and chanted, or, at least repeated, by all the Faithful; a short instruction or lecture, interspersed with some historic traits or facts, whose principal aim is to have us know, love, serve, invoke, and imitate holy Mary; prayers for the spiritual and temporal wants of the people; and, lastly, Benediction of the Blessed Sacrament, when the exercise takes place in a church, with a parting anthem in praise of the Immaculate Virgin, whom they had assembled to venerate, extol, praise and supplicate.

To induce the Faithful worthily to celebrate it, Pius VII. (Rescript of March 21, 1815, issued from the Segretaria of Memorials, and Decree of the Sacred Cong. of Indulg., June 18, 1822) conceded:

1. An Indulgence of 300 days every day of the month, to those who, publicly or privately, honour the Blessed Virgin by some prayers, good works, or other devout exercises.

2. A plenary Indulgence once *during the course of the month*, provided they communicate and pray to the Lord for holy church, &c.  A.*

### 70. EXERCISE IN HONOR OF OUR LADY OF PITY.

It is made up of an hour's pious meditation and prayer, in honor of Our Lady of Dolors, on a day of one's own choosing through the course of the year:

1. A plenary Indulgence, to be gained on that day, by approaching the Sacraments. It is available only once a year (Clement XII., Decree of Feb. 4, 1736; Benedict XIV., July 14, 1757; and Pius VI., July 8, 1785).

During the exercise, the following prayer may be recited, to which Pope Pius IX. (Decree of Dec. 23, 1847) has applied an Indulgence of 100 days every time it is repeated with a contrite heart:

| | |
|---|---|
| Ave, Maria, doloribus plena, Crucifixus, tecum; lacrymabilis tu in mulieribus, et lacrymabilis fructus ventris tui, | Hail, Mary, full of sorrows, the Crucified is with thee; tearful art thou amongst woman, and tearful is the fruit of thy |

---

* Read the note * p. 93, Part II. of this work.

Jesus. Sancta Maria, Mater Crucifixi, lacrymas impertire nobis crucifixoribus Filii tui, nunc et in hora mortis nostræ. Amen. A.

womb, Jesus. Holy Mary, Mother of the Crucified, grant tears to us crucifiers of thy Son, now, and at the hour of our death. Amen. A.

### 71. MONTH OF MARCH.

It is dedicated to St. Joseph, because the glorious Patriarch's principal feast is celebrated in that month. Thus, it serves as a preparation for, and, as it were, an introduction to the delightful month of May. From the Bridegroom we go to the Bride. In truth, Joseph is the way to Mary—*per Joseph ad Mariam.*

As in the case of that of Mary, the chief ingredients of the exercises peculiar to this blessed month are, a tasty decoration of his image or altar with flowers and lights, accompanied with prayers, canticles, sermons or lectures, or meditation on the worship of the Saint, good works, &c.

Although the devotion is in existence only a few years, it has its beneficent branches already extended far and near. Wherefore, on our part, let us try to do something to honor him, as, for instance, to keep a lamp lighting each day of this month before his statue or picture. This generous act of piety, besides carrying out the spirit of the Church, will be more than amply recompensed.*

---

\* A person may extend this virtuous practice to every Wednesday in the year, this day being in a special manner dedicated to our Saint. Read the " Little Manual of the Confraternity of St. Joseph," by F. A. Maurel, S.J., and you will there find the leading motives in behalf of devotion to this mighty Patron, as also its principal practices, e.g.— those of the Seven Joys and Dolors, the Seven Sundays, &c.

By a Decree *Urbis et Orbis*, April 27, 1865, his Holiness Pius IX., deigned to extend to March, consecrated to St. Joseph, the Indulgences attached to the month of May:

1. An Indulgence of 300 days every day of the month, whether the devotion be performed in public or private.

2. A plenary Indulgence on some one day of the month, at the discretion of each client, the conditions being Confession, Communion, and prayer for the Church. A.

### 72. THE SIX SUNDAYS AND FEAST OF ST. ALOYSIUS GONZAGA.

This devotion cannot be too strongly recommended, particularly to the young, to whom St. Aloysius Gonzaga has been given as a special patron by the Holy See. The chief fruits of the devotion, in itself so pleasing to youth, are, preservation of innocence, light as to their vocation, love of Mary, and sanctification of studies.

A plenary Indulgence may be acquired on each of six consecutive Sundays, by all the Faithful who, being truly contrite, shall, after having communicated, employ themselves in some pious meditations, vocal prayers, or other works of Christian piety, in honour of St. Aloysius Gonzaga. The Sundays should be strictly consecutive, without interruption, but may be selected either immediately before the Saint's feast, or at any other time of the year (Clement XII. Decrees of Dec. 11, 1739, and Jan. 7, 1740).

Moreover, they may obtain a plenary Indulgence

on the 21st of June, the feast of St. Aloysius, if they receive the Sacraments, visit his altar in some place where his festival is celebrated, and offer prayers for the Pope's intention. Should the Feast be kept on any other day of the year, *with the permission of the Ordinary*, this Indulgence may be likewise gained under the same conditions (Bened. XIII., Brief of Nov. 22, 1729; Clem. XII., Nov. 21, 1737; et Bened. XIV., Brief, April 22, 1742). A.*

### 73. DEVOTION TO ST. STANISLAS KOSTKA.

1. A plenary Indulgence on the Feast of the youthful Saint, Nov. 13, or the Sunday on which, *de licentia Ordinarii*, it may be celebrated. To partake in the favour, it is requisite to Confess, Communicate, visit a Church or public Oratory where the Feast is observed, and there pray for the intention of the Holy Father.

An Indulgence of 100 days, once a day, to all who shall say a Pater and Ave before a picture exposed in some church or chapel, whether public or not (chapels of seminaries, colleges, convents, &c.), praying, as above, for the Pope's intention.

3. A plenary Indulgence once a month by practising this exercise continuously during said term, and complying with the conditions of Confession and

---

\* See the small treatise entitled, "The Six Sundays and Feast of St Aloysius Gonzaga," by F. A. Maurel, S.J., to be had at M. Pelegaud's. There are also other devotions analogous to this, for example, "The Ten Sundays of St. Ignatius of Loyola," "The Ten Fridays, or Ten Sundays in honour of St. Francis Xavier," "The Six Sundays of St. Stanislas Kostka," &c., to all of which the Sovereign Pontiffs have attached Indulgences in a greater or less extent. Anybody may procure little books explaining them

Communion, with the accustomed prayers. Should one be unable, owing to a lawful hindrance, to recite the Pater and Ave in a church or chapel, in presence of his image, he is free to say it anywhere else on such days as he may be hindered, without forfeiting the Indulgence of the month (Pius VII., Leo. XII., Decrees published by the S. Cong. of Indulg., May 13, 1826, and Decree March 3, 1827).

4. An Indulgence of 300 days, once a day, accorded by Pope Pius IX. to those who recite the three following prayers, to ask of St. Stanislas purity, charity, and a good death, adding each time the Pater, Ave, and Gloria.

5. A plenary Indulgence once a month, if they repeat it once a day during that period, on the ordinary conditions—Confession, Communion, visit to a Church or public Oratory, and prayers offered there for a time, conformably to the mind of his Holiness. (Rescript, March 22, 1847, and Decree of July 10, 1854).

### *For Purity.*

St. Stanislas, my most pure patron, Angel of purity, I rejoice with thee at the extraordinary gift of virginal purity which graced thy spotless heart; I humbly pray thee, obtain for me strength to overcome all impure temptations, and inspire me with constant watchfulness to guard my purity,—that virtue so glorious in itself, and so acceptable to God Pater, Ave. Gloria.

### *For Charity.*

St. Stanislas, my most loving patron, Seraph of

charity, I rejoice with thee at the ardent fire of charity which kept thy pure and innocent heart always at peace and united to God; I humbly pray thee, obtain for me such ardour of divine love, that it may consume away every other earthly affection, and kindle in me the fire of His love alone. Pater, Ave, Gloria.

### *For a Good Death.*

St. Stanislas, my most tender and most mighty patron, Angel of purity and Seraph of charity, I rejoice with thee at thy most happy death, which arose from thy desire to contemplate our Lady assumed into heaven, and was caused by the excess of thy love for her. I give thanks to Mary, because she thus accomplished thy desires; and I pray thee, by the lustre of thy happy death, to be my advocate and my patron in my death. Intercede with Mary for me, to obtain for me a death, if not all happiness like thine, yet calm and peaceful, under the protection of Mary my advocate, and thee, my special patron. Pater, Ave, Gloria. A.

### 74. SPIRITUAL EXERCISES OF ST. IGNATIUS, OR A RETREAT AND MISSIONS.

As far as I know, there are no general Indulgences accorded to the Faithful at large who go through the exercises of Retreats and Missions. Such as have been conceded in that way were dispensed to a certain body of Missionaries or Religious, to the members of some Confraternity, or else in particular circumstances. I shall here indicate the

Indulgences attached to Retreats and Missions of the Jesuit Fathers.

I. *A Spiritual Retreat.*—1. A plenary Indulgence to all who make a Retreat of *eight days* in the houses or colleges of the Jesuits (Alex. VII., Brief, *Cum sicut*, Oct. 12, 1657). 2. The same Indulgence for a Retreat of *five days*, and it is applicable to the Dead (Bened. XIV., Brief, *Quemadmodum*, July 15, 1749). In both cases, by a grant of the same Pontiff, the Retreat may be made anywhere, provided it be conducted by the Fathers of the Society.

Furthermore, it is even sufficient, for obtaining the Indulgence, to devote only a *single day* to the exercise of "The preparation for death," fulfilling the conditions, Confession, Communion, and a visitation of the Church or Chapel assigned for the exercises (Briefs of March 29, and May 16, 1753).

II. *Missions.*—1. A plenary Indulgence once in the course of the Mission, to all who take part in it at least five times during the term of its duration, if, having Confessed and Communicated, they offer some prayers for the wants of holy Church (Greg. XVI., Brief, *Exponendum*, Dec. 20, 1839). But those who, on account of sickness or length of distance, are unable to assist thereat, may gain the Indulgence of the Mission by faithfully accomplishing the works imposed by their confessors. In fact, confessors are empowered to commute the Communion for children not having previously communicated (Pius IX., March 29, 1855). The persons giving the Mission can, at the conclusion of it, either personally impart the Papal Benediction, or depute Parish Priests, or other Ecclesiastics to do so. 2. A plenary Indulgence on the day of the erection of the cross to all the Faithful assisting at this ceremony, if, having Confessed and Communicated, they devoutly visit some church or public oratory, and there piously pray for the Pope's intention. 3. Another plenary Indulgence to anybody who, having shared in the exercises of the Mission, shall approach the Holy Table on a day chosen by himself, in the course of the first six months after the erection of the cross or the close of the mission (Leo. XII., Rescript April 12, 1826). 4. An Indulgence of five years once a day to persons who visit the Cross of the Mission, and, with devotion, recite before it three Paters, Aves and Glorias, in memory of the three hours' agony of our Redeemer, and according to the mind of his Holiness. 5. A plenary Indulgence on some day in December, at their own choice, to all who shall have repeated this pious visit at least three times in each month (Same Rescript of Leo. XII.). 6. Pope Pius IX. granted 100 days' Indulgence for everybody who may visit the Cross of the mission, and say in its presence any prayer whatever (Jan. 19, 1851).

In addition to all these, should there be added a "Quarantine for perseverance," after the mission or Retreat, the Faithful who shall have assisted at these exercises may gain 200 days' Indulgence each day of the Quarantine, if they recite the prayers marked out by the Preacher or Superior of the Mission. Also a plenary Indulgence, under the usual conditions, to all who are punctual in the practice of the exercise during the forty days, both favours being applicable to the Departed (Greg. XVI., Brief *Injuncti Nobis*, July 7, 1843.).

III. *Religious Exercises for men exclusively.*— 1. An Indulgence of seven years and seven Quarantines every time they are present at the instructions or lectures delivered for them by the Jesuit Fathers to whom the Superiors may have confided that office. 2. A plenary Indulgence as often as, after a good Confession, they receive Holy Communion; 3. A plenary Indulgence, *in articulo mortis* to men who perform these spiritual exercises, that is, who make a Retreat, either alone or in conjunction with others, under the direction of the same Fathers without prejudice to the one already noted (No. 1). which the Roman Pontiffs have granted under a similar title (Pius IX., Rescript, May 13, 1852).

*Useful Hints.*—First, it may be asked, is it necessary, after a Mission or Retreat, to give the Apostolic Benediction (if there be permission to impart it at all) in the church, and at the epistle side of the altar? Answ.—It may be given in the church from the pulpit, as is commonly done at Rome, for instance, in the Church of the Gesie, at the end of the Lenten instructions. Not alone that, but, if the church be not spacious enough to contain the multitude present, it may be imparted outside, without erecting an altar for that purpose before the door of the church. The form prescribed by Bened. XIV is rather of direction than of precept and under pain of nullity.

Secondly, the Holy See has dispensed some Indulgences which Missionaries belonging to certain religious associations apply to the Mission-cross erected by them. It is, therefore, doubted, whether such Indulgences are available to the Faithful, even before these crosses have received the blessing? Resp.—Yes, for, properly speaking, it is not essential that the Cross be blessed. in order to gain the Indulgence.

Thirdly, the question has been raised, whether the concession of the Indulgences comprises also the faculty of blessing the Cross? No; the blessing of the mission cross is reserved to the Bishop, who, nevertheless, must have received the power from the Pope. Bishops, too, supplicate from Rome the prerogative of subdelegating Missionaries or other Priests to bless these crosses. As a rule, then, it appertains to the Ordinary to bless crosses which are set up in public places, but Regulars may bless them *intra claustra*.\*

---

## ARTICLE IV.

### Works of Zeal and Charity.

#### 75. The Catechism.

Pursuant to the injunctions of the Council of Trent,† it is the duty of Parish Priests to teach the Christian Doctrine or Catechism to children, on Sundays and Holidays. Schoolmasters should likewise teach it to their pupils, and parents to their children. "This," writes the Sainted Pontiff, Pius V., "is a most holy work."‡ "It is," continues Paul V.,§ "a work conducing very much to the

---

\* N.B.—In virtue of an Apostolical Indult, dated March 14, 1867, Jesuit Missionaries possess the faculty of establishing and blessing these mission crosses, using the formula given in the Ritual, or any other that may have been approved for that purpose.

† Sess. XXIV., Decret. de Reform, cap. 4. The words are: "Iidem (Episcopi) etiam saltem dominicis et aliis festivis diebus, pueros in singulis parochiis fidei rudimenta, et obedientiam ergà Deum et parentes diligenter ab iis ad quos spectabit, doceri curabunt, et, si opus sit, etiam per censuras ecclesiasticas compellent: non obstantibus privilegiis et consuetudinibus."

‡ Bull "Ex debito Pastoralis officii," dating Oct. 6, 1571.

§ Bull "Ex credito Nobis," Oct. 6, 1607.

salvation of souls, and to the prosperity of the Christian commonwealth." The same Pope, not content with having raised to the dignity of an Arch-Confraternity a sodality of the Christian Doctrine founded in the Basilica of St. Peter, which he munificently endowed with various privileges and Indulgences, dispensed, moreover, the ensuing Indulgences for all the Faithful, to stimulate them the more ardently to teach or learn the Catechism.

1. An Indulgence of seven years and seven Quarantines to all the Faithful every time that, after Confession and Communion, they explain the Christian Doctrine, or assist at its explanation.

2. A plenary Indulgence to those having the praiseworthy custom of teaching Catechism, or attending thereat, to be gained on Christmas Day, Easter Sunday, and on the Feast of SS. Peter and Paul, complying with the condition of receiving the sacraments (Clem. XII., Brief, June 27, 1735).

3. Seven years' Indulgence to persons (of whatever age) accustomed to assemble in schools, or at church, to learn the Catechism, available on all Festivals of the Blessed Virgin, if they communicate on these days. But those not yet admitted to Communion, can gain an Indulgence of three years on the same occasions, by merely going to Confession (Paul V., Bull *Ex credito nobis*, Oct. 6, 1607).

4. An Indulgence of seven years, each time, to masters of schools who, on Sundays and Holidays, may bring their pupils to Catechism, and instruct them in it: also 100 days as often as they teach it to them at school, on working days.

5. An Indulgence of 100 days whenever fathers and mothers thus instruct their children or domestics.

6. Finally, 100 days, each time, to all who, for half an hour, study the Christian Doctrine, either to teach it to others, or to learn it themselves (Paul V., same Bull). A.

### 76. PROPAGATION OF THE FAITH.

The institution of this admirable work is, at the present day, a source of the greatest happiness to the Church. It originated at Lyons, in the year 1822, under the inspiration and auspices of our Lady of Fourviere, Queen of Apostles and Martyrs. A few laymen, who brought to their assistance some poor humble females, were the instruments employed by Providence to render this incalculable service to religion. From the 3rd of May, in the above-named year, the Association, properly so called, dates its origin. Then it was that "a dozen of laymen, united by charity, inflamed by zeal, and headed by a Priest, unanimously adopted a system of Association open to all peoples, and contributing to the success of all missions. Like its noble aim, the basis of the work ought to be as wide-stretched as the universe." (*Nouveau coup d'œil sur l' Œuvre*, Lyons, 1856.) Deeply rooted just now, approved, recommended, aye, extolled by the Supreme Head of the Church, and by all the Bishops in the Church, lauded by every Priest and Missionary, and affectionately welcomed by the entire Catholic world, this Heaven-inspired work proudly extends its beneficent branches to every part of the globe. Who, then, be his zeal for the glory of God and the salvation of souls ever so little, could refuse to take part in this grand enterprise, whose only object is to concur, by means of prayer and alms, in spreading our holy faith to the remotest corner of the earth?

The obligations are very few, and very easy: 1, To recite a Pater and Ave every day, and the ejaculation, "St. Francis Xavier, pray for us." 2, To contribute one halfpenny every week, which is handed to the Head or Collector in each circle of ten, himself being a member. The whole sum for the year (2*s*. 2*d*.) may, without inconvenience, be given all at once. Moreover, for the fulfilment of the first condition, it suffices to offer, for that intention, the Pater and Ave of one's morning or night prayer, with the aspiration specified. The poor need only give some trifle, at their own discretion, once every month (Pius IX., Aug. 5, 1851).

The associates are also requested to assist at two masses, which are celebrated every year for the pious undertaking—one on the Feast of the Invention of the Holy Cross, May 3rd, the anniversary of its foundation; the other on the Feast of St. Francis Xavier, Patron of the Association, December 3rd. The favours attached are twofold:—

I. *Plenary Indulgences.*—1. A plenary Indulgence on each of these two feasts, to be gained, once only, by members, at any hour from the commencement of First Vespers to sunset on the last day of the Octaves. To obtain them one should Confess, Communicate, visit a church of the Association, or the parochial church, and pray there for the intention of the Supreme Pontiff. The confessor can substitute for the visit some other good work, to suit the convenience of individuals unable to comply with that condition, either on account of long distance, infirmity, or any other legitimate impediment. Persons living in communities, colleges, seminaries, &c., may satisfy it by visiting their own church, or even a private chapel of the establishment, and there praying as directed. Should these two feasts be transferred by proper authority, the Indulgences likewise accompany them, and therefore may be gained, on the same conditions, from First Vespers of the days to which the transfer has been made to sunset of the same days.

2. A plenary Indulgence twice a month, on any two days chosen by members of the Society.

3. The same on the Festivals of the Annunciation and Assumption, or any day within their Octaves.

4. Once a year, on the day of the solemn commemoration of all the deceased associates.

5. Another plenary Indulgence, once a year, to be gained by members attending at the special commemoration made by each division, council of one hundred, or circle of ten, for its departed associates. And on such days all the altars of the church where the office is recited, are declared privileged as regards masses said in behalf of deceased members. (All these Indulgences are obtainable under the above-mentioned conditions.)

6. Another, *in articulo mortis*, to which I may add the favour of a privileged altar, at every Mass offered in the name of an associate for a deceased member.

II. *Partial Indulgences.*—1. Should there be a Triduo preparatory to the feast on the 3rd of May, or to that of Dec. 3rd, there are 300 days' Indulgence for associates, every time they assist thereat with a contrite heart. The same Indulgence is attainable to those who keep the Triduo privately, if they are sick, or otherwise lawfully hindered from attending publicly. 2. An Indulgence of 100 days, as often as an associate repeats, with heart contrite, the Pater, Ave, and invocation, "St. Francis Xavier, pray for us." 3. 100 days every time he bestows, independently of the weekly subscription, an alms for the same end, or does a work of piety or charity. A.

The other special favours dispensed to members of the Society may be easily ascertained by a perusal of the "Annals of the Propagation of the Faith," since they are copied in each number (Briefs of the Sovereign Pontiffs, Pius VII., Leo XII., Pius VIII., Greg. XVI., and Rescripts of Pius IX., Oct. 17, 1847; Dec. 31, 1853; April 17, 1855; March 7, 1862, &c.).

N.B.—In virtue of a Rescript of Pius IX. (April 17, 1855), children who have not as yet received their first Communion, may acquire all the plenary Indulgences accorded to the Association, by substituting for the Communion, some other good work pointed out by their respective confessors.*

---

* In order that the associates may know something about the mighty work towards which they subscribe, there are embodied in the "Annals of the Propagation of the Faith," published six times a year, most edifying and instructive letters giving an account of foreign Missions. These are presented, free of charge, to the members, one for every circle of ten, so that each may read them in turn.

A pamphlet designated "*Les Missions Catholiques*," is published every Friday in each week. It serves as a supplement to the Annals.

Persons may have their names inscribed at the Office of the Association of the Propagation of the Faith—31, place Bellecour, à Lyon.

N.B.—In our country, this may be done by having the names enrolled in an approved Register.—*Translator*.

## 77. THE HOLY INFANCY.

This interesting work is an association composed of Christian children for the ransom of little infidel children in China and other pagan countries. Thus is rescued from the jaws of death an immense number of poor unfortunate little ones, and the gate of Paradise opened to them. Having been founded at Paris, in 1843, by Mgr. Charles de Forbin-Janson, it was placed under the protection of the Infant Jesus. The Blessed Virgin is its principal Patron. The Guardian Angels, St. Joseph, St. Francis Xavier, and St. Vincent de Paul, are its secondary Patrons. Every baptized child may be enrolled. They are admitted into the Society from the earliest stage of life up to that of First Communion, after which they become aggregated members, and continue so until the age of twenty-one, when they cease to belong to the Association, unless it be affiliated to that of the Propagation of the Faith.

The subscription for each associate is a halfpenny every month, or sixpence per year. The names of all are to be inserted in the registry or report of the Society, and each member has to recite daily one Ave Maria, with the ejaculation, "O Virgin Mary, pray for us, and for poor little infidel children." The Ave Maria of morning or evening prayer may be applied for this intention. Should a child be too young, so as to be unable to say the prayer, anyone of the family may supply it for him. Gregory XVI. and Pope Pius IX. have enriched the work with the subjoined favours:—

1. Two plenary Indulgences, one for living associates, available from the feast of our Lord's Nativity to the Purification; the other, applicable to the dead, to be acquired on any day from the second Sunday after Easter—the Sunday of the Good Shepherd—to the end of May. To share in them it is requisite to assist at a Mass said for the Society, and to communicate thereat. The very young associates are dispensed from Communion, but not from Confession.

2 A plenary Indulgence on the Feast of its Patrons, viz., the Presentation of Mary, the feasts of the Guardian Angels, those of St. Joseph, St. Francis Xavier, and St. Vincent de Paul, the conditions being Confession, Communion, and a special prayer " for the advancement of the Mission of the Holy Infancy."

3, An Indulgence of one year, to all members of the Councils or Committees of the Association, every time they are present at these meetings (Pius IX., Rescript, Jan. 12, 1851).

### 78. SOCIETY OF GOOD BOOKS.

Everybody knows, that the circulation of good books is a most powerful means not alone of preserving faith and morals, but also of improving them in town and country. For this purpose, M. d'Aviau, of venerable and pious memory, in Nov., 1825, organized into a religious association this society of good books, which was founded at Bordeaux about 1820, and already approved by an Apostolic Brief. The numerous blessings heaped on the work by the Almighty, induced Gregory XVI. to confer on it the rank and privileges of an

Archconfraternity, with power to affiliate to itself all other associations of the same title, and to communicate to them the spiritual favours previously accorded to them by Leo XII. and Pius VIII (Brief, Nov. 16, 1830).

I omit to give down the Indulgences and Regulations, as they accompany the diploma of affiliation.\*
O would that all Pastors charged with the care of parishes should bequeath to their flocks a library of good books! It would be the most precious of legacies.

### 79. SODALITY OF SOLDIERS.

"You have heard it said that a soldier need not be devout. Undoubtedly, his piety need not be that of a monk in the cloister; but it would be a gross error to imagine that religion is by no means designed for a soldier. Who has greater need than he of its consolations? Who is more in want of strength to withstand the force of bad example and the occasions of sin? Does anybody more require the protection of the Almighty amidst the dangers to which his profession in the army exposes him every hour of his life? In fact, it is religion alone that will sustain him, encompassed with these difficulties. And it is only by a constant fulfilment of his duties, as a Christian, that he can acquire the necessary aid in his struggles to become virtuous. Those alone who serve God faithfully, are entitled to His pro-

---

\* 1. Gregory XVI. has granted an Indulgence of 300 days to those who aid the Society established to disseminate good books.

2. An Indulgence of 40 days to anyone who denounces a bad book to the Diocesan.

tection. Hence, we see that most of the renowned heroes of old were solidly pious men. Enough to mention Godfrey, Tancréde, St. Louis, Sobieski, Crillon, Turenne, &c. &c."*

From these considerations has sprung the Union called "The Sodality of Soldiers," which, owing to the zeal of worthy Pastors, Missionaries, and lay people, flourishes to day in almost every town where a garrison may be stationed. Our Holy Father, Pius IX., has vouchsafed the following favours in behalf of those branches of it established in Paris and other cities of France :—

1. An Indulgence of seven years to all associates, co-operators or soldiers, as often as they assist at the religious exercises or instructions, either to teach or learn.

2. An Indulgence of one year to each soldier, every time he co-operates, as far as he is able, in the conversion of a fellow-soldier, on condition that he elicit an act of contrition.

3. A plenary Indulgence to all associates, co-operators or military men who, having Confessed and Communicated, shall visit a church or public Oratory and pray there for the usual intentions, to be gained on the four principal Festivals of the year, and on the Feast of St. Maurice, Sept. 22. It is also attainable on any of the fourteen days directly succeeding these feasts, only once, however, within the fifteen days (Pius IX., Brief of May 12, 1851).

N.B.—The chief constituents of the work are, religious instruction, which is given once or twice a week to the soldiers; canticles which they learn, and are taught to sing; prayers offered by them in common;

* "Le Livre du soldat Chretien," an excellent little work written by Fr. Louis Nègre, of the Society of Jesus. 3rd Ed. p. 15.

good books lent to them; pious objects, as chaplets, scapulars, medals, &c., distributed amongst them; reading, writing, figures, &c., and, in fine, games of ball, billiards, draughts, chess, &c., which afford them pleasant, innocent recreation. In many places, some charitable ladies are the chief promoters of the undertaking.

80. ACCOMPANYING THE HOLY VIATICUM TO THE SICK

The Indulgences attached to this pious charitable work are:—

1. Seven years and seven Quarantines, each time, to all who devoutly accompany the Blessed Sacrament to the Sick, with a torch or lighted taper.

2. Five years and five Quarantines, if they accompany it even without a light.

3. Three years and as many Quarantines, when, being unable to go themselves, they send some person in their stead, carrying a light in attendance upon the Holy Viaticum.

4. 100 days to those who cannot accompany the Blessed Sacrament, if they, meanwhile, say a Pater and Ave, according to the intention of the Sovereign Pontiff (Innoc. XII., Bull, *Debitum Pastoralis Officii*, Jan. 5, 1695; and Clement X., Decree of April 23, 1676). A. Nor are these Indulgences suspended during the Holy Year of Jubilee (Declar. of Bened. XIV., Clem. XIV., and Leo. XII.)\*

---

\* At Lyons, Marseilles, &c., there are societies of men who, animated with a lively faith, full of unfeigned piety, and callous to all human respect, are enabled by their easy position in life to accompany the Blessed Eucharist by turns, whenever it is carried to the sick. They thereby do honor to our Lord, and greatly edify the inhabitants of the districts. Why should not the Catholic men of other cities copy so noble an example?

## 81. VISITATION OF THE SICK, AND OF PRISONERS.

It is only in virtue of certain titles a person can obtain the various partial Indulgences annexed to visiting the Sick, whether in hospital or at home, and those in prison. Because they have not been accorded to the Faithful generally.* Thus :—

1. An Indulgence of 200 days to those who, possessed of some blessed pious object, such as a cross, medal, chaplet, &c., visit prisoners or the sick in hospitals.

2. 100 other days if it be a Bridgetine chaplet, provided that, visiting a prisoner or invalid, in honor of our Saviour, Holy Mary, or St. Bridget, they recite three Pater Nosters and three Ave Marias.

3. An Indulgence of 300 days to members of the Confraternity of the Rosary.

4. One hundred days to members of the Confraternities of the Blessed Sacrament, of the Scapular, to associates of the Propagation of the Faith, &c.

5. Seven years, if they belong to a congregation of our Lady, aggregated to the *Prima-Primaria* of the Roman College. A.

## 82. CHARITABLE REPAST IN HONOR OF THE HOLY FAMILY.

It consists simply in feeding three poor persons, in memory and honour of Jesus, Mary, and Joseph. The exercise, doubtless, must be singularly in-

---

\* This was true prior to 1861. Since then, however, the 100 days applied by Pius VI., Feb. 28, 1778, to the visitation of the sick in public hospitals at Rome, exclusively, has been extended to all the Faithful, so that now it may be acquired by anybody visiting hospitals to perform some work of charity (Decree, Aug. 23, 1861).

viting to charitable souls specially devout to the Holy Family. Pius VII. has been pleased to recompense them by granting:

1. An Indulgence of seven years and as many Quarantines, as often as a person does so, penetrated with a sentiment of contrition.

2. A plenary Indulgence if, on the day on which this work of charity shall have been exercised by them, they approach the Sacraments, and pray for the Pope's intention.

3. An Indulgence of 100 days to everybody in the house, not excepting the domestics, who concur in this good work, or who are at least present at the Repast (Pius VII., Rescript of June 13, 1815). A.

### 83. HEROIC ACT OF CHARITY IN BEHALF OF THE SOULS IN PURGATORY.

It is nothing else than a voluntary offering or surrender of all our works of satisfaction in this life, and of all the suffrages that shall be offered for us after our death, into the hands of the Blessed Virgin, to the end that this tender Mother might distribute and dispense them to the Souls of Purgatory, whom it may be Her good pleasure to release from their pains. But, mind, it is only the special personal fruit redounding to us from these satisfactions and suffrages we thus forego in their behalf. Hence, such a transfer would not prevent Priests from offering Mass for the intention of persons who may have given them *honoraria*; neither would it hinder a person from praying for himself, his parents, or friends, nor from practising works of piety, &c. Because, as just stated, it is only the *satisfactory portion*, so to speak, of the works done that is applied or given over by this vow to the Holy Souls. Accordingly, the fruits of merit, propitiation, and impetration always remain with the doer of the acts, since they cannot be communicated to others.

F. Gaspard Oliden, a Theatine, if not the author, was at least a zealous propagator of this *heroic act* or *vow* of charity, which has been enriched with Indulgences by the Supreme Pontiffs Bened. XIII., Pius VI., and recently by his Holiness Pius IX. (Decree of Sept. 29, 1852).*

1. All Priests who have made this vow or oblation, can enjoy the favour of a personal privileged altar every day in the year.

2. A plenary Indulgence, applicable only to the Departed, can be gained by lay persons, whenever they go to Communion, visit a church or public oratory, and there pray, agreeably to the intention of the Chief Head.

3. They will acquire a plenary Indulgence every Monday, by hearing Mass for the relief of the Holy Souls, the conditions being a visit, prayers, &c.

---

* This vow does not bind under sin; to have a share in the Indulgences, it is sufficient to make it in heart, without using any formula ("Raccolta," p. 344). It can be renewed from time to time.

Father Ferdinand de Monroy, a most apostolic man, made in writing, at the hour of death, a donation or transfer to the Souls in Purgatory of all the Masses that might be said for the repose of his soul, and of all the penances offered for him, together with all the Indulgences gained for him ("All for Jesus," by F. Faber, ch. II. 8. 4).

Admonished by the Blessed Virgin herself the Venerable Ximenes made this vow. It was in like manner made by numberless other personages, illustrious in their rank, learning, and sanctity; even by whole communities of Religious. See the little work entitled, "An Heroic Act of Charity," printed at Rome in 1853. It has been lately translated into French, and published at Clermont-Ferand, typog. Hubler, &c.—Nancy, M. Thomas, bookseller, 1854.

Everything we give through charity to the souls of the Departed, says St. Ambrose, is converted into grace for ourselves, so that after death we shall find therein a hundredfold merit.

4. Having made this offering, they can apply to the Dead all the Indulgences then granted, or to be hereafter granted, even though they be not, according to the grants, applicable to them.

N.B.—Invalids, aged persons, labourers, prisoners, &c., unable to hear Mass on Monday, may offer for this purpose the Mass of Sunday. Moreover, as regards children who have not as yet made their First Communion, and others not able to communicate, their Bishops can authorise the confessors to commute the Communion into some other good work (Pius IX., Decree of Nov., 1854).

At the same time, the Mass of Sunday alone can be substituted for that of Monday, and confessors have no authority, up to the present, to assign any other work in its place.

## ARTICLE V.

### Confraternities and Pious Associations.

#### 84. General Observations.

1. Reading the annals of the early ages of the Church, we find no particular Confraternities or Sodalities established amongst the Faithful. In fact, Christianity was then little less than an immense religious congregation, whose members were all of one heart and one soul, animated with the same spirit of faith and piety. But, in the course of time, when the charity and zeal of a great many had grown cold, it became necessary to devise some means of re-enkindling and sustaining them. Next to the founding of Religious Orders, one of the chief

agents for effecting this was the establishment of Confraternities.

One of the first of these, of which we have mention, is the Confraternity of *Confalon* or *Gonfalon*, whose origin is ascribed to St. Bonaventure, and whose statutes were approved by Clem. IV., in 1267.* Its object was to redeem Christian captives from the hands of the Saracens. It derived its name from a banner called *Confalone*, whereon was painted an image of the Blessed Virgin, for in those days the associates usually styled themselves *Commanders*, or *Commandataires* of Holy Mary, having on their shoulders a red and white cross marked with the inscription: "*Insignis Societas Regulae Recommendatorum B. Mariæ Virginis,*" as it was designated by Greg. XIII.

In process of time were organised other associations, whose sole end was to labour for the glory of God, the honour of Mary and the saints, also for their own sanctification, by prayer, alms-deeds penances, and the practice of good works. So marvellous were the fruits produced by the greater number of them, that the Church was pleased not alone to sanction but even to endow them with special gifts and prerogatives. Consequently we should

---

* "To Bonaventure," writes Ciacconius (t. 2, in vit. Greg. X.), "is attributed the glory of being the first who instituted Sodalities composed of lay people, for the purpose of assembling to do works of piety and recite certain prayers daily. This holy undertaking originated at Rome, about 1270, fashioned into the Sodality or Archconfraternity of Confalon, serving as a model for the formation of innumerable other associations through the Christian universe, whose rules comprise every variety of devout exercises."

Thus St. Bonaventure is regarded as the father or founder of Confraternities. Nevertheless, there are some of an earlier date than this; for example, the celebrated one erected at Toulouse by St. Dominick, 1211—*Juvante Legato, obtinuit Tolosæ magnam fieri Confratriam* (see "Theodore of the Holy Spirit." tom. 2, c. ii. p. 118).

always highly esteem them, and never taunt those who think it well to enlist in them. For when a congregation is animated with fervour and wisely governed, it affords to its members advantages the most precious, in the way of piety, charity, and security. "There," says St. Francis of Sales, "a person may acquire everything without losing anything."

2. To become a member, it is necessary to be received by the Priest acting as Director, and specially deputed for that purpose, as also to be enrolled in the Register of the Confraternity. The admission ought to be gratuitous (Clem. VIII., Bull *Quæcunque*, Dec. 7, 1604). It would be desirable not to have one's name inscribed without knowing the rules of the association, or without being disposed to observe them, and, as a consequence, to be present at their meetings, festivals, processions, &c. Furthermore, each individual should evince a great regard for the Sodality to which he may belong, and, by his zeal, his regular edifying life, his charity towards his fellow members, promote its well-being and prosperity, thus rendering himself worthy of persevering in it.

No doubt the rules of these different Confraternities do not bind under pain of sin; still, by neglecting to observe them, a person would deprive himself of the graces and privileges annexed to the Society, and his fellow-associates, of their share of his good works; he would disedify by his inconstancy and carelessness, together with incurring the risk of forfeiting an alliance which he had esteemed, embraced, and loved, and which was to him a source of benediction.

3. Although nothing conduces more to maintain and augment the spirit of faith and piety in a parish than the establishment of one or two Confraternities, yet it would not be profitable to have too many of them there, for, generally speaking, this would interfere with their mutual welfare and prosperity. "The same thing," proceeds the Abbe Geraud in his *Manuel des Principales Devotions et Confreries,* " applies to those Christians who, actuated by an ill-regulated zeal, enrol themselves in a large number of such associations. Because their sanctification is advanced, not precisely by multiplying devotional exercises, but rather by performing them with fervour and exactness."

4. All confraternities and pious congregations are under the jurisdiction of the Diocesan. Hence it is his province to authorise, approve, and canonically erect them, after having modified their statutes, should he deem it expedient to do so.* To the

---

* During the past year, one of the Vicars-General of Orleans solicited from the S. Congregation of Indulgences the solution of four questions, which I think it well to transcribe here, with the answers given on 20th July, 1868 :

1. Cum episcopus obtinuerit facultatem a Sede Apostolica erigendi Confraternitates cum respectivis Indulgentiis, potestne vicarius generalis id præstare absque speciali delegatione episcopi? Resp. *Negative,* Nisi episcopo subdelegandi potestas in Apostolico Indulto concessa fuerit suumque vicarium generalem subdelegaverit.

2. Potestne Vicarius-Generalis auctoritate ordinaria erigere Confraternitates absque delegatione episcopi, ita ut erectio sic peracta canonica sit? Resp. *Negative.*

3. Utrum Vicarius-Generalis possit valide concedere litteras testimoniales ac consensum requisitum a Clemente VIII., pro aggregatione Confraternitatum? Resp. *Negative.*

4. Utrum Vicarius-Generalis possit approbare statuta Confraternitatum? Resp. *Negative, et supplicandum,* SS. *pro sanatione.*

His Holiness approved of and confirmed these responses, 18th Aug., 1868. On the same day he vouchsafed to validate all erections of Confraternities and approbations of statutes made or given up to that date by the Vicars-General, as well as the affiliations issued in virtue of their written authorization.

Bishop also appertains the right of visiting them, of directing them in the use of their privileges and favours, &c. Note, too, that Confraternities not canonically erected, would not be affiliated to the Mother or Archconfraternities at Rome,\* and therefore would not participate in the Indulgences commonly granted to such Societies. The immediate inspection of a Confraternity in a parish is confided to the Pastor or Director, whose duty it is to maintain therein fervour, the observance of rule, and to take precautions against abuses that might creep into it, amongst others, motives of ambition and selfishness.† The title of Director, conferred on the Parish Priest by the Bishop, at the time of the erection of a Society in a parish, does not necessarily descend to the Priests who succeed him in the pastoral functions, unless there be only one Priest in the parish, for, in that case, necessity obliges (Decree of June 7, 1842).

5. There may be several different Confraternities in the same Church (Decision of the Rota, Jan. 18, 1745). But, agreeably to the Bull of Clement VIII. cited before, which has been confirmed by many of his successors, there can be only one Confraternity

---

\* An *Archconfraternity* is one empowered to aggregate to itself other Confraternities of a similar title, and to communicate to them the favours and Indulgences *peculiarly its own*. These particular prerogatives must be procured separately, since the dignity of an Archconfraternity does not carry with it any special Indulgence. An Archconfraternity cannot impart favours or Indulgences not *specially* accorded to itself, and hence not those it may have obtained by some extension or communication.

† Pursuant to the Constitution of Clem. VIII., s. 8, June 11, 1838, there is nothing to prevent a Confraternity from questing according to the Regulations approved of by the Ordinary, whether for the repair or ornamentation of its Church or Oratory, or for other pious uses, but with the consent of the Diocesan.

of the same kind in the same town, and *a fortiori* in the same Church. It is necessary that the churches wherein the same Confraternity is erected, be at least three miles distant from one another. There is an exception, however, in favour of the Confraternities of the Blessed Sacrament (Paul V., 1607), the Christian Doctrine (Decree. Feb. 3, 1610), and of the Sacred Heart (Pius VII., 1805). Furthermore, should an application be made to the Sovereign Pontiffs, as a rule, they unhesitatingly allow exceptions of this kind for every other Confraternity.

6. In an audience, dated January 8, 1861, a fear being entertained that, owing to the formalities prescribed by Clem. VIII. (Constit. *Quæcunque*, Dec. 7, 1604) not having been observed in the erection or in the affiliation to the Archconfraternities or Mother Congregations, several Congregations or Confraternities probably did not enjoy the Indulgences or privileges dispensed to the former, Pius IX. deigned to supply all omissions, thus rendering valid both erections and affiliations. At the same time, he ordained that in future, the formula of erection and aggregation, should at least substantially accord with the one enjoined by Clem. VIII., and contain the points specified in his Bull.

To have this done, the Sacred Congregation got a form of erection and affiliation printed, pursuant to which each Archconfraternity or Mother Congregation may shape its own. A copy may be easily had from the Office of the Secretary of said Congregation.* No formula of this sort is required for

---

* This is its title: *Formula servanda saltem in substantialibus a Superioribus Regularibus Religionum, &c., in erigendis seu instituen-*

Confraternities which Bishops establish in their Dioceses, after having been delegated by the Holy See. They have merely to frame an authentic diploma of erection, to the end that it may be preserved in the Archives of the parish.*

7. Conformably to a decree of 18th November, the Director of a Confraternity is nominated by the Ordinary. In case of lawful hindrance, or otherwise, he cannot substitute his Vicar or another Priest, to admit fresh members. To do so he should have a special faculty. I speak here of an admission properly so called into a Confraternity, and not of a simple inscribing of names in the Register (Decree, August 22, 1842). Finally, in virtue of the former decree, he is not empowered, by the mere fact of his nomination, to bless Chaplets, Rosaries or Scapulars, or to apply to them Indulgences.

8. One altar in the same Church may serve as a *special altar—altare proprium*—for several Confraternities, e. g. for those of the Sacred Heart, Rosary Scapular, &c., provided the respective Directors consent to it. Nevertheless, to obviate troubles or

---

dis *Confraternitatibus ac Communicandis indulgentiis et gratiis spiritualibus quas a Sede Apostolica obtinuerunt*—from which it is manifest that they speak there only of Confraternities or Archconfraternities entrusted to Regulars. The following doubt was proposed to the S. Congregation:

"Is there any fixed form required under pain of nullity?" The reply was "*Negative*," because the formula is prescribed merely for Sodalities erected by Regulars" (Nov. 18, 1842).

* It may be useful to remark that the different faculties bestowed on Bishops by the Holy See, as those of establishing various Confraternities, of erecting the *Via Crucis*, of declaring an altar *privileged* in parochial churches, &c., are considered purely personal favours. Consequently, they alone can exercise them, unless the Papal Rescript permit them to communicate their graces to the people, through their Grand Vicars (Decrees of May 24, 1843, and July 20, 1868).

disputes which might eventually grow out of such an order of things, it would be better, if possible, that each Sodality should have its own altar (Decree of May 29, 1841).

9. The Confraternities and Congregations lawfully and canonically existing in France, prior to the Concordat of 1801, have not lost their privileges or Indulgences, if afterwards re-established under the same title, with the same statutes, and the same dress or *habit* wherever it may be permitted (Decisions of February 22, 1847, and May 14, 1853).*

10. The Director of an Archconfraternity of St. Joseph, which is established in France, proposed to the Sacred Congregation the following doubts:—

I. Seeing that the Pontifical Brief does not give permission to affiliate to said Archconfraternity any Sodalities of St. Joseph but those erected within the limits of the French empire, it is asked whether or not is the reception of individuals living outside France valid? The S. Congregation replied *negatively.*

II. Is it allowable to found in large cities of France many Confraternities of the same name, to satisfy the devotion of the Faithful? The answer was again in the *negative,* at least, generally speaking; but, *should an urgent case arise,* recourse is to be had (to the Holy See).

III. As there are two Archconfraternities of St. Joseph, one at Angers and the other at Beauvais, it is doubted whether that at Angers could associate to itself a Confraternity of the same title erected in a town where there is already a similar one aggregated

---

* There are also other general rules and ordinances, which may be seen by a reference to the Bull of Clement VIII.

to the Mother Congregation at Beauvais? The response is, no—*negative*.

IV. May Confraternities of this kind be established in the churches of religious congregations where young girls, whether day scholars or boarders, are educated? The S. Congregation said that this *would not be expedient—non expedire* (February 19, 1864).

Lastly, according to several Decrees of the Sacred Congregation of Bishops and of Regulars, Confraternities of lay persons cannot, in any hypothesis, *nullimode*, be established in churches belonging to female Religious.

### 85. CONFRATERNITY OF THE BLESSED SACRAMENT.

Its object is to honor Jesus Christ in the Sacrament of His love, and to repair the outrages He there receives from the ingratitude of men. Having originated at Rome in the Church of St. Mary, *supra Minervam*, in the commencement of the sixteenth century, this institution, as praiseworthy as it is salutary, was approved by a Bull of Paul V., dated November 30, 1539. It holds the rank of an Archconfraternity, empowered to communicate the Indulgences with which it has been enriched to all other Confraternities of the same title affiliated to it.\* The principal Indulgences are:

---

\* On the 15th of February, 1608, Pope Paul V. declared that all Confraternities of the Blessed Sacrament erected by the authority of the Holy See or by the Ordinary, enjoy *ipso facto* all the Indulgences attached to the Archconfraternity of St. Mary *supra Minervam* at Rome. The same declaration was repeated by Innoc. XI. in his Bull, *Injuncti Nobis*, 1st October, 1678. A Bishop can therefore establish this Confraternity in the different Churches of his Diocese, with the application of the Indulgences peculiar to it. It belongs likewise to him to examine and approve the statutes of the Confraternity. Though its regulations vary, yet they all agree in this essential point—viz. in

1. A plenary Indulgence on the day of admission, to everybody who, having received the Sacraments, shall become a member.

2. Another plenary Indulgence to each person enrolled, men and women, on the octave day of Corpus Christi, if he approach the Holy Table, assist at the procession on that occasion, and pray for the intention of his Holiness. Innoc. XII., Nov. 27, 1694, transferred this Indulgence to the Friday immediately after the feast of Corpus Christi. Should he be unable to be present at the procession, he can gain the Indulgence by going to Communion, and praying for the designs of the Church.

3. Also a plenary Indulgence on the *third* Sunday of every month, and on Holy Thursday, if persons receive Communion, assist at the procession these days, visit a church or public oratory, and there pray devoutly for the Pope's intention. This Indulgence accorded by Pius IX., 13th June, 1853, supersedes one of seven years and seven Quarantines, previously annexed to those two days by Paul V.

4. A plenary Indulgence at the hour of death.

5. An Indulgence of seven years and seven Quarantines on the Feast of Corpus Christi, by communicating and praying, &c. The same as often as associates accompany the Blessed Sacrament, with or without a light, when carried to the sick; also to all members who, on Holy Thursday, visit it in the place

---

honoring our Lord in the Blessed Eucharist; professing towards **Him** a most tender generous devotion, of which they give practical evidence by numerous acts of homage; assisting at Mass, Benediction, and frequent visits; accompanying the Holy Viaticum, attending to the cleanliness of churches, trimming the lamp which should constantly **burn** before our Redeemer, &c.

where it is preserved; similarly, it is obtainable, once a day, to the same class of persons, who, in the afternoon—*horis vespertinis*—visit the Most Holy Sacrament in some church or public oratory, and there piously pray, with heart contrite, for the wants of the Church. These two latter Indulgences have been accorded by Pius IX.

6. An Indulgence of 100 days each time the associates exercise a work of piety or charity; for illustration, if they convey the body of a deceased Catholic to the grave, if they take part in any procession whatever, authorised by the Ordinary, afford hospitality to a poor person, visit the sick or the imprisoned, co-operate in the reconciliation of enemies, or the conversion of sinners, if they instruct the ignorant, &c. (Paul V., Clem. X., Bened. XIV., Pius IX.). A.

There are various other associations designed to honor the Blessed Sacrament, as the Perpetual Adoration, the Daily Adoration, the Nightly Adoration, &c., each having its own peculiar rules and prerogatives. Any information required concerning them, may be readily acquired by an application to the Directors of these works, to which it is so useful and agreeable to associate oneself, when this is possible, without neglecting the duties of our state in life:

> "Quantum potes, tantum aude,
> Quia major omni laude,
> Nec laudare sufficies."
> —*Hymn* "*Lauda Sion.*"

### 86. CONFRATERNITY OF THE SACRED HEART OF JESUS.

Our Divine Lord Himself manifesting to Blessed Margaret Mary Alacoque the riches of His heart, assured her "that He would open all the treasures of love, mercy, sanctification, and salvation, which that Heart contains, to those who might render to, and procure for it, all the love and honor in their power." "This amiable Heart," writes the holy Nun, "has an infinite desire of being known and loved by its creatures, amongst whom it wishes to establish its empire, as being the source of every good, in order to provide for their wants."

The specific end of the Confraternity is, to honor the Divine Heart of Jesus, to return Him love for love, to thank him for the institution of the Blessed Eucharist, and to make reparation for the coldness, ingratitude and outrages with which His infinite charity is so often repaid. Let us not then refuse to inscribe our names in the Register of the Confraternity of the Sacred Heart; it would be to inscribe them in *The Book of Life*.

The first Confraternity of this title owes its origin to St. Leonard of Port Maurice. It was founded at Rome in the Church of St. Theodore. In February, 1801, the Priests of the Congregation of St. Paul, in Rome, were authorised to establish an Association of the Sacred Heart in the Church of St. Mary *ad Pineam*, called *in capella*. Two years after it was declared an Archconfraternity; later on, it was transferred to the Church of St. Mary *della Pace*. Pius VII. endowed it with numerous Indulgences, and with power to extend a participation in them, to all other Confraternities of the same title aggregated to it.*

---

* A Priest empowered to aggregate to the Archconfraternity of the Sacred Heart, erected in the Church of St. Mary *della Pace*, can do so by simply taking down the names of persons wishing to become members.

Pius VII. (Rescript of March 7, 1801, March 20, and November 13, 1802, and others of 1803, 1815, and 1817), accorded the following favours to all the Faithful, who, being enrolled in a Confraternity of the Sacred Heart, affiliated to the Archconfraternity at Rome, recite devoutly every day, in honor of the Sacred Heart of Jesus, a Pater Ave and Credo, with the ejaculation, "O Sweet Heart of Jesus! grant that I may love Thee more and more."

I. *Plenary Indulgences*: 1. On the day of ad-

---

He preserves these names, and, when occasion requires, sends them to Rome to the Secretary of the Archconfraternity. Meanwhile, these individuals partake of the Indulgences from the very day the names were given to the Priest, because, though desired by the Directors of the work, the inscribing in the great Registry at Rome is not essential. The Holy Sacrifice is frequently offered, and prayers said for the associates.

N. B.—The whole world knows that a magnificent church has been built at Moulins, in honor of the Sacred Heart. It is the first parochial monument in France, dedicated to this adorable Heart. When our loving Saviour vouchsafed to reveal to B. Margaret Mary this charming devotion, Moulins was in the same diocese with Paray-le-Monial, where this holy Nun was living in her Monastery of the Visitation; and it was at Moulins the public adoration of the Sacred Heart commenced.

After having read the Papal Briefs, M. de Dreux Brézé, Bishop of the place, erected, by Apostolic authority, in that new church, on the 3rd of June, 1853, and in presence of a large assembly of people, the Archconfraternity of the Sacred Heart of Jesus, for all France. In conferring this signal favour on the town and diocese of Moulins, and on the French nation, the noble Pontiff Pius IX., designed to reward our country for its zeal in propagating the devotion of the Sacred Heart, as also to stimulate it more and more. Furthermore, to the numerous plenary Indulgences annexed to the Archconfraternity at Rome, and imparted to that at Moulins, his Holiness has added another plenary Indulgence, attainable once a month, by all associates, on a day selected by themselves. Thus, independently of the fact that we thereby correspond with the desire of our Holy Father, wishing us to try to profit by the precious gift, it is both an honor and an advantage to the Catholics of France to join the Archconfraternity founded at Moulins.

See the work entitled : *Instructions sur l' Archiconfrerie du Sacre Cœur de Jesus, pour la France, erigee dans l'eglise du Sacre Cœur, à Moulins, par P. M. Martine, cure du Sacre Cœur, et directeur de l'Archiconfrerie.*—Clermond-Ferrand, 1855.

mission into the Confraternity, the conditions being Confession, Communion, and prayers for the intention of his Holiness. The visit is not required.

2. On the Feast of the Sacred Heart, or Sunday following (same conditions).*

3. On the first Friday or Sunday of every month, conditions unaltered.

4. On one other day in each month, at each one's choice. Do.

5. At the time of death, by invoking, at least mentally, the Sacred Name of Jesus.

II. *Partial Indulgences:* 1, Seven years and as many Quarantines, by approaching the Sacraments on the four Sundays immediately preceding the Feast of the Sacred Heart. 2, Sixty days for every good work done during the day. A.

---

* To gain the plenary Indulgence on the **Feast of the Sacred Heart** (Friday after the Octave of Corpus Christi), it is not necessary to belong to the Confraternity. By a Rescript, bearing date July 7, 1815, Pius VII. renders it available to everyone who may communicate on that day, and visit a church or public oratory where the feast is celebrated, praying according to the intent of his Holiness. By the same Indult, the Feast may be kept any other day of the year, *with the leave of the Ordinary*, and the Mass of the Sacred Heart said on that day ("Raccolta," p. 148).

By a Decree, *Urbis et Orbis*, August 23, 1856, the Feast of the Sacred Heart has been extended to the Universal Church, so that presently it is everywhere celebrated with a proper Office and Mass. To the Bishops of France, where the special public worship (*cultus*) of the Sacred Heart first began, and where it is daily increasing so rapidly, we owe the benefit of having it extended to the whole world. Assembled at Paris for the baptism of the Prince Imperial, their Lordships entreated his Eminence Cardinal Patrizi, *Legate a latere*, to deign to convey their desire to the feet of his Holiness. I give the very words of the Decree, *Ex quo Clemens*, of August 23, 1856:

"The Bishops of France eagerly embracing the opportunity presented to them, of giving a public and solemn testimony, in the person of the Cardinal Legate, of their veneration for the Apostolic See, in a large body collectively waited on him during his stay in Paris; accordingly, having professed their most sincere and devoted attachment to the Roman Pontiff, as being the centre of Catholic unity and Christ's Vicar upon earth, they earnestly implored Him to vouchsafe to ex-

III. *Other Indulgences in favour of associates of the Sacred Heart of Jesus:* They too are applicable to the souls of Purgatory. But, to obtain them, it is not requisite to recite the Pater, Ave, Credo, or elicit the aspiration subjoined (Declaration, March 5, 1840).

1. The Indulgences of the Roman Stations (refer to No. 110), to all who, on the days of the Stations as specified in the Roman Missal, visit a church of the Confraternity, and pray there for the intention of his Holiness.

2. A plenary Indulgence on the Feasts of the Immaculate Conception, Nativity, Annunciation, Purification, and Assumption of the Blessed Virgin; also on those of St. Joseph, SS. Peter and Paul, St. John Evangelist, All Saints' Day, and All Souls! The conditions being Confession, Communion, and a

---

tend the Festival of the Most Sacred Heart of Jesus to the entire Church.

" When the undersigned Cardinal Prefect of the S. R. C. returned to the city, he laid before our Most Holy Father this request of the illustrious French Hierarchy, so obedient to the Apostolic See. His Holiness was pleased to receive it graciously, and, moreover, wishing to hold out to the Faithful fresh inducements to love, cherish, and embrace the wounded Heart of Him who loved us and cleansed us from our sins by His own Blood, he ordered that the Office of the Most Divine Heart of Jesus, approved of by the S. R. C., May 11, 1765, for the kingdom of Poland and the Roman clergy, with its proper Mass, *Miserebitur*, should be annually celebrated throughout the Universal Church, under the Rite of a double-major feast, on the Friday after the Octave of Corpus Christi, it being understood, at the same time, that the Rubrics be observed, and that, as regards Churches privileged to solemnize it with a higher Rite, on another day, or with a different Office, every single Indult hitherto issued by the Apostolic See, remain in full force—notwithstanding anything whatever to the contrary—August 23, 1856.

" C. epis. Albanen. Card. Patrizi, S. R. C., Prefectus
" H. CAPALTI, S. R. C., Secretarius."

(*Place of the Seal*).

visitation of some church of the Confraternity (Pius VII. Two Briefs of April 2, 1805).*

3. Another plenary Indulgence on each of the six Sundays or Fridays before the Feast of the Sacred Heart, supposing a reception of the Sacraments, visit to a church or public oratory where the Feast is observed, and prayers for the Pope's intention (Pius VII., Rescript, March 4, 1806).

4. Seven years and seven Quarantines every day of a Novena kept by any of the associates, preparatory to the Feast of the Sacred Heart, if they visit and pray as above (same Rescript).†

5. Lastly, to increase still more devotion to the Mother of God, the same Pontiff, Pius VII., granted, in perpetuity, an Indulgence of 300 days to all associates who, morning, noon, and night, recite Three *Gloria Patris* in thanksgiving to the Blessed Trinity for the graces and privileges conferred on Mary; also 100 days for each of the three times they may be recited, and a plenary Indulgence once a month, at each one's discretion, provided they shall have been punctual in that devotion during the term, and that they receive the Sacraments, and pray for the usual end. All these Indulgences, whether plenary or partial, are applicable to the Holy Souls (Rescript, Sept. 10, 1814).

*Remarks.*—1. Any members who, on account of

---

* On the other feasts of our Lady, and on those of the other Apostles, there is an Indulgence of seven years and seven Quarantines attached to the visitation of a church belonging to the Confraternity (Brief, April 2, 1805).

† By a Rescript, dating May 21, 1828, Leo XII. accorded to all associates preparing for the Feast of the Sacred Heart by a Triduo, a like Indulgence of seven years and seven Quarantines each of the three days, if they visit a church or public oratory, wherein the Feast may be celebrated, and offer prayers for the general intention.

sickness, absence from home, &c., cannot make the visits prescribed in the foregoing numbers, may, nevertheless, share in the Indulgences, by doing some pious work marked out by their confessors. 2. All the Indulgences dispensed to the Confraternity of the Sacred Heart, as enumerated in the two previous paragraphs, are available to all the Faithful, wherever in the world they may be situated, even in places where it would be impossible to erect a Confraternity, or difficult to aggregate it to the Archconfraternity in Rome, *provided they perform with exactitude the works enjoined* (Pius VII., Rescript, May 15, 1816). 3. Gregory XVI., of holy memory, having, by a Brief of June 20, 1837, confirmed all these Indulgences, granted to associates of the Sacred Heart a plenary Indulgence obtainable on the Feast of St. Gregory the Great, 12th of March, should they receive the Sacraments, visit a church or chapel of the Confraternity, and pray for our holy Mother the Church. The Indulgence commences at First Vespers.

*The Perpetual Adoration.*—Its members are associates of the Confraternity of the Sacred Heart, who unite to render a continual homage (*cultus*) of adoration, thanksgiving, and love to the adorable Heart of Jesus. Persons who join in this Pious Union select one or more days in the year which they consecrate entirely to the Sacred Heart in this manner:—

They approach the Sacraments on that day, visit a church or public oratory, and pray there for the Pope as well as for his intention. They likewise pray there for the clergy, for the conversion of sinners, for all associates of the *Perpetual Adoration*, and for the souls in Purgatory; they devote about one hour to prayer, vocal or mental, on one occasion, or at intervals during the day or at night, should there be a sufficient cause to justify the interruption; during the day they also address some short prayer or ejaculation to the Heart of our Divine Lord; in fine, they renew to Jesus Christ the promises made in Baptism, and any other promises they might have previously made.

Thus the *Perpetual Adoration* of the Sacred Heart becomes that sacred fire which, in the words of Leviticus (vi. 13), "shall always burn, and never go out on the altar." A person faithful to these practices shall gain a plenary Indulgence on the days he observes them (Leo XII.. Decree of Feb. 18, 1826). A.

### 87. THE RED SCAPULAR, OR THAT OF THE PASSION.*

This Scapular was made known to the Faithful after an apparition with which our Lord favoured a Sister of Charity, on the evening of the Octave of St. Vincent de Paul, in the year 1846. On that occasion Jesus held in His hand a scarlet woollen scapular suspended by two cords of the same material and colour. On one side was represented our Divine Saviour nailed to a cross, at the foot of which were the instruments of the Passion, with these words around the crucifix, " Holy Passion of our Lord Jesus Christ, save us;"

---

* I should have ranked the Red Scapular in Article III., amongst devout practices, since it does not properly constitute a Confraternity. Still it approximates to one, because it requires the names of the persons wearing this blessed habit to be inscribed and forwarded, at least annually, to the Office of the Secretary of the Very Rev. Lazarist Fathers, Paris, rue de Sevres, 95. Besides, I did not like to separate it from those of Carmel and the Immaculate Conception.

at the other were seen the images of Jesus and Mary, with these words, "Sacred Hearts of Jesus and Mary, protect us." This is the reason why the diploma delivered to Priests, empowering them to bless and impose this Scapular, styles it "The Red Scapular of the Passion and of the most Sacred Heart of our Lord Jesus Christ, as also of the most loving and compassionate Heart of the Immaculate Virgin Mary."\*

Having been made aware of this remarkable favour bestowed on the virtuous nun, our Holy Father Pius IX., approved of the devotion, and, by a Rescript of June 25, 1847, authorized all Priests of the Congregation of the Mission to bless and confer the Scapular of the Passion. Moreover, to the Superior-General of the same congregation of *Lazarists*, he granted the power of delegating the faculty to other Priests, Secular or Regular (Brief of March 21, 1848).

*Plenary Indulgences:* 1. On the day of receiving the Scapular, provided the new associate Confess, Communicate, visit a church or public oratory, and there pray a while for the intent of the Roman Pontiff.

2. Every Friday in the year, to those who, being invested with the Scapular, receive the Sacraments, meditate for some time on the Passion of our Redeemer, and pray likewise for the intention of Holy Church.

3. *In articulo mortis*, if clients be well disposed by the reception of the Sacraments, or invoke, at

---

\* On the Feast of the Exaltation of the Holy Cross, 1846, our Redeemer appeared again to His servant, and told her that a great increase of faith, hope, and charity was in store every Friday for those carrying this precious livery of His Passion.

least, the Holy Name of Jesus, in heart, if unable to do so orally (Rescripts, March 21, 1848, and July 19, 1850).

*Partial Indulgences:* 1. Seven years and seven Quarantines every Friday to those wearing it, if they receive Communion, and recite five Paters, Aves, and Glorias, meanwhile meditating on the Passion. 2. Three years and three Quarantines on any day of the year, to all who, sorry for their sins, spend at least half an hour in a devout meditation on the sufferings of our Saviour. 3. An Indulgence of 200 days as often as, contrite in heart, persons kiss that Scapular, saying:—

*Te ergo, quaesumus, tuis famulis subveni, quos pretioso sanguine redemisti.* "We therefore pray Thee, help Thy servants whom Thou hast redeemed with Thy Precious Blood."

Note.—On Sept, 13, 1850, the Holy Father permitted that, in case of lawful hindrance, the Communion of Friday may be transferred to the following Sunday, without forfeiting the plenary Indulgence.\*

### 88. CONFRATERNITY OF THE SCAPULAR, OR OF OUR LADY OF MOUNT CARMEL.

*Definition, Origin, and Privileges of the Scapular.*

It consists of two little pieces of brown or black woollen cloth (Decree, 12th February, 1840), connected by two cords made of wool, cotton, thread, &c., or of any other material, no matter what its

---

\* The formula of reception is given at the end of this volume.

colour may be, which will allow it to pass about the neck. The word Scapular is borrowed from the Latin *Scapulæ* (shoulders), because the Scapular hangs over or reclines on the shoulderss. It is called, "The Little Habit of the Blessed Virgin"—*Abitino della Madonna*—to distinguish it from the large Scapular given to the Carmelites by Mary herself, which is composed of two strips or bands of cloth covering the back and front down to the feet.

The devotion of the Scapular traces its origin from the celebrated apparition of the Mother of God to St. Simon Stock, Superior-General of the Carmelites in the West. It took place July 16, 1251, at Cambridge in England. Having appeared to this great Saint who, for a long time previous, had been constantly imploring her protection in behalf of his Order, the Holy Virgin presented to him a Scapular which she held in her hands, saying, "Receive, beloved son, this Scapular of your Order; it is a token of the privilege which I have procured for you and for the children of Carmel; whoever dies invested with this habit shall be preserved from eternal flames (*In hoc moriens æternum non patietur incendium*). It is a sign of salvation, a safeguard against danger, a pledge of peace, and of a special protection."* In his treatise on the Festivals of Mary, the illustrious and learned Pope Bened. XIV. expressly declares that he believes in the vision of St. Simon Stock as a *real fact;* "and," continues he, "we think

---

* Circular of St. Simon Stock to his Religious, dictated by himself, and written by Peter Swanington or Swayngton, companion, secretary, and confessor of the saint. See also the work headed "*De antiquitate et Sanctimonia eremitarum Montis Carmeli*," by F. John Paleonydore, who died in 1507 (Lib. iii., cap. 7).

that the whole world ought, in like manner, to consider it such." *

Arguing from this revelation, which certainly cannot be questioned, we may piously believe that all having the happiness of departing this life with the Scapular on, find favour before God, and are consequently preserved from the fire of hell. For let us be assured that, faithful to her promise, Immaculate Mary will procure for them from the Divine treasures of which she is the depository, the graces necessary either for their perseverance in holiness or for their true conversion. Thus, fortified by grace, freed from sin, and reconciled to God by the Sacraments or by an act of perfect contrition, clients who die wearing this blessed livery shall not fall under the stroke of inexorable justice : *In hoc moriens æternum non patietur incendium* (He who shall die

---

* *De Festis B. Mariæ Virginis*, Lib. ii., cap. 6 : De Festo B. Virginis de Monte Carmelo, die 16 Julii.

A periodical which has usurped the title of *Observateur Catholique*, without the least regard for the authority of Bened. XIV. and his successors, has, with a most flagrant temerity, impudently dared to throw disdain on the origin of this holy Scapular, and on the privileges and Indulgences accorded to those who carry it. It has likewise presumed to combat the far-famed Indulgence of the Portinuncula, and to ridicule it.

But it may be well to know that the publication has been condemned by a Decree of the S. Congregation of the Index, Dec. 6, 1855, which was approved of by the Pope and promulgated on the 15th December of the same year. A bitter anti-Catholic spirit pervaded the entire work. At present, therefore, it is strictly forbidden to edit, read, or have in one's possession the *Observateur Catholique*, in like manner as other works condemned by the Church, which was charged by our Redeemer carefully to attend to the preservation of faith and morals. "Wherefore," says the Decree, "let nobody, whatever his rank or station in life may be, dare henceforth to publish, read, or keep in his possession the aforesaid works condemned or proscribed, no matter where or in what language." To be at liberty to peruse books which are on the Index, one should have obtained permission to that effect, either from the Pope, or from some Bishop delegated by his Holiness for that end.

vested with this (habit) shall be preserved from hell fire). Such is the first favour promised to the members of Carmel by the powerful and merciful Virgin —"This shall be a privilege for you and all the Carmelites."

About half a century later, Mary condescended to renew the vision by appearing to Pope John XXII., to recommend to him the holy Order of Carmel. Extending her solicitude this time even to the other life, she promised him that she would assist and console any of the Carmel brethren that may be in Purgatory, and speedily release them from that prison, especially on the first Saturday after their death —*Sabbato post eorum obitum.*

These prerogatives were promulgated by the same Pontiff in his Bull, *Sacratissimo uti culmine*, which was published at Avignon, and expedited 3rd of March, 1322.* It is called the *Sabbatine* Bull, on account of the release promised on Saturday—*Sabbatum.* It was confirmed by Alex. V. in his Bull, *Tenorem cujusdam privilegii*, Rome, Dec. 7, 1409. Bened. XIV., in fact, has argued from this revelation against certain rash critics, and desires that, in this matter, the people adhere to the Decree of Paul V., Feb. 15, 1613, which allows the Carmelite Friars to preach this pious belief. This is the *second* privilege conferred by the Queen of Heaven on the Scapular, *a privilege of deliverance.*

A great many other Popes have not hesitated to proclaim these signal favours in a most solemn manner, becoming their warmest advocates and defenders. Witness Alexander V., Clement VII., Paul III.,

---

* *Bullarium Carmelitarum*, tom I., pp. 61 and 166

S. Pius V., Greg. XIII., Paul V., Clem. X., Innoc. XI., &c.*

*The Confraternity.*—Many authors are of opinion that the Congregation of Mount Carmel is anterior to the two revelations of which I speak. However this may be, it is only from the apparition of our Lady to St. Simon Stock, that it can claim the title of *Confraternity of the Scapular;* in truth, it is only since the end of the thirteenth or beginning of the fourteenth century, that we see the Popes who successively occupied the chair of Peter favouring with all their might this salutary and holy association. Besides declaring that the Scapular with which the associates are invested entitles them to a share in all the privileges of the holy Order of Carmel, as well as in its merits and good works, the Supreme Pontiffs have unlocked to them the treasury of Indulgences, which they have dispensed to them with a sort of profusion. I give here the chief ones accorded by them severally, in particular by Paul V., Bull, *Cum certus*, Oct. 30, 1606 :—

I. *Plenary Indulgences:* 1. A plenary Indulgence on the day of receiving the blessed habit (Confession, Communion, and prayers for the intention of his Holiness, being supposed).

2. On the Feast of Our Lady of Carmel (July 16), or on the following Sunday. Bened. XIV. extended the faculty of acquiring this Indulgence to all days of the octave (same conditions). The festival may be celebrated on the Sunday within the octave, or, if necessary, on any other Sunday in July, and with a procession.

---

* See an excellent work called *Recueil d' instructions sur la devotion au saint Scapulaire,* b, a discalced Carmelite, *Gand V. J. Poelman-de Pape,* 1846.

3. *In articulo mortis.*

4. By two other Bulls of Paul V. (one dated 3rd Aug., 1609; the other, July 19, 1614), there is a plenary Indulgence for all those attending at the procession made by members of the Confraternity, a Sunday in each month, with the Bishop's permission (Confession, Communion, and the usual prayers). I say, "those attending at the procession," because the presence in the church would not suffice. But persons incapable of taking part in it can obtain the Indulgence by communicating and visiting on that day a chapel of the Order (Clement X., Brief, *Commissæ Nobis*, of 8th May, 1673). Travellers, invalids, prisoners, &c., may secure it by reciting the "Little Office of the Blessed Virgin," or fifty Paters and Aves, and making an act of contrition joined to a firm purpose of confessing and communicating as soon as possible.

5. In virtue of the same constitution of Clem. X., there is a plenary Indulgence on the Feasts of the Immaculate Conception, Nativity, Presentation, Annunciation, Visitation, Purification, and Assumption of Mary.

6. Also on the Feasts of St. Joseph, St. Simon Stock (16th May), St. Anne, St. Michael, St. Teresa, &c.

7. Every Wednesday in the year. This Indulgence is mentioned in the diploma issued at Rome by the General of the Calced Carmelites, *a Santa Maria Traspontina*, between St. Angelo and St. Peter's: "Et tandem omnibus totius anni quartis feriis, sicut de novo eruitur ex Reg. Archivii Ordinis exhibito et approbato a Visitatione Apostolica, anno Jubilæi 1825." The Calced Carmelites of Rome look

upon this Indulgence as positively certain. I see no reason why it should not be regarded as such.

The conditions for acquiring the Indulgences of the three preceding numbers are, Confession, Communion, visit to a church of the Order, and the accustomed prayers. Should the visitation of a Carmelite church be impossible, confessors have power to substitute for it some other works of piety. A Rescript of June 15, 1855, allows it to be made to the parish church, where there is no church belonging to Carmel.

II. *Partial Indulgences:* 1. Seven years and seven Quarantines the Sunday fixed for the procession, when it cannot take place, provided a visit be made to a church or chapel of the Confraternity. 2. Five years and as many Quarantines for those wearing the Scapular, if they Communicate and pray for the Pope's intentions. 3. The same favour to clients accompanying the Holy Viaticum when carried to the sick, for whom they are to pray. 4. Three hundred days to members who abstain from flesh meat on Wednesdays and Saturdays. 5. 100 days every time an associate performs a work of piety or charity, as, e. g. to bury the dead, to relieve the distressed, to reconcile enemies, to instruct the ignorant in the truths of salvation, &c.; in fine, forty days to persons reciting daily seven Paters and Aves in honor of the Blessed Virgin. All these Indulgences are applicable to the souls in Purgatory (Clem. X., Bull *Cum sicut Accepimus*, Jan. 12, 1672). It deserves notice, too, that the churches of the Order of Our Lady of Carmel enjoy the Indulgences of the Roman Stations on the days indicated by the R. Missal (Clem. X., *Commissæ Nobis*, May 8, 1673).

*Conditions of admission, and of participating in the privileges, &c.*—1. To become a member of the Confraternity of Mount Carmel, it is necessary to receive the Scapular from the hands of a Father of the Order, or from a Priest authorised to bless and give it, in places where the Carmelites have no Convent. Having blessed the Scapular, the Priest personally puts it on, or passes it round the neck of the recipient—*benedictio et impositio*—hence persons who, by their own act, might put it on themselves, would not be received, for "in the very *blessing and conferring* of the habit, which are done by authority, consists the formal admission." A Priest, nevertheless, may invest himself (Decree, March 7, 1840).

That one may partake of the privileges and Indulgences, it is also requisite to wear it habitually. Agreeably to an Indult of Pope Gregory XVI., 30th May, 1838, the inscribing of the names in the Register of the Confraternity, though previously enjoined by Paul V., is not a matter of necessity at present. Thus by the mere fact of being received, the Faithful belong to the Confraternity established in a district or locality. It would be well, however, and consoling, to have the names enrolled in it; in order, likewise, that after death a client may not be deprived of the suffrages of his fellow associates (Decree of Sept. 17, 1845).

2. For a participation in the first privilege—that of a good death or exemption from the infernal doom—a person should belong to the Confraternity; in other terms, he should be duly received, carry the Scapular devoutly, and have it at the hour of death—*He who dies invested with this, shall never suffer in the fire of hell.*

3. To enjoy the second favour mentioned in the Sabbatine Bull—a speedy deliverance from the pains of Purgatory—it is obligatory, in addition to the preceding conditions, to observe the chastity proper to one's state of life, and, if able to read, to recite daily the Little Office of the Blessed Virgin, according to the Roman Breviary, or to some Rite sanctioned by the Holy See. The Canonical Office of the Church holds the place of the Little Office of Mary, as regards Priests and all bound to say it. Similarly, the Little Office itself suffices, even when recited by obligation.\* But if a person be unable to say it, he must observe all the fasts of the Church, and abstain on Wednesdays, Fridays, and Saturdays, except when Christmas Day falls on one of those three.

The obligation of the Little Office and the abstinence of Wednesday, may be commuted or changed into some other pious works, and modified or diminished to suit the wants of individuals, at the discretion of him who effects the commutation. But a special power is required for this (Decree, June 22, 1842). It is not enough simply to be authorised to give the Scapular; the faculties forwarded from Rome by the Generals of the Order, must expressly convey the power—"*Nisi expresse enuntietur in Rescripto concessionis pro benedictione et impositione Scapularium,*" says the same Decree of 1842. This is exactly what occurs, for, in the grants issued there, it is stated that the Priest obtaining them can make this commutation. In the diploma given by

---

\* By the Little Office to be recited daily, is meant "A Nocturn of the day, with Lauds and the other Hours of the same Office" (Decree, Aug. 18, 1868).

the Superior of the *Calced* Carmelites, the power is absolute, i. e. unconditional. But in that of the Superior of the *Discalced* Order, it is required that the Priest be approved to hear confessions. He need not, however, be the confessor of the person in whose favour the commutation is effected; it may be made externally to the Sacred Tribunal.*

4. That a person may acquire the above-named Indulgences, it is sufficient to have received the Scapular, and to carry it, complying meanwhile with the prescribed conditions. Hence it is not necessary to recite any special prayers, as seven Paters and Aves every day, or fourteen on Wednesday; no law obliges to this. One will be bound to it only as far as the Priest may substitute such prayers for the Little Office, or abstinence on Wednesday, to insure a share in the privilege of the Sabbatine Bull.

*Practical Observations.*—1. As noticed already, the Scapular ought to be made of woollen stuff or cloth, of Carmel colour, i. e. brown, or black, or nearly so; but the tapes or cords may be of any material or colour whatever, since they do not form part of the Scapular. Iron or metal Scapulars are therefore useless; so, too, as to the acquisition of the Indulgences, are those in tissue of silk, silver, or gold; yet, of course, they may be employed as decorations for statues of Mary. It is even permitted to sew or annex embroidered images to the two woollen

---

* The Sacred Congregation of Indulgences, having been often consulted on this matter, replied, that in cases of a grave impediment, members are not bound either to fast, recite the canonical Hours, or the Office of the Blessed Virgin, or to abstain on Wednesdays and Saturdays. At the same time, in such circumstances, the Faithful ought to be induced to recur to a prudent and learned confessor, to procure a substitution or commutation (Decrees of Aug. 12, 1840, and June 22, 1842, &c.).

pieces of the Scapular. This may be a pious and laudable usage, but the simple Scapular would suffice without any ornaments.*

2. In order to obtain the Indulgences, members must wear the Scapular, even Priests and Religious; it should be worn also in such a way that the two pieces be separated, one suspended on the breast, the other over the shoulders. Hence it would not do to impose or carry it as a girdle, or in the form of a St. Andrew's cross, or as a deacon wears his stole, with the extremities united on one side (Decree, Feb. 12, 1840), for thus the reception would be informal, and consequently no right acquired to the Indulgences or privileges. The reason is, because the little habit of the Blessed Virgin, being a substitute for the great Scapular of the Carmelites, ought to be worn after the manner in which the latter is worn. It matters not whether it be worn inside or outside the dress, but it should not be worn as a deacon wears the stole.

3. The Scapular is to be worn day and night, in sickness and in health, particularly at the hour of death. Wherefore it is wrong to hang it up, day or night, on a peg or at the foot of a crucifix, whether that be done for convenience or through scrupulosity. So true is this, that one who lays it aside, even for a day, for instance, forfeits the Indulgences for that day. Still it may be put off for a while, especially in cases of necessity. But if through negli-

---

* Conformably to a Decree of Aug. 18, 1868, it is allowable to embroider a Scapular with ornaments composed of wool, silk, silver, gold, &c., provided always that the prescribed colour predominates—*prævaleat*. But a Scapular embroidered with blue, red, white, &c., cannot be used instead of the different Scapulars *requiring* those colours.

The Scapular should be square or rectangular in shape, and not round or oval, as some persons would have it. "*Let there be no innovation*," writes the S. Congregation.

gence a person omit to wear it, he ought to lament his fault, and hasten to repair it, by reassuming it. He can then put it on himself, by his own act, because, though he may have ceased to wear it for a considerable time, he does not require to be newly enrolled (Decree, May 27, 1857). On the other hand, should a person have laid it aside or cast it off through contempt or impiety, the ceremony of receiving it must be repeated, for, in that case, he would be reasonably supposed to have wholly renounced the Confraternity. Such is the feeling of the S. Congregation,

No doubt persons can go to Heaven without the Scapular—yet this precious uniform is, as before remarked, a passport to that blessed country—*for he who dies clothed with it, shall never pass through hellfire.*

4. The original Scapular with which a person was invested, the day of his admission, ought to have been blessed by the Priest who receives him. But the others afterwards need not be blessed, for, as is said, *the first blesses all the rest.* Hence, when the primary one is unfit for use, the person can burn it, and himself put on another, even unblessed.

5. In blessing or conferring the Scapular, it is not required that the Priest should use the Ritual or Breviary of the Carmelites. Having been duly empowered to bless and give it, he may employ any formula; yet the Faithful will be always validly enrolled, because, as noted, the essential thing is, to bless the habit and put it round the neck of the postulant, in other words, *to impose it*—the *Benedictio et impositio habitus*—are the substantial requisites enjoined by the Decrees, amongst others, that of Aug. 24. 1844

One blessed Scapular would do to admit several individuals. Still it is requisite that the first Scapular which a client wears should have been blessed (Decree, Aug. 18, 1868). Observe, moreover, that in an urgent case of sickness or otherwise, a person may very well be enrolled by the mere giving or laying on of a Scapular, previously blessed, without any set form of prayers. The conferring of it may take place anywhere, and its blessing does not require the presence of the postulant or client to be admitted. If, therefore, on the occasion of receiving a crowd of persons, or of blessing a number of Scapulars, there remain some over and above, they may serve for other people without a fresh benediction (see Decrees of Aug. 24, 1844, and Aug. 18, 1868, ad II).

6. In virtue of a Decree of Clem. VII. (*Ex Clementi*, Aug. 12, 1530), the power of blessing and imposing the Scapular comprises also the faculty of imparting a general absolution and a Plenary Indulgence at the hour of death to the faithful enrolled. (The Carmelite Fathers give a special form for that purpose, which is inserted at the end of this treatise.) In the absence of a Priest authorised to apply this Indulgence, it may be given *by any other approved by the Ordinary* (*Recueil d'Instructions sur la devotion au saint Scapulaire*, mentioned above).

7. Seeing that in numberless instances throughout the world, the formality of enrolment had been gone through without any observance of the prescribed rules, it pleased the Pope to validate afresh all the informal receptions of the Scapular, which took place in France or other countries, before Sept. 18, 1862.

*Important Note.*—There prevails in some parishes in connection with the Confraternities of Carmel, the

Sacred Heart, and others, an abuse which is totally condemned at Rome. I allude to the obligation imposed on members of both sexes, of presenting themselves every year to the Director of the Confraternity to be newly received and enrolled, and to deposit in the treasury of the Association a certain requital. They ought to know that, once admitted into a Confraternity, a person is admitted for life, and that a new admission or enrolment is not only not necessary, but opposed to all the designs of holy Church (read a Decree of S. Cong. of Indulg., Feb. 5, 1748). The only case where a fresh reception would be required is, as I said, that in which a person having, through irreligion or disrespect for sacred things, abjured his title to the Association or renounced the Confraternity, should, after his conversion, desire to become a member again.

### 89. SCAPULAR OF THE IMMACULATE CONCEPTION.

At the commencement of the seventeenth century, this Scapular was revealed by our Divine Lord and His Blessed Mother to the venerable Ursula Benincasa, foundress of the Oblates and Hermits Theatine at Naples. St. Philip Neri had a high esteem for this holy servant of God, whose admirable virtues have been declared *heroic* by a Decree of Pius VI., Aug. 7, 1793. During her life, Ursula, besides being favoured with frequent ecstacies, had her heart entirely absorbed in divine love, seeking after nothing but the glory of God and the salvation of souls. In one of her raptures, which occurred on the Feast of the Purification, the Queen of Heaven appeared to her holding the Divine Infant in her arms; she was clothed in robes of white, over which she wore another garment of a blue colour, and was surrounded by a band of virgins all dressed in the same style. Full of maternal tenderness, Mary then addressed the fervent Nun in these sweet and consoling terms: "Take courage, Ursula, dry your tears; an unalloyed joy is about to replace your sighs; behold in my arms Jesus, who is yours as well as mine, and listen attentively to the directions He is going to give to you." To these words of the Mother succeeded those of the Son, who thereby clearly made known to the venerable Ursula, that it was His wish that she should build a convent under the title of the Immaculate Conception, wherein were to live conformably to the rule of the Eremites, three and thirty nuns, clad like their good mother Mary. He likewise promised some special graces, together with a superabundance of spiritual blessings to all who might embrace that sort of life, and observe the rule to be afterwards prescribed for them in that holy retreat. Ursula then addressing herself to our Lord, besought Him to deign to extend these favours to those who, though living in the world, should have a special devotion to the *August Virgin conceived without sin,* observe chastity according to their state, and carry the *little blue Scapular.* To assure her that her prayer had been heard, our Blessed Redeemer made her behold, in the same transport, angels holding in their hands a great number of these Scapulars, which they distributed in various directions on the earth.

Immediately after this vision, the venerable servant of God set about making some of these Scapulars, and dealt them out to a multitude of persons, after having got them blessed by a Priest. They were received and worn with piety and respect by the Faithful, so that the heart of the holy religious was overflowing with joy. The devout practice had soon become so universal, that, in addition to the multiplied fruits of sanctification and salvation effected by it, Ursula had the happiness of seeing it every where established before her death.

Since that time, Popes Clem. X. and Clem. XI approved of the Blue Scapular, and enriched it with Indulgences. It is made of two pieces of azure or sky-coloured woollen stuff, to which may be affixed, for the purpose of devotion, a representation of Immaculate Mary. Like that of Carmel, it is worn day and night, hanging over the breast and shoulders. "Over the shoulders," says the Roman gloss, "in such a manner that the front part extend to the breast, the other to the back, as the word Scapular itself implies."*

The two principal ends to be kept in view by those who become invested with the Scapular of the Immaculate Conception are—first, to honour this glorious privilege of Mary; secondly, to pray for the reformation of morals, and the conversion of persons wandering in the ways of sins. There are no fixed prayers for this. Hence, it is left to each one's choice, to offer the prayers and perform the good works which his piety may suggest, to propitiate the Divine justice and induce the Almighty to show mercy to sinners.

* Should a person be already wearing the Scapular of Our Lady of Carmel, he may sew *its* two pieces to those of the Blue Scapular, thus annexing them to one and the same tape or cord. Such was the answer given to me at Rome by M. Prinzivalli, Substitute of the Sacred Congregation of Indulgences. Such, too, was the usage in the Eternal City. For example, when the children of the common people are receiving their first Communion in the house of Ponte Rotto, *in the Travestere*, they are invariably presented with divers Scapulars of the B. Virgin, all attached to the same cord.

*A list of the principal Indulgences that may be acquired by all those wearing the Blue Scapular in honour of the Immaculate Conception of the B. V. Mary.* They have been confirmed by Gregory XVI. (Decree July 12, 1845), *and rendered applicable to the souls in Purgatory by his Holiness Pius IX.,* June 7, 1850. The S. Congregation has also recognised their authenticity, 21st March, 1857.*

*Plenary Indulgences* obtainable under the ordinary conditions—Confession, Communion, prayers, &c.

1. On the day of enrolment. 2. The first Sunday of each month. 3. Every Saturday in Lent. 4. Passion Sunday and the Friday after. 5. Wednesday, Thursday, and Friday of Holy Week. 6. On the feasts of Christmas, Easter, Ascension, Pentecost, of the most Holy Trinity, the Invention and Exaltation of the Holy Cross, and on those of the Immaculate Conception, Nativity, Annunciation, Purification, and Assumption of the Blessed Virgin. 7. On the 2nd of August, the Feast of Our Lady of the Angels, or the *Portiuncula.* 8. On the Feasts of All Saints, of St. Joseph, of St. Michael, of the Holy Angels Guardians, of the Nativity of St. John the Baptist, of the Holy Apostles Peter and Paul, of St. Augustine, of St. Teresa, and of the Saints whose feasts are celebrated in the Order of the Theatine Regular-Clerks. 9. During the Exposition of the Blessed Sacrament for the forty hours, once in the year. 10. During the exercises of a retreat once in the year. 11. For a Priest who is associated, on the day of his first Mass. 12. On a day at each one's

---

* These Indulgences are available either directly, in virtue of concessions accorded to associates of the Scapular, or by a participation in all the Indulgences which the Holy See has granted to the Order of the Theatines.

choice during the year. 13. At the hour of Death. Further, the Indulgences of the *Roman Stations* by visiting, on the days designated in the Roman Missal, a Church of the Regular-Clerks, or *in default of this* any other church, and praying there for some time.*

Associates may likewise gain, *twice a month*, the Indulgences granted to persons who visit the Seven Basilicas of Rome, on condition of adding to Communion a visitation to the seven altars in a Church of the Theatine Fathers. Also, *twice a month*, the Indulgences attached to a visit to the Holy Sepulchre and the Holy Land, by complying with the usual conditions, and praying in a Church of the same Order.

II. *Partial Indulgences.*—Sixty years to those who make a half hour's meditation or mental prayer every day. 2. Twenty years to all who visit and assist, corporally or spiritually, the sick or infirm, or, not being able to do so, recite for them five Paters, Aves, and Glorias. 3. Seven years and as many Quarantines on all the lesser feasts of the B. Virgin. 4. Also, as often as clients confess and communicate; likewise in accompanying the Holy Viaticum; the *same* by reciting daily the *Salve Regina*, and praying for the wants of the Church; a like Indulgence every Monday, by visiting the Blessed Sacrament. 200 days each time a person assists at a sermon; fifty days for respectfully pronouncing the Sacred Names of Jesus and Mary; sixty days for any pious work. A. Finally, all Masses said at any altar whatever for deceased clients enjoy the advantage of a *privileged altar*.

I should direct particular attention to the follow-

* It is the Sovereign Pontiff Pius IX. that has given the permission (December 3, 1847) to visit another church, in which, however, *there is an Altar of the Blessed Virgin Mary*. This authorisation extends to all Indulgences for gaining which is required a visit to the Church of the Reverend Theatine Fathers.

ing very special favour, which, by the way, is most authentic:—*It is granted to all associates reciting six Paters, Aves, and Glorias, in honour of the most Holy Trinity and of Mary conceived without sin*, praying, at the same time, for the exaltation of Holy Church, the extirpation of heresy, &c. Every time they do this—*toties quoties*—they can gain the Indulgences accorded to persons who visit the Seven Basilicas of Rome, the Church of Portiuncula at Assisi, those of St. James of Compostella, and of the Holy Land. To partake of these Indulgences, it is not necessary to recite any other prayers, nor to receive the Sacraments; they are moreover applicable to the Departed. This extraordinary favour has been authenticated and newly approved of by the Sacred Congregation of Indulgences (Decree of March 31, 1856, which was confirmed by Pope Pius IX, April 14, 1856).*

---

* The words of the Decree (March 31, 1856) bestowing the privilege are these:—" The above named Indulgences of the Seven Basilicas of the City, Portinucula, Jerusalem, St. James of Compostella, can be gained—*toties quoties*—as often as the prayers are said, and in any place whatever; neither is it necessary to add other prayers, nor to approach the Sacraments of Penance and the Eucharist; it suffices to recite merely six *Paters*, *Aves*, and *Glorias*, as above; the Indulgences are also applicable to the Souls in Purgatory. Which Decree our Most Holy Father Pope Pius IX. graciously approved of, the 14th day of April in the same year 1856 *(Decreta Authentica*—Appendix n. liv., p. 191)."

To this Decree is furthermore added the subjoined note translated from the Latin: "It must be remarked, that a plenary Indulgence available to the living, and attached to a fixed day, can be acquired but once by those visiting a church or other place, pursuant to the Decree of Innoc. XI., 7th March, 1678, which commences with these words '*Delatæ Sæpius*.'"

Nobody ought either, to count, publish, or publicly announce the number of Indulgences, partial or plenary, annexed to the recital of the six Paters, Aves, and Glorias. To do so would be to act in opposition to the prohibitions of the S. Congregation of Indulgences, which are approved by Clem. XII. and Bened. XIV.

It is a mistake for certain writers or preachers, to extol beyond measure the favours annexed to the Blue Scapular. For, in addition to the fact that such exaggerations are imprudent, they may interfere very much with other devotions, as the Via Crucis, Rosary, Chaplet, Scapular of Carmel, &c., so venerable on account of their origin and

The Scapular of the Immaculate Conception must be blessed and conferred by a Priest who has received power either from the Pope, or from the General of the Theatines, residing at Rome, in the Convent of St. Andrew *della Valle*. The names need not be inscribed in the Register of the Confraternity.* The Rev. Theatine Fathers, of the above named Monastery, have oftentimes assured me of the truth of this assertion. True, they themselves take the names of all receiving the Scapular at their hands, but this is done for the purpose of ascertaining the number of persons enrolled, and consequently the progress of the devotion. I say *devotion*, because the Theatines do not consider it a Confraternity.†

## 90. ROSARY AND CONFRATERNITY OF THE ROSARY.

In its present form, conformably to repeated testimonies of the Roman Pontiffs, the Rosary has for its author St. Dominick. This great Saint had a special revelation from the Blessed Virgin concerning it, about the year 1206. He afterwards exercised all his zeal in establishing and promulgating its use. Thus to this devout practice he owed innumerable conversions of sinners and most marvellous victories over the Albigensian heretics who, at that epoch, had infested all the Southern provinces of France. "*Institute the Rosary, and it will be a remedy against so many evils,*" are the words of Mary to St. Dominick.

antiquity, so salutary to the Faithful, and so dear to the Church, since they only tend to lessen the respect and love in the hearts of the people for these pious practices.

* There are other Scapulars in honour of the Blessed Virgin, as the Scapular of Our Lady of Dolors, and that of Our Lady of Mercy, which may likewise be received from Priests duly authorised to bless them.

† According to Ulrich (p. 117) enrolment on the register is necessary for the Scapulars of the Holy Trinity, and the Seven Dolours.—*Translator.*

The Rosary is made up of fifteen decades, each of which comprises ten *Ave Marias* preceded by a *Pater Noster*. While reciting them, a person should piously meditate, according to his ability, on the principal mysteries of the Life, Death, and Resurrection of our Lord Jesus Christ.* The Church regards these Paters and Aves as so many roses of which are formed fifteen crowns that we present to the Queen of Heaven. Hence the name *Rosary*. The Church puts them into our hands, as a powerful antidote against vice and heresy. Need we wonder then that St. Charles Borromeo seemed to attribute the conversion and sanctification of the Faithful of his diocese to the devotion of the Rosary alone? Pope Gregory XVI. has written, *that the Rosary is a wonderful instrument for the destruction of sin, the recovery of God's grace, and the advancement of His Glory* (Brev. ad Episc. Symac).

A Chaplet is a third part of the Rosary; it may be recited in Latin, French, or English. Should our daily avocations hinder us from saying the entire Rosary, or a Chaplet, let us at least say some part of it ; a slight tribute presented to Mary in this way, will secure for us Her benedictions. St. Francis Xavier effected the cure of diseases by the mere touch of his chaplet. By a Brief, *Sanctissimus*, 13th April 1726, Pope Bened. XIII granted :

1. One hundred days' Indulgence for each *Our Father* and each *Hail Mary*, to all the Faithful who, with contrite hearts, recite either the whole Rosary, or a third part of it.

2. A plenary Indulgence once a year, on some day of their own choosing, to those who shall have repeated, every day of the year, at least the Chaplet

---

* To gain the Apostolic, or the Bridgetine Indulgences, the above meditation is not necessary (*S. C. Indulg.*, July 1, 1839).—*Translator*.

or third part of the Rosary. Pope Pius IX. (Decree May 12, 1851) confirmed these Indulgences, and also added this other. A.

3. Ten years and ten Quarantines to all who, with at least hearts contrite, say conjointly with others, whether publicly, as in a church, for example, or privately in their own houses or elsewhere, a third part of the Rosary.

4. A plenary Indulgence on the last Sunday in every month, on the condition of communicating, visiting a church or public oratory, and there praying for the intent of His Holiness. A.

To obtain these favours, it is requisite—1. That the Beads be blessed by the Reverend Dominican Fathers, or by a Priest specially empowered for this by their General; 2. While saying it, to meditate on the mysteries of the Birth, Passion, Death, &c., of our Divine Redeemer, as before stated (Decree, 12th August, 1726). At the same time, according to a declaration of Bened. XIII. (*Pretiosus*—Bull, 26th May, 1727), it is sufficient for those who, through incapacity, know not how to meditate, say the Rosary devoutly.

*Confraternity of the Rosary:* It was organised at the period when the Devotion of the Rosary itself was introduced amongst the people by the holy Founder of the illustrious Order of Friars Preachers. Some of the greatest Popes approved of it, endowed it with spiritual blessings, and confided its establishment to the Dominicans, in whatever part of the world it may be instituted.* Few Confraternities

---

\* For illustration, Sixtus IV., Clem. VII., Leo X., St. Pius V. Sixtus V. &c.

in the Church are more extensively propagated or more productive of salutary results. Furthermore, as the conditions exacted by it are so easy to be fulfilled, every Catholic ought to be delighted to enlist under its banner. The chief condition for each member is to recite the entire Rosary, at least once a week, meditating on the fifteen Mysteries, which can be found in most Prayer-Books, accompanied with some appropriate reflections.*

The whole Rosary need not be recited on the same day; it may be said in three or more distinct parts or chaplets, or all at once, provided it be recited by the end of the week; this is evident from the Brief of Clem. VII. (May 8, 1534), also from that of Pius IX. (Jan 22, 1858). Accordingly, aggregated clients gain the *Indulgences of the Confraternity* from the time they recite the entire Rosary or fifteen decades once a week, no matter how they take part in its recitation, whether in parts of three, four, five, &c.

These of course, are not the same as the Indulgences attached to the Chaplet or Rosary itself, which may be acquired by persons not at all enrolled in the Confraternity (they are those we have just enumerated, together with those of the Chaplet of St. Bridget, of which later on). Contrary to what

---

* The fifteen Mysteries of the Rosary are as follow :—
*The Joyous Mysteries:* The Annunciation, Visitation of St. Elizabeth, the Birth of Jesus Christ, His Presentation in the Temple, and Finding in the midst of the Doctors by Mary and Joseph.
*The Sorrowful Mysteries:* The Prayer of Our Lord and His sweat of blood in the Garden of Olives, His Scourging, His Crowning with Thorns, His sentence to die and carriage of the Cross, His Crucifixion and Death.
*The Glorious Mysteries:* The Resurrection of Our Saviour, His Ascension, the Descent of the Holy Ghost on Mary and the Apostles, the death and Assumption of the Blessed Virgin, her Coronation in Heaven, and the glory of all the Saints.

was stated in the first edition of this work (p. 235), it is required at present, that the Rosary be not divided into more than three parts or chaplets, and that the Chaplet or third part of the Rosary be said altogether on one occasion (Decree, Jan. 22, 1858). It is not sufficient then to recite the entire Chaplet on the same day; there should be, moreover, between the different parts of the five decades, no notable interruption which would destroy the moral unity of the prayer. But it is not necessary to say either the Rosary or Chaplet *kneeling*.

To become a member of the Confraternity, the only formality requisite is to have one's name inscribed in the Registry belonging to the society. A person ought to take care to have his Rosary or Chaplet blessed by a Dominican Father, or by a Priest who may have received the power from the Pope directly, or from the Very Rev. Superior-General of the Order of Friars Preachers. Otherwise, neither the Indulgences accorded by Bened. XIII., nor those of the Confraternity could be gained.

Note.—This Confraternity of the Rosary can be established only in virtue of a special faculty obtained from the General of the Dominicans (Decrees of the S. Congregation of Indulgences, Aug. 19, 1747, and of the S. Congregation of Rites, April 9, 1661). Even after it has been procured, it ought to be submitted to the inspection of the Bishop of the place, and not exercised without his leave. Remark, also, tha when a Confraternity of the Rosary is erected in a parish, it is always at least under the implied condition, *that the Dominicans have no Monastery in the locality* (see the Decree of April 25, 1735).

The principal Indulgences of the Confraternity of

the Rosary were conceded by several Popes, amongst others by St. Pius V., Sixtus V., Gregory XIII., Innoc. XI. (Brief, *Nuper pro parte,* July 31, 1679), Pius VII. and Pius IX. (Decree, May 12, 1851).

I. *Plenary:* 1. On the day of enrolment in the Confraternity, usual conditions.\* 2. On the same day, if to Holy Communion received in a church or chapel of the Confraternity, clients add the recitation of the entire chaplet, and prayers for the design of His Holiness. 3. The first Sunday of each month, by communicating in a church where the Confraternity exists, or at least visiting it the same day, should the Communion have been received elsewhere. 4. A second plenary Indulgence may be acquired on the same day by those who, having communicated, shall assist at the Rosary-Procession.† 5. On all the feasts of the Blessed Virgin, particularly that of the Rosary, and all days whereon is celebrated one of the Mysteries of the Rosary, the conditions being, as before, Communion and visit to a church or chapel of the Rosary. This Indulgence begins at First Vespers. 6. On Easter Sunday, the feasts of the Ascension, Pentecost, Corpus Christi, Christmas-day, the feast of the Patron of the Church, and on the Sunday within the Octave of the Nativity of the Blessed Virgin (Confession, Communion, and visitation of a chapel of the Rosary). 7. On any two

---

\* This Indulgence is available on the Sunday or festival subsequent to the enrolment.

† Invalids, servants, all who cannot take part in the procession, may obtain the Indulgence by reciting a third part of the Rosary, if, contrite of heart, they desire to Confess and Communicate as soon as possible. The same individuals are dispensed from visiting a church of the Confraternity on the days on which are celebrated the Mysteries of the Rosary; they can gain it by communicating and reciting the Chaplet.

Fridays during Lent, at the free choice of associates
8. *In articulo mortis.*

II. *Partial Ones:* 300 days, for visiting the sick or accompanying the dead to the grave; 100 days *for each visit* to a chapel of the Rosary; 140 days *as often as* a person induces others to say the Rosary; 100 days whenever one assists at the chanting of the *Salve Regina,* after Complin; 60 days for every work of piety or charity, &c. A.

Associates may likewise acquire the plenary and partial Indulgences of the Roman Stations, by visiting five altars of the Church of the Rosary, or, if there be not five altars in it, by repeating the visit five times to the same altar in the church, on the days marked by the Roman Missal. Moreover, the altar of the Rosary is *privileged* for all aggregated Priests saying Mass for a deceased member (Innoc. XI., *Nuper pro parte,* cited above). This favour being local and not personal, is not available where there is no altar of the Rosary.

As a general rule, the members of the Rosary get the Director of the Confraternity to bless for them a wax taper, which they carefully preserve in their houses, and which is put into their hands in their last moments. It is thought that, if they die holding this in their hands, they acquire a plenary Indulgence.*

---

* See a little book published at Rome, under the title: *Il Rosario di Maria Santissima;* it may be procured from the Dominican Fathers of the monastery of the Minerva at Rome.

N. B.—All the Faithful, even non-associates, can gain a plenary Indulgence by approaching the Sacraments and visiting a chapel of the Rosary on the Feasts of Easter, Pentecost, Trinity Sunday, Corpus Christi, and all the Sundays of Lent; also the first Sunday of October, and the days on which are held the feasts of those saints belonging to the Order of St. Dominick.

By a Decree of May 12, 1851, Pope Pius IX. confirmed all the Indulgences accorded by his predecessors, as well to the associates of the Rosary as to the simple faithful.

*The Perpetual Rosary.*—It is supposed that the Society of the *Perpetual Rosary* was founded at Bologna, in the beginning of the seventeenth century, by a Religious of the Order of Friars Preachers. The object is to render to the Mother of God an uninterrupted homage, by having the Rosary recited at each successive hour of the day and night. The Sodality was almost totally abolished in France by the great Revolution; but the zeal and piety of the Bishops and Dominicans have again revived it. At present it numbers thousands amongst its ranks.

Pope Pius IX., by a Brief, dated April 12, 1867, has not alone accorded Indulgences to, but even applauded the modern organization of, this time-honored devotion. One of the principal Indulgences is the plenary one granted to all members of the Association the day they recite the Rosary at the hour assigned to them in each month, under the ordinary conditions of Confession, Communion, visitation of a church, and prayers for the general intentions. A. A copy of the Brief was handed into the holy Congregation of Indulgences, April 13, 1867.

### 91. CONGREGATIONS OF THE BLESSED VIRGIN.

The Congregations of the Blessed Virgin owe their origin to a young Belgian Religious of the Society of Jesus, a professor of grammar in the Roman college.* In 1563, he began to assemble the most fervent of his pupils, particularly on Sundays and Fes-

---

* His name was John Leo, a native of Liege, in Belgium. Some writers style him John Leo Flammingue. The Italian word *Flamingo*, Flamand, led them to this mistake. His family's name was *Leon* (Joannes Leonius, Leodiensis).

tivals, for the purpose of having them pray in a body, to edify them by some pious reading, and stimulate them to honour and serve the Queen of Heaven, especially by imitating her virtues and frequenting the Sacraments. Other students afterwards joined them, so that very soon they grew in strength, and became, in the above-named college, real schools of edification and virtue. At the instance of Father Claude Aquaviva, General of the Jesuits, Pope Gregory XIII., of glorious memory, approved of these assemblies by his Bull, *Omnipotentis Dei*, Dec. 5, 1584, created them into a Congregation under the title of the Annunciation, and enriched them with Indulgences, imparting, at the same time, to the Superior of the Jesuits power to establish similar Congregations in all other colleges subject to his rule, and to affiliate them to the Mother-congregation of the R. College.

Some years later, Sixtus V., subsequently also Clem. VIII., and Greg. XV. extended the favours and prerogatives conferred by Gregory XIII. on the Sodality of Scholars, to every other pious Congregation founded in churches, seminaries, and houses belonging to the Jesuits.

Bened. XIV., in like manner, by his golden Bull, *Gloriosæ Dominæ*, Sept. 27, 1748, added fresh graces to those of his predecessors, complimenting the Congregations in most flattering eulogistic terms." It is incredible," writes the great Pontiff, "all the advantages that have flowed from this pious and laudable institution to men of every rank." He was pleased then to enumerate them. In fine, Leo XII., by a Brief, dated May 17, 1824, deigned to restore to the Jesuit Order, re-established 1814 by the immortal Pius VII., the former rights vested in it by the Holy See in relation to these Congregations of Mary, and to secure to the Sodalities themselves their ancient privileges. Much more, by a special Rescript, bearing date March 7, 1825, he vouchsafed to permit the General of the Jesuits to aggregate to the Congregation at Rome, called the *Prima Primaria*, all other Congregations of men or women, boys or girls, everywhere canonically erected, as well those placed under the direction of the Fathers of the Institute as those not so committed, thus enabling them to share in the Indulgences and faculties of the Mother-congregation.

Such is the importance attached by the Vicars of Jesus Christ to this pious Institution for the strengthening and increase of faith and piety, and for the reformation and maintenance of morals! Besides, our Blessed Lady has on a thousand occasions testified how agreeable these Associations are to Her, inasmuch as she has often miraculously protected them, in all places, and at all times. Who is not aware of the immense good which Confraternities effect in seminaries and houses of education? How appropriately then does St. Bernardin apply to Congregations what the great St. Bernard said of monasteries!

" 1. There a man lives more holily.
2. He falls into sin less frequently.
3. When he falls, it is less grievously,
4. He rises more easily,
5. Walks more cautiously,
6. And reposes more tranquilly.
7. There he is more copiously bedewed with showers of grace and favours from Heaven.

8. There he satisfies Divine Justice, and avoids Purgatory with more facility.

9. There he expires with greater confidence and resignation.

10. Thus, in fine, he is crowned more gloriously in the celestial mansions.

Behold the Decalogue of our Lady's Congregation, the ten prerogatives which she bestows on all those who faithfully fulfil the promises made by them at their entrance into these pious Associations."\*

This is accounted for by the good works practised by the faithful clients of Mary in Her Sodalities; they are mentioned by Father Binet in the eleventh chapter. They learn there to observe the commandments of God; to live well and die happily; to familiarize themselves with the means of gaining paradise; to merit, by slight services, the friendship of Mary, to the end that their names may be registered in the Book of Life; moreover, to tender mutual succour to one another in sickness, and consolation in afflictions; to exercise also all sorts of works of mercy, whether spiritual or corporal; they reciprocally assist one another by pious prayers; they read good books, and hear devout lectures, &c., so that their life and the conduct of their families are regulated by divine maxims.

This is not all. There one is associated with a multitude of persons renowned for rank and virtue; the members have only one heart and one soul, linked together by the strong tie of true charity; they love one another like brothers; those that are strong sustain the weak; and, under the maternal patronage

---

\* *Le Chef d'œuvre de Dieu*, or *Les Souveraines perfections de la Sainte Vierge sa Mère*, by F. P. Etienne Binet, S. J., 3rd Part, ch. XI.

of holy Mary, all hope to arrive at the happy abode offered to Her children. In one word, a true associate of a Congregation of Mary shall never be damned.

The Congregations have a spiritual director, prefect, assistants, secretaries, and other dignitaries or officers. The experience of three hundred years clearly evinces the wisdom of their regulations, which may be found at the commencement of most books or manuals published for the use of aggregated clients. It is noticeable, however, that the election or nomination of officers or dignitaries, so necessary for the well-being and prosperity of a Congregation, is not essential when viewed in connection with the validity of its erection and the obtaining of Indulgences. Subjoined are the favours accorded to the *Prima Primaria*, in which all other Congregations affiliated thereto have a participation.

I. *Plenary Indulgences.*—1. On the day of reception or consecration to Mary, confession and communion being supposed. 2. Once a week, the day of the meeting of the associates, by approaching the Sacraments, visiting a church or chapel of the congregation, and praying there for the intention of the Holy Father. Should the meetings be held in the evening, the Indulgence may be obtained by Communicating on the ensuing morning. 3. The two days of the principal and secondary feasts of the congregation, even though these two feasts may, *de licentia ordinarii*, be transferred to some other days. These two Indulgences of the two Patron-feasts of the Congregation may be gained by persons who are not members, if they comply with the conditions, Confession, Communion, visit to a chapel of the Congregation, and prayers for the Pope's intention. 4. On the day of Communion, after having made a general confession or review of one's past life, once or twice a year. 5. On the festivals of Christmas, the Ascension of our Lord, the Annunciation, Assumption, Nativity, and Conception of the Blessed Virgin, on the above-named conditions. 6. At the hour of death. 7. On the day of a Communion received at the time of grievous illness. This Indulgence is applied to sick members by the Priest who acts as Director, and who should have previously once obtained the sanction of the Ordinary. After a brief pious exhortation he causes the invalid to recite three Paters and Aves in presence of an image of the crucifix. The Indulgence is attainable as often as the Blessed Eucharist is carried to the individual in the course of the sickness.

II. *Partial Indulgences.*—Seven years, for accompanying a deceased person to the grave—*also*, by praying for one in agony, or for one whose death is announced by the tolling of a bell; the same, for being present at some pious assembly, holy services, or a sermon; for hearing Mass on working days; for examen of conscience in the evening before retiring to rest; for visiting the poor, the sick, or the imprisoned, and for reconciling enemies. A.

Associates can, moreover, partake of the Indulgences of the Stations at Rome, by visiting, on the days specified in the Missal, either a church of the Congregation or some other, and there reciting seven *Paters* and *Aves*. Again, the altar of the Congregation is privileged, that is, it has a plenary Indulgence annexed to it at all Masses said there for a deceased member by what Priest soever. Priests also of the Congregation enjoy the favour of a *personal* privileged altar, wherever they offer the Holy Sacrifice in behalf of a departed client.

There are various other privileges vouchsafed to the Congregations of Mary, which may be seen in the printed sheet accompanying the diploma of affiliation.

*Remarks relative to these Congregations.*—1. The mode of reception is indicated in the rules of the Associates. 2. The affiliated, on leaving places of education or the respective parishes, do not on that account cease to belong to the Congregation. Hence they can always acquire the Indulgence, wherever they chance to be, provided they satisfy the conditions. And, instead of visiting a church of the Congregation, they are allowed to pay a visit to a chapel in the locality where they may be situated. 3. The course to be adopted to obtain affiliation to the *Prima Primaria* is this: assuming that the Congregation to be aggregated is canonically erected—that is to say, recognised and approved by the Bishop—the next thing to be done is, to write to the Very Rev. Father Superior of the Jesuits, or to his Secretary. The petition ought to specify the class of persons composing the Congregation—for example, to say whether it is of both sexes, or of men only, or women, young persons, &c.* It should likewise state the titular name or Feast. The Society must of necessity be dedicated to the honour of some mystery or title of our Blessed Lady. But it may furthermore have a secondary Patron or title, as of the

---

* Within the past few years there has been organised at Rome, in the Basilica of St. Agnes—outside the walls—an Archconfraternity of the *Children of Mary*, under the patronage of the youthful Virgin Martyr. Sodalities or Confraternities of young females—*Children of Mary*—are at liberty to affiliate themselves to it, and thus to participate in the Indulgences with which it has been enriched by his Holiness Pius IX.

Angels, St. Joseph, St. Aloysius Gonzaga, St. Anne, &c. Lastly, it ought to indicate the particular church or chapel, the town and diocese, where it is established. It would be well also to translate into the vernacular and hang up in the chapel of the Congregation a summary of the Indulgences and privileges forwarded from Rome.

### 92. ARCHCONFRATERNITY OF THE HOLY AND IMMACULATE HEART OF MARY FOR THE CONVERSION OF SINNERS.

The whole world is aware of the origin of this wonderful Institution, its admirable progress, and the prodigies of grace and conversion constantly effected by it. Just take a glance at a little work entitled: " *Manual of Instructions and Prayers for the use of Members of the most Holy and Immaculate Heart of Mary, established in the parish Church of Notre Dame des Victoires, Paris,*" by the Abbé Desgenettes, and at the " *Annals of the Archconfraternity.*" Who will not admire there the love of Mary's Heart towards France and towards all the souls purchased by the Precious Blood of Her Divine Son? Who will not feel his heart always more and more inflamed with love and confidence in Her whom the Church has aptly designated *the Refuge of Sinners, Comfortress of the Afflicted and Help of Christians?*

Having been approved of in 1836 by Mgr. de Quelen, of ever blessed memory, the association was raised to the rank of an Archconfraternity by His Holiness Gregory XVI. (Brief, April 27, 1838), and endowed with the right of everywhere aggregating to itself other Congregations of the same kind and title, consequently, too, of communicating its graces and Indulgences to them. Since that period it has spread through all parts of Christendom, carrying with it its numerous benedictions.

A person becomes a member of it by having his name inscribed in the Register of the Confraternity which he wishes to join, and which we suppose to have been canonically erected and associated to the Archconfraternity of Notre Dame des Victoires. Each client recites daily a Hail Mary for the intentions of the Archconfraternity, but the Indulgences may be acquired without reciting it (Decision of May 12, 1843). On the day of admission, each new member is presented with a *Miraculous Medal*, which he is recommended to carry always about him with piety, repeating, from time to time, the ejaculation engraved on it "O Mary, conceived without sin, pray for us who have recourse to thee." It is moreover desirable that they should assist at the exercises and go to Communion on the feasts of the Archconfraternity.

### *List of Indulgences.*

*Plenary:* 1. The day of admission, Confession and Communion supposed on the occasion. 2. On the Sunday immediately preceding Septuagesima (Confession and Communion). 3. On the feasts of the Circumcision of Our Lord, the Purification, Annunciation, Nativity, Assumption, Conception, and Dolors of the Blessed Virgin, of the Conversion of St. Paul and St. Magdelene (same conditions).

4. Another plenary, once a year, on the anniversary of each one's baptism, to all associates who daily recite the Hail Mary for the conversion of sinners (the Sacraments to be received).

5. At the hour of death, to members who shall have Communicated, or who, being incapable of doing that, devoutly invoke the Sacred Name of Jesus orally, or at least in heart (Greg. XVI., Brief, *In Sublimi*, April 24, 1838).

6. A plenary Indulgence, applicable to the souls in Purgatory, and attainable twice a month, on days chosen by clients themselves. In addition to Confession and Communion, it is requisite to visit on those days some church or public oratory, and pray there for a time according to the intention of his Holiness. The sick and infirm may obtain these Indulgences, by Communicating and performing some pious works enjoined by their Confessor (Greg. XVI., Rescript of Feb. 4, 1841).

7. On the feasts of St. Joseph, St. John Baptist, and St. John Evangelist (Confession and Communion) (Pius IX., Brief, Dec. 9, 1847).

8. By another Brief of the same date, Pope Pius IX. accorded a plenary Indulgence to all strangers at Paris, who receive Holy Communion in the Church of Notre Dame des Victoires.

*Partial Ones:* 500 days every Saturday of the year, to all associates and others who, in the church of the Archconfraternity, piously assist at the Mass celebrated on those days in honour of the Most Holy and Immaculate Heart of Mary, and pray there for the conversion of sinners; also 500 days for assisting at the public services and prayers offered in the church of the Archconfraternity, or in a church belonging to a Confraternity affiliated to it, for the conversion of sinners (Greg. XVI., Briefs of April 24, 1838, and Nov. 21, 1845).

*Observe:* 1. The Communion prescribed for the above-named Indulgences need not be received in the church of the Confraternity, except, of course, in the case of the strangers mentioned in No. 8. 2. On the first Saturday of each month the adorable Sacrifice is offered at Notre Dame des Victoires for deceased members. 3. At every meeting prayers are said for the conversion of sinners specially recommended. 4. When a person desires to associate to the Archconfraternity at Paris any given Congregation having the same name and object, namely, to obtain, through the mediation of the Most Holy Heart of Mary, the conversion of sinners, application is to be made to the Parish Priest of Notre Dame des Victoires. It should first premise that the Confraternity has been canonically erected by the Diocesan, and that the rules have been approved by him. With the petition addressed to Paris must be sent a copy of the statutes approved by the Ordinary.

### 93. ARCHCONFRATERNITY TO REPAIR BLASPHEMIES AND VIOLATIONS OF THE SUNDAY.

It was established at St. Martin de la Noue, near St. Digier, diocese of Langres, by a Brief of Pius IX., dated July 30, 1847, with power to aggregate to itself all other Associations of a similar title. The Holy Father himself desired that his own name should be the first on the register of the associates. Many dioceses in France have eagerly embraced it.

The first number of its Annals gives an account of its rules, its progress, and the particular favours bestowed on it. References to be addressed to the Parish Priest of St. Martin de la Noue, to procure all necessary instruction.*

### 94. CONFRATERNITY OF THE BONA MORS.

Its object is to prepare us for a happy death. Cemented together by charity, prayer, and the practice of good works, its associates frequently implore for one another the gift of perseverance in virtue, and consequently, too, the most precious of all graces, that of dying in the friendship of God. It was established under the title and invocation of Jesus expiring on the cross, and of Our Lady of Dolors, and placed under the protection of St. Joseph.

Its first founder was the Rev. F. Vincent Caraffa, seventh General of the Society of Jesus. It was

---

* In Belgium there is another Association *for the extirpation of blasphemy*, whose members pledge themselves never to blaspheme, to exert their influence in preventing others from doing so, and to say whenever they hear blasphemies uttered: "*May the holy name of God be blessed!*" or "*Praised be Jesus Christ!*"

A confraternity of this kind also has been founded at Rome, in the Oratory of Caravita. By a Brief of Aug. 8, 1843, Greg. XVI. permitted like Associations, whose object should be the extirpation of blasphemies and curses, to be formed all over the Globe—*ubique instituendæ*—with the sanction of the Bishop, especially at the time of Missions.

The Indulgences granted to its members are: 1. A plenary Indulgence once a month, by approaching the Sacraments and praying for the intention of his Holiness. 2. At the hour of death. 3. Two hundred days when they do pious works prescribed by the Rule. It appertains to the Ordinary to give or approve of that rule.

Finally there exists at Puy, an *Archconfraternity for the observance of Sundays and Festivals*. It was erected in the Church of St. Laurence by a Brief of Pius IX., June 9, 1848.

established at Rome in the Church *del Gesu*, in 1638 Pope Innocent X. confirmed it by his Apostolic authority; and his successors, Alex. VII., Innoc. XII., Bened. XIII., enriched it with Indulgences. In 1821, it was again confirmed by Pius VII., and, in 1827, Leo. XII. accorded to the General of the Jesuits the faculty of affiliating to the Mother-Congregation all other Congregations of the *Bona Mors* already established, or to be hereafter established, throughout the Catholic World, and of thereby making them partakers of the spiritual favours of the *Primaria*. The way to obtain a Diploma of affiliation is analogous to that indicated for the Confraternities of Mary.

*Chief Indulgences.*—*Plenary:* 1. The day of reception or enrolment in the Confraternity, by going to Communion. 2. At the hour of death. 3. Christmas-day, Easter Sunday, feasts of the Ascension, Epiphany, Pentecost, the Holy Trinity, Corpus Christi; also on the five primary feasts of the Blessed Virgin, the Purification, Annunciation, Assumption, Nativity, and Immaculate Conception; on those of St. Joseph, All Saints, and of each of the Apostles, provided Communion be received in a church of the Confraternity, or, if this be not possible, in any other church, and prayers offered there for concord amongst Christian princes, the exaltation of holy church, &c. 4. On a Friday or Sunday in each month, selected by the associates, if however there is a pious custom of exposing the Blessed Sacrament on each of these Fridays or Sundays, it is necessary to approach the Sacred Banquet on that day.

*Partial Indulgences:* 1. Seven years and as many

Quarantines for all members devoutly assisting at the Exposition of the Blessed Sacrament, when it takes place on the Fridays or Sundays noted above, and praying for the wants of the Church. 2. An Indulgence of one year to be acquired by associates *as often as* they perform the following works of piety:—to attend a funeral; to be present at the meetings, public functions, or instructions; to hear Mass on week days; nightly examen of conscience; visitation of the sick poor, of those in hospitals, in prison, &c. A.

Moreover, the *Indulgences of the Roman Stations*, by visiting a church of the Congregation, or a church or chapel of the district where a person may be, are attainable on the days defined in the Missal, and by saying there Seven *Paters* and *Aves*.

Bened. XIV. vouchsafed to grant a plenary Indulgence to associates who devote at least a day of each month to the *preparation for death*. In addition to Confession and Communion, they should pay a visit to the church or chapel of the house in which they make their short retreat on the occasion, and there pray for the usual intention. It is not necessary that it be gone through in a house belonging to the Jesuits.

"One of the great advantages of this Sodality in a parish is, that the members are called on to discharge towards the sick and feeble the ministry of angels of peace, good counsel, and devout assistance; animating them with sentiments of faith and confidence in God; exhorting them to unite their sufferings to those of Jesus Christ, and to receive the Sacraments; and lending their own kind services, worthily to prepare the habitation of the sick for that purpose.*

### 95. THE HOLY SLAVERY OF THE MOTHER OF GOD.

I am not aware that the devotion and Confraternity of *the Holy Slavery of the Mother of God* has ever been approved by the Roman Pontiffs, or enriched with Indulgences. There is a little pamphlet called, "*Devotion au Saint Esclavage de la Mere de Dieu, servant d'un grand secours pour faire son salut,*" wherein is cited Pope Urban VII. as having accorded some Indulgences to these *Captives of the Blessed Virgin,* by his Bull commencing: *Cum sicut accepmius.* But, if I am not mistaken, that Pope, who succeeded Sixtus V., Sept. 15, 1590, and who died on the 27th of the same month, twelve days after his election, published only one Constitution—*Cum dilectus*—bearing date, Sept. 20, 1590, in which there is question of the appointment of Cardinal Pinelli to the presidency of a Roman Congregation. The other Pontiffs adduced in that little work, either have said nothing in favour of such a devotion, or were raised to the Pontificate after the Decree which condemns the Sodality.†

However it may have been in times gone by, a formal Decree of the Congregation of the Holy Office has strictly proscribed and abolished the Confraternities of the Slaves of the Mother of God, together with their external distinctive symbols, medals, chains, &c. The Decree of proscription is dated July

---

\* *Manuel des Principales Devotions et Confreries*, by the Abbe Giraud, p. 180.

† Clement XII., for instance, who is quoted as having favoured them with *great Indulgences*, did not put on the tiara until 1730, whereas Clem. X. had already condemned the Society in 1673.

5, 1673, under Clem. X.\* It appears that a number of abuses had slipped into the devotion. To be convinced on the subject, it suffices to open the *Index Librorum Prohibitorum*, edited by order of Greg. XVI., and printed at Rome in 1841, page xlv. of the Prolegomena No. 3. It declares "that images and medals belonging to Confraternities of the Slaves of the Mother of God, on which may be engraved, painted, or represented some of the associates in chains, are forbidden; so, too, are all books containing the rules of these Confraternities. The Sodalities themselves which distribute chains to the associates, that they might wear them on their arms or round the neck, as a pledge of their promises, are likewise condemned and extinguished. And all Societies observing the rites or usages peculiar to that Slavery, must reject them immediately" (Decree of the Sacred Congregation of Indulgences, Dec. 18, 1821).†

They bring forward a Rescript of Greg. XVI., of Feb. 22, 1833, imparting to Fr. Francis Bernard, Prior of Notre Dame de la Trappe, at Aiguebelle, in the diocese of Valence, power to erect a Confraternity of the Holy Slavery of Mary, with several Indulgences. If the Rescript be authentic, they are

---

\* The Sacred Congregation has condemned this *abuse*, otherwise prohibited in different places by special edicts—"Usum catenularum districte interdicit, sub pœnis gravibus suorum Ordinariorum arbitrio intligendis. Societates quocumque nomine appellentur, quarum institutum in eo mancipatu præcipue versatur, damnat et extinguit; præc.pit ut catenulas statim rejiciant.

† A Brief of Clem. X., *Pastoralis Officii*, Dec. 15, 1675, abolishes in like manner certain Confraternities instituted under the invocation *of the Blessed Sacrament, the Immaculate Blessed Virgin Mary and St. Joseph*, bearing the title, "Flock of the Good Shepherd," which too make use of chains and other sensible signs at variance with the doctrine and practice of the Church. The same Pope condemns all images, books, papers, &c. relative to such associations, interdicting for ever both the use and reading of them.

mistaken as to the signification attached by our Holy Father the Pope to the Latin words: *Sub invocatione servorum B. M. Virginis,* or to the Italian, *Confraternita dei Servi di Maria.* For Gregory intended to approve a Confraternity styled "the Servants of Mary," *Servi di Maria,* and not "Slaves of Mary," *Schiavi di Maria,* which is quite different from the Confraternity or devotion of the Slavery of Our Lady, which he has even reprobated. Hence it is evident that, if the Society in question, or others of a like kind, assume the title of Slavery or Slaves, and distribute to the associates any chains to be borne by them as a token of their Consecration to the Mother of God, they will be acting in opposition to the wishes and ordinances of the Church.

### 96. ASSOCIATION OF THE "*Perpetual Cultus*" OF ST. JOSEPH.

It is very desirable that this pious Association should be established in every parish; it is a fresh fountain of blessings, even temporal ones, poured out upon families and upon all the faithful—*Ite ad Joseph*—Go to Joseph (Gen. xli. 55). Confidence in his powerful protection has never yet been frustrated. Three hundred and sixty-five persons suffice to constitute this society of clients of the Glorious Spouse of Mary, whose aim is to offer him a special tribute of perpetual homage; just as many as are the days of the year. The names of the postulants having been inscribed in a register kept for that purpose, each receives a ticket or card containing the following inscription:—

"With a view of rendering special homage to St.

Joseph, the associate of the *perpetual cultus* dedicates to him the —— day of the month of —— in each year. He will sympathize in the afflictions experienced by this great Saint, which were occasioned by our sins. For this reason, he will most diligently and fervently perform the subjoined practices:

"1. To approach the Sacraments on that day, and, if unable to do so, to supplement the omission by an act of contrition and a spiritual communion.

"2. To assist at Mass with devotion, in memory of the Presentation of the Child Jesus in the Temple.

"3. To make at least a quarter of an hour's meditation on the sufferings and afflictions of St Joseph.

"4. To keep recollected and to entertain some pious thoughts regarding him throughout the day.

"5. To perform some act of mortification in his honour, or some spiritual or corporal work of mercy.

"6. To recite seven *Paters*, *Aves*, and *Glorias*, in honour of his dolors and his joys.

"7. To end the day by a visit to the Blessed Sacrament, and an offering of the heart to that holy Patriarch.

"*Whoever, during life, consoles St. Joseph, shall be comforted by him at the hour of death.*"

*Plenary Indulgences:* 1. On the day of enrolment. 2. The day chosen for the exercise of the *perpetual homage*, once a year, or even once a month. 3. *In articulo Mortis.* 4. On the feasts of St. Joseph viz.: the 19th of March; the feast of his Patronage, the third Sunday after Easter; and Jan. 23, that of his Espousal. 5. On the feasts of the Purification, Annunciation, Assumption, Nativity, and Immaculate Conception of the Blessed Virgin. 6. More over, by a Brief of July 5, 1861, Pius IX. added a plenary Indulgence for a day in each month (under the ordinary conditions).

*A Partial Indulgence* of seven years and seven Quarantines every day on which any of the above-named works may be fulfilled. A. (Pius IX., Rescript Jan. 20, 1856, in the Secretary's office of the Sacred Congregation of the Propaganda.)

Note.—That by multiplying the number of associates, the homages rendered to St. Joseph shall be multiplied in the same proportion. And surely, like Jesus and Mary, Joseph will never allow himself to be surpassed in generosity.

### 97. EJACULATORY PRAYER TO ST. JOSEPH.

Alme Joseph, dux Noster, nos et sanctam Ecclesiam protege.

Good Joseph, our guide, protect us and the holy Church.

By a Brief of Jan. 27, 1863, Pope Pius IX. granted 50 days' Indulgence to associates of the *Cultus perpetuus* of St. Joseph, *as often as* they piously recite this short ejaculation in what language soever.

### 98. APOSTLESHIP OF PRAYER.

To have an adequate idea of this Association, which has already produced such an abundance of happy results for the salvation of souls, and in favour of which his Holiness Pius IX. has unlocked the treasures of the Church, it would be necessary to peruse "The Little Manual of the Apostleship of

Prayer."* This volume, the fruit of piety and zeal, was compiled with method and precision. Having first explained the end, spirit, and advantages of the Association, it then clearly unfolds its nature and organization; it afterwards gives in detail the various Indulgences with which it has been enriched, and proposes a certain number of prayers and religious exercises suitable for members and others devoted to the Sacred Heart of Jesus.

"To take part in the work of the Apostleship of Prayer, is, in the words of the Manual, to take part in the interior life, the Divine Apostleship of the Sacred Heart of Jesus and of the Immaculate Heart of Mary. It is to appropriate to oneself all the intentions of these Divine Hearts, and to pray with them for all the interests forming the object of their supplications—for the extension of the Divine glory, conversion of sinners, advancement of the righteous, and triumph of the Church."

*Indulgences*—I. *Plenary:* 1. The day of admission. 2. On the feast of the Sacred Heart. 3. Feast of the Immaculate Conception. 4. A Friday in each month, and another day of the month, at a person's choice, on condition of Confession, Communion, and visit to a church wherein prayers are to be offered for the Pope's design (Pius IX., Brief of Feb. 26, 1861). 5. Furthermore, the Apostleship of Prayer having been aggregated to the Archconfraternity of the Sacred Heart established at Rome, in the church of St. Mary *della pace*, associates can, in virtue of this title of affiliation, participate in all the plenary In-

---

* It may be procured from Paris, M. Regis Ruffet, Rue Saint Sulpice, 38; or at Lyons, Maison Perisse, Rue Mercière 49.

dulgences annexed thereto (see p. 137, No. 86), (Diploma April 8, 1861). A.

*Partial ones:* 1. An Indulgence of 100 days for all the prayers and good works that members offer according to the recommendations made by the Director of the Association at the commencement of each month. A.

2. All the partial Indulgences granted to associates of the Sacred Heart. The "Little Manual" specifies some other Indulgences available to promoters equally with associates of the Work of the Apostleship.

Again, by a letter of Jan. 3, 1861, the Very Rev. F. General of the Jesuits has accorded to the members of the association a special participation in the merits of the Religious of his Order. A like favour has been extended to them by the Superior-general of the Society of Mary, of the two Congregations of the Sacred Heart (called *de Picpus*), of the Clerics Regular Theatine, and of the Congregation of La Trappe.

Letters of aggregation to the Work are to be procured from the Director, who resides at Vals, pres-le-Puy (Haute-Loire).

### 99. THE LIVING ROSARY.

Everybody knows in what consists the Association of the Living Rosary. Fifteen persons united together, distribute amongst themselves the fifteen Mysteries of the Rosary every month. Each of them undertakes to recite daily, during that term, one decade, meditating on the particular Mystery which may have fallen to his lot. The Institution is admirably organized, and hence, in most countries, it has powerfully contributed to add fresh vigour to faith and piety. Gregory XVI., by two Briefs of Jan. 27, and Feb. 2, 1831, approved of it, and accorded to the faithful joined in it the ensuing Indulgences:—

1. A plenary Indulgence the first feast after their admission, the conditions being Confession, and Communion; it is applicable to the Departed.

2. The Indulgences attached by the Roman Pontiffs to the recitation of the Rosary.

3. An Indulgence of 100 days every time that, on working days, a person recites the part of the Rosary assigned to him, according to the arrangements of the Society. 4. Seven years and seven Quarantines to those who do so every Sunday of the year and on Festivals, including even those on which the hearing of Mass is not of obligation, and during the Octaves of Christmas, Easter, Corpus Christi, Pentecost, the Assumption, Nativity, and Conception of the Blessed Virgin.

5. A plenary Indulgence, applicable to the Dead, on the solemnities of Christmas, the Epiphany, Circumcision, Easter, Ascension, Corpus Christi, Whitsuntide, and on that of the most Holy Trinity, as also on all festivals of the Blessed Virgin, including even the lesser ones; on the feast of the Holy Apostles Peter and Paul, All Saints' Day, and the third Sunday of every month.

To be entitled to these Indulgences, associates ought to have daily recited, at least for the space of a month, unless prevented by some legitimate impediment, the part of the Rosary assigned to them. They must furthermore receive the Sacraments, and offer some prayers in a church. If a legitimate reason prevents this visit to the Church, some other work of piety may be substituted for it by the Confessor.

Here, likewise, let me remark, that it is not true that Pius IX. has retracted the spiritual favours dispensed by his predecessors to the members of the Living Rosary. The Brief of Greg. XVI. has been, on the contrary, registered (Sept. 30, 1862) in the *Segretaria* of the Sacred Congregation of Indulgences.

### 100. ARCHCONFRATERNITY OF THE CORD OF ST. FRANCIS OF ASSISIUM.*

The Sacred Congregation has ranked as *apocryphal* certain Indulgences said to have been granted by Leo X. to persons wearing the Cord of St. Francis. But these are not the Indulgences we wish to recommend in the present instance, whose authenticity has been sealed by the very same Congregation (Appendix to the collection of Decrees, N. 1, p. 3).

After having been called to the Throne from the Order of Friars Minor, Pope Sixtus V. instituted the Archconfraternity of the Cord of St. Francis in the Church of the *Sacro-Convento*, at Assisium, where repose the remains of the Seraphic Patriarch (Constit., *Ex Supernæ*, Nov. 19, 1585). Two years later, Aug. 29, 1587, the same Pope issued another Bull in behalf of the Archconfraternity, and endowed it with a variety of privileges.

Several other Pontiffs, e. g. Clem. VIII. Paul V., Greg. XV., confirmed the concessions of Sixtus V. In fine, Bened. XIII., by a Brief, *Sacrosancti*, Sept. 30, 1724, authorised the Superior-General of the

---

* In 1861, was published a little work under that title; it may be had at Lyons, Maison Perisse, Rue Mercière, 59; or Paris, M. Regis Ruffet, Rue St. Sulpice, 38.

Friars Minor Conventual, to erect in all places, *with the consent of the Ordinary*, the Confraternity of the Cord, with a communication thereto of the spiritual blessings of the Archconfraternity of Assisium. Prior to his entrance into the Third Order of St. Francis, the blessed Joseph Labre had received, at Assisium, the Cord of the Archconfraternity. The Diploma then delivered to him is still preserved at Rome.

The design of the Confraternity is to give special honor to the admirable St. Francis, to merit his patronage by entering into his spirit, and to obtain, by means of his powerful intercession, special graces for oneself, for one's friends, and for holy Church. Read also the advantages of the Association as given in the little treatise referred to.

Needless to remark that those wearing the Cord contract no obligation whatsoever under pain of sin; they carry it habitually round the loins, or at least about their person; the Indulgences would be suspended if it were laid aside. But in the event of its being lost, another, even unblessed, may be substituted in its stead. The first Cord is blessed and given by a Superior of the Order of Friars Minor, or by some Priest possessed of the requisite faculties.

To acquire the Indulgences, the conditions en joined by the R. Pontiffs must be complied with. The Indulgences are very numerous. There is, for in stance, a plenary Indulgence on the day of receiving the Cord, the day of the principal feast, *in articulo mortis*, &c. For a summary of these favours, see the little book cited above, p. 36, and following. Additionally, members of the Association share in all the spiritual fruits and Indulgences dispensed to the

Friars Minor as Religious. The same Work contains a list of the Indulgences available to the Tertians of St. Francis.

N.B.—There are also other Confraternities of the Cord. One of the most celebrated is that of the *Milice Angelique*, or the Cincture of St. Thomas Aquinas. Its aim is to preserve the golden treasure of purity, or to recover it, if it had been lost. The names are inscribed in a Register specially reserved for that purpose by the Rev. F. Dominicans. The Cord having been received from a Dominican, or other Priest empowered to give it, is constantly worn day and night, as specified. (See the small treatise: *Il Giglio della purita, del P. Lorenzo Scupoli.—Roma, tipografia Morini.*)\*

---

## ARTICLE VI.

### BLESSING OF DEVOTIONAL OBJECTS, CROSSES, CHAPLETS, STATUES, MEDALS, &C.,

#### With application of Apostolic Indulgences.

301. GENERAL OBSERVATIONS. APOSTOLIC INDULGENCES.

1. A simple blessing may be and is actually imparted to numberless things which cannot be at all Indulgenced, for instance, new houses, ships, vest-

---

\* A pious Union in honor of St. Joseph has been established at Rome, in the Parish Church of St. Roch. It was dignified with the rank of an Archconfraternity by Pius IX., who also enriched it with Indulgences. Every other Confraternity or Congregation of St. Joseph can be associated to this. The members are furnished with a cord blessed by the Director. Any Priest may get leave to bless the Cords of St. Joseph, by applying to the Sacred Congregation of Rites, which approved of the form to be used on such occasions (Sept. 19, 1859). See the supplement, N. 46.

ments, cords or cinctures, pictures and engravings, eggs of the silkworm, bread, fruits, candles, and persons themselves. The Ritual has peculiar formulas for the benediction of these various objects.

2. Whenever the Faithful present objects to be blessed by Priests, it would be well to act conformably to the recognised ceremonies of the Church, that is, to impart the blessing with a certain solemnity, in surplice and stole, with sprinkling of holy water at the conclusion.

3. Still the sign of the Cross made by the hand, with the intention of blessing and Indulgencing things capable of being thus enriched, is sufficient without any other formality (Decree of April 11, 1840). In truth this is the way the Pope Indulgences articles presented to him. Accordingly, persons should not be surprised, if a Priest, in a hurried moment, or when a surplice, stole, or holy water are not at hand, apply Indulgences to medals, crosses, &c., by simply making the sign of the Cross over them, and repeating by heart a short form of blessing. The Sacred Congregation of Rites (Decision Aug. 12, 1854) even *desires* that, when the Ritual may have no special form for a given object, the Priest merely make the sign of the Cross over the thing to be blessed, saying: *In Nomine Patris, et Filii, et Spiritus Sancti. Amen.* He then sprinkles it with holy water, without a lighted candle, or may altogether dispense with the holy water.\*

\* A Decree of the Sacred Congregation. (Jan. 7, 1843) says the same thing, no matter whether the Indult contain the clause ' *in forma Ecclesiæ consueta*,' or not. But these Decrees of April, 1840, and Jan., 1843, do not include Dominican Rosaries or Chaplets, nor the Chaplet of the Seven Dolors. Hence it is still necessary, in order to apply to these the Indulgences peculiar to them (i.e. the Dominican Indulgences. But no form is needed to attach the Apostolic or the Bridgetine Indulgences), to repeat the formula of blessing, and sprinkle them with holy water. Decree, Feb. 19, 1864, approved by Pius IX., the 11th of April following. *Translator*.

4. Engravings or paintings, crosses, statues, crucifixes, medals of *tin*, *lead*, or any other material that may be easily broken, injured or destroyed, as hollow-glass, plaster, &c., may be blessed, but not Indulgenced. Chaplets not being comprised in this enumeration, may be of tin, lead, iron or steel. This was decided by a Decree of Feb. 29, 1820.

5. But crucifixes, chaplets, &c., of ivory or wood may be Indulgenced.

6. So, too, may crucifixes, crosses, statues, and medals of iron, as also with much greater reason those of steel (Decree, May 14, 1853); in like manner, chaplets, &c., of coral, pearl, amber, enamel, alabaster, marble, crystal, provided the grains or berries be of *solid material* (Decree of Feb. 29, 1820).

7. Indulgences may be annexed to medals or small statues of canonized Saints alone, or of those at least enrolled in the R. Martyrology. Nevertheless they may be applied to medals having on the one side an image of a canonized Saint, and on the other that of a beatified person (Decree, Dec. 22, 1710).*

8. The mere breaking of the string or chain does not cause a chaplet to lose its Indulgences, because the grains alone are Indulgenced. The same holds in cases in which some of the berries are lost, provided the number be not rather considerable.

9. Should an Indulgenced object be given to another, after having been appropriated and used by oneself, it ceases to be Indulgenced. But it is allow-

---

* Still more: In Oct., 1868, the substitute of the Sacred Congregation of Indulgences directed me to state, that it is permitted to bless and Indulgence medals bearing the impress of a Saint on one surface, and on the other some illustrious personage, such as the Pope, Curé of Ars, &c. Thus, in drawings sometimes blessed for churches, we often see images of individuals who unquestionably are far from being beatified, But their chief figure is that of some Saint, and that suffices.

able to Indulgence several pious articles on the same occasion, and to distribute them to others, without prejudice to the Indulgences. Even in this case, the persons to whom they are distributed, may, prior to their using them or appropriating the Indulgences, give the objects to others. But the Indulgence stops there, and cannot proceed farther (Decree of Alex. VII., Feb. 6, 1637, and Decree of the Sacred Congregation of Indulgences Nov. 26, 1714).

10. Pursuant to the same Decree of Alex. VII., if a blessed object be lost, it cannot be replaced by another *at pleasure.*

11. Blessed articles cannot be lent to others, for the purpose of communicating the Indulgences attached to them; if this were done, the Indulgence would be lost both to the lender and him to whom it was lent. (*Ibid.*)

12. Neither can they be sold after having been blessed and Indulgenced (Decree, June 5, 1721). Hence shopkeepers or traders cannot contrive to have Indulgences attached to crucifixes, medals, chaplets, &c., and afterwards sell them, though they may charge only the ordinary price.

13. Again, persons should not buy a number of these objects, in order to get them Indulgenced, and then distribute them to others, requiring in their stead a sum equivalent to the one paid for them. For it is not certain that things given in this way retain their Indulgences; *not safe in practice*, was the reply of the Sacred Congregation of Indulgences to the Bishop of Bruges, June 31, 1837. Not only that, but, agreeably to a response made to the Vicar-General of the Archbishop of Rouen, Oct. 2, 1840, even indigent Priests are not at liberty, when dis-

tributing blessed or Indulgenced objects to the Faithful, to receive in return the amount laid out in purchasing them. It would be different, as we have said, if they were distributed *gratis*.\*

14. Moreover, no Indulgence is gained by making use of an Indulgenced object *found*, or *inherited*. But it may be Indulgenced again.

15. A ring adorned with ten knots or marks, which many would fain to substitute for chaplets, cannot be Indulgenced, conformably to a solution addressed to M. Bouvier by the Cardinal Prefect of the Congregation of Indulgences, in the name of Greg. XVI., July 23, 1836. At least it is necessary to have a special authorization from the Holy Father for that purpose.

16. In the case of an Indulgenced Crucifix, the Indulgence is attached to the figure of Our Lord, so that, the figure may be transferred from one cross to another, of whatever material, without interfering with the Indulgence (Decree, April 11, 1840).

17. The same crucifix may be enriched with several Indulgences—for example, with the Apostolic Indulgences, those of the *Bona Mors*, *Via Crucis*, &c., provided he who applies them has the requisite faculties.†

18. A person possessing a blessed crucifix, to which only the ordinary Indulgences are attached, can

---

\* It has been frequently communicated to me from Rome, that it is not allowable to exact a charge for blessed Cords of St. Joseph. They are to be given *gratis*, after having been blessed. Yet something may be received as alms, provided it be not required as a matter of obligation, whether direct or indirect. The same applies to all objects blessed beforehand.

† Hence it is needless for Missionaries to require, *even from the pulpit*, the faithful to procure two crucifixes, one for receiving the Indulgence of the Bona Mors, the other for those of the Via Crucis.

alone acquire the Indulgence at the hour of death. Therefore, with such a crucifix, this Indulgence cannot be indiscriminately applied to all dying persons, unless there be a special faculty, *in writing*, obtained to that effect from the Holy See, or at least unless the crucifix possess this indulgence privileged and *real.*\*

19. Mass offered at an altar on which there may be an Indulgenced crucifix or medal, or said by a Priest who carries about him one of those pious objects, does not, on that account, enjoy any special privilege (Bened. XIV., Aug. 9, 1752).

20. To gain the Indulgences, it is necessary for one to carry about him the blessed object, or, at any event, to have it in his possession. Moreover, the pious considerations or prayers assigned as conditions for sharing in the Indulgences, must be made either while carrying the articles, or, at least, when kept in one's room or other suitable place in the house, so that the prayers be recited before them.

21. *Apostolic Indulgences* are those which the Holy Father himself attaches to pious articles when blessing them. Sixtus V. was the first Pope who introduced this usage into the Church, about the close of the sixteenth century. On the occasion of re-building the Basilica of St. John of Lateran, done under his direction, there were found amongst the ruins of the old crumbled walls a great many medals of gold, bearing the impress of the cross. In distributing them, the Pope accorded multiplied Indulgences to all who may have had any of them in their possession.†  The Sovereign Pontiffs anterior to him,

---

\* See end of chap. vii., 1st Part.
† See the Constitution, *Laudemus viros* of Sixtus V., Dec. 1, 1587.

whenever they made presents of religious articles of gold, silver, bronze, &c., simply blessed them without annexing Indulgences to them.

The same Indulgences may be attached to pious objects by Priests commissioned to indulgence them, at least regularly speaking.* Here is a *Summary* of them. I have transcribed them word for word from the "Raccolta," p. 372.

*Indulgences annexed to Chaplets, Beads, Crucifixes, Statues, and Medals, blessed by His Holiness, or by one empowered to do so.*

1. A plenary Indulgence, on the following days, to everybody who, *at least once a week*, shall recite the Chaplet of Our Lord, or of the Blessed Virgin, or the Rosary, or the third part of it, or the Divine Office, or that of the Blessed Virgin, or of the Dead, or the Seven Penitential Psalms, or the Gradual Psalms; or who may be in the habit of teaching Catechism, or visiting prisoners, or the sick in hospital, or of helping the poor, of hearing Mass, or saying Mass, if the person be a Priest, *provided that*, truly contrite and having confessed to a Confessor approved by the Ordinary, they Communicate, and pray the same day for the extirpation of heresies and

* A Priest who has obtained from Rome power to Indulgence a fixed number of religious objects, for illustration, 3000 crosses, chaplets, medals, &c., can Indulgence only 3000 in all (Decree of May 29, 1841). For to be empowered to bless 3000 of each kind, the terms of the Brief or Rescript should expressly and formally convey it to him. Wherefore, lest he might exceed his power, it is highly important carefully to read over the grant or diploma of concession. But should he have got the faculty to bless and Indulgence chaplets, he is by that very fact deputed to bless and Indulgence rosaries—*rosaria et coronæ promiscue accipienda sunt* (Decree, Sept. 20, 1775).

schisms, for the propagation of the Catholic faith, for peace and concord amongst Christian princes, and for the other wants of the Holy Church:—Christmas Day, the Epiphany, Easter Sunday, Ascension Day, Pentecost; the Feasts of the Most Holy Trinity, Corpus Christi, the Conception, Nativity, Annunciation, Purification, and Assumption of the Blessed Virgin; the Feasts of St. John Baptist, of the Holy Apostles Peter and Paul, Andrew, James, John, Thomas, Philip and James, Bartholomew, Mathew, Simon and Jude, Matthias, of St. Joseph, Spouse of Mary, and the Feast of All Saints.

2. Whoever may perform the *same works* on the other feasts of Our Lord and the Blessed Virgin, shall gain, on each of these days, an Indulgence of *seven years and seven Quarantines;* and by doing them on *a Sunday or some other feast of* the year, an Indulgence of *five years and five Quarantines;* lastly, if accomplished on any other day in the year, an Indulgence of 100 days is obtained thereby.

3. Moreover, one accustomed to repeat, *at least once a week*, the Chaplet, or Rosary, or Office of the Blessed Virgin, or of the Dead, or Vespers, and at least one Nocturn with Lauds, or the Seven Penitential Psalms with the Litanies and Prayers subjoined, shall obtain an Indulgence of one hundred days.

4. Any person who, *In articulo mortis*, devoutly recommends his soul to God, and, conformably to the Instruction of Bened. XIV. (Constitution, *Pia Mater*, April 5, 1747), is ready to receive death with resignation from the hand of the Almighty, may reap the fruit of a plenary Indulgence, it being assumed that they are truly contrite, have confessed and commu-

nicated, or if unable to do so, invoked, *at least contrite*, the Holy Name of Jesus with the heart, if not with the lips.

5. Fifty days' Indulgence, each time, to him who, by prayer, prepares to say Mass, to receive Communion, or to recite the Divine Office or that of the Blessed Virgin.

6. All who visit the imprisoned, or the sick in hospital, relieving them by some work of charity, or who teach Catechism in a church, or at home to their own children, relatives, or domestics, may each time acquire an Indulgence of 200 days.

7. He who, at the sound of the bell of some church, shall repeat *the Angelus*, in the morning, mid-day, or evening; or not knowing it, a *Pater and Ave;* or in like manner shall say the *De profundis*, &c., when, an hour after nightfall, the signal-bell for the Dead is rung, or not knowing it, a *Pater and Ave,* may obtain 100 days' Indulgence.

8. One hundred days' Indulgence to those who, on Friday, shall devoutly meditate on the Passion and Death of Our Divine Redeemer, and say three *Paters and Aves.*

9. One who, having a sincere regret for his sins and a firm purpose of amendment, examines his conscience and repeats with devotion three *Paters* and *Aves* in honor of the Adorable Trinity, or says five *Paters* and *Aves* in memory of the five wounds of Jesus Christ, can gain a like Indulgence of 100 days.

10. Those who pray with devotion for the agonizing, or who say at least for them a Pater and Ave, shall gain an Indulgence of 50 days.

N.B — In virtue of a concession of the Sovereign Pontiff, all the above-named Indulgences may be acquired for oneself or applied to the Souls in Purgatory. His Holiness also wishes that these Indulgences should in no way derogate from others which the R. Pontiffs, his predecessors, may have attached to some of the works just specified.

## 102. CROSSES, ROSARIES, AND CHAPLETS PROCURED FROM THE HOLY LAND.

The Apostolic Indulgences enumerated in the foregoing number, may be acquired by the Faithful who possess a Cross, or Rosary, or Chaplet (there is no mention of any other pious object), obtained from Palestine, which may have touched the Holy Places and Sacred Relics (Innoc. XI., Brief *Unigeniti Dei Filii*, Jan. 28, 1688). This grant was confirmed by Innoc. XIII. (Decree, June 5, 1721). It is forbidden to sell Crosses, Rosaries, or Chaplets that have been consecrated, so to speak, by the touch of the Holy Places, or to exchange them for other articles, or to lend them with a view of communicating the Indulgences (Decrees of March 11, 1721, and Feb. 11, 1722).

In connection with this matter, it may be well to observe, that sometimes, with a sinister design, persons circulate amongst the people Chaplets and Crosses reported to have touched the Holy Places of Palestine, ascribing to them Indulgences which have no existence at all. Thus it is stated, in the scrap of paper accompanying these articles, "that for every grain in each of these Chaplets, there is granted an Indulgence of 300 days to the individual who recites it and to those who join in the recitation." " An Indulgence of 100 days as often as one of these crosses is kissed with faith." "As to the grains formed in the kernels of the eight Olives of Gethsemani, they have severally a 1,000 days' Indulgence."

Hence, if, in some exceptional case, the Pope may have thus accorded precious Indulgences to a number of these crosses or chaplets from Palestine, it will be requisite to have the Papal Indult conferring the favour publicly *recognised and authenticated*, which indeed is not always attended to. Generally speaking, all Indulgences dispensed in that way are apocryphal.

### 103. INDULGENCES OF A CHAPLET.

*General Observations.*

According to what has been stated in n. 101, chaplets can therefore be enriched with the Apostolical Indulgences.* They may also receive the Indulgences of the Dominican Rosary, together with those of St. Bridget's. This assertion harmonizes with a Rescript of Leo XII., 1823. In No. 91, I have specified the Indulgences attached to chaplets blessed by a Father of St. Dominick's Order, or by a Priest similarly empowered, and the conditions to be fulfilled to acquire them. I shall speak here of the Bridgetine chaplet or Rosary.

---

* Note, however, that Apostolic Indulgences are not attached to the chaplet itself, or to its recital, as those of Sts. Dominick and Bridget, for the chaplet in this case holds the place of some other blessed thing, e. g. a cross, medal, or statue. Hence without reciting it, persons may very well partake of the Apostolical Indulgences, provided they accomplish the works marked out and explained in No. 101.

O what immense riches! Therefore, dear Christians, form the pious habit of daily reciting your chaplet; practise a devotion so pleasing to Mary, so much recommended by the Church, and so singularly esteemed by the greatest saints of later centuries. Besides drawing down upon you a copious shower of graces, it will enable you to afford great relief to the suffering souls of Purgatory, and to open to them the gates of Paradise. The Blessed Berchmans wished to die holding his chaplet in his hand. Is it not a mark of predestination to expire in that manner?

It is customary for persons receiving an Indulgenced chaplet, to commence by reciting it first for the Church, secondly for the Pope, and thirdly for the Priest who blessed and Indulgenced it. But this practice is not essential for participating in the Indulgences.

Although to gain the Indulgences annexed to beads (whether Dominican or Bridgetine), it is necessary to hold them in one's hand, or to touch the berries during the recitation of the Rosary; still, if it be said in union with others or in common, it is enough that one of the individuals present hold his Indulgenced chaplet in his hand. Nor is this prerogative confined to the Bridgetine beads alone. For, in virtue of a recent Decree of the Sacred Congregation of Indulgences, Dec., 1857, approved by His Holiness, Jan. 22, 1858, when several persons say the Dominican Rosary or ordinary chaplet in common, they can gain all the Indulgences accorded to it by Bened. XIII. (No. 90), even though they have no blessed Rosary or chaplet. It is sufficient that one of them hold in his hand, while reciting it, an Indulgenced chaplet. The Pope, nevertheless, desires that persons assembled together to say the Beads or chaplet, should lay aside every other concern, and prepare attentively to join in prayer with him who holds the Rosary in his hand: *Addita tamen expressa conditione, quod fideles omnes, cæteris curis semotis, se componant pro oratione facienda una cum persona quæ tenet Coronam, ut Rosarii Indulgentias lucrari queant.* This Decree was solicited by the Rev. F. Superior-General of the Dominicans.

Indeed my own opinion is, that, in these circumstances, each of those present need not have a blessed or Indulgenced Beads. Such, too, appears to be the view maintained in the *votum* of the Consultor, Rev. F. Anthony-Mary de Rignano, Minor Observant. "If not, the fact of granting such a favour to those who have a Rosary, but are not able to make use of it, would be a rather restricted advantage." Still it is always safer for each to have in his possession a Beads that has been blessed and Indulgenced. Hence, the following decision of the Sacred Congregation May 29, 1841, *In una Briocen*:—

"When the possessor of a Beads of our Saviour, or a cross, to which are applied the Indulgences of the Via Crucis, recites the prescribed prayers in conjunction with others who have no such privileged beads or cross, do those present assisting and reciting gain the same Indulgence as that person? The answer says—*No, without a special faculty.* This faculty, in point of fact, has been conceded in favour of the Rosary and chaplet of the Blessed Virgin.*

Call to mind what is put forth in No. 90, viz., that to acquire the Indulgence of the chaplet, it

---

* At present one Indulgenced Crucifix would enable many to gain the Indulgences of the Via Crucis. *Vide.* p. 154.—*Translator.*

must be all recited without *interruption*, or at least without a notable one.

### 104. LITTLE STATUES OF ST. PETER.

In the Vatican Basilica at Rome there is a large statue in bronze of St. Peter. The Prince of the Apostles is represented sitting down, holding his right hand raised, as it were, to bless the people. This time-honored image is an object of special veneration; thus, when going to pray at the *Confession* of St. Peter, near which is located this statue, the Faithful kiss its feet. Wishing to encourage and recompense their devotion, the Pope has granted an Indulgence of 50 days to those who, with contrite hearts and praying for the necessities of the Church, kiss the feet of this statue as aforesaid (Pius IX., Brief, May 15, 1857).

Furthermore, since the date of that grant, there have been moulded other small metal statues of the same Apostle, after the model of the one in the Vatican. The Holy Father blesses them, and annexes to them the same Indulgence.

### 105. THE AGNUS DEI.

The rite according to which the R. Pontiffs have been accustomed to bless and consecrate certain figures or medals of wax, called *Agnus Deis*, is of great antiquity in the Church. It is spoken of in the Roman Ordo, which, in the opinion of the learned, is anterior to the eighth century; even the R. Ceremonial clearly defines the matter, form, and prayers to be employed in their consecration, wherein everything has a spiritual and sacred signification.

*Agnus Deis* are made of white, pure, virgin wax, to denote the human nature assumed by Jesus Christ, through the sole operation of the Holy Ghost, without the slightest blemish, in the most pure womb of the Virgin Mary. The image of a lamb is stamped upon them, emblematical of the Immaculate Lamb immolated on the altar of the Cross for the Redemption of the human race. In blessing it, they make use of water, an element chosen by God, in the Old and New Testament, to be the instrument of numerous wonders. With the water is mixed balsam and holy chrism, and it is in this liquid the *Agnus Deis* are immersed, whilst the Supreme Pontiff implores of God to bless, sanctify, and consecrate them, in such a way that the Faithful who, with a sincere and lively faith, piously use them, may obtain the following graces:—

1. That the sight or touch of the lamb impressed on these figures, exciting the hearts of the Faithful to contemplate the Mysteries of our Redemption, may induce them to thank, and bless, and adore the Divine goodness, and thus obtain for them pardon of their faults.

2. That the sign of the Cross represented on these figures, may remove from them evil spirits, hail, thunder, storms and tempests.

3. That, through the efficacy of the Divine blessing, they may escape the wiles and temptations of the dragon.

4. That women bearing children be preserved from all harm, and favoured with a happy delivery.

5. That pestilence, falling sickness, water or fire may have no power over them.

6. That both in prosperity and adversity, these

pious Christians be fortified with the Divine protection; and that, through the Mysteries of the Life and Passion of Our Lord, they may be preserved from a sudden and unprovided death, from every other danger and from every other evil.

Such are the signal favours which, in the name of Holy Church, the Vicar of Jesus Christ implores from the Divine Mercy for all the Faithful who piously carry or keep about them these *Agnus Deis;* they have been oftentimes confirmed by most remarkable prodigies. When we are deprived of them, we are to attribute the privation to our own want of faith and piety, or to some other latent cause which prevents our Saviour from enriching us with such extraordinary benefits.

(Translated from the Roman printed form of 1856. *Ex typographia Reverendæ Cameræ Apostolicæ.*)\*

---

\* As explained in by-gone days, the marvellous efficacy of this sacred symbol was set forth in these verses:

"Pellitur hoc signo tentatio dæmonis atri,
   Et pietas animo surgit, abitque tepor.
Hoc aconita fugat, subitæque pericula mortis,
   Hoc et ab insidiis vindice tutus eris.
Fulmina ne feriant, ne sæva tonitrua lædant,
   Ne mala tempestas obruat, istud habe.
Undarum discrimen idem propulsat, et ignis,
   Ullaque ne noceat vis inimica valet.
Hoc facilem partum tribuente, puerpera fœtum
   Incolumem mundo proferet, atque Deo.
Unde, rogas, uni tam magna potentia signo?
   Ex Agni meritis, haud aliunde fluit."

Other figures of the same shape, but darker in colour, styled *Paste dé Santi Martiri*, are likewise distributed at Rome. From the first ages of the Church, they have been held in veneration. They are composed of Paschal candles and the dust of Martyrs' bones; they are esteemed and honored as sacred relics.

## 106. CROSS OR MEDAL OF ST. BENEDICT.

During his life, St. Benedict had a great devotion to the Cross, the instrument of our Redemption and Salvation; hence, as may be seen in the second book of Pope St. Gregory's Dialogues, he often employed the Sign of the Cross to work miracles. He was the Father of the renowned Order of Benedictines. We cannot trace the exact origin of this cross or medal. The little treatise sent from the Eternal City by the Very Rev. F. Abbot of St. Paul's to Priests who procure from him the faculty to bless these articles, dates it as far back as the beginning of the eleventh century. It was on the occasion of the miraculous cure of Bruno, son of Count d'Eginsheim in Germany, who was born in 1002, and became Pope St. Leo IX. In his "Sixth Benedictine Age," Mabillon relates the fact, corroborated afterwards by the illustrious Abbé de Solesme, D. Prosper Gueranger.*

In the Monastery of Metten in Bavaria, in the year 1647, there was discovered a manuscript wherein St. Benedict is pictured holding in his right hand a staff terminated by a cross; on the staff was written this inscription:

"*Crux sacra sit M. Lux non draco sit michi dux.*"

The saint bore in his hand a flag whereon were these verses:

"*Vade retro Sathana nuq suade m vana
Sunt mala quæ libas ipse venena bibas.*"

---

* *Essai sur l'origine, la signification et les privilèges de la médaille ou croix de saint Benoît, par le R. P. Dom Prosper Guèranger, abbé de Solesme*, page 24.

In that interesting little work, will be found, in detail, all the

These are precisely the words whose initials are on the face of the medal.

On one side of the medal is represented the holy patriarch holding a cross in his hand; and on the other are engraved those mysterious characters:

In the four triangular parts, are the letters C. S. P. B., that is, *Crux sancti Patris Benedicti*, or cross of Holy Father Benedict; on the middle perpendicular line, C. S. S. M. L., which signifies: *Crux sacra sit mihi lux;* in English, *May the holy cross be my light.* And on the transverse line, N. D. S. M. D., or, *Non draco sit mihi dux*, *May the dragon be not my guide.* Moreover, around the medal is the monogram of the Sacred Name of Jesus, I. H. S.; then the following symbols, V. R. S. N. S. M. V. S. M. Q. L. I. V. B., which denote:

"*Vade retro, Satana; nunquam suade mihi vana:
Sunt mala quæ libas; ipse venena bibas*"—

"Begone, Satan, never counsel me to do vain things; the drink you offer is bad, yourself take draughts of poison." The Roman notice has *ipsa* instead of *ipse*.

The medal may be borne or worn by persons; it may be also fastened to the doors or walls of houses, or buried in their foundations; it is even permitted to immerse it in water which is given as a drink to animals, *for their increase and safety.*

The Roman document enumerates the graces obtained by means of this holy medal, and through the intercession of St. Benedict. It is chiefly a most effectual preservation against the molestation and special favours and prodigies with which Our Lord was pleased to reward the confidence reposed by the people in this medal.

snares of evil spirits. When used with faith and piety, it often powerfully conduces to the relief and recovery of the sick, to freedom from temptations and scourges, as also to the conversion of sinners. To participate in these privileges, it suffices to carry or make use of the medal as blessed by the Benedictine Fathers, or by a Priest furnished with the necessary faculty. There is no particular prayer prescribed. It is advisable, however, to say on every Tuesday, five *Gloria Patris* in remembrance of the Passion of Our Lord, three *Hail Marys* in honor of the Immaculate Conception, and three *Gloria Patris* to secure the patronage of St. Benedict. In fact they may be said as often as one may desire to acquire some special favour from the Almighty through the merits of that holy Patriarch.

By a Brief, *Cœlestibus Ecclesiæ*, March 12, 1742, Pope Bened. XIV. has approved the medal with the cross, the Saint's image, and the letters accompanying it. He has likewise approved of the form to be employed in blessing the medal, granting at the same time very many Indulgences to all who carry it about them.

I. *Plenary Indulgences:* 1. On the Feasts of Christmas, Epiphany, Easter, Ascension, Pentecost, the Trinity, Blessed Sacrament, Immaculate Conception of our Lady, her Nativity, Annunciation, Assumption, Purification, All Saints, and on the Feast of St. Benedict (March 21). The conditions for gaining these are, piously to carry the medal after it has been blessed by proper authority, and to discharge what is indicated in page 260, in order to share in the *plenary* Apostolic Indulgences.

2. At the hour of death, to those who commend

their souls to the Most High, after having Confessed and Communicated, if they can do so; if not, they must elicit an act of contrition, and invoke, at least in heart, should this be impossible *orally*, the Names of Jesus and Mary.

3. All who, on Holy Thursday and Easter Sunday, shall have Confessed and Communicated, praying also for the designs of Holy Church and the preservation of His Holiness the Pope, will acquire the Indulgences which he grants on these days, by giving the Solemn Papal Benediction.

N.B.—All these are applicable to the Departed.

II. The partial Indulgences are very numerous; they are detailed in the little work of the Rev. F. Gueranger.

Observe, that, conformably to the Papal grant, the medals ought to be made of gold, silver, bronze, copper, or some other solid material (See Appendix to the *Decreta Authentica*, no. iii., p. 8.).

---

## ARTICLE VII.

### Special Indulgences.

#### 107. Indulgences of St. Bridget's Chaplet.

*Observations:*—1. This chaplet is so called because we are indebted for it to St. Bridget, who first conceived the notion of circulating its use. She intended, by means of the devotion, to honor the sixty-three years which, in the opinion of many, the Blessed Virgin spent upon earth. Consequently, it is composed of six decades, each containing one *Pater*, ten *Aves*, and a *Creed* instead of the *Gloria Patri*. To make up the number seven, a *Pater Noster* is added in honor of the seven Dolors and seven joys of Mary, together with three *Aves*, to complete the sixty-three years (Archives of the Segretaria of the Sacred Congregation of Indulgences, tom. vi., p. 144).

2. Nevertheless, the Indulgences of this chaplet can be applied as well to Rosaries as to the ordinary Beads of five decades. But, for this application, a special faculty is requisite, since, agreeably to a Decree of Jan. 28, 1842, the ordinary power of indulgencing chaplets is not sufficient. At the same time, the Briefs from Rome to bless and Indulgence crosses, chaplets, medals, &c., generally contain that faculty. Bear in mind also, that, in according the power to apply the Bridgetine Indulgences to chaplets or Rosaries, the Briefs do not by that act give power to bless and Indulgence the real chaplets of St. Bridget, constituted of six decades as above. The faculty was reserved to the Superiors of the Order of St. Saviour, or of St. Bridget, or to other Priests of the same Order, deputed for that object (same Decree). Hence, as this Order does not exist at present, the Popes grant permission to annex to ordinary chaplets the *Indulgences of St. Bridget*. Yet, as already stated, this delegation exclusively regards chaplets of five decades, without any reference to the chaplets of St. Bridget, made up of six decades. This has been repeatedly declared by the Sacred Congregation, particularly through the Decrees of Jan. 15, 1839, Sept. 25, 1841, and Jan. 28, 1842.*

---

* Plures sacerdotes diœcesis Rothomagensis sac. Congregationi dubia quædam solvenda proponunt, ut infra:—

3. The Indulgences of St. Bridget's chaplet were granted by Leo X. (Bull, July 10, 1515), and Clem. XI. (Bull, *De salute Domini gregis*); they were confirmed and augmented by a Brief of Bened. XIV., dated Jan. 15, 1743.

4. To participate in the Indulgences of the chaplet of St. Bridget, it is not necessary to meditate on the Mysteries of Our Lord and the Blessed Virgin, as is the case in regard to the Indulgences of the ordinary Rosary (Decrees of July 1, 1839 and Oct. 2, 1840). Pursuant to the latter one of 1840, it is not requisite to reflect on the Dolors or Joys of Holy Mary. True, indeed, according to a response given, Jan. 28, 1842, to several Priests of Rouen, it would seem that this meditation is essential. But the context of the Decree of 1726, on which the Sacred Congregation rests, shows evidently that the reply comprises merely Rosary Indulgences for which meditation on the Mysteries is required.

1. An benefaciant benedicendo coronas ordinarias quinque decadum cum applicatione Indulgentiarum divæ Birgittæ nuncupatarum?

Sac. Congregatio respondit:—"*Negative*, nisi sacerdotes peculiares habeant facultates ab Apostolica Sede impetratas, quaeque in concessionibus exprimuntur per illa verba, aut similia, *ac etiam applicandi Indulgentias sanctæ Birgittæ nuncupatas;* per ista enim verba, aut similia, non datur facultas benedicendi coronas Birgittinas (quæ sex pecadibus constant, totidemque orationibus Dominicis et Apostolicis Symbolis, atque in fine una alia Oratione dominica tribusque Salutationibus Angelicis); sed traditur potestas benedicendi coronas communes (id est quinque vel quindecim decadum) cum Indulgentiis quoque, quæ propriæ sunt coronarum divæ Birgittæ." Ita S. Congregatio in Strebatensi 25 Sept. 1841, in Rothomagensi 24 Januar. 1842, et nunc 28 ejusdem mensis.

2. An fideles illas coronas sic benedictas recitando revera Indulgentias Birgittinas lucrentur?

Sacr. Congr. respondit:—Satis responsum in primo. Die 28 Januarii 1842

*Catalogue or List of the Indulgences attached to the Chaplet of St. Bridget.*

1. An Indulgence of 100 days for each *Pater*, 100 for each *Ave*, and the same for each *Credo*, to whomsoever shall recite the chaplet or Beads of St. Bridget.

2. All who say the entire Rosary (to which the Bridgetine Indulgences have been applied), gain an Indulgence of seven years and as many Quarantines.

3. By saying the Rosary or chaplet of St. Bridget with one or more individuals, each person will gain the partial Indulgences annexed to the recitation of the Pater, Ave, and Credo, just as if he were to say it privately by himself. Neither is that communication of Indulgences peculiar to this chaplet, as was remarked in the foregoing number.

4. He who shall recite at least five decades of said chaplet daily, throughout the year, will gain a plenary Indulgence on a day determined by himself, after the lapse of the year, provided he Confess, Communicate, and pray for Holy Church.

5. All in the habit of reciting, at least once a week, the chaplet of five decades, may obtain a plenary Indulgence on the Feast of St. Bridget (Oct. 8), if on that day they Confess, Communicate, visit a parochial or some other church, and pray there as above.

6. A plenary Indulgence, at the hour of death, to those accustomed to say this chaplet at least once a week.

7. Whoever may recite it each day for a month, will gain a plenary Indulgence on a day of his own

selection, when, having Confessed and Communicated, he shall visit a church and offer there the usual prayers.

8. An Indulgence of 40 days to him who, having about him this chaplet, shall pray on bended knees, at the sound of the bell, for a person in his agony.

9. He who, having on his person this chaplet, shall, with contrite heart, make an examen of conscience, and say three Paters and Aves, will acquire an Indulgence of 20 days.

10. An Indulgence of 100 days to one who, having about him the chaplet, shall hear Mass on a Festival, or a working day, or accompany the Holy Viaticum, or bring back to the way of salvation some strayed soul, or, in fine, accomplish any other pious work in honor of Our Lord, the Blessed Virgin, or St. Bridget, and recite the Our Father and Hail Mary three times.

### 108. CHAPLET OF THE SEVEN DOLORS.

It owes its origin to the Venerable Order of Servants of Mary, which sprang up towards the middle of the thirteenth century, on Mount Senario near Florence. The chaplet is composed of seven divisions or septenaries in remembrance of the seven Dolors of the Blessed Virgin, on which the Faithful are to piously meditate while saying it. Each division contains one *Pater* and seven *Aves*. It is terminated by three Hail Marys in honor of the tears shed by our sorrowful Mother in Her great afflictions, and also to obtain true contrition, together with an application of the Indulgences. The seven Dolors of Mary are :—

1. When the aged St. Simeon, in the temple of Jerusalem, predicted that a sword of sorrow should one day pierce Her soul.

2. When, to escape the cruelty of Herod, She was forced to fly into Egypt with Her Son Jesus and St. Joseph.

3. When She lost Her Divine Son at the age of twelve years, and sought Him for the space of three days, Her heart being a prey to the most anxious cares.

4. On the occasion of Her beholding Jesus all covered with bruises and laden with the heavy burden of the cross, on the road to Calvary.

5. When She witnessed Her adorable Son nailed to the cross, and the blood trickling from his wounds.

6. At the time She received in Her arms Jesus taken down from the cross, after His side had been opened with a spear.

7. Lastly, when She accompanied the body of Her Blessed Son to the grave.

To stimulate the Faithful to recite this chaplet, Pope Bened. XIII. (Brief *Redemptoris*, Sept. 26, 1724), accorded an Indulgence of 200 days for each *Pater* and *Ave*, to those who, truly contrite and having confessed, or firmly resolved to confess, shall say it in the churches of the Servites. The same Indulgence may be acquired by reciting it anywhere, on Fridays, on every day of Lent, the Feast of the Seven Dolors, and on the Octave. 100 days for each *Pater* and *Ave*, wherever it may be repeated, any other day during the year. In fine, seven years and seven Quarantines, to anybody who recites it either alone, or with others.

Pope Clement XII. (Bull, *Unigeniti*, Dec. 12,

1734), confirmed these Indulgences, and moreover conceded:—

1. A plenary Indulgence to those who, having recited the chaplet of the Seven Dolors during a month, shall then select a day to approach the Sacraments and pray for the intentions of the Church.

2. An Indulgence of 100 years, *each time*, to everyone who says it with heart contrite, and having confessed, or at least formed a resolution of confessing.

3. An Indulgence of 150 years to all who recite it on Mondays, Wednesdays, Fridays, and Holidays of obligation, supplying the conditions, Confession and Communion.

4. A plenary Indulgence to persons in the habit of repeating it four times a week, to be gained some day of the year defined by themselves, conditions being as just specified.

5. Two hundred years' Indulgence, to those piously reciting it after Confession.

6. In fine, an Indulgence of ten years, *each time*, to all who, carrying the chaplet of the Seven Dolors about them, and reciting it frequently, shall, after Confession and Communion, assist at Mass, or a sermon, or accompany the Blessed Sacrament to the sick, or reconcile enemies, or reclaim sinners; or, at any rate, to the recital of the seven *Paters* and *Aves*, add some other good work, temporal or spiritual, in honor of Our Redeemer, Holy Mary, or some Patron Saint.

All these Indulgences were corroborated by Bened. XIV. (Decree of Jan. 6. 1747), and by Clem. XIII. (Decree March 15, 1763). However, to partake of them, it is requisite that the chaplets should have been blessed by the Superiors of the Order of Servants of Mary, or by another Priest of the same Order deputed for that purpose, or finally by some Priest specially endowed with power either from the Pope, or from the Very Rev. Father-General of the Servites at Rome.*

Observe, these chaplets, like the ordinary blessed and Indulgenced ones, cannot be sold, or lent with the design of communicating the Indulgences annexed to them; otherwise, they would at once cease to be privileged (Brief of Bened. XIII., cited above). A.

### 109. PAPAL BENEDICTION OR INDULGENCE.

It is a plenary Indulgence which the Holy Father accords at Rome to all the Faithful who, having Confessed and Communicated, receive the solemn Benediction given by himself personally on some greater Festivals, when he officiates pontifically, as at Christmas, Easter, &c. In France, most of the Bishops have obtained from the Holy See the faculty of imparting this solemn Benediction once or twice a year, with an application of the plenary Indulgence.

The people may acquire it by communicating on these days, assisting at this Benediction, and praying for the Church, its Head, and for the officiating Bishop. In its own place, I have mentioned, that the Communion of Easter Sunday may serve both to satisfy the Paschal precept and gain the Papal Indulgence.†

---

* Read note 3, n. 101, where it is stated that the mere sign of the cross is not sufficient to bless and Indulgence chaplets of the Seven Dolors.

† See in the *Formula* at the end of this volume, the rite to be observed by Missionaries authorised to give the Papal Benediction.

## 110. INDULGENCES OF THE ROMAN STATIONS.*

The practice of visiting the Churches of the Stations, at Rome, dates as far back as the first ages of Christianity. At certain times the people, the Clergy, and even the Popes themselves used to go there to honor the memory of the Saints, especially of the Martyrs. Wishing to systematize and add solemnity to so commendable and salutary a devotion, St. Gregory the Great instituted the Roman Stations, by specifying the churches to be visited, not alone during Lent, but also on other days of the year; he furthermore had them inserted in the R. Missal ("Raccolta," from the narration of John the Deacon, in his life of the Saint).

To induce the Faithful to visit these churches, and pray there pursuant to the intentions of the Sovereign Pontiff, St. Gregory first, and afterwards his successors, attached to this pious exercise various Indulgences, which were confirmed afresh for ever by His Holiness Pius VI. (Decree of July 9, 1777).†

### *Indulgences of the Stations.*

Jan. 1., *Circumcision of Our Lord;* Indulgence of thirty years and thirty Quarantines.

---

\* Amongst the Romans, the word *statio* signified a post, where soldiers or sentinels are stationed for a certain time. By analogy, then, pilgrimages, *watches*, prayers before the tombs of the Apostles and Martyrs were called *stations.*

† In 1827, Leo XII. accorded other Indulgences to all who might visit the Churches of the Stations during Lent, conformably to a method published at Rome through the Press of the *Camera Apostolica* (see "Raccolta, 348)."

Jan. 6, *The Epiphany;* thirty years and thirty Quarantines.

*Septuagesima, Sexagesima, and Quinquagesima Sundays;* same Indulgence.

LENT: *Ash-Wednesday* and the *4th Sunday;* fifteen years and as many Quarantines.

*Palm-Sunday;* twenty-five years and twenty-five Quarantines.

*Holy Thursday;* plenary Indulgence, assuming Confession and Communion.

*Good Friday* and *Holy Saturday;* thirty years and as many Quarantines.

*Every other Sunday and every other day in Lent*; ten years and ten Quarantines.

*Easter Sunday;* plenary (Confession and Communion).

Easter Monday and Tuesday, each day of the Octave, including *Quasimodo,* or Low Sunday; thirty years and thirty Quarantines.

April 25, Feast of St. Mark, Evangelist; same Indulgence.

*The Three Rogation Days;* thirty years and thirty Quarantines also.

*Ascension-Day;* plenary (Confession and Communion implied).

*Vigil of Pentecost;* ten years and ten Quarantines—Feast of Pentecost, and all days within the Octave, thirty years and thirty Quarantines.

Ember-days of September, Wednesday, Friday, and Saturday; ten years and ten Quarantines.

ADVENT: 1st, 2nd, and 4th Sundays; ten years and as many Quarantines. 3rd. Sunday, fifteen years and fifteen Quarantines. Quatuor-tense days in December, ten years and ten Quarantines.

Vigil of Christmas, Christmas-night, and Mass of the Aurora.

*Christmas-Day;* plenary (Confession and Communion).

December 26, *Feast of St. Stephen;* thirty years and thirty Quarantines.

December 27, *Feast of St. John, Evangelist;* the same.

December 28, Feast of the Holy Innocents; the same. A.

*Visit to the Seven Churches and Seven privileged Altars.\**

In the Holy City, there is also a custom of paying a visit to the seven principal churches, namely, those of St. Peter on the Vatican, St. Paul, St. Sebastian (outside the walls), St. John Latern, the Holy Cross in Jerusalem, St. Laurence (outside the walls), and St. Mary-Major. It is usual likewise to visit the seven privileged altars of the Basilica of St. Peter, to wit, those of the Madonna, of St. Gregory (the *Gregoriana*), S.S. Processus and Martinianus, St. Michael Archangel, St. Petronilla, Virgin; the Madonna of the Pillar, the Holy Apostles Simon and Jude, and of St. Gregory the Great.

Whoever, having Confessed and Communicated,†

---

\* This devotion is most ancient; *Antichissima,* says the "Raccolta," p. 366. In his Bull, *Egregia Populi Romani pietas,* Feb. 13, 1586, Sixtus V. notices the approbation given to it by the Sovereign Pontiffs. It was extremely dear to St. Philip Neri, and to a multitude of other Saints. At Rome, persons of all ranks daily visit these august sanctuaries, there to venerate the memory of the Glorious Apostles and Martyrs of Jesus Christ.

† Communion is required, to partake of the plenary Indulgences, attainable through this devout observance.

shall piously perform this devotion of visiting those churches or altars, praying for the intention of His Holiness, may gain numerous Indulgences, with which, from time to time, the Vicars of Christ have enriched them, as is evident from the original Bulls and Briefs kept chiefly in the Archives of the Vatican. They are most authentic, though it would be difficult to define the exact number.*

### 111. INDULGENCE OF THE PARDON, OR PORTIUNCULA.

The little church of St. Mary of the Angels, near Assisium, also called *della Portiuncula*, from a small villa adjoining it, was bestowed to St. Francis of Assisium by the R. Benedictine Fathers of the Monastery of Mount Soubaze. Francis, who had repaired this decayed and neglected church, always cherished a special predilection for it, because it had been dedicated to the Queen of Angels, was the first temple and cradle of his Order, and the sanctuary where he received most signal favours from Our Divine Lord and His Blessed Mother. Before his death, the saint expressly ordered all his *Brothers* to

---

* St. Pius V., Sixtus V., Paul V., Clem. VIII., and Urban VIII., have confirmed these time-honored Indulgences annexed to the visitation of the seven privileged altars of St. Peter's. Bened. XIV., March 26, 1752, defined afresh the following Indulgences, dispensed by Innoc. XII., Feb. 22, 1738:

1. A plenary Indulgence, available for ever to any of the Faithful, as often as, truly contrite, and, having confessed, if necessary, and Communicated, they shall visit the august Basilica of St. Peter, and pray there, &c.; applicable to the Departed.

2. A plenary Indulgence for the seven privileged altars. See the *Bullarium Vaticanum*, tom. iii., p. 309.

In confirming the Indulgences accorded by his predecessors to the Basilica of St. John Lateran, Bened. XIV. speaks of them in a style calculated to engender a belief that they are rather numerous (Bullar Bened. XIV., tom. iii., p. 366).

entertain great veneration for this church, "so singularly chosen," said he, "by Jesus Christ and His Holy Mother."*

About the month of October 1221, on the occasion of an apparition of our Saviour, Immaculate Mary, and a host of heavenly spirits, Francis ventured to ask of our Saviour, through the intercession of His Virgin Mother, a plenary Indulgence for all who, heartily contrite and after Confession, should visit the church of our Lady of Angels or of Portiuncula. The Redeemer graciously heard the prayer of his faithful servant, on condition, however, that the Saint should obtain from the reigning Pontiff (Honorius III.), a confirmation of the favour granted to him. In point of fact, Pope Honorius did confirm it the same year, but it was only two years afterwards in 1223, he accorded it for ever, attaching it to the 2nd of August, conformably to the will of Jesus Christ, as manifested to St. Francis in a second vision, and having it commence with First Vespers, that is, towards the decline of the day on which St. Peter the Apostle had been delivered from his chains.

By order of the Pope, it was solemnly published at St. Mary of the Angels, on the 1st of August, same year (1223), through the Bishops of Assisium, Perugia, Lodi, Spoletto, Foligni, Nocera, and Gubio. The announcement of the Indulgence was preceded by a discourse replete with fervor, delivered by the saint himself.†

---

* It had then become a magnificent church. Boned. XIV., March 22, 1754, raised the church of St. Mary of Angels to the dignity of a *Patriarchal Basilica.*

† *Life of St. Francis of Assisium,* by F. Candido Chalippe, a Recollect—Tom. 2, lib. iv.; in tom. 3 is given a very full account of the Indulgence of the Portiuncula.

This extraordinary privilege, commonly styled the Indulgence of the *Sacred Pardon*, or of Portiuncula, was subsequently extended to all the churches of the three Orders of St. Francis,* by several Popes, notably by Gregory XV. (Bull, *Splendor Paternæ Gloriæ*, July 4, 1622), who, to the confession already required for acquiring the Indulgence, added Communion also. By a Brief of Jan. 22, 1689, Innoc. XI. made it applicable to the Faithful departed.†

The peculiarity of the Indulgence of the "Sacred Pardon" is, that it can be acquired, *toties quoties*, that is to say, several times the same day, or as often as a person shall, with an intention of gaining it, visit the church of Portiuncula, or some other church privileged in that way, at any hour from First Vespers to the Eve of the 2nd. of August. But to the visit and prayers for the Pope's intention, ought to be added Confession and Communion. Let us not forget, especially, to apply these Indulgences to the holy souls in Purgatory.

* These three Orders are:—1. The Friars Minor, a title given to them by their holy Founder, through a spirit of humility. 2. The Order of *Poor Clares*, or Religious of St. Clare, originally called Poor Ladies. 3. The Tertians, whose first title was *the Order of Brothers and Sisters of Penance*.

† The Feast of the dedication of the Church of Portiuncula is annually celebrated in the three Orders of St. Francis. According to F. Chalippe, it is thus published in their Convents:—"At Assisium in Umbria, the dedication of the Church of St. Mary of Angels, also called Portiuncula, which our Seraphic Father, St. Francis, singularly honored, which he chose to make the centre of his Order, and in which, through the mediation of the Blessed Virgin Mother of God, he obtained for all the Faithful from Our Lord Jesus Christ, a plenary Indulgence, confirmed by Pope Honorius III., as Vicar of Christ, and by his command."

Innoc. XII. extended this Indulgence, perpetually, to every day of the year, for the spiritual benefit of the Faithful who, through devotion, are ever attracted thither, from all parts, to the Church of St. Mary of Angels (Bull, Aug. 18, 1695). This daily grant has been renewed by Bened. XIV., under the ordinary conditions of Confession and Communion.

Never, writes the "Raccolta," has this pious custom of repeatedly visiting the same church on the same day, with a view of oftentimes participating in the Indulgence of the Portiuncula, been disapproved, as was declared by the Sacred Congregation of the Council (July 17, 1700, and Dec. 4, 1723). Nay more, the Sacred Congregation of Indulgences has confirmed the prerogative of the *toties quoties* by a Decree of Feb. 22, 1847, declaring at the same time that the prescribed Communion need not be received in a Franciscan church. His Holiness Pius IX. sanctioned this Decree, July 12, 1847.*

In virtue of a Decree of Feb. 10, 1819, churches which formerly enjoyed the Indulgence of the Portiuncula, on account of their having belonged to the Franciscans, have lost their Indulgence since these Religious abandoned them. Hence, in order that they should continue privileged, it would be necessary to procure the favour newly from the Holy See (*Analecta Juris Pontificii*, 15th. ed., July 1856). Moreover, except in the case of a particular Indult, this Portiuncula privilege is confined to public churches of the Franciscans, and does not extend to private chapels of their convents (Decree of June 15, 1819).

---

* The clause *toties quoties* is then to be understood literally. Such is the common feeling of all the Faithful at Rome without exception, as well Priests, Religious, and men of learning, as the people generally.

Some persons require the lapse of a considerable time between two consecutive visits to a privileged church, while others even ridicule those who repeatedly enter a church, without leaving any interval, so to speak, between the visits. The former have no foundation for their view, and the latter are quite astray. Let us pity them and bring to their minds the words of our Lord (Matt. xi., 25), "Father, thou hast hidden these things from the wise and prudent, and revealed them to little ones."

What has been said in reference to churches relinquished by the Franciscans, does not apply to those in France, since Pius VII. has made an exception in favour of them. The Rev. F. Adrian Joseph Humbert, Minor-Conventual, fearing that since the suppression of the Monastic Orders in France, the churches formerly belonging to the Franciscan Religious, had forfeited the Indulgence of the Portiuncula, solicited from Pope Pius VII. a confirmation, and, if necessary, a fresh concession of the prerogative for the entire of France. His Holiness was pleased to accede to his wishes, by a Brief, *Exponi Nobis*, dated from Castelgandolfo, June 20, 1817.*

Observe, the Decree of Feb. 10, 1819, has not revoked the ordinances of the Brief of 1817, relative to France; for, less than three months after, May 5, 1819, by a second Brief, commencing *Alias Nos*, Pius VII. confirmed the grant of *Exponi Nobis*. Furthermore, for the greater spiritual advantage of the Faithful, in confirming it he wished that, in those French churches of which we speak, the Indulgence of the Portiuncula should be transferred to the Sunday following the 2nd of August, when that day does not fall on a Sunday.

Thus, notwithstanding the Decree of Feb. 10, 1819, to which there has been made an exception, the churches of France, which, prior to the revolution of '89, belonged to the Friars Minor or Franciscans, are still enriched with all the Indulgences of the Portiuncula; and they can be gained the Sunday after the 1st of August. A special Indult would be required, in order to acquire them on the 2nd of

---

* The Brief of Pius VII. comprises all the churches in France, which formerly appertained to any of the three Orders of St. Francis.

August (Decree of August 29, 1864). But in the churches actually appertaining to a branch of the Franciscan Order, the Indulgence is obtained on the 2nd of August; so too as regards those that have obtained from His Holiness this favour, one of the most valuable that has emanated from the treasures of Divine Mercy.*

### 112. INDULGENCES OF THE HOLY YEAR.

The *Holy Year* is that in which the Great Jubilee is celebrated at Rome every twenty-fifth year: Thus the year 1875 will be a Jubilee or *Holy Year* at Rome, unless there be some derogation emanating from the Apostolic See. It will open at First Vespers on Christmas-Eve in 1874. It is only after a year the Pope extends the "Great Jubilee" to all the dioceses of the world.

It is worthy of note, that during the entire year of this Great Jubilee at Rome, all Indulgences hitherto dispensed in favour of the Living are suspended. The Church thus wishes her children to have a higher appreciation of the Indulgence of the Jubilee. There are a few exceptions, however, such as Indulgences attainable at the hour of death, those of the Angelus and Quarant-Ore, those accorded to

---

* Through a declaration of Pius IX. (April 14, 1856), all the Indulgences, privileges, communications of favours, &c., accorded to the Tertians of St. Francis by Bened. XIII. (Bulls *Paterna Sedis*, Dec. 10 1725, and *Singularis Devotio*, July 5, 1726), together with those recently dispensed by the first named Pope to the Tertians living in France, are extended to the same body (Tertians), whatever their rule may be. At present, therefore, these spiritual favours are available to all Tertians of St. Francis, whether they are under the direction of Franciscans of the Observance, or of the Recollects linked to them, or Conventuals, or Capuchins, or if governed even by any Priest whatever, secular or regular, who may have been duly empowered to establish and rule congregations of Franciscan *Tertians*.

persons accompanying the Blessed Sacrament to the sick, with some local Indulgences—for example, that of Portiuncula, obtained by visiting the Chapel of St. Mary of Angels at Assisium; the prayer *Sacrosanctæ* is also an exception, &c. But any in behalf of the Dead, as that of a 'privileged altar,' &c., are by no means suspended during that epoch. One may even gain, for these suffering Souls, all the other Indulgences, which, at other times, are available only for the Living (Bened. XIII., Bull *Salvatoris*, April 28, 1725,—Bened. XIV., Clem. XIV., and Leo XII., June 20, 1824).

At the end of the Jubilee of Rome, all the Indulgences suspended become again effectual without a fresh grant from His Holiness. I may remark, furthermore, that the faculty of blessing and Indulgencing devotional objects, remains in full force through the Holy Year. But those who get them blessed at that period, should be told that the Indulgences can be acquired for the Souls in Purgatory alone.

### 113. INDULGENCE OF A PRIVILEGED ALTAR.

A privileged altar is one to which, by a special favour, our Holy Father annexes a plenary Indulgence applicable only to the Departed, and obtainable by a Priest saying Mass for them at that altar. Behold how Pope Pius VI. expresses himself on the subject of a privileged altar, in his Brief of Aug. 30, 1779. "Every time a Priest, secular or regular, shall celebrate at this altar, we grant a plenary Indulgence, by way of suffrage, to that one of the Faithful Departed for whom the Holy Sacrifice shall have been offered, so that, in virtue of the Treasure of the Church, that is, of the merits of Christ, the Blessed Virgin and Saints, this soul may be delivered from the pains of Purgatory." Such is the sentiment of St. Peter's successors, in reference to a privileged altar. As to the application of the Indulgence, read what is laid down in Part I., n. v.*

*Conditions for obtaining the Indulgence:*—1. The Priest should determine in his mind the particular soul to whom he may wish to apply the Indulgence of the privileged altar. 2. The Mass must be said for the deceased person to whom the Indulgence is to be applied, because the Indulgence is attainable and applicable only through the celebration of Mass; neither can the Indulgence be applied to one soul, and the Mass to another, as is evident from the Papal Indults. The Substitute of the Sacred Congregation of Indulgences assured me of the truth of this conclusion, in Oct. 1868. If the Indulgence be applied to the dead in general, the Mass ought to have the same general application. This, however, it seems, cannot be done except on the Feast of All Souls, whereon, by a Decree of May 19, 1761, every altar is privileged; and pursuant to a decision of the Sacred Congregation of Rites, the Mass may be applied, same day, *tam in genere pro omnibus quam in specie pro aliquo defuncto.*†

---

* Episcopus Sancti Flori in Gallia exposcit: Utrum, per Indulgentiam altari privilegiato annexam, intelligenda sit Indulgentia plenaria animam statim liberans ab omnibus Purgatorii pœnis; an vero tantum Indulgentia quædam, secundum divinæ misericordiæ beneplacitum applicanda?

Sacra Congregatio, votis Consultorum auditis, respondit: "Per Indulgentiam altari privilegiato annexam, si spectetur mens concedentis, et usus clavium potestatis, intelligendam esse Indulgentiam plenariam quæ animam statim liberet ab omnibus Purgatorii pœnis; si vero spectetur applicationis effectus, intelligendam esse Indulgentiam cujus mensura divinæ misericordiæ beneplacito et acceptationi respondet." (28 julii 1840.)

† The Bishop of Angers proposed this doubt: "Utrum privil. gium

Note, that a Priest who may have received an offering or intention for saying Mass at a privileged altar, is bound in justice to celebrate Mass at that altar, and to apply both the Mass and Indulgence to the soul of the deceased for whom the *honorarium* has been offered and accepted. We except, of course, instances wherein he is possessed of a personal privileged altar, for then, conformably to a declaration of the Sacred Congregation, March 15, 1852, he may celebrate at a non-privileged altar.*

3. It is necessary to say a *Requiem* Mass, *diebus non-impeditis*, i.e., on days when the Rubrics permit or prescribe to celebrate in black vestments.† This condition is required also in the case of one who, enjoying the favour of a privileged altar—of which just now—says Mass at any altar whatever (Decree of April 11, 1840). But on forbidden days, such as Doubles,

---

altaris applicari possit pluribus defunctorum animabus in cujuscumque diei Missa (servatis servandis), sicuti declaratum fuit die 19 maii 1761, pro Missa in die Commemorationis omnium defunctorum?" The S. Cong. answered *negative*. (February 29, 1864.)

* Caius Sacerdos habens privilegium personale altaris privilegiati bis aut ter in hebdomada, accepto stipendio pro Missa celebranda in altari privilegiato ex prætextu personalis privilegii ejusdem altaris privilegiati, celebrat in altari non privilegiato.—Quæritur an bene se gerat, et utrum oneri suscepto satisfaciat? Sacra Congregatio respondit *Affirmative*, die Mart. 15, 1852.

† Should the body of the deceased be present in the church, but not entombed, it is permitted to sing a Requiem Mass even on Doubles of the first class, though of obligation, unless these festivals are celebrated with great pomp. And if they be not of obligation for the Faithful, yet kept with much outward solemnity, it may be also sung, provided they happen not to be titular feasts of a given church (Congregation of Rites, April 8, 1808). So, too, may solemn Requiem Masses on Doubles of the second class which are of precept, even if accompanied with the dignified grandeur of the first mentioned class of feasts (ibid.). But they cannot be said at all the three last days of Holy Week, whether the body be present or not (Decree, Aug. 11, 1736).

The annual anniversary Masses offered for the Dead on the day of their demise, to carry out the design of their last Wills, may be chanted on a double-Major feast not observed as a holiday. The same extends to the 3rd, 7th, and 30th day after the death of the deceased, or after

Sundays, and within privileged Octaves, as those of Christmas, Epiphany, &c., the Indulgence of a privileged altar can be obtained by celebrating the Mass corresponding with the Office of the day, and using its proper colour. This is plain from several decisions.\*

For Masses of the Dead, according to a Decree of the Sacred Congregation of Rites, approved by Pius IX., July 23, 1868, it is no longer allowable to use violet-coloured vestments. The sole case in which they may be employed is the 2nd Nov., if the Blessed Sacrament were exposed for the Forty Hours' Adoration (Decree, Sept. 16, 1801); in such circumstances the Priest might still partake of the Indulgence of a privileged altar.†

Notes: — 1. On All Souls' Day, Nov. 2, every altar is privileged (Decree of May 19, 1761); not so, however, during the Octave. Hence, if any church enjoy this favour throughout the Octave, it is owing to some special grant. The same applies, during the term of the Quarant-Ore, to all the altars of churches wherein Exposition takes place, at what

---

the burial, according to the custom of different churches (Nov. 22, 1664, and July 20, 1669), (Aug. 23, 1766). For more ample instructions see " Le Guide pratique de Liturgie Romaine," chap. v., art. vii., Mass of the Dead.

\* Missa Defunctorum, seu de Requiem omnino dicenda est, quando a Rubrica permittitur; nam juxta Constitutiones Summorum Pontificum Romanorum Alexandri VII., Clem. IX. et Innoc. XL, Indulgentia altaris privilegiati in Duplicibus lucratur per celebrationem Missæ officio diei respondentis et cum colore paramentorum conveniente cum applicatione sacrificii (S. Congreg. Rituum, die Julii 22, 1848).

† Utrum color niger sensu exclusivo debeat intelligi, ita ut Indulgentiam altaris privilegiati non consequatur qui, verbi gr., ad ministrandam Eucharistiam per modum Sacramenti, cum paramentis violaceis Missam de Requiem celebret? S. Congreg. die Feb. 16, 1852, respondit: Ut fruatur altari privilegiato sacerdos diebus non impeditis, celebrare debet Missam Defunctorum, et uti paramentis nigris, vel ex rationabili causa violaceis. At present the only reasonable cause is the circumstance mentioned in the text.

time soever it is held in the year. But while the Blessed Sacrament is exposed Mass cannot be said in Black.*

2. In the same church there can be but one privileged altar (Bened. XIII., Clem. XIII.). The Indults have this clause in express terms. Nevertheless the Holy See often accords the favour of two privileged altars to a parish church; and sometimes as many as three or four, &c., altars—*ex gratia speciali*—for a church wherein there may be a great number of Masses said. As a matter of fact, this prerogative has been vouchsafed to the Sanctuary of Notre Dame de Fourviere, at Lyons.

3. Some altars are privileged in perpetuity; but not unfrequently the prerogative is only for the space of seven years, to be computed from the day on which the Indult may have been issued. In such instances an extension or renewal is commonly solicited towards the end of the seventh year.

4. It is usual to hang over the altar a tablet or card bearing in large characters the inscription:—ALTARE PRIVILEGIATUM. But of course the absence of this would by no means affect the validity of the privilege.

5. The Indulgence of a privileged altar is not lost if the altar be repaired, or reconstructed, even of a different material. It can also be changed to another place in the church, provided its name or title be not altered (Decrees, February 16, 1846, and August 30,

---

* The subjoined question was proposed to the Sacred Congregation: An sacerdos celebrans in altari privilegiato, legendo Missam de festo simplici, semiduplici, votivam, vel de feria non privilegiata, sive ratione expositionis SS. Sacramenti, sive Stationis ecclesiæ, vel alterius solemnitatis, fruatur privilegio ac si legeret Missam de Requiem per Rubricas eo die permissam ? The Sacred Congregation replied, *Affirmative* (Feb. 29, 1864). The Pope sanctioned the response, 11th of April ensuing. The difficulty had been previously solved, in this sense, by the Sacred Congregation, July 1751 (see p. 261).

1847).* Yet if the privilege had been conferred on account of an ancient venerated picture, the privilege no longer remains, when the image or picture is destroyed by fire, or otherwise.

6. An altar ceases to be privileged, as soon as the church falls into ruin or decay. But the privilege revives when the church is rebuilt *in the same place* (Decree, Aug. 30, 1847).

7. According to a decision of the Sacred Congregation of Indulgences, March 19, 1847, a Priest who celebrates Mass, at a privileged altar, for a deceased person, and applies to him the plenary Indulgence, may on the same day, in virtue of the Communion received by him, acquire another plenary Indulgence, either for himself or for the Dead.

8. As we can never know whether the Indulgence of a privileged altar has been communicated in its entire extent to the soul for which the Holy Sacrifice is offered, it would be very laudable and beneficial to have several Masses said for it, even at a privileged altar. Besides, that soul may not be in Purgatory at all, in which case, the Indulgences will, doubtless, be applied, through the goodness of God, to the parents or friends of the person who gets the Masses offered, particularly if the Priest, in offering them, had added this secondary intention to his primary and direct one.

9. *A personal privileged Altar:* In this case the favour of the Indulgence is attached, not to a given

---

* Episcopus N. exponit quod anno 1835 altare majus ecclesiæ parochialis B. privilegiatum in perpetuum declaratum fuit : cum vero idem altare marmoreum hodie constructum sit, supponitur quod privilegium peremptum sit; supplicatur hinc pro opportuna declaratione.

S. Congregatio respondit : *Dummodo altare sit iterum sub eodem titulo constructum, non amisisse privilegium ab Apostolica Sede concessum.* Die Aprilis 21, 1843.

altar, in such or such a church, but to the person of the Priest himself. The Pope ordinarily grants it for two, three, or four days in each week; he accords it for ever or for a time. A Priest enjoying this sort of prerogative may obtain a plenary Indulgence for the Dead at whatever altar he celebrates. The conditions required to gain it are the same as those mentioned above.* Whether the altar be a personal privileged one or not, it is expressly forbidden to receive a larger *honorarium*, by reason of the privilege (Clem. XIII., May 19, 1761).

10. Agreeably to a recent declaration of Pius IX., it is not necessary, when soliciting from Rome (through the Congregation of Briefs) a privileged altar for a church, to specify the material of the altar, whether marble, bronze, wood, &c.; nor even to say whether it is fixed or portable. But the name of the church wherein the altar is erected, ought to be expressed, and the title of the altar itself, as, e. g. if it were dedicated to the Sacred Heart, Immaculate Mary, St. Joseph, &c. Remark, too, that this privileged altar cannot be transferred to another church.† These statements have been delivered to me from the Office of the Sacred Congregation of Briefs.

11. An liceat recipere onera perpetua ac fundationes ad altaria privilegiata? S. Congregatio respondit *Negative*, die 14 Dec. 1711.

---

* Sacerdos qui gaudet privilegio altaris personalis, si sit aggregatus alicui Congregationi quæ etiam dicto privilegio gaudet, potest adhuc frui hoc alio privilegio, licet aliunde jam habeat per tres aut quatuor vices in hebdomada tale privilegium, dummodo in Indultis aliter expresse non disponatur (S. Cong. Maii 27, 1839).

† I just add a note here which might have been inserted amongst the general remarks: The Indulgences annexed to a church are not lost when, it having been destroyed, a new church is constructed in the same place, and under the same title. But they are not attainable, if it be built in a cemetery or place different from that in which the former one had been situated (Decree of Aug. 9, 1843).

114. PLENARY INDULGENCE AT THE HOUR OF DEATH.

As can be seen, by reading over this work, the plenary Indulgence at the hour of death may be obtained on many titles; thus, for instance, all who shall have frequently recited, during life, the Acts of Faith, Hope, and Charity, have a right to it; so too have the possessors of devotional objects enriched with Indulgences, as crucifixes, chaplets, medals, &c., also those who, through life, invoked the Sacred Names of Jesus and Mary, and then invoke them in their last moments; or members of the Confraternity of the Sacred Heart, Rosary, Scapular, or of a Congregation of our Lady affiliated to the *Primaria* at Rome, if they have fulfilled the requisite conditions.

To partake of this Indulgence it is necessary—1. to Confess and Communicate, if possible; if not, to be truly contrite for one's faults, since a state of grace is ever indispensable for the acquisition of Indulgences. 2. To invoke in heart, if impossible to do so verbally, the Holy Name of Jesus; at least this condition is not unfrequently enjoined. 3. Above all, to accept with resignation, in expiation of one's sins, both the sufferings of our agony and death itself as coming to us from the hand of God.

Thus the dying person can, in a manner, by his own act, apply to himself this precious Indulgence, and as often as it may be available; the presence of a Priest is not necessary. The same is true of the plenary Indulgence, *in articulo mortis*, oftentimes accorded by the Holy Father either *viva voce*, or by a special Rescript. A person may apply it to himself on the same conditions. Still Pius IX. desires that, if the choice can be made, we should ask our Confessor or some other Priest to impart it to us, reciting the formula of the Ritual.

Besides these Indulgences for the hour of death, there is another much more solemn and of great antiquity in the Church, which, through a special grant of the Roman Pontiffs, Bishops impart personally, or by delegated Priests, to the sick in agony. At first they acquired the privilege merely for a limited period, but, by his Constitution, *Pia Mater*, of April 5, 1747, Benedict XIV. extended it to the entire term of their Episcopate or as long as they held their Sees, together with the power of sub-delegating their Priests, secular and regular, to apply the Indulgence to the dying. He furthermore declared, that this power does not expire at the death of the Pope who granted it, as it does not for the Priests possessed of it, whether by the death of the Ordinary, or through his being transferred to another See.

In giving this Benediction, with the plenary Indulgence, Priests ought to use the formula framed and prescribed by Bened. XIV.; it is to be found at the end of the Bull, *Pia Mater*, and in all the Roman Breviaries and Rituals. The present volume has it in the Formulary at the end. They can use no other. Yet if the sick person were so near his end, that the Priest would not have time to recite the whole form, he should commence with the words "Dominus noster Jesus Christus," or even, if necessary, say simply, "Indulgentiam plenariam et remissionem peccatorum tibi concedo: In Nomine Patris✠, et Filii, et Spiritus Sancti. r. Amen."

This Indulgence should be communicated even to the dying who have lost the use of their senses; for we may always presume, at least in ordinary cases, that it would be their desire to receive this blessing, had they the use of reason. It may be also applied to children who, by reason of their age, have not made their First Communion. Such was the decision of the Sacred Congregation of Rites, Dec. 16, 1826.

In the same danger, or in the same *articulus mortis*, said the ancient decrees, it is not permitted to recite many times the Benediction for a dying person, with an application of the plenary Indulgence. But Pius IX. has given leave to repeat the form of the Indulgence over the same invalid and in the same danger. He furthermore allows Priests vested with the power to impart several times—*pluries*—to a dying person the different plenary Indulgences *in articulo mortis*, to which he may have a right under various titles.

Notwithstanding this, the Indulgence cannot be gained more than once, and is not truly applied to a sick person, except when death actually ensues. Thus the *articulus mortis* is that moment which is followed by death—*cui subsequitur mors*. The intention of the Supreme Pontiffs, in granting the Indulgence, being, according to Theodore a Spiritu Sancto, "that the Faithful might have nothing to expiate after this mortal pilgrimage."*

O let us then strive, at this last moment, before entering on our road to eternity, to gain as many Indulgences as possible; for how do we know what debts we have to pay to the Divine Justice, or whether these plenary Indulgences have been applied to us in

---

* Sometimes the Popes have accorded an Indulgence, *in articulo mortis*, with this modification: "Etiamsi tunc mors non subsequatur," or "toties quoties incideris in mortis articulum." Plainly, in such cases, the Indulgence may be repeated and obtained, even though death does not ensue (Theodore a Spiritu Sancto, part II., cap 2, §5).

their full extent, or in what proportion they are applied? It is also of the utmost importance to us to qualify ourselves in life for such an abundant application of the merits of Jesus Christ, the Blessed Virgin and Saints, at the hour of our death. The most effectual means for attaining this end is, carefully to keep ourselves in the friendship of God, especially by a frequent worthy reception of the Sacraments, as also by being devout to the Blessed Virgin, and to St. Joseph, the Great Patron of a happy death.

## ARTICLE VIII.

### Indulgences peculiar to Religious.

#### 115. Observations.

1. Religious of both sexes, to whatever Order or Institute they may belong, can, by fulfilling the works enjoined, participate in the greater part of the Indulgences mentioned in the preceding articles.

2. The Sovereign Pontiff, Paul V., by his general Brief, May 23, 1606, commencing, "*Romanus Pontifex*," revoked all Indulgences previously granted to Regular Orders, whether Monastic or Mendicant—*quibuscumque Regularium Ordinibus*—that make the three solemn vows, as was declared by the Sacred Congregation of Indulgences, May 8, 1713 and April 23, 1714. But there are exceptions in favour of the Indulgences annexed to churches belonging to them, according to a decision of the Sacred Congregation of Indulgences (Sept. 7, 1607), and another of the Sacred Congregation of Bishops and Regulars (Aug. 21, 1615).

3. However, in the same Constitution—*Romanus*—Paul V. granted anew for ever the following Indulgences to all Religious of any Order whatever, Mendicant or Monastic, and to all Nuns whose rule has been approved, and who, consecrated to God by the three solemn Vows, live in perpetual cloister.*

4. In virtue of a response of the Sacred Penitentiary to Mgr. Bouvier, Jan. 2, 1836, the Nuns in France, though their vows be not solemn, nevertheless enjoy the spiritual favours accorded to their Order, and consequently the Indulgences. The same applies, pursuant to a reply of the Sacred Congregation of Indulgences (Feb. 22, 1847), to Congregations of females existing in France, not even approved by the Holy See. Hence, they can gain the Indulgences accorded to similar Congregations existing at Rome or elsewhere, with requisite sanction.† In fine, according to several other declarations, these Indulgences are likewise vouchsafed to all Religious Bodies of Men, as also to Monasteries, Congregations, and Religious Communities, who are not cloistered—

---

* All Nuns, of what title soever, subject to Bishops, share in the Indulgences of their respective Orders or Congregations, whose Constitutions and Rite they observe in the recitation of the Office (Decree, May 18, 1744).

† The question has been proposed to the Sacred Congregation: "Whether Nuns not approved by the Holy See, as commonly happens in France, could acquire the Indulgences available to their respective Religious Orders at Rome or elsewhere, and which are approved?" The Sacred Congregation replied (Feb. 22, 1847) in the affirmative, *et detur Rescriptum Sacræ Pœnitentiariæ.*

The Rescript to which the Sacred Congregation alludes, is that addressed by the Sacred Penitentiary (in 1846) to the Carmelites of the diocese of Bordeaux; it runs thus: "Sacra Pænitentiaria, perpensis expositis, respondit Oratrices, uti et cæteras Sorores Monasteriorum Galliæ, lucrari posse Indulgentias omnes, quæ Religioni, seu Instituto aliarum Monialium solemnia vota emittentium secundum Institutum, seu Regulam respectivam concessæ fuerunt, idque ex Indulto Sa: Me: Pii VII., a SS. D. N. Papa Gregorio XVI. iterum confirmato.

*senza clausura*—and bound to God only by simple vows (see "Raccolta," p. 379).

5. Agreeably to a declaration of Paul V., infirm Religious may obtain the Indulgences in bed, if unable to go to church, by performing the works of piety prescribed by their Confessors.

### 116. THE INDULGENCES.

*Plenary.* 1. The day of receiving the habit, Confession and Communion being implied. 2. The day of solemn profession, under the same conditions, after an entire year of noviceship. 3. The day of the principal Feast of the Order, careful to Confess, Communicate, or say Mass, and pray for the Church. 4. *In articulo mortis.* 5. To Religious, newly ordained Priests, the day of celebrating their first Mass; likewise to Religious who shall assist thereat, provided they Communicate or offer Mass if they are Priests. 6. To all Religious of both sexes, who, with the permission of their respective Superiors, go through the spiritual exercises for ten days, making each day at least two hours meditation on the Last Things, the Passion of Our Lord, the goodness of God, &c., and practising other acts of virtue, mortification, &c. They should, moreover, during this Retreat, make a general Confession, or that of a year, or at least an ordinary Confession, and approach the Holy Table. This Indulgence is attainable as often as the Retreat is made in the manner described. 7. Religious sent by the Pope, or going, with the leave of their Superiors, into infidel or heretical countries, to preach the faith, shall gain a plenary Indulgence the day of their departure, as also the day of arrival at their destination, if they Confess and Communicate or offer the Adorable Sacrifice. 8. When in his General Visitation, the Superior orders a continual prayer of forty hours in the Convents of his Order, for a prosperous issue thereof, each Religious can obtain a plenary Indulgence, by praying for two hours, even at different times, adding prayers for concord amongst Christian princes, &c., for the increase and observance of religious discipline, and Communicating or celebrating Mass. 9. The Indulgences of the Roman Stations to all Religious who, on the days marked in the Roman Missal, devoutly visit their respective churches, to pray there for some time (see n. 110).

*Partial:* 1. An Indulgence of sixty years and sixty Quarantines to all Religious, if, having each day during a month made half an hour's meditation, they Confess, Communicate or say Mass, the last Sunday of the month. 2. Five years and five Quarantines each day, if they recite five Paters and Aves before the altar of their church. This Indulgence may be also gained by Religious who, for a legitimate cause and with the sanction of their Superiors, are on a journey or outside the monastery, by saying the five Paters and Aves before any altar whatever. 3. Three years and three Quarantines *each time*, to those who, with contrite heart, accusing themselves of their faults and imperfections, say their fault at the Chapters, and hold spiritual conferences together.

In addition to these Indulgences, which are common to all Religious Institutes, each particular Order, each Congregation, nay, oftentimes each House of Religious, possesses others that have been in modern times either confirmed, renewed, or freshly granted by the Vicars of Jesus Christ. It is for each member of these communities to ascertain everything about them, should he wish to participate in the spiritual treasures with which the Holy See vouchsafes to enrich them.

---

## ARTICLE IX.

### APPENDIX.

INDULGENCES PECULIAR TO THE CHURCH OF NOTRE-DAME DE FOURVIERE, LYONS.

#### 117. NOTRE-DAME DE FOURVIERE.

For seventeen centuries, devotion to the Mother of God has ever been one of the chief characteristics of the people of Lyons. This pious regard to Mary was transmitted to them by their first Apostles, their Christian ancestors, the illustrious Pontiffs SS. Pothin and Irenæus, who had themselves imbibed it from a virgin source, the heart of St. John, or at least from the heart of the disciples of this great Apostle, so dearly loved by Jesus and Mary. It was at Lyons the first Church dedicated in France to the Queen of Heaven, was consecrated by St. Pothin, about the middle of the second century. Ever since, the fathers of succeeding generations have continuously handed down to their children these traditions of veneration, confidence, and love, which have merited for Lyons the happy title of *Ville de Marie* (City of Mary).

The first oratory dedicated to the Blessed Virgin, in Lyons, occupied, it is said, the place at present occupied by the subterraneous chapel in the church of St. Nizier. Other oratories were soon afterwards founded, and it is even thought that in the primitive ages the Mother of God had a little chapel under the porticoes of Trajan's *Forum*, or on the summit of Fourviere.*

However that may be, the immense porticoes of the ancient Forum having fallen into decay in the ninth century, the Lyonese either erected in their stead, or re-established the Chapel of our Lady of Fourviere, under the title of *Notre-Dame-de-bon-Conseil*. For more than three centuries, this poor, narrow, little church had been very badly frequented, as the people preferred to go to the crypt of St. Pothin—the cradle of their faith—or to *Notre-Dame-des-Graces*. in the Isle of Barbara, or finally to the Sanctuary of the Immaculate Virgin at Ainay. But, having been enlarged, and its collegiate Church founded about the close of the twelfth century, the devotion of the inhabitants was imperceptibly directed towards this blessed chapel, which became the sanctuary of favours from their most powerful Protectress.

The Calvinists having, through strategy, obtained possession of Lyons, in 1562, made it a prey to the most frightful ravages; they pillaged and destroyed the churches; and the Chapel of Fourviere, foremost in the fall, had only its walls preserved. But, in destroying the holy temples consecrated to Mary, they did not destroy the devotion cherished for her

---

* *Notre-Dame-de-Fourviere*, by Abbé A. M. Chaour, p. 22. The details given in that number are little better than a very brief analysis of a learned work published at Lyons by Mgr. Pelagaud, about 1835.

in the hearts of the Lyonese. For when the altar of Fourviere had been re-erected, August 1586, the inhabitants hailed with transports of joy, the new bell as a celestial thunder-rod, a symbol of hope and salvation.

I should remark that, in 1630, the Virgin of Fourviere, hitherto styled *Notre-Dame-de-bon-Conseil*, then acquired the title of *Notre-Dame-des-Graces*, which had been bestowed on the Virgin in the Isle of Barbara, at the time the famous sanctuary existed in the Isle.

The first link of the new chain of countless miraculous tokens of Her protection, so lavishly conferred by the Blessed Virgin on Her dear city of Lyons was annexed to Fourviere, September 8, 1643. Almost without interruption, the plague had been devastating the city. Hence the magistrates conceived and realized the idea of consecrating it for ever to our Lady of Fourviere. The plan was accomplished on the Feast of the Nativity, 1643, and accordingly from the date of that memorable alliance entered into between Mary and the people of Lyons, there is no mention of plague or epidemic in the histories or archives of Lyons. Hence, too, up to the time of the Revolution, the Provosts went annually to Fourviere to fulfil the vow of their ancestors. Still more, as soon as ever any calamity threatened this territory, or even the empire, the whole city at once earnestly raised its hands towards that mount whence they were sure to derive speedy relief.

During the dismal years of the latter part of the last century, the Church of Fourviere was sold, pillaged, and profaned. Yet the Faithful were not on that account deterred from going, animated with a spirit of religion, to pray at its gates, the church itself being closed. The turbulence having ceased, Religion once more made its appearance in France, whose soil it had enriched with glory and blessings for fourteen centuries. Wherefore the sanctuary of our Lady was recovered; the old statue was found under the roof, beneath a large pile of rubbish; and a few months afterwards, on Friday, the 19th April, 1805, the immortal Pius VII. came from Paris, opened the valued church, and celebrated there the Sacrifice of Expiation, to the great satisfaction, joy, confidence, and love of the Lyonese. He, then, from the summit of the holy eminence, blessed the city and its inhabitants who had been a long time designated *the special children of the Holy See—Sedis Apostolicæ. . . . filios speciales* (Innoc. IV.).

After the reopening of the church, numerous miracles were wrought through the powerful mediation of Mary. They are embodied in the annals of the Lyonese and other families, partly also exhibited in the *ex-voto* offerings hung around the walls of this miraculous retreat. In 1832, 1835, and much later still, the cholera impending over the city, it had recourse each time to that Heavenly Queen, who, particularly since 1643, had taken it under Her protection, and each time the calamity was averted. The marble and engravings will transmit to future generations a remembrance of this signal favour, which at present engenders unbounded confidence in the hearts of the Lyonese and others, even in the remotest parts of France, as may be inferred from the latest visitations of the cholera.

Thus it was befitting, that the Church of Fourviere, so worthy of being revered on so many titles, situated in the centre of a most religious city, on a soil fertilized by the blood of thousands of Martyrs, should likewise become a prolific source of Indulgences to the pilgrims who come in crowds to it from all parts of the globe. The Vicars of Christ perceiving this, and being themselves devotedly attached to Lyons and Fourviere, have generously vouchsafed to treasure up in this august holy sanctuary, some of the ineffable riches of the merits of Jesus, Mary, and the Saints.

118. INDULGENCES ATTACHED TO THE CHURCH OF FOURVIERE.

*Plenary Indulgences:* 1. The first plenary Indulgence, singularly remarkable and very rare, is recorded in the Pastoral addressed by His Eminence Cardinal Fesch, Archbishop of Lyons, to the Faithful of his diocese, April 18, 1805, on the occasion of the opening of *Notre-Dame-de-Fourviere.* The Prelate's words are:—" The Holy Father (Pius VII.) has been pleased to commute all the old Indulgences and spiritual favours of this sanctuary into: 1. One daily plenary Indulgence, applicable to the Living and the Dead, and attainable by the Faithful *once a day only*, provided that, being in a state of grace, even without having Confessed or Communicated, they visit that Basilica, and there pray for the Church, the State, our City, and our Diocese. 2. A *privileged altar* for every day, that of the Blessed Virgin," &c.

2. Another plenary Indulgence accorded by His Holiness Gregory XVI. (Brief, *Nuper Venerabilis,* issued at St. Mary Major, Sept. 15, 1837). It may

be acquired by everybody who, truly penitent, after Confession and Communion, shall visit the Church of Fourviere, and pray there for peaceful union amongst Christian princes, for the extirpation of heresy and exaltation of our Holy Mother the Church. A.

*Partial Indulgences:* 1. Those annexed to the recitation of the *Angelus*, to anyone who piously recites in the evening, at the sound of the Bell of Fourviere,* the *De profundis*, or three Paters and Aves for the Faithful Departed.

2. The same Indulgence to all who devoutly pray for the sick whose agony is announced by the Bell of said church (Pius VII. and Gregory XVI, Brief cited above).

*Other Indulgences:* By a most signal favour, His Holiness Gregory XVI. (same Brief) deigned to impart and annex to the Church of Notre-Dame-de-Fourviere, *all the Indulgences, remission of sins, relaxation of punishments*, and *other spiritual prerogatives* dispensed by the Sovereign Pontiffs to the holy chapel of the Church of Loretto, on condition that the Faithful accomplish therein the pious works enjoined for acquiring them. Thus the tutelary church of the Lyonese partakes of the privileges of the holy house of the Mother of God—*la Santa Casa*—that house wherein was accomplished the ineffable Mystery of the Incarnation, and which was literally the tabernacle of God amongst men.†

---

* The Bell of the Church at Fourviere announces the prayer for the Dead, every evening, an hour after the Angelus.

† In the reign of St. Celestine V., the natal dome of the Virgin, which had been consecrated by the Divine Mysteries, was first removed from the power of the infidels into Dalmatia, and afterwards transferred to the territory of Loretto in the province of Carthage. That

The following is a catalogue or summary of the Indulgences accorded by the Roman Pontiffs to the holy Chapel of Loretto; it has been extracted from authentic documents.*

Paul II., in 1464, granted an Indulgence of seven years and seven Quarantines to all the Faithful who, sincerely penitent, having Confessed and Communicated, might visit the holy House of Loretto, on the Feasts of the Assumption and Nativity of the Blessed Virgin, and on every Sunday of the year. Julius II. added a plenary Indulgence for the Feast of the Annunciation (1503). Leo X. extended the favour to the Festivals of Christmas, and in the Church of Loretto, attached the Stations of Rome to the seven altars distinguished by inscriptions (1513).

In 1573, Gregory XIII. desired to have the Indulgence conceded by Julius II. and Leo X. obtainable every day in Holy Week, also on the Festivals of our Lord and those of Mary, including their Octaves respectively. Furthermore, to the altar of St. Anne, through a Brief, dated Jan. 10, 1578, he annexed the privileges of the Gregorian altar.

Again, Clement VIII., 1592, accorded seven years and as many Quarantines, to all who go round the circuit of the holy chapel (*la Santa Casa*) on bended knees; similarly to persons devoutly assisting at the

---

the same was the very house in which the WORD WAS MADE FLESH AND DWELT AMONGST US, is clearly proved as well by the Papal Indults and most renowned veneration of the entire universe, as by an unbroken evidence of miracles and a profusion of celestial gifts (Brev. Rom. in festo translat. almæ Domus Lauret., die 10 Decembr., Lectio VI.).

* The Italian copy from which I have taken them, word for word, was forwarded to me from Loretto, October 18, 1855, by the R. F. Francis Orsini, then Rector of the Jesuit College in that city. The same list had been sent to me by Mgr. Thomas, Bishop of Loretto and Recanati, Jan. 17, 1868.

Divine Offices celebrated therein. He also vouchsafed to pilgrims and other strangers coming to Loretto to visit the Sanctuary, a plenary Indulgence attainable once a day. This grant was confirmed by Clem. XI. (Brief of 1700), and the Indulgence rendered applicable to the Souls of Purgatory.

Benedict XIII., 1724, dispensed an Indulgence of forty days, to the Faithful whom the Penitentiaries may touch with their reed.

Pius VI. corroborated the favour of the R. Stations bestowed by Leo X. on the seven altars of the Basilica (1775). And Pius VII, (Brief, Dec. 19, 1806) enriched the keepers or guardians of the holy chapel with power to apply to crucifixes and medals the Indulgence *in articulo mortis*, in favour of pilgrims and other strangers, and to attach the Bridgetine Indulgences to Chaplets, by touching the sacred *scutellum* of the Blessed Virgin with these devotional objects.

Moreover, by a second Brief of Aug. 29, 1815, the same Pope accorded a plenary Indulgence, applicable to the Dead and attainable once a day, to the Faithful of Loretto, who, having Confessed and Communicated, should pay a visit to the *Santa Casa*.

Such are the spiritual favours in which the chapel of Fourviere has a participation. "In days gone by," writes F. Cahour, "on occasions of any impending calamity, the people of Lyons used to go to supplicate our Lady of Loretto; but, behold, through a loving condescension, *Notre-Dame-de-Loretto* is become, in a manner, *Notre-Dame-de-Fourviere*. After having, at different times, graciously heard the deputies of Lyons, in days of plagues, She ended by saying to them: Why cross the Alps? I also inhabit the hill of your martyred ancestors." The people assembled there with the magistrates, and the scourge which had been always reappearing vanished for ever more. Even in our own day She said to a Pastor accustomed frequently to confer with Her concerning the interests of his flock: "Ask, and I will disclose at Fourviere a treasure of graces like to that from which pilgrims from all parts of the Christian world, draw in my ancient house of Nazareth. *I love those who love me, and those who desire to seek me in the morning, shall find me."**

*Plenary Indulgence for the 8th of September:* This new blessing, the immortal Pius IX., inheritor of the love of Innoc. IV., Pius VII., and Gregory XVI. for the *special children of the Holy See*, has granted, for the occasion of solemn Benediction of the Blessed Sacrament, which takes place annually on the hill of Fourviere, and for the Feast of the Nativity of the Blessed Virgin. The Brief is dated July 29, 1856, and runs thus :—

"We have heard, by official report, that, in the city of Lyons, it is a practice of long duration, to commemorate the visible patronage of the Virgin Mother of God, the effect of which that city has experienced, by a solemn Benediction each year, on the Nativity of Immaculate Mary, at the summit of the hill of Fourviere, in the presence of the people, so that thereby the whole city is put under the protection of the Mother of God," &c.†

The conditions for obtaining this Indulgence are: to Confess, Communicate, piously visit, on the day

---
* *Notre-Dame-de-Fourviere*, 6th Epoch, p. 373.
† The entire Brief is given in a number of the *Gazette* (Lyons Tuesday, Aug. 26, 1856).

of the Feast, either one's own Parish Church or that of Fourviere, and pray there with fervour for the intentions of the Supreme Pontiff, and devoutly assist at the solemn Benediction to which we refer. The Indulgence is applicable to the Souls in Purgatory.

N.B.—Besides the altar of the Miraculous Virgin, there are likewise *privileged* the small altar of the Annunciation, located beneath the Bell, and the altar of St. Thomas (Greg. XVI., Brief, Aug. 4, 1837). Moreover, agreeably to a testimony whose genuineness cannot be questioned, the altar of *Notre-Dame des Sept-Douleurs* enjoys the same prerogative.

Finally, in virtue of a Papal Indult, dated June 2, 1864, every Priest may say a votive Mass of the Blessed Virgin, at Her own altar: "Occurrente licet ritu duplici, dummodo," adds the Indult, "non discrepet color paramentorum occurrentis officii, atque omnino exclusis a præsenti concessione duplicibus 1mæ et 2ndæ classis, festis de præcepto servandis, feriis, vigiliis, et octavis privilegiatis—

"LAUS DEO SEMPER
VIRGINIQUE IMMACULATÆ."

# PART III.

## FORMULARY.

### Formulas of Blessings.

#### § I.

##### 119. OBSERVATIONS.

1. Read No. 101, Part II., page 254.
2. Bear in mind, also, that no others are to be employed but the formulas of Benedictions corresponding with those of the Roman Ritual: *Illi soli libri adhibendi, et in illis tantum Benedictionibus quæ Rituali Romano sunt conformes* (Decree of the Sacred Congregation of Rites, April 7, 1832—Gardellini, n. 4532). All ecclesiastical Benedictions not approved by the Sacred Congregation of Rites are prohibited under the penalties of the Index.*
3. *In omni benedictione extra Missam, Sacerdos saltem superpelliceo et stola, pro ratione temporis, utatur, nisi aliter in Missali notetur.*
 *Stando semper benedicat, et aperto capite.*
 *In principio cujusque benedictionis dicat:*
  v. Adjutorium nostrum in nomine Domini;
  ʀ. Qui fecit cœlum et terram.

---

* See the *Analecta Juris Pontificii*, part 7, January, 1855.

v. Dominus vobiscum;
r. Et cum spiritu tuo.

*Deinde dicatur oratio propria, una vel plures, prout suo loco notatum fuerit.*

*Postea rem aspergat aqua benedicta; et, ubi notatum fuerit, pariter incenset, nihil dicendo.* (Rit. Rom. de Benedictionib. Reg. Gener.).\*

### 120. BENEDICTO CRUCIS.

v. Adjutorium nostrum, etc.
r. Qui fecit coelum, etc.
v. Dominus vobiscum;
r. Et cum spiritu tuo.

*Oremus.*

Rogamus te, Domine sancte Pater omnipotens, æterne Deus, ut digneris benedicere ✠ hoc signum crucis, ut sit remedium salutare generi humano, sit soliditas fidei, profectus bonorum operum, redemptio animarum, sit solamen et protectio ac tutela contra sæva jacula inimicorum. Per Christum Dominum, etc.

*Deinde aqua benedicta aspergat.*

(Si fuerint plures, mutetur numerus).†

---

\* See the *Guide pratique de liturgie romaine*, sec. 6, chap. II, IV, v.
† When there is question of Blessing a Cross of the Mission, the Priest who blesses it, adds the following prayer, taken likewise from the Ritual.

OREMUS.

Benedic ✠, Domine, hanc crucem tuam per quam eripuisti mundum a dæmonum potestate, et superasti passione tua suggestorem peccati qui gaudebat in prævaricatione primi hominis per ligni vetiti sumptionem. (*Hic aspergat aqua benedicta.*) Sanctificetur hoc signum crucis in nomine Patris ✠ et Filii ✠ et Spiritus Sancti ✠, ut orantes clinantesque se propter Dominum ante istam Crucem inveniant corporis et animæ sanitatem. Per Christum Dominum nostrum. Amen.

*Postea sacerdos genuflexus ante crucem devote adorat et osculatur, et idem faciunt quicumque voluerint.*

### 121. BENEDICTIO IMAGINUM.

Jesu Christi D. Nostri,—B. Virginis Mariæ,—et aliorum Sanctorum.*

v. Adjutorium, etc.   r. Qui fecit, etc.

*Oremus.*

Omnipotens sempiterne Deus, qui Sanctorum tuorum imagines, *sive* effigies sculpi aut pingi non reprobas, ut quoties illas oculis corporeis intuemur, toties eorum actus et sanctitatem ad imitandum memoriæ oculis meditemur; hanc, quæsumus, imaginem, *seu* sculpturam in honorem et memoriam unigeniti Filii tui Domini nostri Jesu Christi, *vel* beatissimæ Virginis Mariæ, Matris Domini nostri Jesu Christi, *vel* Beati N. Apostoli tui, *vel* Martyris, *vel* Confessoris, *aut* Pontificis, *aut* Virginis adaptatam benedicere ✠ et sanctificare ✠ digneris; et præsta, ut quicumque coram illa unigenitum Filium tuum, *vel* beatissimam Virginem, *vel* gloriosum Apostolum, *sive* Martyrem, *sive* Confessorem, *aut* Virginem suppliciter colere et honorare studuerit, illius meritis et obtentu a te gratiam in præsenti, et æternam gloriam obtineat in futurum. Per eumdem Christum Dominum nostrum. r. Amen.

### 122. BENEDICTIO ROSARIORUM B. MARIÆ V.

(Propria Ordinis Prædicatorum.)

v. Adjutorium, etc.   r. Qui fecit, etc.

---

* Without a delegation from the Ordinary, a Priest cannot bless a cross, images or statues of the Blessed Virgin and Saints, whenever the blessing takes place publicly.

*Oremus.*

Omnipotens et misericors Deus, qui, propter eximiam charitatem tuam qua dilexisti nos, Filium tuum unigenitum Dominum nostrum Jesum Christum de cœlis in terram descendere, et de Beatissimæ Mariæ Dominæ nostræ utero sacratissimo, Angelo nuntiante, carnem suscipere, crucemque ac mortem subire, et tertia die gloriose a mortuis resurgere voluisti, ut nos eriperes de potestate diaboli: obsecramus immensam clementiam tuam, ut hæc signa Rosarii in honorem et laudem ejusdem Genitricis Filii tui ab Ecclesia tua fideli dicata bene✠dicas et sancti✠fices, eisque tantam infundas virtutem Spiritus Sancti, ut quicumque horum quodlibet secum portaverit, atque in domo sua reverenter tenuerit, et in eis ad te, secundum ejusdem sanctæ Societatis instituta, divina contemplando mysteria devote oraverit, salubri et perseveranti devotione abundet, sitque consors et particeps omnium gratiarum, privilegiorum et indulgentiarum quæ eidem Societati per Sanctam Sedem Apostolicam concessa fuerunt, ab omni hoste visibili et invisibili semper et ubique in hoc sæculo liberetur, et in exitu suo ab ipsa Beatissima Virgine Maria Dei Genitrice tibi plenus operibus præsentari mereatur. Per eumdem Dominum. ℟. Amen.

123. ALTERA BENEDICTO ROSARII, VEL CORONÆ PRECATORIÆ.

℣. Adjutorium, etc.     ℟. Qui fecit, etc.

*Oremus.*

Bene✠dic, Domine Jesu Christe, Fili Dei, Fili Mariæ, hæc Rosaria (*sive* has Coronas) ad honorem

SS. Virginis Genitricis tuæ instituta: et præsta, ut quicumque illa pie gestaverint, et devote recitaverint, per viscera misericordiæ et per intercessionem ejusdem Beatissimæ Virginis exaudiri mereantur, et tam animæ quam corporis recipere sanitatem et pacem. Qui vivis et regnas in sæcula sæculorum. ℟. Amen.

*Deinde sacerdos aspergat aqua benedicta.*
(Authorised for the diocese of Nantes).*

### 124. BENEDICTIO CANDELARUM EXTRA DIEM PURIFICATIONIS B. MARIÆ V.

℣. Adjutorium, etc.   ℟. Qui fecit, etc.

*Oremus.*

Domine Jesu Christe, Fili Dei vivi, benedic ✠ candelas istas supplicationibus nostris; infunde eis, Domine, per virtutem sanctæ Crucis ✠ benedictionem cœlestem, qui eas ad repellendas tenebras humano generi tribuisti; talemque benedictionem signaculo sanctæ Crucis ✠ accipiant, ut quibuscumque locis accensæ sive positæ fuerint, discedant principes tenebrarum et contremiscant, et fugiant pavidi cum omnibus ministris suis ab habitationibus illis, nec præsumant amplius inquietare aut molestare servientes tibi omnipotenti Deo: qui vivis et regnas in sæcula sæculorum. ℟. Amen.

### 125. BENEDICTIO LOCI, VEL DOMUS.

℣. Adjutorium, etc.   ℟. Qui fecit, etc.

* The Benedictions peculiar to certain Religious Orders can be used only by Priests who have derived the faculty from them. The same is to be said of the formulas of Benedictions approved for dioceses different from that to which a person belongs. I shall cite many of the kind in this Formulary.

*Oremus.*

Benedic ✠, Domine Deus omnipotens, locum istum *vel* domum istam, ut sit in eo *vel* in ea sanitas, castitas, victoria, virtus, humilitas, bonitas, et mansuetudo, plenitudo legis et gratiarum actio Deo Patri, et Filio, et Spiritui Sancto, et hæc benedictio maneat super hunc locum et super habitantes in eo, nunc et semper. R. Amen.

### 126. BENEDICTIO COMMUNIS SUPER FRUGES ET VINEAS.

V. Adjutorium, etc.  R. Qui fecit, etc.

*Oremus.*

Oramus pietatem tuam, omnipotens Deus, qui has primitias creaturæ tuæ quas aeris et pluviæ temperamento nutrire dignatus es, benedictionis tuæ imbre perfundas, et fructus terræ tuæ usque ad maturitatem perducas. Tribue quoque populo tuo de tuis muneribus tibi semper gratias agere; ut a fertilitate terræ esurientium animas bonis omnibus affluentibus repleas, et egenus et pauper laudent nomen gloriæ tuæ. Per Christum Dominum nostrum. R. Amen.

*Aspergat illas aqua benedicta.*

### 127. BENEDICTIO CUJUSLIBET VESTIMENTI HONESTI.

V. Adjutorium, etc.  R. Qui fecit, etc.
V. Dominus vobiscum.  R. Et cum spiritu tuo.

*Oremus.*

Domine Jesu Christe, qui pro salute generis humani de cœlo in terram descendere, et in utero gloriosæ Virginis Mariæ incarnari voluisti: bene ✠ dic hanc vestem (*vel* has vestes, *vel* hoc cingulum), ut ea (*vel* iis, *vel* eo) indutus, ab omnibus animæ et corporis hostibus protegatur. Qui vivis et regnas in sæcula sæculorum. R. Amen.

*Deinde sacerdos indumentum aspergat aqua benedicta.*

(Sanctioned for the diocese of Nantes.)

### 128. BENEDICTIO PUERORUM ET PUELLARUM.

v. Adjutorium, etc.  R. Qui fecit, etc.

*Oremus.*

Quæsumus, omnipotens Deus pueris istis pro quibus tuam deprecamur clementiam, bene✠dicere dignare, et per virtutem Sancti Spiritus corda eorum corrobora, vitam sanctifica, castimonia decora, et sensus eorum in bonis operibus munitos informa; prospera tribue, pacem concede, salutem confer, charitatem largire, et omnibus diabolicis atque humanis insidiis, tua protectione et virtute, semper defende, et in finem ad requiem Paradisi eos perducas. Per Dominum nostrum, etc.

*Oremus.*

Domine Jesu Christe, qui parvulos tibi oblatos et ad te venientes complectebaris (*hic ponat manus super capita puerorum*) manusque super illos imponens benedicebas atque dicebas: Sinite parvulos venire ad me, et nolite prohibere eos, talium est enim regnum cœlorum; et Angeli eorum semper vident faciem Patris mei; respice, quæsumus, ad pueri *vel* puellæ (*si fuerit unus*) *seu* puerorum *vel* puellarum præsentium innocentiam, et ad suorum parentum devotionem: et

clementer eos hodie per ministerium meum bene✠
dic, ut in tua gratia et misericordia semper proficiant,
te sapiant, te diligant, te timeant, et mandata tua
custodiant, et ad finem optatum feliciter perveniant
per te, Salvator mundi, qui cum Patre et Spiritu
Sancto, etc.

Benedictio Dei omnipotentis Pa✠tris, et Fi✠lii,
et Spiri✠tus Sancti descendat super vos, et custodiat atque dirigat vos, et maneat semper vobiscum.
R. Amen.

*Aspergantur aqua benedicta.*

(Authorised in many dioceses.)

### 129. BENEDICTIO AD OMNIA.

V. Adjutorium, etc.    R. Qui fecit, etc.

*Oremus.*

Deus, cujus verbo sanctificantur omnia, benedictionem tuam effunde super creaturam istam (*vel*
creaturas istas), et præsta: ut quisquis ea (*vel* eis)
secundum legem et voluntatem tuam cum gratiarum
actione usus fuerit, per invocationem sanctissimi
Nominis tui, corporis sanitatem, et animæ tutelam,
te auctore, percipiat. Per Christum Dominum, etc.
R. Amen.

*Deinde aspergit aqua benedicta.*

(Approved by the Sacred Congregation of Rites.
Every Priest may use this to bless any object what-
ever whose Benediction is not embodied in the Roman
Ritual.)

## 130. MODE OF IMPARTING THE PAPAL BENEDICTION.*

*Methodus indictionis præmittendæ Pontificiæ Benedictioni statutis diebus super populum elargiendæ.—Ritusque in ea servandus a regularibus, quibus a S. Sede hujusmodi facultas indulta est, vel indulgebitur.*

*Admoneatur populus de Indulgentia a Sede Apostolica concessa, de præceptis operibus pro ea lucrifacienda; de die quo visitanda est designata ecclesia; de hora denique qua dabitur Pontificia Benedictio. De quibus, quatenus opus sit, etiam schedis impressis, et consuetis locis palam affixis certior fiat.*

*Postquam statutis die et hora, populus ad ecclesiam convenerit, alta voce legantur Apostolicæ Litteræ, seu Decreta, quibus Indulgentia conceditur, una cum potestate Benedictionem Apostolicam super populum effundendi, ut de delegatione audientibus constet; et concessio ex latino sermone in vulgarem accommodatum ad populi intelligentiam conversa pronuntietur,† populus ad suorum scelerum detestationem pio brevique sermone excitetur, post quæ sacerdos, nullis circum-*

---

\* In conferring on Jesuit Missionaries power to give the Papal Benediction, His Holiness Pius IX. wishes the Benediction to be given, not with the hand, but with a crucifix—detur cum imagine D. N. Jesu Christi.

The reference is solely to the Benediction imparted in every parish, city, town, &c., at the conclusion of a Mission. Under the name Mission are comprised Retreats of eight days observed in parishes. But Retreats for Religious Communities are not included. Yet, if the Stations of Advent and Lent were being terminated, especially when gone through as Missions, they are embraced.

The Benediction is not given except with the consent of Ecclesiastical Superiors. On May 4, 1851, the Pope allowed Jesuit Missionaries to yield to the senior, or to the highest in dignity among the ecclesiastics present at the Mission, the favour of imparting this Benediction.

† Should there be a justifying cause, one may simply say, *in the vernacular,* "*in virtue of the faculties received from the Holy See,*" &c. (Decree of June 30, 1840). It is enough to make the people aware of the Apostolic delegation.

*stantibus ministris, stola et superpelliceo indutus (ut in Rituali hoc præscribitur cum agitur de benedictionibus quæ extra Missam præsbyteris permittuntur), ante altare genuflexus, sequentibus verbis Dei opem imploret;*

℣. Adjutorium nostrum in nomine Domini;
℟. Qui fecit cœlum et terram.
℣. Domine, exaudi orationem meam;
℟. Et clamor meus ad te veniat.
℣. Dominus vobiscum;
℟. Et cum spiritu tuo.

*Diende stans sequentem recitet orationem:*

*Oremus.*

Omnipotens et misericors Deus, da nobis auxilium de sancto, et vota populi hujus in humilitate cordis veniam peccatorum poscentis, tuamque benedictionem præstolantis et gratiam, clementer exaudi: dexteram tuam super eum benignus extende, ac plenitudinem divinæ benedictionis effunde, qua bonis omnibus cumulatus, felicitatem et vitam consequatur æternam. Per Christum...

℟. Amen.

*Post quam, ad cornu Epistolæ accedat, ut in Actis Ecclesiæ Mediolanensis (par. 4.), benedicet in ecclesia ad altare, stans in cornu Epistolæ: Et stans in cornu Epistolæ, non trina, hoc est, triplici signo crucis, sed una benedictione, unico videlicet signo crucis, benedicat, proferens alta voce hæc verba:*

Benedicat vos Omnipotens Deus ✠ Pater, et Filius, et Spiritus Sanctus. ℟. Amen.

*Sic præcipitur in Epistola Encyclica Benedicti XVI., ad PP. Generales Ordinum Regularium.*

*Dat. Romæ, apud Sanctam Mariam Majorem*, die 19 Martii, 1748; Pontificatus sui anno VIII.

### 131. BENEDICTIO CINGULORUM IN HONOREM S. JOSEPHI, SPONSI B. MARIÆ VIRGINIS.

*In diœcesibus quibus a Sancta Apostolica Sede privilegium conceditur benedicendi Cingula in honorem sancti Josephi sponsi beatæ Mariæ Virginis, sacerdotes adhibere debent hanc formulam a sacra Rituum Congregatione approbatam, die* 19 *Septembris*, 1859:

v. Adjutorium nostrum in nomine Domini,
r. Qui fecit cœlum et terram.
v. Dominus vobiscum,
r. Et cum spiritu tuo.

*Oremus.*

Domine Jesu Christe, qui virginitatis consilium, et amorem ingeris, atque castitatem præcipis: oramus clementiam tuam, ut hæc Cingula castitatis tesseram bene✠dicere et sancti✠ficare digneris, ut quicumque pro castitate servanda illis præcincti fuerint, intercedente beato Josepho Sanctissimæ Genitricis tuæ sponso, gratam tibi continentiam, mandatorumque tuorum obedientiam servent, atque veniam peccatorum suorum obtineant, et sanitatem mentis et corporis percipiant, vitamque consequantur æternam. Qui vivis regnas cum Deo Patre in unitate Spiritus Sancti Deus, per omnia sæcula sæculorum. r. Amen.

*Oremus.*

Da, quæsumus, omnipotens æterne Deus, ut purissimæ Virginis Mariæ, ejusque sponsi Josephi integerrimam virginitatem venerantes, eorum intercessionibus puritatem mentis et corporis consequamur. Per Christum Dominum nostrum. R. Amen.

*Oremus.*

Omnipotens sempiterne Deus, qui castissimo viro Josepho purissimam Mariam semper Virginem et Puerum Jesum commisisti, te supplices exoramus ut fideles tui, qui his Cingulis in honorem, et sub protectione ejusdem sancti Joseph, præcincti fuerint; te largiente, et ipso intercedente, in castitate semper devote persistant. Per eumdem . . . R. Amen.

*Oremus.*

Deus, innocentiæ restitutor et amator, quæsumus ut fideles tui, qui hæc Cingula adhibuerint intercedente beato Josepho sanctissimæ Genitricis tuæ sponso, in lumbis suis sint semper præcincti et lucernas ardentes gestent in manibus suis, ac similes sint hominibus exspectantibus Dominum suum quando revertatur a nuptiis, ut cum venerit et pulsaverit, confestim aperiant ei, et in æterna gaudia recipi mereantur. Qui vivis et regnas in sæcula sæclorum. R. Amen.

*Deinde sacerdos, imposito thure in thuribulo, aqua benedicta aspergit Cingula, dicens:* Asperges me, etc.; *postea incensat, et tandem dicit:*

V. Salvos fac servos tuos,
R. Deus meus, sperantes in te.
V. Mitte eis, Domine, auxilium de sancto;
R. Et de Sion tuere eos.
V. Domine, exaudi orationem meam;
R. Et clamor meus ad te veniat.
V. Dominus vobiscum;
R. Et cum spiritu tuo.

*Oremus.*

Deus misericors, Deus clemens, cui bona cuncta placent, sine quo nihil boni inchoatur, nihilque boni perficitur : adsint nostris humillimis precibus tuæ pietatis aures, et fideles tuos, qui in tuo sancto nomine Cingulo benedicto in honorem, et sub protectione sancti Josephi præcincti fuerint, a mundi impedimento, vel sæculari desiderio defende ; et concede eis, ut in hoc sancto proposito devoti persistere, et remissione percepta, ad electorum tuorum valeant pervenire consortium. Per Dominum nostrum . . .
ʀ. Amen.

132. FORMULA BENEDICENDI NUMISMATA SEU CRUCES S. PATRIS BENEDICTI, A SS. D. BENEDICTO PP. XIV. APPROBATA.

ᴠ. Adjutorium nostrum in nomine Domini,
ʀ. Qui fecit cœlum et terram.

*Oremus.*

Exorcizo vos Numismata per Deum Patrem ✠ omnipotentem, qui fecit cœlum et terram, mare, et omnia quæ in eis sunt. Omnis virtus adversarii, omnis exercitus diaboli, et omnis incursus, omnia phantasmata Satanæ eradicare et effugare ab iis Numismatibus, ut fiant omnibus qui eis usuri sunt salus mentis et corporis, in Nomine Patris ✠ omnipotentis, et Jesu ✠ Christi Filii ejus Domini nostri, et Spiritus Sancti Paracliti et in charitate ejusdem Domini Nostri Jesu Christi, qui venturus est judicare vivos et mortuos, et sæculum per ignem. ʀ. Amen.

Kyrie eleison. Christe eleison. Kyrie eleison
Pater noster, etc.

v. Et ne nos inducas in tentationem;
r. Sed libera nos a malo.
v. Salvos fac servos tuos,
r. Deus meus, sperantes in te.
v. Esto nobis, Domine, turris fortitudinis,
r. A facie inimici.
v. Dominus virtutem populo suo dabit;
r. Dominus benedicet populum suum in pace.
v. Mitte eis, Domine, auxilium de sancto;
r. Et de Sion tuere eos.
v. Domine, exaudi vocem meam,
r. Et clamor meus ad te veniat.
v. Dominus vobiscum;
r. Et cum spiritu tuo.

*Oremus.*

Deus omnipotens, bonorum omnium largitor, supplices te rogamus, ut per intercessionem S. P. Benedicti his sacris Numismatibus, litteris ac characteribus a te designatis, tuam benedictionem infundas; ut omnes qui ea gestaverint, ac bonis operibus intenti fuerint, sanitatem mentis, et corporis, et gratiam sanctificationis, atque indulgentias nobis concessas consequi mereantur, omnesque diaboli insidias et fraudes per auxilium misericordiæ tuæ effugere valeant, et in conspectu tuo sancti et immaculati appareant. Per Dominum nostrum, etc.

*Oremus.*

Domine Jesu Christe, qui voluisti pro totius mundi redemptione de Virgine nasci, circumcidi, a Judæis reprobari, Judæ osculo tradi, vinculis alligari, spinis coronari, clavis perforari, inter latrones crucifigi, lancea vulnerari, et tandem in cruce mori; per hanc tuam sanctissimam Passionem humiliter exoro, ut omnes diabolicas insidias et fraudes expellas ab eo, qui nomen sanctum tuum his litteris et characteribus a te designatis devote invocaverit, et eum ad salutis portum perducere digneris. Qui vivis et regnas, etc.

Benedictio Dei Patris ✠ omnipotentis, et Filii ✠, et Spiritus Sancti descendat super hæc Numismata ac ea gestantes, et maneat semper. In nomine Patris ✠, et Filii ✠, et Spiritus Sancti ✠. Amen.

*Aspergantur aqua benedicta.*

### 133. METHODUS PRO ERIGENDIS STATIONIBUS VIÆ CRUCIS.

(Propria Ordinis Minorum Observantium S. Francisci.)

*Sacerdos superpelliceo et stola violacei coloris indutus, uno saltem clerico adhibito, qui ei opportuno tempore porrigere possit vasculum aquæ benedictæ cum aspersorio, et thuribulum cum incensi navicula, ascendit altare, ibique stans brevi sermone super præstantia et utilitate pii exercitii Viæ Crucis populum alloquetur; deinde genuflexus infimo gradu intonabit hymnum: Veni, Creator Spiritus, ect.*

v. Emitte Spiritum tuum, et creabuntur.
r. Et renovabis faciem terræ.

*Oremus.*

Deus, qui corda fidelium Sancti Spiritus illustratione docuisti: da nobis in eodem Spiritu recta sapere, et de ejus semper consolatione gaudere.

Defende, quæsumus, Domine, Beata Maria semper Virgine intercedente, populum istum (*vel* familiam istam) ab omni adversitate, et toto corde tibi prostratum (*vel* prostratam) ab hostium propitius tuere clementer insidiis.

Actiones nostras, quæsumus, Domine, aspirando præveni, et adjuvando prosequere, ut cuncta nostra oratio et operatio et operatio a te semper incipiat, et per te cœpta finiatur. Per Dominum nostrum, etc.

*Benedictio tabularum pictarum* (si adsunt).*

v. Adjutorium, etc.     r. Qui fecit, etc.

*Oremus.*

Omnipotens sempiterne Deus, etc., page 316, No. 121.

*Tunc Sacerdos eas aspergit aqua benedicta, et incensat. In oratorio privato omitti potest incensatio.*

*Benedictio crucium* (quæ ex ligno esse debent).

v. Adjutorium, etc.     r. Qui fecit, etc.

*Oremus.*

Rogamus te, Domine sancte, etc., page 315

*Oremus.*

Benedic☩, Domine, has cruces, quia per crucem sanctam tuam eripuisti mundum, etc., page 315, note

*Deinde cantatur hymnus:* Vexilla Regis prodeunt; *et* Stabat Mater dolorosa *usque ad strophen:* Fac ut ardeat cor meum, *inclusive.*

*Post* Amen, *Sacerdos accedens ad locum I. stationis osculatur crucem et tabulam, easque vel per se, vel per laicum decenti habitu indutum, collocat in loco ad id præparato; deinde legit meditationem et preces huic*

---

* In the chapter on the Way of the Cross, I have cited a Decree of Jan. 30, 1839, in reference to the blessing of the pictures or images.

*stationi respondentes: quod et fiet in cæteris stationibus. Quibus finitis, cantatur Hymnus:* Te Deum, *cum Oratione:* Deus cujus misericordiæ, etc.

*In fine, Sacerdos benedicit populum cum cruce.*

---

## § II.

### Formulas of Receptions.

134. RITUS BENEDICENDI ET IMPONENDI SCAPULARE RUBRUM PASSIONIS SACRATISSIMIQUE CORDIS DOMINI NOSTRI JESU CHRISTI, NECNON ET CORDIS AMANTISSIMI AC COMPATIENTIS BEATÆ MARIÆ VIRGINIS IMMACULATÆ.

*Genuflexo qui suscepturus est Scapulare, Sacerdos superpelliceo et stola rubra indutus, capite detecto, dicat:*

v. Adjutorium nostrum in nomine Domini;
r. Qui fecit cœlum in terram.
v. Dominus vobiscum;
r. Et cum spiritu tuo.

*Oremus.*

Domine Jesu Christe, qui tegimen nostræ mortalitatis induere dignatus temetipsum exinanivisti, formam servi accipiens, et factus obediens usque ad mortem Crucis, tuæ largitatis clementiam humiliter imploramus, ut hoc genus vestimenti quod in honorem et memoriam dolorosissimæ Passionis tuæ tuique sacratissimi Cordis, necnon et Cordis amantissimi ac compatientis Immaculatæ Matris tuæ institutum fuit, atque ut illo induti hæc mysteria devotius recolant, benedicere ✠ digneris, ut hic famulus tuus qui (*vel* hæc famula tua quæ) ipsum gestaverit, te quoque, per tua merita et intercessionem beatissimæ Virginis Mariæ, induere mereatur. Qui vivis et regnas in sæcula sæculorum. Amen.

*Hic Sacerdos S. Scapulare aqua benedicta aspergit, et illud imponit, dicens:*

Accipe, carissime frater (*vel* carissima soror), hunc habitum benedictum, ut veterem hominem exutus (*vel* exuta) novumque indutus (*vel* induta) ipsum digne perferas, et ad vitam pervenias sempiternam. Per Christum Dominum nostrum.

*Deinde subjungit.*

Et ego, ex facultate mihi concessa, recipio te (*vel* vos) ad participationem omnium bonorum spiritualium quæ per Sanctæ Sedis Apostolicæ privilegium huic sancto Scapulari, in gratiam Congregationis Missionis, concessa sunt. In nomine ✠ Patris, et Filii, et Spiritus Sancti. Amen.

*Denique dicatur trina vice versiculus sequens:*

Te ergo quæsumus, tuis famulis subveni, quos pretioso sanguine redemisti!

135. RITUS SERVANDUS IN BENEDICTIONE HABITUS, AC RECEPTIONE CONFRATRUM B. VIRGINIS MARIÆ DE MONTE CARMELO.

(Proprius Ordinis Carmelitarum.)

*Sodalitati Carmeli nomen daturus, ipso die ad Pœnitentiæ, atque Eucharistiæ Sacramenta accedat ut Plenariam Indulgentiam a Paulo V. concessam, lucrari valeat.*

*Si fieri potest, Scapulare benedicendum est ad Altare B. V. Mariæ de Monte Carmelo, duobus cereis accensis.*

*Sacerdos superpelliceum, vel Regulare Pallium induat, una cum Stola albi coloris.*

*Genuflexo qui habitum recipit, Sacerdos stans dicat:*
Suscepimus, Deus, misercordiam tuam in medio templi tui: secundum nomen tuum, Deus, sic et laus tua in fines terræ: justitia plena est dextera tua.

Kyrie eleison. Christe eleison. Kyrie eleison. Pater noster.

   v. Et ne nos inducas in tentationem;
   r. Sed libera nos a malo.
   v. Salvum fac servum tuum, *vel* (ancillam tuam);
   r. Deus meus sperantem in te.
   v. Mitte ei, Domine, auxilium de sancto;
   r. Et de Sion tuere eum, *vel* eam.
   v. Nihil proficiat inimicus in eo, *vel* in ea;
   r. Et filius iniquitatis non apponat nocere ei.
   v. Domine, exaudi orationem meam;
   r. Et clamor meus ad te veniat.
   v. Dominus vobiscum;
   r. Et cum spiritu tuo.

*Oremus.*

Suscipat te Christus in numero fidelium suorum, et nos, licet indigni, te suscipimus in orationibus nostris. Concedat tibi Deus per unigenitum suum Mediatorem Dei et hominum, tempus bene vivendi, locum bene agendi, constantiam bene perseverandi, et ad æternæ vitæ hæreditatem feliciter perveniendi: et sicut nos hodie fraterna charitas spiritualiter jungit in terris, ita divina pietas, quæ dilectionis est auctrix, et amatrix, nos cum fidelibus suis conjungere dignetur in Cœlis: Per eumdem Christum Dominum nostrum. ℟. Amen.

℣. Adjutorium nostrum in nomine Domini;
℟. Qui fecit cœlum et terram.
℣. Sit nomen Domini benedictum;
℟. Ex hoc nunc et usque in sæculum.
℣. Domine, exaudi orationem meam;
℟. Et clamor meus ad te veniat.
℣. Dominus vobiscum;
℟. Et cum spiritu tuo.

*Oremus.*

Æterne Pater, et omnipotens Deus, qui Unigenitum tuum vestem nostræ mortalitatis induere voluisti: obsecramus immensam tuæ largitatis bene✠dictionem in hoc genus effluere vestimenti, quod sancti Patres ad innocentiæ et humilitatis indicium a renuntiantibus sæculo gestari sanxerunt, et sic ipsum bene✠dicere digneris, ut quicumque eo usus fuerit, induere mereatur ipsum Dominum nostrum Jesum Christum Filium tuum, qui tecum vivit, ea regnat in unitate Spiritus Sancti Deus, per omnia sæcula sæculorum. ℟. Amen.

*Oremus.*

Suppliciter te, Domine, rogamus, ut super hunc habitum servo tuo (*vel* ancillæ tuæ), imponendum bene✠dictio tua benigna descendat, ut sit bene✠dictus, atque divina virtute procul pellantur hostium nostrorum visibilium et invisibilium tela nequissima. ℟. Amen.

*Aspergat habitum aqua benedicta, et imponendo dicat:*

Accipe, vir devote (*vel* mulier devota), hunc habitum benedictum, precans Sanctissimam Virginem, ut ejus meritis illum perferas sine macula, et te ab omni adversitate defendat, atque ad vitam perducat æternam. R. Amen.

Adesto, Domine, supplicationibus nostris, et hunc famulum tuum (*vel* hanc famulam tuam), quem (*vel* quam) sacræ Religioni Carmelitarum sociamus, perpetua tribue firmitate corroborari, ut perseveranti proposito, in omni sanctitate tibi valeat famulari.

Protege, Domine, famulum tuum (*vel* famulam tuam) subsidiis pacis, et B. Mariæ semper Virginis patrociniis confidentem a cunctis hostibus redde securum (*vel* securam).

Bene✠dicat te Conditor cœli et terræ Deus omnipotens, qui te eligere dignatus est ad Beatissimæ Virginis Mariæ de Monte Carmelo societatem, et Confraternitatem, quam precamur, ut in hora obitus tui conterat caput serpentis, qui tibi est adversarius, et tandem tanquam victor (*vel* victrix) palmam et coronam sempiternæ hæreditatis consequaris. Per Christum Dominum nostrum. R. Amen.

*Si autem habitus solum sit benedicendus, incipitur a* v. Adjutorium nostrum *usque ad orationem* Suppliciter *inclusive.*

*Deinde aspergat confratrem aqua benedicta et subjungat:*

Ego auctoritate, qua fungor, et mihi concessa, recipio te ad Confraternitatem sacræ Religionis Carmelitarum, et investio, ac participem te facio omnium bonorum spiritualium ejusdem Ordinis. In nomine Patris, et Fi✠lii, et Spiritus Sancti. Amen.

*His expletis describatur confratris nomen in Codice*

*Confraternitatis\*, et paucis sed efficacioribus verbis eum adhortetur ad caute, pie, sancteque vivendum, ne Deiparam offendat, quam in posterum peculiari devotionis obsequio et affectu colere, ac veluti singularem ac dulcissimam Matrem prosequi fas erit.*

### 136. A SHORTER FORM FOR ADMISSION INTO THE CONFRATERNITY OF CARMEL.

v. Adjutorium nostrum . . . r. Qui fecit . . .
v. Sit nomen Domini benedictum ;
r. Ex hoc nunc et usque in sæculum.
v. Domine, exaudi orationem meam;
r. Et clamor meus ad te veniat.

*Oremus.*

Æterne Pater, et omnipotens Deus, qui unigenitum Filium tuum vestem nostræ mortalitatis induere voluisti; obsecramus immensam tuæ largitatis benedictionem in hoc genus effluere vestimenti, quod sancti Patres ad innocentiæ et humilitatis indicium a renuntiantibus sæculo gestari sanxerunt, et sic ipsum benedicere✠digneris, ut quicumque eis usus fuerit, induere mereatur ipsum Dominum nostrum Jesum Christum Filium tuum, qui tecum vivit et regnat in sæcula sæculorum. Amen.

*Aspergat aqua benedicta Scapulare, et illud imponens dicat:*

Accipe jugum Christi suave et onus ejus leve, in nomine Patris ✠, et Filii ✠, et Spiritus ✠ Sancti. Amen.

\* The inscription is *not a matter of necessity*, but merely of *expediency* (Read the Article on the Scapular of Carmel).

*Oremus.*

Adesto, Domine, supplicationibus nostris, et hunc famulum (*vel* famulam) quem sacræ Religioni sociamus, perpetua tribue firmitate corroborari, ut perseveranti proposito in omni sanctitate tibi valeat famulari, qui vivis et regnas, etc.

Auctoritate mihi concessa, ego te recipio et adscribo Confraternitati sanctissimi Scapularis in honorem Deiparæ Virginis instituti, teque facio participem omnium gratiarum, Indulgentiarum, privilegiorum, bonorumque spiritualium ejusdem Confraternitatis, in nomine Patris, et Filii, et Spiritus Sancti. Amen.

137. RITUS BENEDICENDI ET IMPONENDI SCAPULARE CÆRULEUM IN HONOREM CONCEPTIONIS BEATÆ MARIÆ VIRGINIS IMMACULATÆ, QUOD A CLERICIS REGULARIBUS, TEATINIS NUNCUPATIS, EX SPECIALI PRIVILEGIO CLEMENTIS PAPÆ X. DISTRIBUITUR, ET A CLEMENTE PAPA XI., APPROBATUS ANNO 1710.

*Genuflexo qui suscepturus est scapulare, Sacerdos superpelliceo et stola alba indutus, capite detecto, dicat absolute:*

V. Adjutorium nostrum in nomine Domini;
R. Qui fecit cœlum et terram.
V. Dominus vobiscum;
R. Et cum spiritu tuo.

*Oremus.*

Domine Jesu Christe, qui tegimen nostræ mortalitatis induere dignatus es, tuæ largitatis clementiam humiliter imploramus, ut hoc genus vestimenti, quod in honorem, et memoriam CONCEPTIONIS BEATÆ

Mariæ Virginis Immaculatæ, nec non ut illo induti exorent in hominum pravorum morum reformationem institutum fuit, bene ✠ dicere digneris, ut hic famulus tuus, qui eo usus fuerit (*vel* hæc famula tua quæ eo usa fuerit) eadem Beata Maria Virgine intercedente, te quoque i nduere mereatur. Qui vivis et regnas in sæcula sæculorum. Amen.

*Postea Sacerdos, nihil dicendo aspergit Scapulare aqua benedicta; deinde illud imponit dicens :*

Accipe, frater (*vel* soror), Scapulare Conceptionis Beatæ Mariæ Virginis Immaculatæ, ut, ea intercedente, veterem hominem exutus (*vel* exuta), et ab omni peccatorum inquinamento mundatus (*vel* mundata), ipsum perferas sine macula, et ad vitam pervenias sempiternam. Per Christum Dominum nostrum. Amen.

*Postea subjungit :*

Et ego ex facultate mihi concessa, recipio te ad participationem bonorum omnium spiritualium, quæ in Clericorum Regularium Congregatione, ex gratia Dei, fiunt : et quæ per Sanctæ Sedis Apostolicæ privilegium concessa sunt.

✠ In nomine Patris, et Filii, et Spiritus Sancti.
R. Amen.

**138. Ritus imponendi habitum confratribus Societatis septem dolorum B. V. M.**

(Proprius Ordinis Servorum B. M. V.).

*Sacerdos indutus superpellicio et stola vialacea dicat*

V. Adjutorium nostrum in nomine Domini ;
R. Qui fecit cœlum et terram.

℣. Dominus vobiscum;
℟. Et cum spiritu tuo.

*Oremus.*

Omnipotens sempiterne Deus, qui morte Unigeniti tui mundum collapsum restaurare dignatus es, ut nos a morte æterna liberares, et ad gaudia Regni cœlestis perduceres: respice, quæsumus, super hanc familiam Servorum in nomine Beatissimæ Virginis septem Doloribus sauciæ congregatam, de cujus gremio hic famulus tuus (*vel* hæc famula tua) esse cupit (*vel* hi famuli tui, *vel* hæ famulæ tuæ esse cupiunt), ut augeatur numerus tibi fideliter servientium: ut omnibus sæculi, et carnis perturbationibus liberatus (*liberata*) (*liberati*), et a lacqueis diaboli securus (*secura*) (*securi*), intercessione ejusdem Beatæ Mariæ Virginis, et Beatorum Augustini, et Philippi, ac septem nostrorum Beatorum Patrum Ordinis nostri Fundatorum, vera gaudia possideat (*vel possideant*). Per Christum Dominum nostrum. Amen.

*Inde benedicat Habitum et Coronam, dicens:*

*Oremus.*

Domine Jesu Christe, qui tegmen nostræ mortalitatis induere dignatus es, obsecramus immensam largitatis tuæ abundantiam, ut hoc genus vestimentorum, quod sancti Patres nostri ad innocentiæ humilitatisque indicium, in memoriam septem Dolorum B. Mariæ Virginis nos ferre sanxerunt, ita benedicere ✠ digneris, ut qui illis fuerit indutus, corpore pariter et animo induat te Salvatorem nostrum. Qui vivis et regnas in sæcula sæculorum. Amen.

*Oremus.*

Omnipotens et misercors Deus, qui propter nimiam charitatem, qua dilexisti nos, Filium tuum Unigenitum Dominum nostrum Jesum Christum pro redemptione nostra, de cœlis ad terram descendere, carnem suscipere, et Crucis tormentum subire voluisti; obsecramus immensam clementiam tuam, ut hanc Coronam, in memoriam septem Dolorum Genitricis Filii tui ab Ecclesia tua fideli dicatam benedicas ✠ sanctifices ✠ et ei tantam Spiritus Sancti virtutem infundas, ut quicumque eam recitaverit, ac secum portaverit, atque in domo sua reverenter tenuerit, ab omni hoste visibili, et invisibili, semper, et ubique in hoc sæculo liberetur, et in exitu suo a Beatissima Virgine Maria tibi bonis operibus coronatus præsentari mereatur. Per Dominum nostrum. Amen.

*Tandem aspergit dicens:* Asperges me, etc.
*Præbendo Habitum et Coronam dicat:*

Accipe, carissime frater (*vel* carissima soror) Habitum B. M. Virginis singulare signum Servorum suorum, in memoriam septem Dolorum, quos ipsa in vita, et morte Unigeniti Filii sui sustinuit, ut ita indutus (*vel* induta) sub ejus patricinio perpetuo vivas. Amen.

Accipe Coronam B. Mariæ Virginis, in memoriam septem Dolorum suorum contextam, ut dum eam ore laudaveris, ejus pœnas toto corde compatiaris. Amen.

### 139. FORMULA FOR A SOLEMN RECEPTION INTO ANY CONFRATERNITY WHATEVER.

For example, of the Blessed Sacrament, Sacred Heart, Holy Rosary, &c.

Those to be received kneel at the Communion-rail, holding a candle in their hands; the Priest duly authorised, vested with surplice and stole, on his knees before the altar, recites the "Veni Creator," and the prayer "Deus qui corda fidelium;" then, turning towards the postulants he says:

Auctoritate mihi concessa, ego te (vos), recipio et adscribo Confraternitati (SS. Sacramenti, *vel* SS. Cordis, etc.) teque participem (vosque participes( facio omnium gratiarum, Indulgentiarum, privilegiorum, bonorumque spiritualium ejusdem Confraternitatis, in nomine Patris, et Filii, et Spiritus Sancti. Amen.

He afterwards says the *Te Deum*, and inscribes the newly admitted in a register. Strictly speaking, this inscription alone would suffice, to belong to the Confraternity of the Holy Scapular.

The admission into the Confraternity of the Rosary ordinarily follows the blessing of the chaplets and candles for the fresh associates. Enrolment in the Confraternity of the Blessed Sacrament, which Paul V. (1607) desired to see established in every parish, is often preceded by a profession of faith in the Real Presence.*

## § III.

### 140. ORDO ET MODUS COMMUNICANDI INDULGENTIAM PLENARIUM MORIENTIBUS.

(Juxta formulam præscriptam a Benedicto XIV., in Bulla *Pia Mater*, Aprilis 5, 1747).

* *Manuel du Missionnaire*, by Fr. Nampon, S. J.

℣. Adjutorium, etc.
℟. Qui fecit cœlum et terram, etc.

*Antiphona.* Ne reminiscaris, Domine, delicta famuli tui (*vel* ancillæ tuæ), neque vindictam sumas de peccatis ejus.

Kyrie eleison. Christe eleison. Kyrie eleison. Pater noster.

℣. Et ne nos inducas in tentationem;
℟. Sed libera nos a malo.
℣. Salvum fac servum tuum (*vel* ancillam tuam); *et sic deinceps.*
℟. Deus meus, sperantem in te.
℣. Domine, exaudi orationem meam;
℟. Et clamor meus ad te veniat.
℣. Dominus vobiscum;
℟. Et cum spiritu tuo.

*Oremus.*

Clementissime Deus, Pater misericordiarum, et Deus totius consolationis qui neminem vis perire in te credentem, atque sperantem, secundum multitudinem miserationum tuarum respice propitius famulum tuum N., quem tibi vera fides et spes Christiana commendant. Visita eum in salutari tuo, et per Unigeniti tui passionem, et mortem, omnium ei delictorum suorum remissionem, et veniam clementer indulge; ut ejus anima in hora exitus sui te judicem propitiatum inveniat; et in sanguine ejusdem Filii tui ab omni macula abluta transire ad vitam mereatur perpetuam. Per Christum Dominum nostrum.
℟. Amen.

*Tum dicto ab uno ex clericis adstantibus*, Confiteor, *Sacerdos dicat:* Misereatur, etc. *Deinde:*

Dominus noster Jesus Christus, Filius Dei vivi, qui beato Petro Apostolo suo dedit potestatem ligandi atque solvendi, per suam piissimam misericordiam recipiat Confessionem tuam, et restituat tibi stolam primam, quam in Baptismate recepisti; et ego facultate mihi ab Apostolica Sede tributa, Indulgentiam plenariam et remissionem omnium peccatorum tibi concedo.

In nomine Patris, etc.

Per sacrosancta humanæ reparationis mysteria, remittat tibi omnipotens Deus omnes præsentis et futuræ vitæ pœnis, Paradisi portas aperiat, et ad gaudia sempiterna perducat. Amen.

Benedicat te Omnipotens Deus, Pater, Filius, et Spiritus Sanctus. Amen.

*Si vero infirmus sit adeo morti proximus ut neque confessionis generalis faciendæ, neque præmissarum precum recitandarum tempus suppetat, statim Sacerdos benedictionem ei impertiatur.*

### 141. MODUS IMPERTIENDI GENERALEM ABSOLUTIONEM MORIBUNDIS CONFRATRIBUS BEATISSIMÆ V. M. DE MONTE CARMELO.

*Cum Sacerdos ingressus fuerit infirmi cubiculum, dicat:*

v. Pax huic domui;
r. Ex omnibus habitantibus in ea.

*Deinde imposita stola violacei coloris, aspergat ægrum et circumstantes aqua benedicta in modum crucis dicens:*

*Antiphona.*

Asperges me hyssopo, etc.

Miserere mei, Deus, secundum magnam misericordiam tuam. Gloria Patri, etc.

*Et repet. Ant.* Asperges me, etc.

v. Salvum fac servum tuum (*vel* ancillam tuam) ;
r. Deus meus, sperantem in te.
v. Nihil proficiat inimicus in eo (*vel* in ea);
r. Et filius iniquitatis non apponat nocere ei.
v. Mitte ei, Domine, auxilium de sancto.
r. Et de Sion tuere eum (*vel* eam).
v. Domine, exaudi orationem meam ;
r. Et clamor meus ad te veniat.
v. Dominus vobiscum ;
r. Et cum spiritu tuo.

*Oremus.*

Exaudi nos, Domine sancte, Pater omnipotens æterne Deus, et mittere digneris sanctum Angelum tuum de Cœlis, qui custodiat, foveat, protegat, visitet atque defendat omnes habitantes in hoc habitaculo. Per Christum Dominum nostrum. r. Amen.

*Diende genuflexus dicat Litanias B. Virginis Mariæ.*

Kyrie eleison. Christe eleison, etc.

*Pater noster*, et *Ave Maria.*

Sub tuum præsidium confugimus, Sancta Dei Genitrix, nostras deprecationes ne despicias in necessitatibus nostris, sed a periculis cunctis libera eum (*vel* eam) semper, Virgo gloriosa et benedicta. Domina nostra, mediatrix nostra, advocata nostra, tuo eum (eam) Filio reconcilia, tuo eum (eam) Filio repræsenta.

v. Ora pro eo (ea), Sancta Dei Genitrix ;
r. Ut dignus (digna) efficiatur promissionibus Christi.

v. Domine, exaudi orationem meam;
r. Et clamor meus ad te veniat.
v. Dominus vobiscum;
r. Et cum spiritu tuo.

*Oremus.*

Protege, Domine, famulum tuum (*vel* famulam tuam) subsidiis pacis, et Beatæ Mariæ semper Virginis patrociniis confidentem a cunctis hostibus redde securum (*vel* securam).

Sanctissimæ Genitricis tuæ Sponsi, quæsumus Domine, meritis adjuvemur, ut quod possibilitas nostra non obtinet ejus nobis intercessione donetur.

Omnipotens et misericors Deus, qui humano generi et salutis remedia, et vitæ æternæ subsidia contulisti: respice propitius famulum tuum (*vel* famulam tuam) infirmitate corporis laborantem, et animam refove quam creasti; ut in hora exitus illius absque peccati macula tibi Creatori suo per manus sanctorum Angelorum repræsentari mereatur.

Deus, infirmitatis humanæ singulare præsidium, auxilii tui super infirmum famulum tuum (*vel* infirmam famulam tuam) ostende virtutem, et sic eum (eam) gratia tua confirmare digneris, ut in hora mortis ejus non prævaleat contra eum (eam) adversarius, sed cum Angelis tuis transitum habere mereatur ad vitam.

Omnipotens sempiterne Deus, qui Montis Carmeli Ordinem gloriosæ Virginis Matris Mariæ sacrato titulo insignitum Sanctorum tuorum Eliæ, Angeli, Cyrilli, Alberti, Teresiæ, et aliorum plurimorum Sanctorum meritis decorasti, tribue, quæsumus, ut per eorum merita et suffragia ab instantibus animæ et corporis malis, et periculis liberatus (*vel* liberata) ad te verum Carmeli verticem gaudens pervenire mereatur. Per Christum Dominum nostrum. ℞. Amen.

*His absolutis dicatur* Confiteor, *deinde Sacerdos stans dicat :*

Misereatur tui omnipotens Deus, et dimissis peccatis tuis perducat te ad vitam æternam. ℞. Amen.

Indulgentiam, absolutionem, et remissionem peccatorum tuorum tribuat tibi omnipotens, et misericors Dominus. ℞. Amen.

*Oremus.*

Deus omnipotens Salvator et Redemptor generis humani, qui Apostolis suis dedit ligandi et solvendi potestatem, ipse te absolvere dignetur ab omnibus iniquitatibus tuis, et quantum meæ fragilitati permittitur, auxiliante ipso, sis absolutus (*vel* absoluta) ante faciem ejus. Qui vivit et regnat, etc.

*Deinde conferat Indulgentiam Plenariam in hac formula :*

Concedo tibi Indulgentiam Plenariam peccatorum tuorum facultate mihi concessa, et commissa virtute Bullarum Ordinis Carmelitarum, quod si præsens mortis periculum, Deo favente, evaseris, sit tibi hæc Indulgentia pro vero mortis articulo reservata. In nomine Patris, et Fi✠lii, et Spiritus Sancti. Amen.

*Preces in casu necessitatis possunt omitti, et illico ægro Absolutionem impertiri antequam e vita discedat.*

## 142. MODUS APPLICANDI INDULGENTIAM PLENARIAM MORIBUNDIS CONFRATRIBUS IMMACULATÆ CONCEPTIONIS BEATÆ MARIÆ VIRGINIS.

*Dicatur ab infirmo, si vires habeat, vel ab alio, si*

*infirmus nequeat :* Confiteor Deo, etc. ; *a Sacerdote vero* Misereatur, *et* Indulgentiam, etc.

*Deinde:*

Dominus noster Jesus Christus, Filius Dei vivi, qui Beato Petro Apostolo suo dedit potestatem ligandi atque solvendi, per suam piissimam misericordiam te absolvat ; et ego auctoritate ipsius, et Beatorum Apostolorum Petri et Pauli, ex speciali gratia mihi tradita tibique concessa a Sanctissimo Domino nostro Papa Clemente Decimo, et a Pontifice Clemente Decimoprimo confirmata, absolvo te ab omni vinculo excommunicationis majoris et minoris, suspensionis, et interdicti, si teneris, in quantum possum et tu indiges ; et restituo te sanctis sacramentis, Ecclesiæ communioni, et unitati Fidelium, in nomine Patris ✠, et Filii ✠, et Spiritus ✠ Sancti. ℟. Amen.

Item eadem auctoritate mihi tradita, et tibi concessa, ego te absolvo ab omnibus peccatis tuis, quæcumque toto decursu vitæ tuæ, quomodocumque commisisti, de quibus corde contritus (*vel* contrita), et ore confessus (*vel* confessa) es, et quorum memoriam non habes usque in præsentem diem, et de quibus confiteri minime recordatus (*vel* recordata) fuisti, et restituo te illi innocentiæ, in qua eras, quando baptizatus (*vel* baptizata) fuisti, et puritati eidem, in quantum claves sanctæ Matris Ecclesiæ se extendunt. Remitto tibi etiam pœnas Purgatorii, quas per culpas et offensas contra Deum, et proximum et teipsum (*vel* teipsam) commissas incurristi. Claudo tibi portas inferni, januas aperio Paradisi: bona per te facta, et facienda, sint tibi in remissionem peccatorum, in augmentum gratiæ, et præmium vitæ æternæ: et hoc, si in infirmitate qua ægrotas decedas: alias, **ex** misericordia Dei, salva sint tibi, donec fueris in articulo mortis constitutus (*vel* constituta). In nomine Patris ✠, et Filii ✠, et Spiritus ✠ Sancti.  ℟. Amen.

### ⁑43. Forma applicationis Indulgentiæ plenariæ Confratribus sanctissimi Rosarii in articulo mortis.

*Dicto* Confiteor, *Sacerdos dicet:* Misereatur, etc. Indulgentiam, etc.

*Oremus.*

Dominus noster Jesus Christus Filius Dei vivi, qui Beato Petro Apostolo suo dedit potestatem ligandi atque solvendi, per suam piissimam misericordiam recipiat confessionem tuam, et remittat tibi omnia peccata quæcumque et quomodocumque in toto vitæ decursu commisisti, de quibus corde contritus, et ore confessus es (*vel* contrita et confessa es), restituens tibi stolam primam, quam in baptismate recepisti. Et, per Indulgentiam Plenariam a Summis Pontificibus Innocentio VIII. et Pio V., Confratribus sanctissimi Rosarii in articulo mortis constitutis concessam, liberet te a præsentis ac futuræ vitæ pœnis ; dignetur Purgatorii cruciatus remittere, portas Inferi claudere, Paradisi januam aperire, teque ad gaudia sempiterna perducere, per sacratissima suæ vitæ, passionis et glorificationis mysteria in sanctissimo Rosario comprehensa. Qui cum Patre et Spiritu Sancto, Deus unus, vivit et regnat in sæcula sæculorum. Amen.

*Conclusion.*

Let us conclude by a few words extracted from a letter which St. Ignatius of Loyola wrote from Rome, at the commencement of the year 1540, to his fellow citizens, inhabitants of Aspezia:

"It appears to me that I should delight and console your souls in the Holy Spirit, by sending to you a Diploma through which the Supreme Pontiff grants to you two or three Indulgences. But, since Indulgences are of such value, that I find myself unable to appreciate them adequately or extol them sufficiently, I entreat and exhort you all, for the love and reverence you owe to God, to set the highest esteem on the favour thus conferred upon you: *Tales vero (Indulgentiæ) quoniam eæ sunt, tantique faciendæ, ut nec a me pro illarum meritis laudari, nec verbis posse confidam convenienter extolli; quod restat unum, omnes vos propter amorem Dei ac reverentiam hortor et obsecro, maximo eas in pretio habere curetis.*"

N.B.—Indulgentiarum libri omnes, Diaria, Summaria, libelli, folia, etc., in quibus earum concessiones continentur, non edantur absque licentia Sacræ Congregationis Indulgentiarum. (Decrata de libris prohibitis, § iii, n. 12, in Indice, page xlvi.).

A. M. D. G.

# INDEX.

|  | PAGE |
|---|---|
| Preface to the Second English Edition. | iii |
| Approbations of the Irish Hierarchy. | v |
| Bishop's authorisation to publish the Translation. | xv |
| Father Maurel's letter to the Translator. | xvi |
| Translator's Preface. | xvii |
| Approbations of the Consultors of the Sacred Congregation of Indulgences. | xxi |
| Decree of the Sacred Congregation of Indulgences. | xxiii |
| Other Approbations. | xxiv |
| Dedication. | xxv |
| Preface to the Fourteenth Edition. | xxvii |

## PART I.

### DOGMATIC AND GENERAL PRINCIPLES.

|  |  |
|---|---|
| I. Definition of an Indulgence. | 1 |
| II. Grounds of Indulgences. | 10 |
| III. Power of granting Indulgences- Exercise of that Power. | 21 |
| IV. Salutary effects of the use of Indulgences. | 34 |
| V. Application of Indulgences to the Souls in Purgatory. | 41 |
| VI. Various kinds of Indulgences — Important observations regarding them. | 49 |
| VII. Dispositions necessary for gaining Indulgences. | 61 |
| VIII. The transferring of Indulgences. | 78 |
| IX. Recapitulation. | 79 |

## PART II.

### SPECIAL PRACTICAL POINTS

|  |  |
|---|---|
| Preliminary observations. | 84 |
| Decree of April 17, 1856, to prevent the circulation of Apocryphal Indulgences. | 87 |

|   | PAGE |
|---|---|
| Translation of Prayers—Decree | 87 |
| When the Briefs, &c, mention a Plenary Indulgence to be gained on the Feasts of our Lord, of the Blessed Virgin, and the Apostles. What feasts are meant? | 90 |
| Other observations. | 91 |

# ARTICLE I.

## PRAYERS.

| No. | | Page |
|---|---|---|
| 1 | Angelic Trisagion. | 92 |
|   | Important note. | 93 |
| 2 | Three *Gloria Patris*, &c. | 97 |
| 3 | Three Offerings to the Most Holy Trinity. | 95 |
| 4 | Triduo or Novena in honor of the Most Holy Trinity | 96 |
| 5 | Praises to the Holy Name of God. | ibid. |
| 6 | Prayers and Petitions. | 97 |
| 7 | Acts of Faith, Hope, and Charity. | 98 |
| 8 | An Act of Conformity to the Will of God. | 99 |
| 9 | Use of Indulgenced prayers, during our daily occupations | ibid. |
| 10 | Prayer in the form of an offering. | 100 |
| 11 | Prayer of St. Francis Xavier, for the conversion of Infidels. | ibid. |
| 12 | The Hymn "*Veni Creator Spiritus*," and the Sequence "*Veni Sancte Spiritus*." | 102 |
| 13 | Prayer, "*En Ego*," &c., before a Crucifix. | 105 |
| 14 | Prayer, "*Ego volo celebrare Missam*," &c., | 107 |
| 15 | Prayer, "*Obsecro Te, Dulcissime,*" &c. | ibid. |
| 16 | Prayer, "*Anima Christi*," &c., "Soul of Christ," &c. | 108 |
| 17 | Ejaculatory prayer, or offering of the Precious Blood of our Saviour Jesus Christ. | 109 |
| 18 | Ejaculation to the Blessed Sacrament. | ibid. |
| 19 | The Hymn "*Pange Lingua*," or the "*Tantum Ergo*." | 110 |
| 20 | Offering to Jesus Christ. | 113 |
| 21 | Pious ejaculation: "My Jesus, Mercy." | ibid. |
| 22 | Another invocation. | 114 |
| 23 | Devout aspiration. | ibid. |
| 24 | The Holy Names of Jesus and Mary. | ibid. |

| No. | | Page |
|---|---|---|
| 25 | Another pious salutation. | 115 |
| 26 | Litany of the Sacred Name of Jesus. | ibid. |
| 27 | Ejaculation to the Sacred Heart of Jesus. | 116 |
| 28 | Invocation of Jesus, Mary, and Joseph. | 117 |
| 29 | The prayer, "*Sacrosanctæ*," &c. | ibid. |
| 30 | Prayer for Confessors. | 118 |
| 31 | Office of the Blessed Virgin. | 119 |
| 32 | Little Office of the Immaculate Conception. | ibid. |
| 33 | Litany of the Blessed Virgin. | 120 |
| 34 | The "*Angelus Domini*," or the "*Regina Cœli*," &c. | ibid. |
| 35 | The "*Salve Regina*," &c., and the "*Sub Tuum*," &c. | 122 |
| 36 | Ejaculation "Sweet Heart of Mary," &c. | 123 |
| 37 | Prayer to the Sacred Heart of Mary. | ibid. |
| 38 | The "*Stabat Mater*," &c. | 125 |
| 39 | The "*Memorare*," or "Remember, O Most Pious Virgin," &c. | ibid. |
| 40 | Ejaculation in honor of the Immaculate Conception. | 126 |
| 41 | The prayer "O My Queen," &c. | ibid. |
| 42 | Prayer to the Blessed Virgin and to St. Anne. | 127 |
| 43 | Little Chaplet of the Immaculate Conception. | 128 |
| 44 | The "*Memorare*," or "Remember," &c., to St. Joseph. | 129 |
| 45 | Prayer "O glorious St. Joseph," &c. | ibid. |
| 46 | Prayers to St. Joseph, before and after Mass, for Priests. | 130 |
| 47 | Hymn of St. Michael. | 131 |
| 48 | Prayer to the Angel Guardian. | 133 |
| 49 | Prayer to St. Aloysius Gonzaga, with a Pater and Ave. | 134 |
| 50 | Three Paters and Aves, for the Faithful in their Agony. | 135 |
| 51 | The "*De profundis*," for the Dead. | 136 |
| 52 | Office of the Dead. | ibid. |
| 53 | Prayer for Peace. | 137 |

## ARTICLE II.

### DEVOUT EXERCISES.

| | | |
|---|---|---|
| 54 | The Sign of the Cross. | 138 |
| 55 | Meditation or Mental Prayer. | 139 |
| 56 | Holy Sacrifice of the Mass. | ibid. |

| No. | | Page |
|---|---|---|
| 57 | Frequent Communion. | 141 |
| 58 | Examen of Conscience. | ibid. |
| 59 | Assisting at a Sermon. | ibid. |

## ARTICLE III.

### SPECIAL DEVOTIONS.

| | | |
|---|---|---|
| 60 | Way of the Cross. | 142 |
| | Useful Observations. | 147 |
| 61 | Crucifix Indulgenced for the Stations of the Cross. | 153 |
| 62 | Devotion to the agonizing Heart of Jesus. | 155 |
| 63 | Prayer of the Quarant' Ore. | 156 |
| 64 | Visit to the "Altar of Repose" on Holy Thursday and Good Friday. | 158 |
| 65 | Feast of the Blessed Sacrament, or Corpus Christi. | ibid. |
| 66 | The Holy Hour. | 159 |
| 67 | Novena in honor of the Sacred Heart of Jesus. | 160 |
| 68 | First Friday of the Month. | ibid. |
| 69 | Month of Mary. | 161 |
| 70 | Exercise in honor of our Lady of Pity. | 162 |
| 71 | Month of March. | 163 |
| 72 | The six Sundays and Feast of St. Aloysius Gonzaga | 164 |
| 73 | Devotion to St. Stanislas Kostka. | 165 |
| 74 | Spiritual exercises of St. Ignatius, or a Retreat and Missions. | 167 |
| | Religious exercises for men exclusively—Useful hints. | 169–70 |

## ARTICLE IV.

### WORKS OF ZEAL AND CHARITY.

| | | |
|---|---|---|
| 75 | The Catechism. | 171 |
| 76 | Propagation of the Faith. | 173 |
| 77 | The Holy Infancy. | 177 |
| 78 | Society of Good Books | 178 |

| No. | | Page |
|---|---|---|
| 79 | Sodality of Soldiers. | 179 |
| 80 | Accompanying the Holy Viaticum to the Sick. | 181 |
| 81 | Visitation of the Sick, and of Prisoners. | 182 |
| 82 | Charitable repast in honor of the Holy Family. | ibid. |
| 33 | Heroic act of charity in behalf of the Souls in Purgatory. | 183 |

## ARTICLE V.

### CONFRATERNITIES AND PIOUS ASSOCIATIONS.

| | | |
|---|---|---|
| 84 | General observations, ten in number. | 185 |
| 85 | Confraternity of the Blessed Sacrament. | 193 |
| 86 | Confraternity of the Sacred Heart of Jesus. | 195 |
| | Archconfraternity of the Sacred Heart, erected at Moulins, for France. | 197 |
| | Remarks. | 200 |
| | The Perpetual Adoration. | 201 |
| 87 | The Red Scapular, or that of the Passion. | 202 |
| 88 | Confraternity of the Scapular, or of our Lady of Mount Carmel. | 207 |
| | Conditions of admission and of participating in the privileges, &c., &c. | 211 |
| | Observations Seven in Number | 213 |
| | Important note. | 216 |
| 89 | Scapular of the Immaculate Conception. | 217 |
| | Privilege of the Six Paters and Aves and Glorias, &c. | 222 |
| 0 | The Rosary. | 223 |
| | Confraternity of the Rosary. | 225 |
| | The Perpetual Rosary. | 230 |
| 91 | Congregations of the Blessed Virgin. | ibid. |
| | Indulgences accorded to the *Prima-Primaria* at Rome. | 234 |
| | Observations, and course to be adopted to obtain affiliation to the *Prima-Primaria*. | 236 |
| 92 | Archconfraternity of the Holy and Immaculate Heart of Mary for the Conversion of Sinners. | 237 |
| 93 | Archconfraternity to repair blasphemies and violations of the Sunday. | 240 |

| No. | | Page |
|---|---|---|
| 94 | Confraternity of the *Bona Mors*. | 241 |
| 95 | The Holy Slavery of the Mother of God. | 244 |
| 96 | Association of the "*Perpetual Cultus*" of St. Joseph. | 246 |
| 97 | Ejaculatory prayer to St. Joseph. | 248 |
| 98 | Apostleship of Prayer. | ibid. |
| 99 | The Living Rosary. | 250 |
| 100 | Archconfraternity of the Cord of St. Francis of Assisium. | 252 |

## ARTICLE VI.

### BLESSING OF DEVOTIONAL OBJECTS, CROSSES, CHAPLETS, STATUES, MEDALS, &c.

| | | |
|---|---|---|
| 101 | Twenty general observations. | 254 |
| | Apostolic Indulgences. | 259 |
| 102 | Crosses, Rosaries, and Chaplets procured from the Holy Land. | 263 |
| 103 | Indulgences of a Chaplet—General Observations. | 264 |
| 104 | Little Statues of St. Peter. | 267 |
| 105 | The Agnus Dei. | ibid. |
| 106 | Cross and Medal of St. Benedict. | 270 |

## ARTICLE VII.

### SPECIAL INDULGENCES.

| | | |
|---|---|---|
| 107 | Indulgences of St. Bridget's Chaplet. | 273 |
| 108 | Chaplet of the Seven Dolors. | 277 |
| 109 | Papal Benediction or Indulgence. | 280 |
| 110 | Indulgences of the Roman Stations. | 281 |
| | Visit to the Seven Churches and seven privileged altars. | 283 |
| 111 | Indulgence of the *Pardon* or Portiuncula. | 284 |
| | Briefs of Pious VII., in behalf of Churches no longer belonging to the Franciscans, in France. | 289 |

| No. | | Page |
|---|---|---|
| 112 | Indulgences of the Holy Year. | 289 |
| 113 | Indulgence of *a privileged altar*. | 290 |
| | Observations. | 292 |
| | A personal privileged altar. | 295 |
| 114 | Plenary Indulgence at the Hour of Death. | 297 |

## ARTICLE VIII.

### INDULGENCES PECULIAR TO RELIGIOUS.

| | | |
|---|---|---|
| 115 | Observations (Five). | 300 |
| 116 | The Indulgences. | 302 |

## ARTICLE IX.

### APPENDIX.

#### INDULGENCES PECULIAR TO THE CHURCH OF NOTRE-DAME DE FOURVIERE, LYONS.

| | | |
|---|---|---|
| 117 | Notre-Dame De Fourviere. | 304 |
| 118 | Indulgences attached to the Church of Fourviere. | 308 |
| | Catalogue or Summary of the Indulgences accorded by the Roman Pontiffs to the Holy Chapel of Loretto. | 310 |
| | Plenary Indulgence for the 8th of September (Pius IX.). | 312 |

## PART III.

### FORMULARY.

#### 1st. FORMULAS OF BLESSINGS.

| | | |
|---|---|---|
| 119 | Observations. | 314 |
| 120 | Benedictio Crucis.—Cross of the Mission. | 315 |
| 121 | Benedictio Imaginum. | 316 |

| No. | | PAGE |
|---|---|---|
| 122 | Benedictio Rosariorum B. Mariæ Virginis. | 316 |
| 123 | Altera Benedictio Rosarii, vel coronæ precatoriæ. | 317 |
| 124 | Benedictio Candelarum extra diem Purificationis B. Mariæ V. | 318 |
| 125 | Benedictio Loci, vel Domus. | ibid. |
| 126 | Benedictio communis super fruges et vineas. | 319 |
| 127 | Benedictio cujuslibet vestimenti honesti. | ibid. |
| 128 | Benedictio puerorum et puellarum. | 320 |
| 129 | Benedictio ad omnia. | 321 |
| 130 | Mode of Imparting the Papal Benediction. | 322 |
| 131 | Benedictio cingulorum in honorem S. Josephi, Sponsi B. M. V. | 324 |
| 132 | Fomula benedicendi numismata seu cruces S. Patris Benedicti, A. SS. D. Benedicto P.P. XIV. approbata. | 326 |
| 133 | Methodus pro erigendis stationibus Viæ Crucis. | 328 |

2NDLY. FORMULAS OF RECEPTIONS.

| 134 | Ritus benedicendi et imponendi Scapulare rubrum Passionis D. N. Jesu Christi. | 330 |
|---|---|---|
| 135 | Ritus benedicendi et imponendi Scapulare B. M. Virginis de Monte Carmelo. | 331 |
| 136 | A shorter form for admission into the Confraternity of Carmel. | 335 |
| 137 | Ritus benedicendi et imponendi Scapulare Cœruleum. | 336 |
| 138 | Ritus imponendi habitum Septem Dolorum B. M. V. et benedicendi ejusdem Coronam. | 337 |
| 139 | Formula for a solemn reception into any Confraternity whatever. | 339 |

3RDLY.

| 140 | Ordo et Methodus communicandi Indulgentiam plenariam Morientebus (Benedictus XIV.). | 340 |
|---|---|---|
| 141 | Methodus eamdem Indulgentiam impertiendi moribundis confratribus B. V. Mariæ de Monte Carmelo. | 342 |
| 142 | *Idem*, pro Confratribus Immaculatæ Conceptionis B. Mariæ V. | 345 |
| 143 | Forma ejusdem applicationis pro Confratribus Sanctissimi Rosarii. | 347 |
| | Conclusion. | 348 |

www.ingramcontent.com/pod-product-compliance
Lightning Source LLC
Chambersburg PA
CBHW030358230426
43664CB00007BB/645